THE MIRACLE

THE
MIRACLE

THE EPIC STORY OF ASIA'S QUEST FOR WEALTH

MICHAEL SCHUMAN

HARPER
BUSINESS

An Imprint of HarperCollinsPublishers
www.harpercollins.com

HarperCollins books may be purchased for educational, business, or sales promotional use. For information, please write: Special Markets Department, HarperCollins Publishers, 10 East 53rd Street, New York, NY 10022.

FIRST EDITION

Designed by Renato Stanisic

Library of Congress Cataloging-in-Publication Data is available upon request.

ISBN 978-0-06-134668-2

09 10 11 12 13   OV/RRD   10 9 8 7 6 5 4 3 2 1

TO MY MOTHER, EMILY,
WHO FIRST INSPIRED ME TO WRITE

CONTENTS

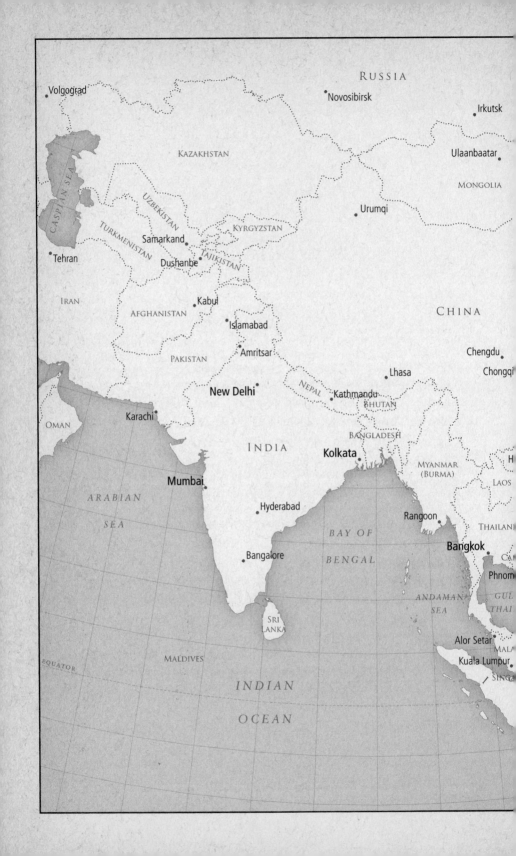

THE CAST

MONTEK SINGH AHLUWALIA: A civil servant in India, Ahluwalia advocated for the dismantlement of the License Raj and assisted Manmohan Singh and P. Chidambaram in their market-reform program of the early 1990s.

ANWAR IBRAHIM: As Malaysia's finance minister, Anwar challenged Mahathir Mohamad's radical economic policies during the Asian Financial Crisis. He became the leader of a Malaysian reform movement.

PRAMOD BHASIN: As chief of GE Capital in India, Bhasin, in cooperation with Raman Roy, turned India's fledgling business-process outsourcing sector into a large and influential Indian industry.

CHAN CHIN BOCK: As a member of Singapore's Economic Development Board, Chan was responsible for attracting some of the earliest and most important foreign investors to the island.

MORRIS CHANG: A former Texas Instruments executive, Chang was invited to Taiwan by the government to develop new technology industries. He founded the first independent chip foundry, Taiwan Semiconductor Manufacturing Company.

CHIANG KAI-SHEK: The leader of China's Nationalists, Chiang lost control of the country in a bloody civil war with Mao Zedong's Communists. He reestablished his regime on Taiwan, where he and a team of skilled technocrats transformed the island into one of Asia's earliest and most impressive economic success stories. Chiang served as president of the government on Taiwan from 1950 to 1975.

PALANIAPPAN CHIDAMBARAM: A lawyer and ally of Manmohan Singh, Chidambaram, as commerce minister in the early 1990s, played a key role in dismantling the License Raj during India's market-reform drive.

CHUNG JU YUNG: Founder of South Korea's giant Hyundai group of companies, the bold Chung rose up from poverty to develop the country's powerful car and ship industries. He became known as "King Chairman."

CHUNG MONG KOO: Chung Ju Yung's son, Chung took over management of Hyundai Motor in the late 1990s and surprised the auto industry by transforming the second-rate carmaker into a major global competitor.

DAIM ZAINUDDIN: As finance minister of Malaysia, Daim, a close protégé of Mahathir Mohamad, was the country's most powerful economic official and led the government's liberalization and privatization efforts.

DENG XIAOPING: As China's paramount leader, Deng championed the reforms in the late 1970s and 1980s that transformed the economy from a centrally planned Communist model to a system based on trade, foreign investment, and private enterprise. He is responsible for making China the world's budding superpower, but his brutal crackdown on protestors in Tiananmen Square in 1989 tarnished his reputation.

FUNG HON-CHU, VICTOR FUNG, AND WILLIAM FUNG: The Fungs manage Hong Kong trading firm Li & Fung. They played a pioneering role in developing "borderless manufacturing," in which products are assembled from components from many countries to lower costs.

GOH KENG SWEE: A long-serving minister in Singapore, Goh was Lee Kuan Yew's right-hand man and a tireless proponent of industrialization in Singapore.

BACHARUDDIN JUSUF (B. J.) HABIBIE: An Indonesian government minister and aviation engineer, Habibie oversaw an expensive effort to build a heavy industry sector. His ideas on state-led development challenged the free-market ideology of the Berkeley Mafia. He became president of Indonesia after Suharto's resignation in 1998.

MOHAMAD "BOB" HASAN: A golfing partner of Indonesia autocrat Suharto, Hasan was the prototype "crony" businessman who became the country's top timber tycoon. He once called himself "King of the Jungle."

ALAN HASSENFELD: The former chairman of U.S. toymaker Hasbro, Hassenfeld developed ties to Asian industrialists in the late 1960s and 1970s, including Hong Kong's Li Ka-shing, as American industry began to shift production to Asia.

SOICHIRO HONDA: The most successful automobile entrepreneur of the post–World War II era, Japan's Honda aggressively built his upstart business with important technical breakthroughs. Honda is famous for challenging the dictates of the powerful bureaucrats at Japan's Ministry of Trade and Industry (MITI). His company was the first Japanese carmaker to open a factory in the United States.

HU YAO-BANG: A general secretary of China's Communist Party, Hu was a key supporter of Deng Xiaoping and one of the country's most aggressive reformers and champions of free expression. His death sparked the protests in Tiananmen Square in 1989.

MASARU IBUKA: Co-founder of Japan's Sony, the brilliant Ibuka was the engineering genius behind many of the company's most famous gadgets.

HAYATO IKEDA: As Japanese prime minister in the early 1960s, Ikeda built confidence in Japan's economy by launching a plan to double national income in ten years.

SHOICHIRO IRIMAJIRI: The manager of Honda's first car plant in America in the 1980s, the quirky Irimajiri became the face of Japanese automakers in America. He was known as "Mr. Iri."

JOHN JOYCE: As IBM's chief financial officer, Joyce negotiated the sale of the firm's PC unit to Chinese PC maker Lenovo.

KIM DAE JUNG: South Korea's leading democracy advocate, Kim challenged the country's dictators for more than two decades. He was elected president in 1997 and guided Korea through the Asian Financial Crisis.

KIM WOO CHOONG: The flamboyant founder of the Daewoo Group, Kim became South Korea's most international and well-known tycoon. His mismanagement created one of the world's biggest bankruptcies during the Asian Financial Crisis.

F. C. KOHLI: The dictatorial Kohli is known as the father of India's IT industry. He turned Tata Consultancy into India's first international IT services provider.

LEE KUAN YEW: The first prime minister of Singapore, Lee instituted creative economic policies that transformed the island into a major industrial and finance center. His "Asian values" argument and criticism of Western democracy also make Lee one of the Miracle's most controversial figures.

LI KA-SHING: Chairman of Hong Kong conglomerate Hutchison Whampoa, Li rose from a small plastic-flower maker to one of Asia's richest men. His amazing success has earned him the nickname "Superman."

LI KUO-TING: A physicist, Li was a key policymaker in Taiwan for four decades. His ideas helped the island become a major exporter and electronics manufacturer.

LIU CHUANZHI: A former government researcher, Liu took great risks in founding PC maker Lenovo. As China's first multinational enterprise, Liu's purchase of IBM's PC unit signaled the country's growing global ambitions.

MARY MA: As chief financial officer of Chinese computer maker Lenovo, Ma led the company's quest to acquire IBM's PC unit.

MAHATHIR MOHAMAD: As prime minister of Malaysia for twenty-two years, Mahathir, a former medical doctor, strove to develop his tropical nation with policies adopted from Japan and South Korea. He is known more for his tirades against the West and Jews than for his economic achievements.

SRIDHAR MITTA: A talented engineer, Mitta played an instrumental role in the 1980s in the emergence of India's Wipro as a computer and IT firm.

AKIO MORITA: Co-founder of Sony, and Asia's best-known businessman, Morita was the marketing mastermind behind the company's success. Morita became a passionate defender of Japan as trade disputes flared with the United States in the 1980s.

NARAYANA MURTHY: A former socialist, Murthy built India's Infosys from a tiny firm housed in his apartment into one of the world's major IT services providers.

TAIICHI OHNO: An engineer at Toyota, Ohno was the creator of the Toyota Production System, the highly efficient method of making cars that became known as "lean" manufacturing.

PARK CHUNG HEE: A general who claimed control of South Korea in a 1961 coup, Park ruled for eighteen years. He was the driving force behind Korea's government-led development and is responsible for the policies that created the country's giant family-run business conglomerates, called *chaebols*.

PARK TAE JOON: A South Korean military officer and colleague of Park Chung Hee, Park is the founder of the country's steel industry.

AZIM PREMJI: As chairman of Wipro, Premji transformed the family vegetable oil firm into one of India's most powerful IT service providers. Today, he is one of the country's richest men.

SUBRAMANIAN RAMADORAI: As Tata Consultancy's first representative in New York, Ramadorai was instrumental in building the IT services provider into a major international enterprise. He later became the company's chief executive.

P. V. NARASIMHA RAO: A longtime functionary of the Indian National Congress party, Rao became prime minister amid the financial crisis of 1991. He surprised the nation by acting as the political backbone of the effort to reform the economy.

RAMAN ROY: Known as the father of India's business-processing outsourcing industry, Roy was responsible for setting up the country's first call center.

ROBERT RUBIN: As U.S. secretary of the treasury, Rubin helped organize rescue programs for Asia's faltering economies during the Asian Financial Crisis.

SHIGERU SAHASHI: Sahashi was a controversial vice minister of Japan's powerful Ministry of Trade and Industry (MITI). He personified the intrusiveness of Japan's state in guiding the economy.

EMIL SALIM: A long-serving minister in Suharto's government in Indonesia, Salim was a core member of the Berkeley Mafia, the team of economists who guided the country's policy for nearly three decades.

STAN SHIH: Founder of PC maker Acer, Shih is the grandfather of Taiwan's computer sector. He also left his mark on the global PC industry by inventing the "fast-food" model of assembling computers.

MANMOHAN SINGH: A soft-spoken economist, Singh as finance minister in the early 1990s led the effort to reorient the Indian economy toward the international marketplace that jump-started the country's rapid growth. In 2004, he became India's prime minister.

SUHARTO: A former army general who ruled Indonesia from 1966 to 1998, Suharto brought about a stellar record of poverty alleviation in the world's fourth-most-populous nation. However, his authoritarian regime was also riddled with corruption and nepotism, and he was forced to resign in 1998 amid the Asian Financial Crisis. Like many Indonesians, he has only one name.

SUN YUN-SUAN: A premier of Taiwan, Sun supported key policies that helped develop the island's influential technology industries.

H. C. TING AND KENNETH TING: As father and son, the Tings built Kader Industrial into a major Asian toymaker and one of the earliest companies to shift production to China.

EIJI TOYODA: A member of Toyota's founding family, Toyoda oversaw the development of the Toyota Production System and the company's successful expansion into the the U.S. market.

WAN LI: Communist Party official and protégé of Deng Xiaoping, Wan Li took the lead in reforming China's agricultural sector by advocating for family farming over collectivization.

ALI WARDHANA: A key member of Indonesia's Berkeley Mafia and a long-serving finance minister, Wardhana helped design the free-market economic policies that brought about the country's Miracle.

JACK WELCH: As CEO of GE, Welch helped develop India's IT and business-process outsourcing industries by bolstering the sector's international credibility.

WIDJOJO NITISASTRO: A skilled economist, Widjojo was the unofficial chief of Indonesia's economic policy team, the Berkeley Mafia. He pushed the other members to put their economics training to practical use developing the nation.

ALBERT WINSEMIUS: The Dutch economist became a key advisor to Lee Kuan Yew in Singapore and influenced some of the country's most important policies.

YANG YUANQING: As an aggressive young executive, Yang devised the strategy that turned Lenovo into China's largest PC maker. As chief executive, Yang has played a key role in managing Lenovo after its historic acquisition of IBM's PC unit.

ZHANG RUIMIN: As chief executive of Haier, China's largest appliance maker, Zhang made history by opening the first Chinese factory in the United States, to make refrigerators.

ZHAO ZIYANG: As general secretary of China's Communist Party, Zhao was the most inventive economic reformer and the most important figure in the economy's transformation, after Deng Xiaoping.

ZHU RONGJI: A premier of China, Zhu's creative economic policy-making solidified Deng Xiaoping's reforms and further liberalized the Chinese economy. His most important achievement was steering China's entry into the World Trade Organization.

INTRODUCTION
A FEW THOUGHTS ON HOW MIRACLES HAPPEN

The ambition of the greatest man of our generation has been to wipe every tear from every eye. —JAWAHARLAL NEHRU

The spies called as soon as I returned to my desk.

I was the South Korea correspondent for the *Wall Street Journal*, living in Seoul, and the country at that moment—December 1997—was in the deepest depths of the Asian Financial Crisis. Companies toppled into bankruptcy, unemployment soared, and the local stock market and currency (the won) plummeted in value. The country had nearly run dry of foreign currency and faced the possibility of defaulting on its international debt. In November, the president had turned to the International Monetary Fund for a rescue—a national humiliation in Korean eyes—but the promised $58 billion support package had done little even to slow the economy's downward spiral. Gripped by uncertainty and confusion, Koreans feared the worst was yet to come. The economy was on the verge of complete collapse.

Thus the phone call from the spy agency. I had just attended an hour-long meeting at the U.S. embassy with Stephen Bosworth, the recently installed ambassador, who briefed me and two other journalists on Washington's position on the Korean economic crisis. Afterward, I decided to enjoy the clear winter day and take the twenty-minute walk from the boxy embassy compound down Seoul's main thoroughfare, Sejong-ro, to the *Journal* bureau near City Hall. I got that phone call shortly after I arrived.

The caller identified himself as a member of the intelligence service, but did not bother to give his name. "We want to know what the ambassador told you," he said.

I was a bit stunned. Calls from the spy agency were not unusual at the bureau. Though Korea had been a democracy for a decade, the old authoritarian practices of media control died hard, but I was startled that the Korean government knew of the briefing so soon. The spies were never this well informed.

I decided they knew enough already. In my two years in the bureau, I had learned that the best way to handle such calls was to say nothing. The less the government knew about what I was doing, the better. "I don't know what you're talking about," I said.

The mystery man persisted. "We know you were in the ambassador's office. We want to know what he told you."

I began to surmise what was afoot: Paranoid government officials had most likely assumed that the ambassador was dictating the next day's press reports—a common practice within the Korean media—and they had worked themselves into a lather that some kind of conspiracy against Korea was being hatched by American diplomats and the international press. I had already come under suspicion in Korea for my stories about the Crisis. My colleagues and I had been the earliest journalists to warn of the country's impending calamity and the Korean press blamed us for *causing* the Crisis. I spent weeks parrying complaints and angry letters from a panicked finance ministry.

Whatever the government thought, however, I had no intention of blabbering out Bosworth's briefing to Korea's version of the CIA. "You'll have to read about it in the newspaper tomorrow like everybody else," I said, then got off the phone.

I was usually easily angered by Korea's meddlesome spies, but that time, I felt bad for them. I, too, was moved by the trauma the Crisis was causing in Korea, a country that was turning into my second home. Over the previous four decades, Koreans had become accustomed to economic growth and rising incomes. The Crisis hit them as an incomprehensible nightmare. All of their tremendous gains, won with Herculean effort, seemed to be slipping away—and in a matter of days. Stunned, unemployed managers, too embarrassed to inform their families they had lost their jobs, donned the dark blue suits of Korean salarymen and pretended to head for the office each morning. They spent the day hiding out in the mountainside parks on Seoul's outskirts. Housewives volunteered to sell their precious gold jewelry to the government for worthless won in a selfless yet futile attempt to refill the country's depleted coffers. The elderly finance minister, unfortunate enough to be in office when the Crisis hit, was later tossed into prison by vengeful prosecutors.

Americans and Western Europeans who suffered through the global recession of 2008–09, with its tremendous destruction of wealth, jobs, and hope, can begin to empathize with the insecurity and dread experienced by the average Korean at that time. Any Korean over thirty years old remembers the poverty the nation endured and the agonizing sacrifices made to crawl out of it. Since the early 1960s, Koreans worked in miserable factories, scrimping and saving to build themselves better lives. They surrendered civil liberties and personal freedoms to authoritarian regimes in a national quest for economic development. And they had triumphed. In only thirty-five years, Koreans transformed a nation poorer than Liberia, Zimbabwe, and Iraq into a member of the rich countries' club, the Organization for Economic Cooperation and Development.

Korea's economic boom was far more than just a route to wealth. It defined the nation's purpose, engendered a sense of pride and confidence rarely matched in Korea's five-thousand-year history, and elevated the country to a position of respect and power in the global economy. The same can be said of nearly all of Asia. From India to Japan, countries only recently emerged from centuries of colonial domination or the devastation of war and revolution forged themselves into modern nations through the trials of economic hardship, sacrifice, and, eventually, success.

Fortunately for Korea and its neighbors, even the Financial Crisis proved a brief hiatus from Asia's relentless progress. Since the 1950s, the economic gains achieved in Asia are almost impossible to comprehend. Asia has produced the most sustained economic boom in modern history, a massive surge in income that has brought unprecedented gains in wealth and economic opportunity to three billion people.

The Miracle created an almost unbelievable increase in wealth.

GROWTH OF GROSS NATIONAL INCOME PER CAPITA (IN CURRENT US$)

COUNTRY	1965	2007	PERCENT CHANGE
South Korea	130	19,690	15,046%
Taiwan	204	15,078	7,291%
Singapore	540	32,470	5,913%
Hong Kong	710	31,610	4,352%
Japan	890	37,670	4,133%
Thailand	130	3,400	2,515%
China	100	2,360	2,260%
Indonesia*	70	1,650	2,257%
Malaysia	330	6,540	1,882%
India	110	950	764%

*Earliest year available is 1969.
Source: World Bank; Taiwan Directorate General of Budget, Accounting and Statistics.

Economists call it the Asian Economic Miracle, and a miracle it certainly was. In 1981, East Asia had the highest poverty rate of any region in the world, with nearly 80 percent of its people living on an income of less than $1.25 a day. By 2005, the rate had fallen to only 18 percent. (By comparison, the percentage of the population of sub-Saharan Africa suffering in absolute poverty has remained almost unchanged over that same time period, at 50 percent.)[1] Hundreds of millions of Asians who would have been stuck knee-deep in muddy rice paddies, living in thatch huts, and surviving on subsistence diets now work in air-conditioned glass-and-steel skyscrapers, inhabit glitzy high-rises with stuffed refrigerators, and sip Starbucks cappuccinos. Forty years ago, most Asians were lucky to get a primary school education; now many send their children to the best American universities. In the 1950s, Asian economies could barely feed their own people; today, Asians make more memory chips, LCD panels, and notebook computers than anyone else in the world.

This transformation drew me toward Asia. I had read quite a bit about economic development as a university student, and I wanted to experience the process in real life and real time. Asia has not let me down. Each time I ride the Skytrain through congested Bangkok, take an old Ambassador taxi around New Delhi, or stroll down the busy streets of Shanghai, the cities look wealthier and more modern than they had on my previous visit. Asia is changing by the day.

My first visit to Asia was in 1991, as a graduate school intern at *Far Eastern Economic Review* magazine in its New Delhi bureau. I had never been to a country as underdeveloped as India. The poverty shocked me. In Kolkata (formerly Calcutta), I could not step from my hotel without getting swarmed by street children, all tugging at my shirt and begging for money. I bought them bunches of bananas. In Varanasi, the holiest city in Hinduism, parked on the edge of the sacred Ganges River, the townspeople spent each morning bathing, brushing their teeth, and washing clothes in the smelly water, polluted by raw sewage streaming down from the city in open ditches. At first, I found myself emptying my pockets, but after several weeks, the scale and scope of the suffering was so great that the only way to survive it was to immunize myself. I felt guilty, but the desperation of India left me no choice.

Today, that poverty still exists in many parts of India, but so does an economic vibrancy that was unimaginable during my first

visit. From Mumbai to Chennai, young, well-dressed professionals cram multiplex cinemas while taxi drivers jabber on mobile
phones. In the old Muslim town of Hyderabad in southern India,
sleek technology parks exist only a short drive away from the city's
traditional market, where craftsmen still bang out silver and gold
leaf with old hammers. Even Kolkata has been resurrected. The restaurants along Park Street, a thoroughfare famous for its nightlife
and eateries, are abuzz with raucous diners and unlimited hope.

This rush of new wealth has had repercussions well beyond
Asia. The Miracle has given this continent more influence in world
events than it has held for hundreds of years, perhaps all the way
back to the fourteenth century, when the Mongol Khans reigned
from Moscow to Baghdad to Guangzhou. For the first time, stock
markets in Hong Kong and Shanghai help determine what happens on Wall Street. The statements of central bankers in Tokyo
and Beijing are almost as closely monitored as those of the Federal
Reserve chairman. Asian investors have become important players
in global securities, currency, and real estate markets. With that
economic power has inevitably come political power. Backed by
their growing economies, Asian nations are pursuing their strategic
interests more aggressively than they have in centuries. Their voracious quest for natural resources has sparked fierce competition
for global sources of energy and raw materials. Asian countries
have launched a diplomatic offensive from the halls of the United
Nations to the capitals of Africa. China especially has flexed its
new financial and diplomatic muscle in such crucial international
issues as climate change, trade liberalization, nuclear-weapons
proliferation, and human rights. The Miracle is the single most
important trend in world history since the end of World War II—
with a longer-lasting and deeper impact on the future than either
the fall of Communism or the war on terror.

In the United States and Europe, Asia's rise has generated fears
that the region will eclipse the West. British historian Niall Ferguson wrote that "the relative decline of the West became unstoppa-

ble" once Asia modernized, and the result "was nothing less than the reorientation of the world."[2] For three decades, politicians, journalists, and economists have warned of the threat from Asia. Trade negotiator turned anti-free-trade pundit Clyde Prestowitz has been predicting since the late 1980s that a rising Asia would doom the American economy. The first conqueror was supposed to be Japan, and then the menace switched to China and India. "Whether slowly or quickly, the forces now bringing wealth and power to the East will also bring crisis and painful adjustment to the West," he wrote in 2005. "Far from leading the world on a global march to freedom, the United States could find itself hard-pressed to maintain a reasonable standard of living and defend its vital interests." The conditions could be in place, he alerted his American readers, for an "economic 9/11."[3]

Though we need to keep this kind of fearmongering in perspective—the Chinese economy, for example, is still less than one-fourth the size of America's—it is indisputable that over the next several decades the United States will face an Asia that possesses greater and greater economic power. The West is not in "decline." The East is on the rise. The ascent of Asia is creating a world in which the global economy has more than one dominant power. "As the world's economic center of gravity shifts to Asia, U.S. preeminence will inevitably diminish," economist Jeffrey Sachs wrote in 2004. "The 21st century could well be a period of unprecedented prosperity and scientific advance, but one in which the U.S. will have to learn to be one of many successful economies rather than the world's indispensible country."[4] Investment bank Goldman Sachs in an influential 2003 report predicted that China could overtake the United States as the world's largest economy by 2041. India could race past Japan by 2032 to become the third-biggest. By 2050, the Chinese and Indian economies combined would, by Goldman's reckoning, be more than twice the size of America's. Goldman's report ends with a simple, but ominous, question: "Are you ready?"[5]

The Miracle is reshaping the global economy. By 2050, China will have over-taken the United States as the largest economy in the world; India will not be far behind.

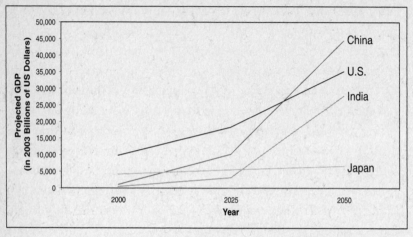

Source: Wilson, Dominic, and Roopa Purushothaman, "Dreaming with BRICs: The Path to 2050."

We all better be ready. There is little reason to believe the Miracle will come to an end anytime soon. It will remain the primary force determining global economic relationships and events for the foreseeable future. Asia may experience an occasional crisis along the way, like the one that roiled Korea in the late 1990s. Economies may slow down or even slide into recession, as they did during the global financial conflagration of 2008, or get side-tracked by political upheaval and social turmoil. But we are, after all, talking about a Miracle, and like all miracles, real or perceived, they become forces in and of themselves. In 2005, I was traveling in China's far west and met Chen Xiangjian, then a bespectacled thirty-two-year-old salesman for a state engineering firm, in Chongqing, which, at 32 million people, is among the world's largest urban centers. Chen told me how his life had changed in just the previous five years. His income had tripled, he owned a Sony digital video camera, a notebook computer, and two apartments, and was thinking of buying his first car. Though excited about his own future, he was even more buoyant about the prospects for his daughter Youyou, then one year old. "By the time she's my age," he predicted, "her life will be as good as the best in America."[6] In modern Asia, that dream is coming true.

. . . .

IN ORDER TO appreciate just how miraculous the Miracle has been, we need to look back at how pitiful Asia was in the early 1950s, when our story begins. Just about every corner of the continent was in chaos. In Japan, the desperate and ruthless conflict with the United States had eviscerated the country's once formidable economy. By the end of World War II in 1945, a quarter of Japan's wealth had been lost. Some 40 percent of the sixteen largest cities targeted by Allied bombers were destroyed. Millions were homeless; many were malnourished and even starving. Foreign correspondent Russell Brines, upon arriving in Tokyo after the war's end, said that "everything had been flattened. . . . Only thumbs stood up from the flatlands—the chimneys of bathhouses, heavy house safes and an occasional stout building with heavy iron shutters." One American official reported that "the entire economic structure of Japan's greatest cities has been wrecked."[7]

The war brought similar devastation to much of Asia as Japanese armies rampaged from Shanghai to Singapore. In 1937, Japan launched a brutal invasion of China, punctuated by the infamous Rape of Nanjing, one of the twentieth century's greatest atrocities. After Japan's defeat, China descended into a destructive civil war between the U.S.-backed Nationalists under Chiang Kai-shek and Mao Zedong's Communists. Mao emerged victorious and proclaimed the People's Republic of China in 1949, while Chiang fled to Taiwan and set up his own regime. Less than a year later, war erupted in Korea. The Korean peninsula was a Japanese colony that after World War II was split in two—one sphere controlled by the Soviet Union in the north, the other by the United States. Three years later, the zones became North and South Korea. In 1950, the North invaded the South in an attempt to unite the peninsula under Communism. U.S. forces rushed to defend the South and, shortly after, Mao's China jumped in to save the North. The three-year conflict left the Koreans with smashed cities and little industry. A legacy of this period is a Korean stew called *budae jjigae*. Starving Koreans picked through leftover army rations in the garbage dumps outside U.S. military bases for scraps of Spam, spaghetti, and American cheese—anything that could bolster their diets—and cooked them in traditional Korean spicy red pepper soup. The dish is still served today, though the ingredients are no longer pilfered from waste bins.

In South and Southeast Asia, the nations we know today were just coming into existence as modern nation-states. After Indonesia declared its independence from the Netherlands in 1945, the country's first president, the dynamic nationalist Sukarno, had to fight off Dutch forces attempting to reclaim their colonial empire before knitting together 17,500 islands that were home to a disparate collection of ethnic groups speaking myriad languages. India won its independence from Great Britain in 1947 after Mahatma Gandhi's legendary nonviolent mass disobedience movement. India, like Indonesia, emerged as a modern nation-state for the first time, cobbled together from a collection of princely states and colonial provinces. Malaysia did not exist until 1957, when it was formed by merging semi-independent sultanates under the thumb of the British with Crown-controlled territories. Singapore became an independent country after splitting from Malaysia in 1965.

These mid-twentieth-century convulsions, revolutions, and wars, however, were only the latest calamity in centuries of stagnation. There was a time when the societies of Asia were much richer and more developed than those of Europe. In the year 1600, Asia accounted for two-thirds of world GDP, compared to about 20 percent for all of Western Europe. China and India were the world's two largest economies, representing 29 percent and 23 percent of global GDP respectively.[8] François Bernier, a Frenchman who traveled in India in the seventeenth century, wrote of the country's Mughal emperor: "I doubt whether any other monarch possesses more of this species of wealth [i.e. gold, silver and jewels] . . . and the enormous consumption of fine cloths of gold, and brocades, silks, embroideries, pearls, musk, amber and sweet essences is greater than can be conceived."[9]

Yet by the 1500s, Asia began a long, slow decline relative to the West. European societies invented new technologies (advanced weaponry and navigational tools) and forms of economic organization (the modern corporation) that gave them a military and economic edge. The spices, silks, porcelains, and other valuables of Asia were among Europe's most coveted items, so it is no surprise that Europe's new technologies were employed in a worldwide quest to find their sources and control their trade. By the late sixteenth century, the tiny country of Portugal dominated East-West economic ties by conquering or founding a series of trading colonies stretching from West Africa to the Persian Gulf to Japan. The Industrial Revolution in Great Britain in the eighteenth century gave Europe an advantage in manufacturing that Asia would not match for two centuries. By the late nineteenth century, most of Asia had even been subjugated by European colonial powers. China, too vast to be taken over by the Europeans, was nevertheless under their control. Led by Britain, the Europeans, using the threat or actual use of force, extracted "unequal" treaties from China that gave them special concessions, such as control of pieces of Chinese territory. Hong Kong, for instance, was ceded to Britain in 1842.

By the late 1950s, Asia was generally free from colonialism but far from its former glory. Development economists had much greater hope for other parts of the developing world, such as the more advanced countries of Latin America or resource-rich nations in Africa, such as Ghana or the Congo. The depleted economies of East Asia, including Korea, Taiwan, and Singapore, with few sources of money and practically no existing industry, seemed especially hopeless. Yet it was here, supposedly the bottom of the international economic barrel, that the Miracle was born.

East Asia outperformed every other region in income growth.

AVERAGE ANNUAL GROSS DOMESTIC PRODUCT PER CAPITA GROWTH, 1965–1999

REGION	PERCENT CHANGE
East Asia	5.6
South Asia	2.4
High-income nations	2.4
World	1.6
Latin America	1.4
Middle East and N. Africa	0.1
Sub-Saharan Africa	−0.2
E. Europe and Central Asia	−1.5

Source: World Bank.

. . . .

HOW DID THESE countries defy economic logic and ascend to the forefront of the global economy? *How did the Miracle happen?* The answer to that question has been one of the most hotly debated in modern economic history. The result is a library of literature and an avalanche of explanations. Yet no single theory tells the whole story.

One school of thought argues that there is *something special about Asians themselves* that gave birth to the Miracle. Asian cultures, the argument goes, contain the necessary ingredients to cook up rapid economic achievement. Proponents of this view have been especially focused on Confucianism, the ancient moral and ethical code of China. Among its main tenets are a stress on societal order, respect for hierarchy, bureaucratic excellence, and devotion to a strong work ethic and education—all elements that laid the groundwork for economic development. Confucianism, wrote British politician Roderick MacFarquhar in 1980, "is as important to the rise of the east Asian hyper-growth economies as the conjunction of Protestantism and the rise of capitalism in the west."[10]

It is true that Asians across the region exhibit certain behavior patterns that contributed to their economic success. Foremost is a propensity to save rather than spend, which built up the capital necessary for industrial investment. Furthermore, the societies that entered the Miracle in its first stages—Japan, South Korea, Taiwan, Hong Kong, and Singapore—are all tinged by Confucian culture. However, as the Miracle spread across the continent, countries with an increasingly wide range of cultural influences achieved the same results—from India's Hindus to Malaysia's Muslims to Thailand's Buddhists. The cultures of Asia are too diverse to be bunched together, so it is impossible to credit any one culture or clear set of cultural practices for the entire Miracle. Most of all, the culture thesis falls apart when put into historical perspective. Confucianism has been a pillar of many Asian societies for centuries, but that did not stop Asia, and especially China, the Confucian heartland, from falling far behind the West in economic development and technology. Asia had to *do* something, and something *new*, to make the Miracle happen.

A second category of thought claims that that is *exactly* how the Miracle was created. *Asia designed unique and superior economic policies and institutions* that brought about the region's spectacular growth. The focal point of this argument has been the unusual role the state played in economic development. Rather than adopting a pure, American laissez-faire ideology, most Asian governments intervened in their economies in ways that classical economics considers unwise and potentially catastrophic. The ultimate government sin was playing a direct role in allocating resources within the economy, a task, according to economists, best left to impartial markets. Government bureaucrats "picked winners" by choosing specific industries to nurture, then devised a mix of policies to support and accelerate their growth. Asian governments directed finance and investment, created special banks, and set up biased trade regimes to turn

chosen industries—and in some cases, individual companies—
into top-notch global competitors. As many Asian governments
pursued similar programs, some experts believe that Asia created
its own model for development.

The "Asian model" theory has been highly influential, and we
will continue to examine it in coming pages. However, it has its
limitations. The model was adopted in some form by many—but
not all—countries that joined the Miracle. In fact, two of the most
important entrants—China and India—sparked their Miracles
by *removing* state influence from the economy. Furthermore, the
debate over the true effectiveness of Asia's state-led development
rages to this day. Advocates argue that the model produced economic results above and beyond what would have happened in a
free-market environment. Detractors contend the role of the state
in the Miracle has been exaggerated and the record of Asia's attempts to "pick winners" is riddled with failures and hidden costs.

Those who harbor reservations about the "Asian model" tend
to lean toward a third type of explanation for the Miracle—that
Asia did nothing special to create it, crediting instead the basic
forces of capitalism. Asia took full advantage of the global system
of free trade that emerged under American auspices after the
end of World War II to generate exports, investment, jobs, and
growth. Every country—from Japan to India—capitalized on its
comparative advantages in the world economic system to generate rapid development. Government policies fostered private enterprise—what the World Bank called "getting the basics right."[11]
Policymakers, for example, invested heavily in education to build
up human capital and in infrastructure to reduce business costs,
and they maintained healthy, stable macroeconomic environments
by keeping inflation and budget deficits low. From this standpoint,
Asia followed a route to growth that was essentially classical in
its economics. "Developing nations," Goh Keng Swee, one of the
architects of Singapore's Miracle, counseled, "need not go beyond
Adam Smith for guidance on their economic policies."[12] The Miracle was in this way a textbook case of the power of free markets

and free enterprise. Perhaps the Miracle was not that miraculous after all.

Yet even this explanation is incomplete. Purely theoretical reasons for the Miracle tell us *how* growth happened but not *why*. If the Miracle was so easy to achieve, *any* country could have done it. The persistence of grinding poverty in large swaths of the world, especially Africa, reveals that is not the case. Setting in place the proper conditions for development never happens automatically. *There is something special about Asia.*

. . . .

SO THE QUESTION remains, at best, only partially answered. *What really caused the Asian Economic Miracle?* My own theory completes the puzzle with a missing piece that economists tend to ignore: *the people.*

The story of economics is at its heart the story of human endeavor. Behind the statistics, charts, and graphs that are the standard tools of the professional economist lay the decisions and deeds of people, both great and ordinary. Economies are built not by policies but by the people who craft them; not by capital flows, but by the people who use them to invest; not by data on production and exports, but by the people who take the bus to work each day and spend twelve hours on an assembly line making the goods counted by statisticians. Theories on economic development tend to leave out the human element. Yet it is in the lives of people that the secret to Asian success is found. As South Korea's great nation builder, Park Chung Hee, once wrote, his country's economic transformation "is not so much the work of a miracle as the fitting results of many years of hard work to make ourselves stand on our own feet."[13]

Since the 1950s, Asia has been blessed by a series of determined, devoted, and inventive leaders, in both government and business, who, to a substantial degree, believed their own success depended on economic achievement. The group was a diverse one—bureaucrats and technocrats; politicians and generals; Communists and capitalists; democrats and dictators; engineers, economists, and entrepreneurs; even a medical doctor. But they all shared common goals: to elevate their people from poverty, to build thriving economies on war-torn landscapes, to forge new nations from disaggregated colonies, to hoist Asia into its proper place in the world. Jawaharlal Nehru, India's first prime minister, summed up this spirit on the eve of Indian independence from British rule in August 1947. "The achievement we celebrate today is but a step, an opening of opportunity, to the greater triumphs and achievements that await us," he said. "The service of India means the service of the millions who suffer. It means the ending of poverty and ignorance and disease and inequality of opportunity. The ambition of the greatest man of our generation has been to wipe every tear from every eye. That may be beyond us, but as long as there are tears and suffering, so long our work will not be over."[14]

Nationalists throughout the developing world expressed similar sentiments, but few held to these ideals and doggedly pursued the well-being of their countries. All too often they turned into power-crazed tyrants or persisted with economic programs that brought their countries to ruin. Asia has had its share of poor leadership as well. But eventually, most of Asia's misguided leaders and wrong-headed policies got washed away and replaced by new faces and intelligent ideas. Once again, though, we need to ask ourselves, *Why Asia?* Why did this exceptional group of leaders appear in Asia and not Africa or the Middle East? Why were Asian nationalists devoted to economic growth while those in other parts of the emerging world were not? These questions are hard to answer. One economist simply chalked it up to "luck."

I am not such a fatalist. I believe there were factors at work—historical, political, and economic—that created the Miracle. The leaders of the Miracle faced remarkably similar economic and political conditions and they set in place the policies that produced rapid growth during a period of tremendous weakness and political upheaval. They either forged entirely new states, as did Lee

Kuan Yew in Singapore (chapter three) or Chiang Kai-shek and his technocrats in Taiwan (chapter five), or founded new, often illegitimate regimes, as did Park Chung Hee of South Korea (chapter two) and Suharto of Indonesia (chapter seven), both of whom were generals who claimed political power. Simultaneously, these same leaders all confronted severe threats from Communism. Korea's Park faced off with North Korea and Taiwan's Chiang with China, while Singapore's Lee and Indonesia's Suharto contended with powerful domestic Communist movements. To tackle these threats and challenges, all of these leaders made rapid growth a top priority. Park, Chiang, Lee, and Suharto realized that they needed strong economies to ensure the survival of their states or governments. Not only was there a need to build weapons and arm men, but Asia's battles were fought as much with ideas as guns. To defeat Communism, the regimes of Park, Chiang, Lee, and Suharto had to prove to Asians that their governments and ideologies offered a better future than that promised by Communism. This group of leaders realized that improving the livelihoods of their citizens was the surest way of achieving their goals.

Facing similar problems, Asia's leaders tended to pursue similar economic strategies. The "early movers"—Japan, South Korea, Hong Kong, Taiwan, and Singapore—all lacked natural resources and had to import important raw materials, such as oil, to survive. All of them (except Japan) had poor, small populations unable to support industry on their own. These factors forced them to turn to the international economy. First Japan's bureaucrats (chapter one), then Park's, Lee's, and Chiang's technocrats all became obsessed with exports. They linked their economies to the global marketplace more tightly than most other emerging nations.

This "export-led" growth strategy was adopted by every one of the Miracle countries and was perhaps the most important single factor in achieving Asia's rapid growth. Though it sounds like common sense today, the export route was not seen that way in the 1950s and 1960s. Back then, Asia's policies were often considered heretical in development circles. Many experts maintained that the newly independent nations of the Third World would never achieve economic development if they did not *disengage* themselves from a world economy dominated by their former colonial masters. The global economic system, the thinking went, kept developing nations trapped as bonded servants to the West, which simply extracted their raw materials and, in the process, stifled their own industrialization. The idea was called "dependency theory." Development specialists in both the West and emerging countries advocated restricting trade and foreign investment and pursuing "import substitution," through which countries replaced goods imported from abroad by producing them at home. The emergence of the Soviet Union as a superpower in the 1950s also provided a noncapitalist alternative to development. These ideas took hold in large parts of Latin America and Africa. The results were often disastrous.

In Asia, the leaders of the Miracle flouted convention and ideology in forming their policies. Asia's choice to hitch onto the forces of globalization and ignore the prevailing economic wisdom is what caused the Miracle to happen. The region's leadership discovered the true path to attaining fantastic gains in human welfare and economic power in a remarkably short period of time. The Miracle showed that "the global economy was not, as so many 'dependency' theorists had claimed, rigged against latecomers," wrote economist Paul Krugman. "On the contrary, it offered the opportunity for countries . . . to achieve two centuries' worth of economic progress in little more than a generation. And that discovery energized not only the Asians but capitalism in general."[15] The Miracle leaves no doubt that globalization creates wealth.

To many readers of this page, such an emphatic endorsement of globalization may appear misguided, even startling. Critics charge that globalization has led to the exploitation of the poor, the abuse of labor, and the impoverishment of the developed world's middle class. During times of economic stress, such as the 2008–09 global economic meltdown, those voices only grow louder. It is undeniable, of course, that the greater integration of the world economy will bring more pain than profit in times of recession. However, the past forty years of economic history in Asia prove that the building blocks of globalization—free trade, free flows of investment, free enterprise, and free markets—have generated wealth and opportunity on an unprecedented scale. Though the global economic system may occasionally need reform, the Miracle is clear evidence that policymakers in both Asia and the West should avoid the temptation to construct protectionist barriers or withdraw from the international economy. Reversing globalization will only prevent the hundreds of millions of remaining poor from experiencing the Miracle. Asia's story provides important lessons for central bankers and government leaders around the world on how to restore growth, increase incomes, and improve human welfare.

Making the hard, but correct, choices in favor of globalization, often in the face of furious political opposition, takes guts—as Asia's leaders have learned again and again since the 1950s. Why Park, Lee, and the rest of Asia's leaders fearlessly headed off on their own economic course is a major theme of this book. They were less ideological than many other leaders of developing nations, and more open to adapting policies to the needs of their economies. This may be because hardly any of the Miracle leaders—with one major exception, Manmohan Singh in India (chapter nine)—were economists. They tended to be lawyers, engineers, or generals. Once the key policies were set in place by the "early movers," they spread across Asia, one country to the next. Policies that worked in one country were snatched up and implemented in another. The process started with Japan. The ideas generated by Japan's bureaucrats and political leaders provided a ready roadmap to development, which many Miracle countries followed in some form. Park, for example, copied Japan's economic system. The "late movers"—Deng Xiaoping in China (chapter six), Manmohan Singh, and Mahathir Mohamad in Malaysia (chapter ten)—were all heavily influenced by the "early movers." Mahathir, for example, launched a "Look East Policy" in Malaysia that advocated mimicking Japanese and South Korean economic practices as a way of sparking Malaysia's own Miracle. The Miracle had a self-sustaining quality. Success bred more success.

In setting in place policies that supported rapid growth, the leaders of the Miracle created conditions that nurtured entrepreneurial ingenuity. The role of Asia's business leaders is often overlooked in development theory. Their creativity and uncanny ability to invent new products, overcome barriers, and compete in international markets were crucial to Asia's success. Electronics genius Akio Morita (chapter one) and auto innovator Soichiro Honda of Japan (chapter eight), Hong Kong plastics maker Li Ka-shing (chapter four), industrialist Chung Ju Yung of South Korea (chapter two), computer entrepreneurs Stan Shih of Taiwan (chapter five) and Liu Chuanzhi of China (chapter twelve), and Indian tech gurus Azim Premji and Narayana Murthy (chapter thirteen) forever altered the global marketplace by building companies of international stature, usually against nearly insurmountable odds. At its heart, the Miracle was a victory for private enterprise.

It was also a triumph for the United States, the chief underwriter of the Miracle, which provided aid, military protection, guidance, and access to the large American market for Asian-made products, thus setting in place the regional and international conditions that allowed Asia to thrive. The United States wished to erect a "barrier" of friendly governments across Asia to contain Communism, and most of the "early movers" were along this line of defense—Japan, South Korea, and Taiwan. The critical role the United States played in encouraging economic development in Asia is often underestimated. "Without the United States providing security and stability throughout the region, there would have been no growth," says Singapore's patriarch Lee Kuan Yew.[16]

. . . .

ASIA'S ACHIEVEMENT HAS created the world we know today. The continent's success has shifted the global balance of economic and political power, forever altering the structure of the world economy and propelling forward the globalization of international markets. New multinationals have been created to compete with those of America and Europe. Budding superpowers have emerged to challenge the dominance of the West.

This is not to say that all of the Miracle's leaders were saints. Some suppressed democracy and human rights and employed torture and murder to cement their rule. They have sometimes been guilty of corruption, occasionally on a massive scale. Business tycoons have been as quick to secure a monopoly or peddle political influence as to create jobs. Though it is impossible to justify such actions, it is equally impossible to deny the results they achieved. As Nehru hoped, they wiped the tears from the eyes of Asia.

What follows is the story of who they are and how they did it. The tale is one of great hardship and sacrifice, of innovation and inspiration, of a dramatic, continent-wide effort to uplift the fortunes of half of the world's population. We start in an unlikely place—the demoralized nation of Japan. Within the charred ruins of postwar Tokyo, the Miracle was about to take flight.

CHAPTER ONE

THE RADIO THAT
CHANGED THE WORLD

We should all join to try to make more Japans in other parts of the world. —AKIO MORITA

Akio Morita was not amused. The Japanese businessman was in a restaurant in Dusseldorf in 1953 and ordered a dish of ice cream. Stuck into a scoop was a miniature decorative paper parasol. "This is from your country," the smiling waiter informed Morita. He probably intended to make Morita feel welcome in a foreign land, but instead he inadvertently bruised Morita's pride. "That was the extent of his knowledge of Japan and its capabilities, I thought, and maybe he was typical," Morita later wrote. "What a long way we had to go."

At that moment, Morita was not confident that Japan could get as far as it needed. More than eighty years earlier, Japan had determined to catch up with the West, yet despite all of its efforts, the Japanese were still far behind, especially in the realm Morita knew best—technology. The importance of technology was made devastatingly clear to him while he served as a naval officer during World War II. He was assigned to a team of researchers developing heat-seeking weaponry and night-vision gun sights. The Imperial military headquarters believed that breakthrough technologies would turn the tide of a war that was fast becoming a hopeless cause. At the time, Morita believed that the technology gap between Japan and the United States was not great.

That illusion, however, was shattered when America dropped atomic bombs on Japan. He heard about the first—Hiroshima—while eating lunch with his colleagues on August 7, 1945, one day after the blast. The news report stated that "a new kind of weapon that flashed and shone" had been used by the Americans, but Morita, a highly trained physicist, knew exactly what it was. The news came as a revelation. "We might as well give up our research right now," a despondent Morita told his team at the lunch table. "If the Americans can build an atomic bomb, we must be too far behind in every field to catch up." His superior officer was furious with him for such defeatism, but Morita believed he was simply being realistic. "The news of Hiroshima was something truly incredible to me," he later recalled. "It struck me that American industrial might was greater than we realized, simply overwhelming." The bombs also convinced Morita that educated young Japanese like himself must persevere and lead Japan's postwar renewal. "It was brought home to me more than ever that Japan would need all the talent it could save for the future," Morita later wrote. "I don't mind saying that even then, as a young man, I felt that somehow I had a role to play in that future."

Morita pursued that role through a start-up venture he founded in 1946 with a partner, Masaru Ibuka. They called it the Tokyo Telecommunications Engineering Corporation. Their first headquarters was in the ruins of a Tokyo department store. Then they moved to a wooden shack on the outskirts of the capital. When it rained, the staff opened umbrellas over their desks to protect them from water leaking through the bomb-damaged roof.[1] But like garage entrepreneurs anywhere, they had ambitions well beyond their meager resources. Amid the destruction of the war, they hoped their efforts could contribute to their nation's recovery. In a founding prospectus, Ibuka wrote that the company determined "to reconstruct Japan and to elevate the nation's culture through dynamic technological and manufacturing activities."[2]

As Morita sat glumly with his ice cream in Dusseldorf seven years later, however, he was disheartened. Morita felt that Germany's rapid recovery from its own disastrous war effort "made Japan's postwar progress seem slow."[3] His spirits were also dampened by a preceding trip through America. The size and scale of the United States made him doubt that his tiny firm could ever be successful in the American market. "I thought it would be impossible to sell our products here," Morita later wrote. "The place just overwhelmed me."

Yet just before his return to Tokyo, Morita's hopes lifted during a stop in Eindhoven in the Netherlands, then the home base of electronics giant Philips. He toured the factory—not as a VIP executive, but as an ordinary tourist—and was wowed by its technical prowess. Morita was impressed that the Netherlands, a small, agricultural nation much like Japan, had produced such a world-class technology firm. Encouraged, he wrote a letter to Ibuka. "If Philips can do it," he scribbled, "maybe we can too."

It was not such a far-fetched idea. The enterprise Morita and Ibuka formed would become the famous Sony Corporation, arguably Asia's best-known company. Sony came to symbolize the growing economic and technical power of Japan and Asia and the intensifying threat they posed to the Western-dominated economic order. Sony, in some ways, became the Miracle's brand name.

Likewise, the gregarious Akio Morita was probably the Miracle's single most famous personality. Morita became so well known in the United States that he was enlisted to pitch American Express cards in a commercial on American television. ("Do you know me?" Morita asks. "As chairman of Sony, I expect great reception.")[4] Morita operated in the most elite circles of American society, fraternizing with the likes of the Rockefellers and calling Leonard Bernstein a good friend. When Sony wished to break into the China market, Henry Kissinger arranged a meeting for Morita with China's supreme leader.[5] Morita, Kissinger once commented, was "a great patriot yet an individual who had learned that, in the current world, Japan had to excel by relating to other countries rather than by separating itself from them."[6] Despite his respect for the United States, Morita was also one of Japan's stoutest defenders when trade disputes turned the relationship between the two countries confrontational in the 1970s and 1980s.

As a businessman, Morita displayed an innate talent for understanding consumer behavior and identifying future technological and social trends. Those talents helped place Sony at the forefront of the global electronics industry. His inspiration came from an almost childlike curiosity and enthusiasm. A lifetime lover of toys, he collected music boxes and player pianos, and never resisted a visit to New York City's famous toy store FAO Schwarz.[7] The study at his home featured an antique American nickelodeon, complete with a stash of nickels to make it play.[8] Morita started skiing at sixty, windsurfed at sixty-five, and learned to scuba dive at sixty-seven. "Idleness leads to sickness," he once said.[9] An incessant tinkerer, Morita was always fascinated by the latest electronic gadgetry. Yotaro Kobayashi, a former chairman of Fuji Xerox and a close friend of Morita's, recalls contacting Morita in 1967 when his company had just released its first desktop copier in Japan. Morita wanted one immediately. The next day, Morita called Kobayashi and proclaimed: "We know everything about the Xerox machine." No sooner had the new product arrived at Morita's office than he and a team of engineers dismantled it to figure out how it worked. Perturbed, Kobayashi gently reminded Morita that he had rented, not purchased, the copier, so Morita had just destroyed Kobayashi's property. "I know that," Morita said. "It's back in complete shape and working."[10]

Morita's greatest contribution to the Miracle may be his success in improving the perception of the capabilities of Asian companies. As Sony was starting out, Japan was known as a purveyor of inferior knock-offs of Western-designed goods or cut-rate trinkets, like the paper parasol Morita discovered in his ice cream. Yet from its earliest years, Sony's labs produced technological innovations and lifestyle-altering gadgets—most famously, the Walkman portable cassette player—that became integral to the daily lives of consumers around the world. "Sony's technological achievements in product design, production and marketing helped change the image of MADE IN JAPAN from a notion of cheap imitations to one associated with superior quality," wrote management guru Kenichi Ohmae.[11]

Morita set Sony on this course in 1953 when he got access to the transistor. He believed the transistor was a "breakthrough" technology that would replace the bulky and unreliable vacuum tube used in electronics at the time, allowing companies to develop smaller, high-quality radios and other products. This idea was visionary. The global technology community was still uncertain about the transistor's potential. Invented by Bell Labs, the transistor was not powerful enough to work even in a small radio. The executives at Western Electric, the firm that held the patent to the technology, thought it could be used in little more than hearing aids.

It was Ibuka who first became enamored with the transistor during a trip to the United States in 1952. He failed to get a meeting with Western Electric, but before returning to Tokyo he enlisted a Japanese friend in New York to inquire about the company's willingness to license the technology and lobby on Sony's behalf.[12] In 1953, these efforts paid off. Ibuka received a letter from Western Electric inviting Sony to discuss a license agreement, and he dispatched Morita to New York to finalize a deal.

Morita, disheartened by his U.S. visit, suffered a serious crisis of confidence the night before the meeting. In despair, he visited an old friend from Japan, Yuzuru Tanigawa, who was also conducting business in New York, at his hotel. Why, he asked Tanigawa, would a well-established firm like Western Electric bother with a nobody like him? "I'm afraid they really won't take this seriously tomorrow," Morita confessed, "so I may give it up now." Tanigawa gave Morita a pep talk. "What are you saying? Americans aren't like that," he said. "Whenever they find something interesting, they will just come out and tell you. This is where Americans differ from Japanese."[13]

Morita emboldened himself and met the next day with Frank

Mascarich, Western Electric's vice president of licensing. As Morita feared, Mascarich had misgivings about Sony. Any agreement required the approval of the Japanese government, which Morita did not yet have. Morita spoke almost no English at that time and had to conduct the complex negotiations through a translator. Nevertheless, Morita's ebullience and charm worked. "I wasn't terribly pleased with the arrangement," Mascarich later recalled. "But [Morita] was so persuasive, and so anxious to proceed with his plans." Mascarich gave Morita two technical manuals not available to the public before Sony had paid him a dime. They became the basic textbooks with which Sony's engineering team educated themselves about the transistor.[14]

Ibuka was thrilled, though Sony still needed government approval. For that, Morita and Ibuka had to contend with the powerful Ministry of International Trade and Industry, or MITI. In the 1950s, MITI exerted tremendous authority over corporate Japan. Political scientist Chalmers Johnson, who wrote the definitive study of MITI, called the ministry Japan's "economic general staff."[15] The specific problem MITI presented for Sony concerned foreign exchange. Morita and Ibuka needed to pay Western Electric $25,000 as an advance on royalties to get the rights to the transistor technology, but MITI controlled the allocation of Japan's hard currency. Sony could not complete its agreement with Western Electric until MITI gave its consent.

The ministry's initial reaction was not encouraging. Ibuka said he got "laughed out of the room" when he first asked for approval.[16] The bureaucrats were also angered that Sony had proceeded to sign a formal agreement with a U.S. company without the ministry's prior consent.[17] "The bureaucrats at MITI could not see the use for such a device and were not eager to grant permission," Morita later explained. "MITI thought that such a small company . . . could not possibly undertake the enormous task of dealing with brand-new technologies. In fact, they were adamant against it at first."[18]

The task of changing the bureaucrats' minds fell to Ibuka. He hosted teams of MITI officials at Sony's leaky headquarters and regaled them with his vision of how the transistor would forever alter the electronics industry. "We intend to proceed with or without you," he told them, "but if you approve our deal with Western Electric, you will look smart!"[19] After six months of haggling and waiting, Sony received approval from MITI.[20]

MITI's decision proved a turning point in global economic history. It ensured the future of Sony and was one of the earliest and most important steps taken in the creation of Japan's influential electronics and semiconductor industries. Sony's tussle with MITI also tells us a lot about how Japan achieved its Miracle. It explains why many Americans held misperceptions about the Japanese economic system that later generated fear and hostility about Japan's rise to global prominence. To understand this history, we have to go back in time—way back—to the deck of an American naval vessel off the coast of Japan in the year 1853.

· · · ·

COMMODORE MATTHEW PERRY had little patience for the Japanese, whom he considered "semi-barbarous" and "deceitful."[21] Yet his actions in Japan in the 1850s helped propel the Japanese leadership to make economic modernization their top priority. Perry inadvertently reordered the global balance of power, launched Asia's challenge to the dominance of the West, and laid the groundwork for the Miracle.

The crusty Perry was assigned to a special mission by U.S. President Millard Fillmore to open trade relations with Japan. The Tokugawa shoguns, who had ruled Japan since the early seventeenth century, kept the country sealed from foreigners, save for restricted trade conducted from the southern port of Nagasaki. Influence from abroad, the shoguns feared, would undermine the nation's culture, religion, and economy. As Perry sailed in his giant frigates near Tokyo Bay, the Japanese resisted his entreaties. Government representatives asked him to depart for Nagasaki, where Japan would parlay with him.

To Perry that seemed like retreat. Fillmore had entrusted him with a letter addressed to Japan's leadership, and he intended to deliver it. On July 9, 1853, Perry informed the Japanese that if they would not accept Fillmore's letter, then he would go ashore "in sufficient force" to hand it over—"whatever the consequences." To clarify his position, two days later he sailed his mighty frigate, the *Mississippi*, up Tokyo Bay and closer to the city (then called Edo), certain this would sway the minds of Japan's dithering ruling council.[22] Perry's actions panicked Tokyo. Its residents feared he would turn his impressive guns on the town, and they "carried their valuables and furniture in all directions to conceal them in the house of some friend living further off," according to one Japanese chronicler. The government reversed course and agreed to receive Fillmore's letter. The next year, Perry returned and completed a treaty that unlocked two ports to American trade. In his formal report, a triumphant Perry predicted what might happen in Japan after his departure. "The Japanese are, undoubtedly, . . . a very imitative, adaptative, and compliant people," he wrote, "and in these characteristics may be discovered a promise of the comparatively easy introduction of foreign customs and habits."[23]

Perry was prescient. The humiliation inflicted by Perry, and later by other foreign powers who followed his lead, mixed with growing dissatisfaction with the Tokugawa government acted as a catalyst for major change. Perry's mission, with its imposing warships and weaponry, awoke many in Japan to how far behind their nation had fallen during its centuries of isolation. If Japan was going to defend itself from these rapacious barbarians, the nation had to reform itself—and fast. In 1868, a coalition of regional leaders overthrew the shogunate and restored the emperor as the preeminent power in the Japanese government. However, this political rebellion—called the Meiji Restoration after the name of the emperor—was anything but a return to the ancient days of imperial rule. Led by a group of nationalists determined to upend the old order, whose slogan became *fukoku-kyohei*, or "enriching the country, strengthening the military," the Meiji mission was to catch up to the economic, technological, and military prowess of the West. Korekiyo Takahashi, a Meiji-era reformer and prime minister, captured the spirit in an address to university students. "Gentlemen," he told them, "it is your duty to advance the status of Japan, bring her to a position of equality with the civilized powers and then carry on to build a foundation from which we shall surpass them all."[24]

Meiji Japan began importing foreign technology and institutional frameworks at a furious pace. Missions were sent abroad in search of the best models to follow. Banking and university systems were created on American lines, commercial and civil legal codes were influenced by Britain and Germany, and the latest technical know-how and machinery in railroads, communications, and industry were imported from everywhere. Japan, however, had no intention of simply aping foreign ways. The country would borrow from the world's most advanced economies what it needed to compete with them, but would still preserve the basic elements of Japanese culture. "One who wants to resist alien ideas and religion should thrust himself into its bosom [*sic*] and make its weapon his own," counseled Jo Niijima, a prominent Meiji educator.[25]

The Meiji leadership did not dare entrust their nation's future to the forces of laissez-faire economics. The state was heavily involved in launching Japan's industrialization from the beginning. Toshimichi Okubo, one of the most powerful Meiji leaders, warned that Japan must move quickly "to stimulate domestic production and increase our exports so as to repair our weakness by attaining national wealth and strength." He believed that Japanese merchants were not capable of achieving these goals on their own. State-run industries were "absolutely necessary," he insisted, "even though they go against the laws of political economy." Japan was "something different" and therefore needed "different laws" to develop.[26]

Meiji's efforts were spectacularly successful. Japan became the first non-Western nation to industrialize. As Japan moved into heavier industries, massive corporate conglomerates called *zaibatsu* formed. The economic expansion, however, had a sinister, militaristic edge. In the 1930s, the bureaucracy marshaled the nation's industrial resources for a military conquest of Asia. By World War II, as the world discovered to its dismay, Japan's technology and industrial capabilities matched those of Europe.

Japan's defeat in World War II only intensified the desire of its government and business leaders to catch up to the West. The desperate conditions in the country at the war's end made it imperative to get the economy moving again as quickly as possible. The fierce nationalistic energy, once poured into the war effort, now went into economic development. The *fukoku-kyohei* of the Meiji period became *Obei ni oikose*, "overtake Europe and America," in the 1960s.[27] Japan's postwar leadership combined some of the features of the Meiji and wartime economies with new elements to produce what became known as a specific "Asian model" of development, one that later influenced much of the region.

The creation of this "model" was a collaborative effort. No one ever sat down and drafted a complete program for Japan's development. The system formed over time in response to the specific needs of the economy at specific moments. When it took shape, by the mid-1950s, the "model" operated like a well-oiled machine—a "GNP machine," in the words of one Japanese official.[28] The cast of civil servants who created the "Asian model" all eschewed American-style laissez-faire economics. The state, they determined, had to play a leading role in the economic development of Japan. In this way, they were all disciples of Meiji's Okubo.

The prototype for Japan's development-minded bureaucrats was Shigeru Sahashi, a career MITI man and one of its powerful vice-ministers. Among the most influential postwar government officials, he left an indelible mark on Japan's "model." Combative, outspoken, and arrogant, Sahashi set in place Japan's bureaucratic traditions and then broke them. He was a lifelong critic of the government's system of promotion based on seniority and believed merit should take precedence. In that spirit, he hired women onto the MITI staff in contradiction to the bureaucracy's strict bias toward men.[29] Nicknamed "Mr. MITI" by the local press, the hard-boiled Sahashi was feted as a hero by his supporters, who dubbed him a "samurai among samurai." But his fierce reputation also earned him the epithet "Monster Sahashi."[30]

Like many of Japan's economic mandarins, Sahashi was neither from an elite family nor a trained economist. He was born in 1913 in the town of Izumi in central Japan, where his father was a photographer. In elementary school, Sahashi, a rough-and-tumble child, was a top sumo wrestler who often competed in local tournaments. His skills earned him the nickname "Yama Arashi," or "mountain storm." An equally excellent student, Sahashi reached Japan's academic pinnacle when he enrolled in the prestigious University of Tokyo to study law. As was true for many top college graduates, Sahashi's first choice of career was government. A die-hard nationalist, Sahashi believed joining the powerful bureaucracy was the surest way to contribute to the country's development. In Japan, economic policy was devised and implemented primarily by career bureaucrats, unlike in the United States, where elected leaders have greater influence. "I thought the best shortcut to ensure people had 'really human-like lives' would be to become a bureaucrat," he later wrote. "I thought I would become a bureaucrat to work for society."[31] The premier job choices for graduates like Sahashi were at MITI* and the Ministry of Finance, the two most influential arms of the bureaucracy. After a grueling series of interviews, both ministries offered him positions on the same day. He chose MITI.[32]

MITI, with Sahashi's help, became command central for the "Asian model" in Japan. Sahashi's views on the economy, like Okubo's, rested on the belief that Japan could not properly advance

---

* When Sahashi first joined the government, the ministry was called the Ministry of Commerce and Industry. MITI was formed in 1951.

without the guiding hand of the state. It would be best "if human beings became perfect and the harmony between the individual and the whole was formed in an ideal fashion," he wrote. "But our reality in normal social life or the economic realm is far from this ideal. Therefore, [the bureaucrats] have to contribute to human welfare and social development."[33] Sahashi and other MITI officials worried that, left to the market, the Japanese economy would not develop in the *right* way. Market forces would direct the country's scarce resources into businesses in which Japan had a clear advantage. In the years immediately after the war, for instance, labor-intensive industries like toys and textiles utilized the country's large pool of low-wage workers. Officials like Sahashi, however, wanted to create *new* comparative advantages.* They intended to push the economy into heavy industries that required greater technical expertise and larger investments, thus generating higher wages and top-value exports. The only way these industries would develop, Japan's officials determined, was through state intervention. The government had to ensure that the necessary resources got allocated to designated sectors. This practice is called "industrial policy."

There is nothing new about the idea that governments are capable of engineering specific economic results. One of industrial policy's early proponents was America's founding father Alexander Hamilton. In a report to Congress in 1791, Hamilton argued that the newborn American government needed to offer "extraordinary aid and protection" to nurture manufacturing industries vital to the national economy and defense to ensure the United States could compete with the more advanced economies of Europe.[34] Japan's strategy resembled Hamilton's. Postwar Japan set in place an advanced and complex economic system aimed

---

* A country has a "comparative advantage" when it can produce a certain good more efficiently than other countries. For example, a country has a "comparative advantage" in growing corn if it has cheap, available land and good farming practices that can produce corn at lower cost than other countries. Or a country has a "comparative advantage" in making shirts if it has a large pool of low-wage labor to sew them together.

at developing certain specified industries. Japan's "high growth system," Johnson wrote, "was one of the most rational and productive industrial polices ever devised by any government."[35]

Sahashi and his fellow bureaucrats at MITI "picked winners" by "targeting" certain industries they thought had growth potential and could become globally competitive.[36] The early "winners" included steel and shipbuilding; later, high-tech industries like semiconductors were "targeted." MITI, the finance ministry, and the central bank then cooperated to create incentives to attract the private sector into those "targeted" industries. These incentives included easy access to low-cost finance, duty-free imports of necessary machinery, infusions of foreign technology, and trade barriers that protected the favored industries from foreign competition. The goal of the incentives was to reduce the costs and risks for private companies to undertake projects in "targeted" sectors and thus prod them to invest on a larger scale and at a faster pace than would otherwise have taken place under free-market conditions. Lowering the barriers to investment was crucial as the favored heavy industries required hefty up-front outlays but provided little hope of a quick return. The purpose of Japan's industrial policy was not only to produce rapid growth, but also to alter the entire *structure* of the Japanese economy toward advanced industries and create companies that could compete in the global marketplace in new, high-value sectors. In orchestrating this shift, Japan's bureaucrats set in place a pattern of development followed by most of the other Asian countries that experienced the Miracle. Economies first generated rapid growth by producing low-cost, low-tech products with their low-wage labor, then steadily transitioned into more expensive, more technologically complex goods as development progressed.

For the Japanese businessman, the MITI-driven "Asian model" had a clear upside—all kinds of government perquisites and protection that helped build new corporations. But the "model" also had a clear downside. Japan's bureaucrats required much greater control over the economy than their more free-market American

counterparts to make their industrial policy work. MITI held tremendous formal authority through much of the 1950s, which allowed the ministry to interfere in corporate decision making. Its
grip on the allocation of foreign currency that gave Sony headaches was just one example. By the early 1960s, MITI began to
lose some of its legal powers in a liberalization effort, but Sahashi
and the other bureaucrats saw it as unthinkable that the private
businessman would be left to run his own affairs without their
oversight. "It is an utterly self-centered point of view [among
businessmen] to think that the government should be concerned
with providing only a favorable environment for industries without telling them what to do," Sahashi once commented.[37] He and
his colleagues perfected a method of informal control in which
MITI issued "recommendations" to private industry that became
known as "administrative guidance."

These policy decisions were often "extra-legal"—MITI was
not officially able to enforce them—but the government maintained enough levers of control in the economy that executives ignored "administrative guidance" at their own peril. Sahashi took
an especially hard line against corporate leaders who defied his
orders. In 1965, a steelmaker named Sumitomo Metals rejected
"guidance" from MITI that the industry should reduce production amid a recession. Organizing such production cartels had
become a regular feature of MITI activity to protect Japanese industries from the ill effects of market downturns. However, Sumitomo's irate president, Hosai Hyuga, considered the production
quotas unfair. Convinced Sumitomo "argued for the sake of their
benefit under the name of justice," Sahashi threatened to cut off
the company's imports of coking coal, a crucial raw material for
steel production. In a rare public challenge to MITI, Hyuga held
a press conference where he insisted he could make as much steel
as he wished. Yet Sahashi held his ground on coal imports, and
with no option, Hyuga soon fell in line. Though Sahashi took a
beating in the press for being imperial, the unrepentant Mr. MITI

believed he served the good of the economy. "I still don't think even slightly that I did anything wrong," he later wrote.[38]

The government's most important lever of control was its command of finance, managed by MITI's powerful industrial-policy partner, the Ministry of Finance. One journalist called this ministry "a political, economic, and intellectual force without parallel in the developed world."[39] Though the commercial banks in Japan were private, the finance ministry manipulated much of their decision making. The bureaucrats directed the flow of resources to make sure loans got to companies undertaking investments in MITI-targeted industries. It achieved this through its oversight of the lending practices of the central bank, the Bank of Japan, which, unlike in Western economies, was under the thumb of the finance ministry. When financing from private banks was not sufficient to support a "targeted" venture, the government ordered state-owned financial institutions to provide further funds, especially the Japan Development Bank. To smooth the process of directing finance, the government reconstituted the large business groups, including some of the old *zaibatsu*, which had been dismantled by General Douglas MacArthur during America's military occupation of Japan after the war. Now called *keiretsu*, each had a bank and a trading firm at its core, with industrial firms attached around them. All of a *keiretsu*'s affiliates were linked through cross-shareholdings. The *keiretsu* were responsible for bringing MITI industrial policy to life—by taking the plans, proposals, and incentives and transforming them into new enterprises. These big groups became globally recognized names, such as Mitsubishi, Sumitomo, Fuji, and Mitsui.

Though the *keiretsu* were protected at home, Japan's bureaucrats never intended for them to become bloated, inefficient behemoths. From their start, MITI's nurtured projects were meant to be globally competitive. This foresight was an important difference between Japan's industrial-policy "model" and the state-led development methods of much of the rest of the emerging world.

The success of a MITI-sponsored venture was determined by its ability to export. With few natural resources of its own, exports were considered a lifeline for Japan. Japan's industrial policy was therefore intimately linked to the demands of international trade.

The devotion to exports also forced corporate Japan to tussle with American and European competition in world markets from an early stage. Japanese companies had no choice but to become efficient, high-quality producers as rapidly as possible. In this way, Japan's "model" introduced the influence of markets into development strategy, an element which other state-led efforts often ignored. Competition is "the way to realize a better economy," Sahashi wrote. "We see free competition as good because that's the best measure to exploit human creativity." It is here that we find the real secret to Japan's "model"—the way in which it linked state intervention to market forces.

Inside the domestic market, however, Japanese companies were shielded from the heated competition of the international economy. MITI, and Sahashi in particular, was decidedly nationalistic in its outlook. Its goal was to create homegrown industries. It did not want multinational companies charging into Japan, claiming market share, and stifling the advancement of Japanese business. MITI carefully monitored and restricted the inflow of foreign investment into Japan. This policy frequently brought MITI into conflict with foreign firms. One of the more famous cases involved IBM. When the American giant tried to form a local subsidiary, MITI demanded that it be majority-owned by Japanese, knowing full well that IBM would never accept such a stipulation. IBM, though, circumvented MITI and its foreign investment regulations by founding a fully yen-based local operation. Outsmarted, a furious Sahashi blocked IBM's local outfit from importing equipment for its factories. The conflict was eventually resolved in a series of tense meetings between Sahashi and IBM's local managers. Sahashi wanted access to IBM's computer patents, but the American firm was wary of turning over its proprietary technology to

Japanese competitors. Sahashi resorted to extortion. "If you don't agree to our conditions," Sahashi bluntly threatened, "we will take any measures necessary to deter IBM from operating in Japan." With no option, IBM surrendered its patents.[40]

. . . .

The actions of "Monster Sahashi" and his fiercely nationalistic colleagues gave rise to the concept of "Japan Inc." As the economy advanced under MITI's "guidance," the perception grew around the world that Japan was a monolithic entity in which government, business, and banking acted as the coordinated departments of one, big corporation. This "Japan Inc.," like any company, was out to forward its own interests in the global marketplace at its competitors' expense. Japan's economy became characterized as a sinister organization bent on world domination. In 1990, Bennett Bidwell, then a senior executive at Chrysler, described Japan as "a centrally orchestrated, totally committed, economic aggressor."[41]

Despite Japan's coordinated business patterns, the "Japan Inc." concept is one of the great misperceptions of the Miracle. MITI bureaucrats may have manipulated policy and finance, but they could not possibly have micromanaged every aspect of a primarily private economy. There are examples of successful uprisings against MITI "guidance" by companies or entire industries. In the early 1960s, for example, Sahashi hatched a plan to force mergers in the automobile industry in an attempt to form bigger companies he believed could better compete against the American Big Three. He met such resistance that the plan was scrapped. MITI's bureaucrats also had their share of embarrassing failures when the "winners" they picked turned out to be losers. One of its most glaring errors was its high-profile but unsuccessful bid to build a commercial aircraft industry. On the other hand, some of Japan's most successful industries, including motorcycles, robotics, fax machines, and consumer electronics, prospered *without* significant assistance from MITI.[42] "MITI," complained Morita, "has not been the great benefactor of the Japanese electronics industry that some seem to think it has."[43]

In fact, MITI's mixed record has sparked a vicious debate among Japanese economists over the true importance of its industrial policies in generating Japan's spectacular growth. Was the "Asian model" really that effective? *Is the model the chief cause of the Miracle?*

Proponents of the "Asian model," like Chalmers Johnson, believe MITI accelerated Japan's industrialization and economic growth beyond what it would have been under a laissez-faire system. In Johnson's words, MITI "single-handedly" transformed Japan's economic structure in the 1950s and early 1960s.[44] The proof, this camp contends, is in the results: Several industries picked as winners by MITI were among Japan's most successful. Government intervention, therefore, was *decisive.*

Others are not so sure. They contend that advocates like Johnson award MITI too much credit. The "'Japan, Inc.' views," wrote economist Takafusa Nakamura, "tend to exaggerate the importance of only one aspect of the Japanese economy."[45] Johnson and those who share his views tend to downplay the role of entrepreneurs, corporate management, and the Japanese worker and attribute Japan's success to the bureaucracy. "Rapid growth was not simply the result of growth policies; still less was it the result of a 'plot' on the part of a segment of the elite," wrote Japanese economist Yutaka Kosai. "Rather it was the . . . prompt responses to market conditions by firms and households at the grassroots level that was decisively important."[46] In this view, MITI merely set in place the conditions that allowed growth to happen. The hard work was achieved by Japan's private companies. The real source of Japan's rapid development, their argument goes, is not the guiding hand of the bureaucracy, but the power of markets. "While the government has certainly provided a favorable environment, the main impetus to growth has been private—business investment demand, private saving, and industrious and skilled

labor operating in a market-oriented environment," wrote economists Hugh Patrick and Henry Rosovsky. Japan's development,
they concluded, "was not unique at all; thus, while government
policy may have been important, its impact on economic performance was not 'uniquely Japanese.'" MITI, in this view, played a
supportive, not a decisive, role in the Miracle.[47]

The story of Sony shows the dangers of attributing too much
influence to MITI and its industrial policies. In their pursuit of
the transistor, Morita and Ibuka did not follow "administrative
guidance" or respond to specific MITI incentives. They identified the future ramifications of transistor technology and found
a way to acquire it without MITI's involvement. MITI failed to
recognize the importance of what Sony had done and opposed
its initiative. "The episode," wrote political economist Daniel
Okimoto, "belies the myth of MITI's prescience."[48] Throughout
its history, Sony was never part of MITI's system. The company
benefited from certain MITI and Ministry of Finance policies—
such as preferential taxes on some of its early products, which
made them more affordable to consumers[49]—but Morita's firm
did not receive any "targeted" financial aid, such as policy-driven
loans.[50] In the mid-1950s, Sony's request for state funds to help
the firm develop a video recorder was outright rejected by the government.[51] The company was "free-market from the beginning,"
says Nobuyuki Idei, a former Sony CEO. "I don't think MITI
had a strong interest" in the firm, or the electronics industry in
general, he says.[52]

MITI advocates respond that most economists have been
simply too trapped in an outdated, American free-enterprise ideology to appreciate the factors that created Japan's Miracle. Classical economists, they contend, are conditioned to believe that state
interference can do no more than muck up markets; they fail to
comprehend how government policy can guide and enhance market
forces. Japan's version of industrial policy, its supporters say, directed and accelerated the actions of markets; it did not replace
them. In economist lingo, MITI pursued "market-conforming"

rather than "market-defying" policies. Journalist James Fallows, one of the leading advocates of the "Asian model," wrote that the "lesson" to be learned from the success of the model "concerns the *combination* of markets and planning that lies behind Asia's modern growth." By utilizing government policy to make markets work *better*, Japan flouted the traditions of classical economics and the basis of America's free-market ideology. In Fallows's words, Japan "reinvented the rules of economics."[53]

The belief that Japan had devised some superior form of capitalism became increasingly widespread as Japan's Miracle accelerated. The classical economic view of Japan's success got shunted aside as out-of-touch with the new realities of global economics, yet the debate over the "Asian model" never faded away. Even the most die-hard advocates of the "Asian model" could not account for the success of firms like Sony. Fallows attributed Sony's rise to global prominence not to MITI, but to old-fashioned, against-the-odds entrepreneurship. Calling Morita a "buccaneer entrepreneur . . . in a way we think of as American," Fallows said that he "built a wonderful company more or less on his own, in what we would think of as the American tradition."[54] Perhaps Japan did not "reinvent" economics after all.

. . . .

MORITA WAS "FULL of excitement and wonder" when his father purchased an electronic phonograph for the family's large home in Nagoya. Morita, then a junior high school student, was astounded by the clear sound it produced. A music lover, he played his favorite Bach, Mozart, and Ravel records over and over again. From that moment, Morita was forever hooked on electronic gadgetry. "I was obsessed with this new discovery and all the questions it raised in my mind," he later wrote. Morita began devouring books and articles on the latest radio and electronics technologies and spent his after-school hours building devices from diagrams in his favorite magazine, *Wireless and Experiments*.

The Moritas were a venerable and wealthy business family who had been brewing sake for three centuries. Asian tradition demanded that Morita, as the oldest son, should take over the family firm, and his father brought Morita to the sake factory for board meetings beginning at a mere ten years old. "I learned while I was still in elementary school something about what goes on in business discussions," Morita wrote. "After a while I got to enjoy it."

Not enough, however, to choose sake over electronics—he studied physics at Osaka Imperial University. When World War II broke out, Morita preemptively joined the navy as part of a special program in which he could remain in his lab and "avoid throwing my life away in some futile sea battle thousands of miles from home," as he explained later. While working on that team developing heat-seeking missiles, he met Masaru Ibuka. A civilian, Ibuka owned his own company, which had devised an important component in a system to detect submerged American submarines, and he acted as a consultant to the group.[55] Ibuka and Morita were very different characters. Moody and obsessive, Ibuka could sometimes be gruff and tactless. He became so consumed by a favorite project that he could focus on little else. Quickly bored, he was well known within Sony for cutting off long-winded visitors in mid-sentence.[56] Yet the two became fast friends and remained so for the rest of their lives. In business, they were a perfect pair—Ibuka, an exceptionally creative engineer; Morita, with a genius for marketing and identifying consumer trends. Morita once called meeting Ibuka the biggest turning point of his life.[57]

After the war, Ibuka started a new company in Tokyo in the abandoned, charred remains of a department store in the rubble of what was once a ritzy part of town. He tried perfecting an automatic rice cooker made with a wooden basket and an electric coil, but never got it to work properly. Then he designed a device that attached to a regular radio to allow it to receive shortwave signals. Many Japanese had gone to great lengths to preserve their radios during the war—they were the main source of new information—and Ibuka's attachments sold well. Morita, meanwhile, had lost touch with Ibuka in the later stages of the war and only rediscovered Ibuka's whereabouts when he read a newspaper article about his friend's firm. Morita wrote Ibuka a letter offering to help out and he joined Ibuka in the burnt-out department store.[58] "The two of us talked about our dreams," Morita later recalled, "which amounted to wanting a car and building a factory with an elevator."[59]

Morita and Ibuka needed a hot product. While visiting Japan's national radio station in 1949, Ibuka saw his first tape recorder, an American model. Ibuka was enthralled, and he and Morita resolved to make one of their own. They knew little about the technology, but that was not nearly enough to dissuade them. Japanese studies professor John Nathan, who wrote the definitive work on Sony, called their effort to develop a homegrown tape recorder "a vintage example of the ingenuity and determination that drove Japan's postwar recovery."[60]

The most difficult part of producing the recorder proved to be the magnetic tape. Ibuka, Morita, and their team had no idea how the tape worked, nor did they have access to the proper supplies. The plastic used in the tape was unavailable in Japan at that time. They experimented with cellophane, but it stretched as it passed through the machine. Morita decided to try a thick paper instead. Magnetizing the tape was the biggest challenge. Through trial and error, one of their chief researchers, Nobutoshi Kihara, ingeniously took a chemical found in a local pharmacy, sautéed it in a frying pan, and mixed the resulting brown powder with lacquer to make a magnetic coating for the tape. The paper was sliced into thin strips and then painted with Kihara's mixture, using delicate paintbrushes made from the hairs of a raccoon's belly. In early 1950, Sony produced its first bulky recorder.

Sales were dismal. Potential customers who saw the machine in action were impressed but could not find a use for it, especially with its hefty price tag—the equivalent of $475 at the time. Morita and Ibuka thought that "all we had to do was make good products and the orders would come," Morita wrote. "We both had a lesson to learn." Morita, never one to give up, lugged the machine around in a Datsun truck to show it off to potential customers. Eventually Japanese courts purchased their recorders to replace stenographers, who were hard to find in postwar Japan.

This effort was a high-school science experiment compared to Sony's struggles with the transistor. When Ibuka and Morita first acquired the technology, they had to reinvent the transistor in their own labs in order to make it powerful enough to work in the mini-radio they envisioned. Sony's engineers brainstormed for possible ways to boost the transistor's output, but with few practical results.[61] Ibuka put Sony researcher Kazuo Iwama, Morita's brother-in-law, in charge of the transistor project. In early 1954, Ibuka and Iwama flew to the United States and Mascarich took them on a tour of Western Electric's transistor factory in Allentown, Pennsylvania. The visit did not lift their spirits. "It was some complicated business," Ibuka later said of the manufacturing process, "and I got pretty worried and asked Iwama if we maybe weren't over our heads here?"

Iwama, a geophysicist from the University of Tokyo, stayed behind in the United States for three months, visiting Bell Labs, Westinghouse, and Western Electric and bombarding their techni-cians with questions. At night in his hotel room, he wrote up his findings from memory and mailed them to Tokyo. These handwrit-ten pages laid the foundation for transistor production in Japan. Back home at Sony's headquarters, engineers used Iwama's notes to produce Sony's first transistor by mid-1954. Over the next sev-eral months, Iwama perfected a process, which had been rejected by Bell Labs, to boost the transistor's power. With amazing speed, Sony had produced a radio-ready transistor.

Meanwhile, Kihara and other engineers were at work designing the tiny components the radio required.[62] In January 1955, Sony produced its first prototype transistor radio. It was not the world's first—an American company called Regency had beaten Sony to market in late 1954—and a disappointed Ibuka blamed the bureau-crats at MITI. "If only MITI had issued our permit a little sooner," Sony's official history records Ibuka thinking at the time.[63] The first Sony model to hit the market, called the TR-55, was introduced in

August 1955. Two years later, a smaller, higher-quality version was released on a large scale.[64] Morita badly wanted to dub his mini-radio "pocketable" for the marketing effect, but it was not quite tiny enough to fit into a standard men's shirt pocket. To compensate, he ordered shirts with slightly wider pockets for his sales staff so they could just slip it in for dramatic effect.[65]

With a unique product in hand, Morita looked to the global marketplace.

. . . .

IN A MARCH 1960 weekly internal report, Morita wrote that "Sony must move from the domestic to the global stage."[66] It was a remarkable statement for a company so new and inexperienced. Sony was small enough at the time that Morita and Ibuka still shared an office.[67] But they, like nearly everyone in corporate Japan, had been infected with the export bug from their firm's inception. With Japan's consumers still cash-strapped, selling in major markets was the only route to advancement. "It was the consensus among Japanese industrialists that a Japanese company must export goods in order to survive," Morita later explained. "It became obvious to me that if we did not set our sights on marketing abroad, we would not grow to be the kind of company Ibuka and I had envisioned."[68] For Japan, "marketing abroad" was a synonym for exporting to the United States. By far the largest consumer market in the world, the United States was the perfect target.

Morita was also personally drawn to the United States. As Idei says, Morita "had a yearning for America."[69] Morita tried selling his transistor radios in the United States before they had even hit the market at home. In 1955, he took Sony's prototype to New York and shopped it to major retailers. He got nowhere. Buyers questioned why anyone needed a radio that small. In the 1950s, consumer electronics were household items. Families listened to their favorite radio shows in the living room; televisions were almost like furniture. Morita and Ibuka correctly surmised that people would come to see radios, TVs, and tape players as personal products. In 1955, that concept had yet to emerge in America.

Morita met with an executive at Bulova, a well-known brand at the time. After Morita made his pitch, the executive told him, "We definitely want some of these." He ordered 100,000 radios. Morita was "stunned." "It was an incredible order," he later wrote, "worth several times the total capital of our company." But Bulova wanted to put its own name on the radio, not Sony's. "Nobody in this country has ever heard of Sony," the executive told Morita.

For Morita, this stipulation was a deal breaker. He was determined not to allow Sony to become just an anonymous supplier to other companies but a brand name in its own right. He cabled Sony headquarters in Tokyo to get its opinion before making a decision. His colleagues responded that he should accept Bulova's terms. "Forget the name, get the order," the cable read. It was just too big to pass up.

Sony's official history says that Morita and the board debated Bulova's offer for several days, with Morita eventually convincing them to reject it. Morita, in his memoirs, mentions no such exchange. It is likely that Morita returned to Bulova and turned the order down on his own initiative. The Bulova executive was shocked, but Morita explained to him that he possessed an original product that gave Sony a unique opportunity to build its own brand. "Fifty years from now," he told the Bulova executive, "I promise you that our name will be just as famous as your company name is today." Ibuka thought Morita was foolish, but Morita later wrote that "it was the best decision I ever made."[70]

Morita instead committed himself to building Sony's U.S. business on his own. By the late 1950s, he was practically commuting back and forth between Tokyo and New York. "I began to feel that to establish our company more firmly in the U.S. I had to get to know the country better, and . . . I felt I needed to know more about how Americans lived and how they thought," he wrote. Morita told Ibuka that Sony should establish an American subsidiary and set up its own sales network so it would not have to rely on trading firms or unreliable distributors. Ibuka resisted at first, but eventually relented. In February 1960, Morita founded the Sony Corp. of America.[71] He threw his usual frenetic energy into the new operation, spending ten days a month in New York despite overwhelming responsibilities in Tokyo. The head office was in the storefront of a former textile warehouse on Broadway. Morita hopped from desk to desk, getting updates and sending reports back to Tokyo by telex. He often worked until midnight, stopping afterward for late dinners at all-night delis. Morita acquired a taste for matzoh ball soup.[72]

Morita, though, realized Sony needed a much higher profile if it was going to be an American success story. Back in Tokyo, he had opened a showroom in the city's tony Ginza shopping district to introduce new products in Japan. The marketing value proved incalculable. New York, he decided, needed a similar showroom, and for him, there was only one possible location. "I surveyed the city and realized that if the people I wanted to reach were people who had money and could afford to buy our rather high-priced products, Fifth Avenue was the place to find them," he wrote. Morita spent hours walking up and down Fifth Avenue, marveling at the luxury stores—Tiffany, Bergdorf Goodman, and Saks Fifth Avenue. He also noted that the flags of many nations hung over the storefronts—but not Japan's. His national pride again wounded, "I decided . . . we would be the first to fly the Japanese flag on Fifth Avenue," he wrote. The most elegant stretch, Morita believed, was on the street's east side, between Forty-fifth and Fifty-sixth streets. That was the spot.[73]

Sony, with only a line of radios in the U.S. market, could hardly afford such a ritzy address. Morita ignored the costs, focusing instead on the marketing benefits. As he once wrote: "Being in style is important."[74] It took him two years to find the right location, and even then, the storefront was so cramped Morita mirrored one wall to make it appear roomier.[75] At the grand opening in October 1962, Morita and his wife stood among the four hundred guests near the centerpiece of the exhibit, Sony's new five-inch micro-TV. Morita hung a Japanese flag outside, the first on the street.[76] Sony and Japan were firmly planted in America.

. . . .

"What will you do if you become prime minister?" Hayato Ikeda's secretary asked him. Ikeda, then MITI minister, knew what was most important in Japan. "Isn't it all a matter of economic policy?" he answered. "I'll go for income doubling."[77] In 1960, Ikeda became prime minister, and, as he promised, he implemented a plan that aimed to double national income by 1970.

By that point, Ikeda had already played a central role in Japan's postwar economic success. Ikeda "will be remembered as the man who pulled together a national consensus for economic growth and who strove unceasingly for the realization of that goal," Nakamura wrote. So devoted was he to the mission of economic expansion that French President Charles de Gaulle derisively dubbed him the "transistor radio salesman."[78] As a former MITI and finance minister, Ikeda championed many of the crucial elements of Japan's industrial policy. Ikeda also had a reputation for speaking his mind. He was forced to resign as MITI minister in 1952 after he blurted out in parliament that "it makes no difference to me if five or ten small businessmen are forced to commit suicide" due to the government's aggressive economic program.[79]

His crowning achievement was the National Income Doubling Plan of 1960. Its greatest impact might have been on the national psyche. By bolstering the public's faith in Japan's economic future, it exerted great influence over the economy's development. The plan, Ikeda said in a 1964 speech, "has given the nation self-awareness and self-confidence."[80] Corporate investment and wages surged. Consumers, usually savers rather than spenders, splurged in the early 1960s on the "three sacred treasures"—a television, washing machine, and refrigerator—and later that decade, on the "three c's"—a car, color TV, and cooler.[81] Due to Ikeda's plan, Nakamura said, the average Japanese "began to take it for granted that rapid growth and what went with it—rising incomes and living standards—had come to stay."[82]

By 1970, Ikeda's plan had been fulfilled—and then some. Ikeda had targeted gross national product of 26 trillion yen in 1970; the economy actually grew to 40 trillion yen.[83] The world began to realize something special was happening in Japan—that perhaps Japan had come up with an entirely new model for economic development. Japan's success "must also be regarded as a harbinger of future possibilities for the rest of Asia and Africa," the *Economist* suggested in an influential survey in 1962. "We have here a practical case study in that most over documented but least satisfactorily solved of all economic problems—how a very poor country can at last start to shake grinding poverty off."[84]

Akio Morita told *Time* magazine: "Just as the U.S. helped Japan rise from nothing, we should all join to try to make more Japans in other parts of the world."[85] The rest of Asia learned the lessons of Japan, and put its new theories to work to create Miracles around the region.

CHAPTER TWO

WHY KOREANS WANT TO CLONE A DICTATOR

In human life, economics precedes politics or culture.
—PARK CHUNG HEE

Park Chung Hee calmly lit a cigarette. Dawn had not yet broken on the morning of May 16, 1961, and Park, a major-general in the South Korean army, was approaching Seoul, with his men, from the city outskirts. His target was not the hated Communists of North Korea, but his own government. Park and a group of young officers believed a military coup was the only method of ridding the nation of a political leadership they condemned as inept and corrupt.

Their operation got off to a rough start. A contingent of marines who had promised to join the putsch showed up late because its devout Christian officer decided a last-minute prayer session was in order. Park, annoyed at the delay, raced off in a jeep in search of the laggards. With the coup finally under way, Park found himself blocked by a troop of military police deployed on the northern end of a bridge across the Han River, the waterway that bisects Seoul. They opened fire as Park's men approached from the south bank. It was at that moment when Park decided he needed that cigarette.

Park pulled his pistol from its holster and walked out onto the bridge. At the end of the first span, he turned and signaled for

his men to follow. Frightened, they barely budged. Park continued across the bridge. At the end of the second span, he ordered
them again to follow. This time they built up the courage to rush
forward. The defenders fled. That one nail-biting incident was the
most resistance Park faced. By 5 a.m., he was at the national telecommunications center, handing a radio announcer a prepared
statement informing South Koreans of their new government.[1]

From that moment, Park became enshrined as one of the
most important and dominating figures in Korea's long history.
His reign lasted eighteen years, a time marked by brutality and
intolerance. Yet, that May morning, he did not see himself as a
power-crazed conqueror. He believed he was the savior of the
nation, the defender of the South Korean people against government injustice and Communist annihilation. "We saw ourselves
as standard-bearers to guide the people toward the attainment of
their long-cherished hope," Park later wrote.[2] His coup was not a
coup, but a "revolution," an opportunity for national renewal, a
chance to overcome centuries of backwardness, foreign domination, and decay—"our last chance for a National Renaissance,"
Park wrote.[3] Many military despots have couched their blatant
self-serving quest for power in the lofty language of reform. Park
Chung Hee actually meant it.

South Korea is arguably the Miracle's most unlikely success
story. At the time of Park's coup, the country was among Asia's
most feeble. Many of South Korea's 24 million people were going
hungry and more than half of the national budget was American
aid. What few factories and power stations survived the Korean
War ended up in the North after the peninsula's partition. The
South had so little industry, Park griped, that it produced less electricity than the Ford Motor Company.[4] Yet by the end of his rule in
1979, Korea was manufacturing cars, consumer electronics, ships,
and steel. Park built an industrialized economy from scratch, a
remarkable achievement, rightly called the Miracle on the Han.

The case of Korea is convincing proof that state intervention
can produce high rates of economic growth. Park, influenced by

Japan's Miracle, took the MITI model of development—and put it on steroids. His regime exerted government control over the economy with a ferocity out of reach of even "Monster" Sahashi and his meddlesome cohorts. In the process, he created the same ties between government, business, and finance, and earned his own country the similar moniker of "Korea Inc." Park, as its CEO, practically a one-man MITI, controlled and designed much of Korea's economic program. His strategy defied the wisdom of classical economics, even more so than in Japan, due to the personalized nature of Park's rule. Political economist Alice Amsden, in her definitive study of Park's economic policies, called Korea "an example of a new way of industrializing that challenges long-held assumptions of generations of economic thinkers."[5]

Park's success also contributed to one of the most controversial themes of the Miracle—that rapid economic development requires authoritarian rule. His regime has been called a "developmental dictatorship." Authoritarian governments, the thinking goes, insulate technocrats from the potential pressures imposed by politicians, civic groups, and business interests, allowing them to implement long-term growth strategies without worrying about short-term political repercussions. The highly hierarchical structure of the government also permits clean, quick decisions. Democracies, on the other hand, are too fractured, its politicians too susceptible to the concerns of their electors to pursue the consistent policy needed to achieve rapid economic growth.

Liberal-minded Americans and Europeans, with their long legacy of democracy *and* economic growth, are often quick to dismiss the "developmental dictatorship" argument. However, the dual nature of Park's legacy—astounding economic success combined with intensifying political repression—leaves a thorny question. Would democratic rule have derailed Korea's Miracle? Park thought so. Korea, he concluded, was not ready for multi-party democracy. Unlike the political systems of Western nations, the democratic experiment in Korea in the 1950s, he believed, did not emerge naturally from the course of societal development. It was imposed from the outside on an impoverished, premodern nation. Koreans were unable to enjoy the fruits of that system, as it became dominated by special interests and ended up corrupt and ineffective—thus creating the need for his "revolution." Korea, he argued, needed to develop a strong economy *before* democracy could succeed. Political freedom, he believed, meant nothing without economic growth. "The gem without luster called democracy was meaningless to people suffering from starvation and despair," he wrote. Park even argued that what was true for Korea was true across Asia. "The Asian peoples want to attain economic equality first, and build a more equitable political machinery afterwards," he proclaimed.[6]

Park, as we will see, was not the only leader to hold these views. Was Park correct? *Is there a link between authoritarianism and rapid industrialization?* It is startling that nearly all of the economies that experienced the Miracle either had dictatorial regimes (South Korea, Taiwan, China, Indonesia), periods of military rule (Thailand), or systems with limited freedoms dominated by one political movement (Singapore, Malaysia). Even Japan was a kind of one-party state. Though the country holds free elections, the same party, the Liberal Democrats, has controlled the government since the mid-1950s (save for a short period in the early 1990s). However, over time, the connection between dictators and development weakened in Asia, and Park's arguments appeared increasingly self-serving and less valid.

There has also been a terrible downside to this "developmental dictatorship"—the abuse of human rights. Park—if we can take him at his word—may never have wanted to claim power for himself, but once he had it, he would not let it go. He became more repressive as his tenure progressed. Opponents were jailed and tortured; protestors, usually students, were beaten by police squads. For the most part, however, Koreans willingly sacrificed civil liberties in return for national economic advancement. The legitimacy of Park's rule became inexorably linked to his ability to produce the economic goods. There was, however, a limit to their tolerance. Poor people might be willing to trade liberty for improved living standards for a while, but eventually the expanded middle class will demand political rights to match their economic rights. The Park era ended in violence and protest.

Nevertheless, South Koreans remember Park as their national champion, the man who built the nation into a modern state. In a 1996 poll, Koreans named him the person they would most like to clone.[7] Still, he remains something of an enigmatic figure. Unlike the better-known, more flamboyant nationalist leaders of the day, Park was withdrawn and austere, an inspiration to his nation through example, not passionate oratory. "It was certain," noted Kim Chong Shin, a journalist who wrote about Park in the 1960s, "that the many sides of his personality were revealed, not by words, but through actions carried out in silence."[8] When journalist Don Oberdorfer interviewed Park in June 1975, he found the powerful figure "reticent and shy, almost smaller than life." Park "toyed with a tiny chihuahua dog in his lap and rarely looked me in the eye."[9] In public, he appeared aloof and icy. Novelist Michael Keon witnessed Park at a 1966 ceremony in which he presented land deeds to a group of North Korean refugees "with a dourness, detachment, and dignity that might have marked some Aztec warrior-king presiding over the commencement of a pyramid."[10] Perhaps no single incident shows Park's steely personality better than his reaction to a horrifying assassination attempt in 1974. As Park delivered a speech at the packed National Theater, a man rose from his seat and ran down the auditorium's aisle firing a pistol. Park escaped unharmed by ducking behind his lectern, but his wife, sitting behind him, slumped forward in her seat, a bullet in her head. After aides carried her blood-splattered body from the theater, Park returned to the microphone. "Ladies and gentlemen," he told a stunned audience, "I will continue my speech." His wife died several hours later.[11]

When Park did speak in public, he exhorted the Korean people to devote themselves to his economic program and the development of the nation. His speeches are cluttered with calls for ever greater productivity. In his annual national address in January 1965, he declared that year a "year to work"[12]; twelve months later, he humorlessly named 1966 a "year of harder work."[13] A tireless workaholic himself, Park often sat in his office in the presidential palace, called the Blue House, notepad in hand, figuring his own calculations with economic statistics.[14] Even after long days of meetings with policymakers, Park retired to his personal apartments within the Blue House only to scribble out more ideas to present the next morning. He attempted to lead a life similar to those of the average Korean worker. His Blue House lunches were often simple bowls of noodles and he insisted on mixing his rice with poor-man's barley.[15] "As far as merriment is concerned," Park once said, "the shorter and rarer the better."[16] Koreans responded. By the late 1970s, the average workweek of a Korean manufacturing employee was more than 30 percent longer than an American's.[17]

However Park and his methods may be judged, it is impossible to question his devotion to building an economically vibrant South Korea. On the morning of the coup, Park collected the young officers who supported him in a room at a military command headquarters and promised they would take Korea to a level of wealth few thought possible. He talked of building an industrialized state, where Koreans would not go hungry, and which had enough money to defend itself against the Communist North. Listening intently, a colonel and Park protégé, Park Tae Joon,* held faith in his message. "There were many people who would follow him, whatever he would do," he said of Park Chung Hee. "Everybody believed he would do good things for the country."[18]

With these exalted intentions in mind, Park Chung Hee set out that morning to claim control of South Korea. He was about to take on one of the greatest challenges of the Miracle, yet he approached this task with confidence and optimism. "Coolly, I ordered the advance of the revolutionary army," he wrote. "I was

---

* Park Chung Hee and Park Tae Joon are not related. Park is a very common Korean name.

not one bit excited." Watching the soldiers advance through Seoul "was a noble human image, one that made me tearful. I looked down upon the Han River and realized that the waves were new, the water fresh, nothing was the same as yesterday."[19]

. . . .

PARK'S ROAD TO power is packed with as many mysteries as his personality. He was born in the town of Kumi in southern Korea in 1917. His father passed the tough examinations needed to enter the civil service, but, unable to find a proper position, he ended up a farmer. He was not good at it, and the family was destitute. Park was the last of seven children and his mother feared he would so tax the family's feeble resources that she drank raw soybean sauce and willow soup to try to induce an abortion. Fortunately for Korea, it did not work, and Park grew up in the family's two-room clay-and-thatch hut. An excellent student, he was admitted to the prestigious Taegu Normal School, claiming one of the few slots open to Koreans under Japanese colonial rule. After graduation, he became a teacher at a primary school in a remote mountain village.

It was there that Park had a life-altering experience. A visiting Japanese provincial school inspector treated the staff with such disdain that Park had a revelation—there was no hope of true advancement for Koreans under the thumb of the Japanese. The country's only hope was to toss them out. To achieve that goal, he made an ironic decision—he enlisted in the Japanese army. It was classic pragmatic Park. He figured he needed military training and experience to fight the Japanese and saw the Japanese army as the only place to get it. For Park, the end always justified the means.

While in the Japanese army, Park skirmished with Chinese Communists in Japan-controlled Manchuria during World War II. After Korea's liberation at war's end, he enrolled in Korea's new military academy.[20] It was there that one of the strangest events

in Park's life took place. After a 1948 Communist-inspired uprising in the country's far south, in which rebellious soldiers briefly
formed a "people's republic," Park was arrested as the chief of a
Communist cell inside the academy and sentenced to death. However, President Syngman Rhee commuted the sentence at the insistence of army brass and Rhee's American military advisor James
Hausman, who considered Park "a damned good soldier." Park
then switched teams. He joined military intelligence with the
task of rooting out Communists from the armed forces. (When
Park first took power in 1961, this incident had American officials
worried that he was a closet Communist. Park sent Hausman to
Washington to vouch for him.)[21]

Park fought bravely during the Korean War and was a brigadier
general by the time the armistice was signed in 1953. As the 1950s
wore on, however, Park became increasingly disgruntled with the
weak, economically prostrate state of the nation and the inability
of the Rhee administration to do much about it. He eviscerated
the country's politicians for their "dictatorship, corruption, in-
competence and sloth" and for having "wasted the rare opportunity to establish a new and viable nation for the first time in our
five thousand years of history." Since Korea's independence, Park
complained, "we have lost far more than we have gained!"[22] If
the South's feebleness was not remedied, Park believed the country was vulnerable to an aggressive North Korea. As South Korea
deteriorated, Kim Il Sung's regime in Pyongyang was thriving,
bolstered by Soviet aid. If "the situation worsened, this country
would eventually become Communist," Park warned, and as a
result, the "history and tradition of the country would then have
come to an end."[23]

Student protests led to the end of Rhee's regime; the elderly president resigned in April 1960.[24] The government that replaced him
was democratically elected, but weak and disorderly. For Park, the
situation had become intolerable, and he thought more and more
of taking action himself. "When my thoughts reached this point, I
was overwhelmed with sorrow that I had been born in this land at

such a time. I stayed awake nights, planning how I might save the nation from its crisis, by whatever means were available to me." He claimed that he was uncomfortable with the idea of holding power himself. "Nevertheless, there is a point beyond which one cannot simply be an onlooker," he wrote. "With the nation on the verge of ruin . . . , my conscience would not allow me to remain concerned with the duty of national defense only."[25]

The plotting of the coup began long before it took place. Park wrote that he was prepared to launch his putsch in early 1960, but delayed it due to the student uprising and Rhee's overthrow. He may not have been the lead planner of the coup—historians often award a junior officer, Kim Jong Pil, that distinction—and after the military took power, Park was one member of a junta of generals who ran the government. Within months, however, it became clear that Park was taking charge, first as chairman of the junta's council and then as acting president. His dramatic overhaul of South Korea began immediately.

· · · ·

" 'YOU TOOK over a burnt down, robbed house.' This is what I told myself when I took over the government," Park wrote. His first task was taking out the "trash"[26]—Park's term for the officials and supporters of the previous regimes. Thousands of people were arrested;[27] some were executed. "I resolved to uproot all the existent germs by cleaning the entire contaminated area as if digging with a shovel," Park wrote. He claimed, or feigned, to be pained by his ruthless purge. "With tears, with true tears, I had to punish them," Park wrote.

This "clean-up" was simply a prelude to what he considered his most pressing task: building the economy. He was sickened by the pathetic conditions in which Koreans lived.[28] "I had to break, once and for all, the vicious cycle of poverty and economic stagnation," he determined.[29] "In human life, economics precedes politics or culture." Park's obsession with economic development was also driven by his concern for security. For Park, an industrialized state was a strong state, one capable of building the weaponry and supporting an army large enough to defend the South from the North. Even more, Park deeply believed that Koreans could simply not be a true sovereign people without a thriving economy. "The hope for the wholeness of a nation without its economic independence is literally to look for fish in a forest," he wrote.[30]

Like MITI's Sahashi in Japan, Park believed economic development could not be entrusted to the private sector alone. Park and his junta, as political scientist Woo Jung En explained, "were men of peasant origin and harbored . . . a peasants' suspicion of the wealthy." Free capitalism, they held, was a cover for a conspiracy of the rich.[31] Park worried further that Korea's private enterprises did not have the resources and skills necessary to build a strong economy unaided by the state. He also thought that economic development had to be a national effort, in which scarce resources were marshaled and utilized to their utmost by the country's leadership.[32]

The economic system Park created was influenced by Japan's. He imported wholesale the "Asian model" of capitalism—the MITI practice of "picking winners" and supporting them with financing and protective barriers. Park set in place institutions to manage the economy that mimicked those in Japan. Korea's ministries of finance and industry functioned in a similar fashion to Japan's, as did the Korea Development Bank, a copy of the Japan Development Bank. "In sector after sector, no nation has profited more from an understanding of Japanese success than South Korea," wrote Harvard University Asia studies professor Ezra Vogel.

Park, however, took the "Asian model" to a new level by centralizing state control to a degree unseen in Japan. Two months after the coup, Park and his junta created the Economic Planning Board (EPB), an über-committee set above the individual ministries that controlled the entire development process. The EPB held greater powers than Japan's planning agency;[33] it not only outlined the government's policy priorities and coordinated between the different ministries, but also allocated budgetary resources to implement its program and could even determine the monetary policies of the central bank.[34] One task of the EPB was devising and overseeing Korea's five-year plans, which laid out the government's targets for the economy and the programs it deemed necessary to meet them.[35] The first five-year plan was thrown together in a few months after Park's coup and implemented beginning in 1962.[36]

Park also took measures to ensure the business community served the government's interests. One month after the coup, his regime passed the Law for Dealing with Illicit Wealth Accumulation, which allowed Park to arrest big businessmen who had grown rich under the old regimes as "profiteers" and threaten them with prison and confiscation of their property. In the end, the wily Park allowed most of the businessmen to escape punishment. In return, they had to pay off their obligations to the state by investing in industries favored by Park. Four months later, Park extended his grip on the economy even further. Rather than managing the banking system indirectly, as in Japan, Park nationalized Korea's banks and took direct control over their lending practices. Park and his technocrats decided which industries and projects received loans.[37]

Those that got such support were inevitably major exporters. Park, like his Japanese counterparts, rushed headlong into an export promotion campaign, and for similar reasons. In a country reliant on imports, Park needed foreign exchange to purchase necessary capital goods and energy, and he also wanted to replace U.S. foreign aid as the country's main source of hard currency. Park once called exports "the economic life line."[38] Beginning in 1964, the government undertook a series of policies aimed at expanding exports, including devaluing and then floating the won and liberalizing the country's strict import regime to make it easier for Korean companies to bring into the country the machinery, raw materials, and components needed to manufacture ex-

ports. In 1965, the government then "targeted," MITI-style, thirteen products it considered "winners" for special promotion. The
list, which included silk, textiles, rubber, and radios, was composed of labor-intensive industries, in which Park's bureaucrats
believed Korea had a special comparative advantage due to its
plentiful, hard-working—and inexpensive—workforce. Companies in these sectors got special perquisites from the government,
such as low-interest loans, tax credits on income earned from exports, and tariff reductions on necessary imported inputs.[39] In this
way, the Korean government altered the incentive structure of the
economy—or in the words of Amsden, got prices "wrong"—to
encourage investment in export industries by making it unnatu-
rally profitable to do so.[40]

An energized Park watched over the state's development plans in
excruciating detail. According to Vogel, Park behaved "like a frontline commander."[41] He set up a "situation room" next to his office
to supervise and track programs, and held monthly and quarterly
meetings with ministers, politicians, bankers, business leaders, and
even labor chiefs to check their status. He harassed ministers with
persistent phone calls to make sure they were meeting deadlines
and targets. "President Park monitored the progress of every single
project, both public and private," wrote Kim Chung Yum, who
served Park as a finance minister and chief of staff. Even obscure
projects received the Park treatment. For one scheme to improve
groundwater usage, Park held dozens of meetings until every aspect
was determined, then visited the project site himself.[42]

Despite his heavy hand on policy, Park admitted he had little
experience or training in economics.[43] However, he was surprisingly open to the advice of economic experts whom he enlisted
as ministers and aides. Kim Chung Yum was one of the most enduring. At the time of the 1961 coup, Kim, a staffer at Korea's
central bank, was posted in New York as the bank's liaison to
the Federal Reserve. As Park began to purge officials of the previous regime, Kim remained in the United States, wary that if he
returned home, he would meet the same fate. Yet living in exile

in the United States did not seem a good option either. He lacked the confidence that he could provide for his family in a foreign country. Seeing no other choice, Kim returned to Seoul. "I was definitely scared," Kim says. "There was a danger I would be put in prison." He hoped his expertise, especially in currency matters, would keep him safe.

He was right. Drafted into the economics research department of the Korean Central Intelligence Agency, he was soon asked to prepare a report on implementing a major currency reform that the junta was considering. The government would replace the old currency with a new one, the won, and alter banking regulations, all to spur investment. Kim designed the entire implementation scheme, all the while convinced that such an effort would be calamitous for the economy.

His expertise impressed the junta. Summoned into a meeting with Park, his first, Kim entered a conference room to find Park looking imperial, sitting stiffly with his arms apart, "a silent figure" with "fire in his eyes," Kim remembers. Other military officers sat on either side of him. Park asked Kim to explain his currency plan to everyone. It was an intimidating scene, but Kim felt so strongly about the dangers of the planned reform that he believed, for the good of the economy, he had to speak up. He told Park that less drastic methods could be used to achieve the same goals. Park, unperturbed by the critique, listened to Kim's advice and then outlined his own thinking. The economy was a mess, Park said, and drastic measures were necessary. Park not only did not punish Kim for his opposition, Kim gained Park's respect. He served Park for nearly the president's entire time in power.[44]

. . . .

PARK MAY HAVE been willing to tolerate the criticism of experts, but he did not always take their advice. He ignored Kim's warnings about the currency reform plan, and it ended up failing badly. Some of the measures had to be reversed.[45] That experience did not deter the hardheaded Park from ignoring his economic team in the future. As his rule progressed, he became more and more willing to take unilateral action. The steps he took, often in the face of furious opposition, reshaped the economy and fashioned Korea Inc.

A classic case was Korea's first cross-country expressway. Park became obsessed with building a system of freeways in Korea after a visit to West Germany in 1964. He sped down an autobahn and was so impressed that he stopped the driver on two occasions to examine the road surface, dividing barriers, and other elements of the construction. A German official spread out a map of West Germany, charted out for Park the country's extensive road network and outlined its economic benefits. Park was convinced Korea needed a highway system of its own, to spur commerce and boost efficiency. Linking Seoul and Pusan, the country's two largest cities, with an expressway became Park's top priority.

Few agreed. In 1965, the government asked the World Bank to conduct a study on Korea's road transport, and its report advocated a much more modest building program, with no major expressways. Park rejected the study. The economy was exceeding the targets of his five-year plans, he figured, so Korea needed expressways much more quickly than the World Bank believed. Yet even within the government, Park's plans met resistance. The projected cost of the Seoul-Pusan expressway alone was larger than the entire 1967 national budget.[46] A usually compliant National Assembly initially refused to fund his plan—even members of his own party.

Undeterred, Park took the project on personally. He ordered aides to gather information on highway construction from the Andes to Siberia, which he devoured himself. He flew up and down Korea in a helicopter with Ministry of Construction engineers plotting a projected route on a sketchpad balanced on his knees. During the construction, Park's helicopter was omnipresent, darting from site to site troubleshooting. "If he didn't know the answer [to a problem] on Tuesday, Mr. Park was back with it on Thursday or Friday," said one engineer who worked on the expressway.[47] In the end, Park got his road, and in record time. The entire 266-mile (428-kilometer) stretch, completed in 1970, was finished in just two years and five months.[48]

Another of Park's famous against-all-odds project was the Pohang Iron & Steel Company, better known by its acronym, POSCO. Of all of Park's countless industrial missions, none meant more to him than the dream of constructing a steel mill. For Park, steel was core to Korea's industrial development, a necessary component for construction, heavy industry, and infrastructure. Even more important, Park saw steel as crucial to the defense against North Korea.[49] "Steel is national power," Park wrote in his own hand on a banner presented to POSCO (which still hangs today in the company's Seoul headquarters).

The mill, however, was considered an even more fanciful project than Park's expressway. Korea had no technology, no trained engineers with experience in steel, no money, no raw materials, and a small domestic market that could not support the giant integrated mill Park favored. Another World Bank study concluded that Park's idea was "a premature proposition without economic feasibility."[50] Nevertheless, Park's new regime included the development of a mill in its first five-year plan, and Park was highly dismayed that the country could not get the project off the ground.[51]

He turned to Park Tae Joon, the young colonel who had supported his coup. The two Parks had similar backgrounds. Park Tae Joon was born to a poor family and worked up through the Japanese education system, attending Japan's prestigious Waseda University, where he studied mechanical engineering. After the 1961 coup, Park Chung Hee named the younger Park as his first chief secretary. Three years later, he was dispatched to take on a different assignment—to repair a scandal-ridden, loss-making state tungsten company, which he quickly turned around even though he had no business experience.[52] Impressed, the president decided that his hardworking young protégé was just the man to build his steel mill. In 1965, he asked Park Tae Joon to lead the project. At first, he refused. The steel mill was too daunting even for him. "What can I do about it?" he responded. But as usual, Park Chung Hee had made up his mind. "It has been a failure so far," the president responded, "so you have to take this on." Park Tae Joon relented. The president, he says, "had this weird belief that if he gave me work to do, I would do it."[53]

The main hurdle was money. In 1967, the Korean government arranged a technical assistance agreement with a consortium that eventually comprised companies from five countries. Pohang Iron & Steel was incorporated as a state enterprise the next year, with Park Tae Joon in charge. Construction was slated to start in early 1969. That date, however, came and went, and no money had been raised for the mill. Concerned, Park Tae Joon flew to Pittsburgh to meet with Fred Foy, chairman of an influential engineering firm called Koppers, who had been instrumental in forming the consortium. Citing the negative World Bank study, the consortium, Foy said, was unable to support or secure financing for POSCO. Despite Park's pleas in a midnight session with Foy, the American executive insisted that a steel mill in Korea was not viable. As a dejected Park packed to return home, Foy offered to arrange a stay in a Hawaiian oceanfront condominium owned by one of Foy's colleagues. Physically and mentally exhausted, Park accepted the invitation.[54]

Sunny Hawaii did not lift Park's spirits. The mill was all he could think about. "Nobody was willing to invest in a steel mill because they believed the economic base of Korea was too weak to justify a plant," Park explains.[55] While he lounged on a towel on the beach, Park got his breakthrough idea. Why not, he wondered, use war reparations from Japan to fund POSCO?[56] In 1965, Park Chung Hee had raised an uproar by normalizing relations with Japan; in return, Tokyo promised a package of aid and loans. The money was already earmarked for other development projects, but Park thought the remaining funds could be redirected to POSCO. He called Park Chung Hee in Seoul. "Why didn't I think of that? It's a good idea," the president responded.[57] Park Tae Joon worked his contacts in Japan, while the president and his ministers lobbied the Japanese government. Eventually Seoul got Tokyo's approval.[58] POSCO was set for takeoff.

Itching to make up for lost time, Park Tae Joon put his construction teams on a grueling schedule. Wielding a baton to direct the work, Park oversaw the construction, even in the middle of the night, while workers labored under bright lights. His baton became a symbol of his relentless drive and an object of fear.[59] Through the entire process, Park believes he rarely slept more than two to three hours a night.[60] These antics earned Park some colorful nicknames—"Dynamite Park" was one, "the man with iron blood" another.[61] Beyond speed, what distinguished Park's management of POSCO was an obsessive-compulsive attention to quality—something often missing from state-led projects in the developing world. On one occasion, he decided to inspect the frame of the steel mill, all the way to its top, 300 feet high. He noticed that some of the bolts were loose—a potentially disastrous flaw. Together with a team of managers, he inspected all 240,000 bolts and marked those that needed fixing with white chalk.[62]

In July 1973, the two Parks together pushed a flaming rod into the blast furnace at POSCO's mill, inaugurating Korea's steel age.[63] Park Tae Joon continued to manage POSCO with an iron will until 1992. During that time, Park's relentless quest for quality and technology turned POSCO into one of the largest and most efficient steel producers in the world. The company, as Park Chung Hee had hoped, laid the foundation of the country's next step along the Miracle. Korea had proved the experts wrong.

. . . .

FOR PARK, STEEL was only one part of a much larger plan to remake the Korean economy. Exports of shoes and shirts had succeeded at jump-starting growth in South Korea, but by the early 1970s, Park believed the country, facing rising costs, could not rely on such labor-intensive manufactures indefinitely. Like Sahashi, Park wished to shift the structure of the economy into the heavy industries that required big factories, big money, highly trained management, and POSCO's steel. The economic transformation in Japan and its success with heavy industry convinced Park that Korea had to do the same. As usual, national security guided his thinking. Park wanted to develop a defense industry so the country could produce its own armaments.

Once again, not everyone in Park's government agreed. His economic ministers generally opposed the shift. The powerful EPB argued that the Korean economy was simply too small and fragile to take on such a massive industrial program. The disagreement turned into heated debates in cabinet sessions between the president and representatives of the EPB. Park called a series of special sessions to resolve the differences, but to no avail.[64]

Park again chose to act on his own. His heavy industrialization program, announced in 1973, is often dubbed the "Big Push." In the words of Woo Jung En, the plan was a "reflection of a political obsession." To bypass his cranky ministers, Park set up a special office within the Blue House, called the Corps for the Planning and Management of Heavy and Chemical Industries, which usurped the EPB's power in these sectors. The president and this corps selected six industries for special focus: shipbuilding, electronics, steel, metals, machinery, and chemicals. The new team also set out to create large industrial complexes around the country to house these new factories and shipyards. The companies that took up the projects received preferential financing and discounts on freight rates and electricity bills. Park's plans were grandiose, almost fantastic in size and scope. "Every new plant had to be one of the *best* and the *largest* in the world and boasted of as such, the quickest ever built, or the most efficient ever operated," quipped Woo, "almost as if the program jostled for a place in the *Guinness Book of World Records*."[65]

The Big Push did more to create Korea Inc. than any other initiative. The program prodded the economy into the industries for which Korea is well known today—its vibrant shipbuilding, automobile, and electronics sectors—and defined the country's corporate structure. The government selected not only industries and projects but also the businessmen who would run them. Park forged professional, and in some cases personal, relationships with a handful of driven business leaders who implemented the heavy industry plan. As a result, Park nurtured the massive conglomerates that came to dominate the economy's trade—the *chaebols*. These sprawling, family-run business groups, modeled roughly on Japan's *keiretsu*, became the engines of Korea's growth and today are recognized household names—Samsung, Hyundai, LG, and others.

What separates Park's industrial program from other state-led efforts in the developing world was that secret of the "Asian model" of development—the mixing of government action and market forces. In the same fashion as MITI's bureaucrats, Park expected results—quality products and strong exports—from his favored companies as payment for government support. While protected at home, the *chaebols,* like the *keiretsu*, were forced, from an early stage, to compete internationally against the most advanced companies of their industries. The ferocity of international competition imposed high standards onto Korean production. Where international markets did not push the *chaebols* to perform, Park was there to inflict punishment himself. Those managers who failed were removed; those who succeeded got access to more projects and privileges. The system was far from perfect, but it forced the *chaebols* to strive to excel. This element was a key factor in Korea's development story.[66] Park, in his own way, tried to be "market conforming" rather than "market defying," as the "Asian model" demands.

Park Chung Hee strove to shift the Korean economy into heavy industry.

THE HEAVY AND CHEMICAL INDUSTRIES PROGRAM IN KOREA, % OF MANUFACTURING

	1971	1975	1980	1984
Output	41	48	56	62
Exports	14	26	40	60

Source: Amsden, *Asia's Next Giant*, p. 58.

One of Park's favorite businessmen was Chung Ju Yung, founder of the Hyundai group of companies. Both men rose from poverty through hard work and chutzpah; both believed in building the national economy; and both possessed a penchant for dictatorial rule. One evening in 1984, Chung ordered the entire staff at Hyundai's Seoul headquarters to move to a new office tower—immediately. The employees, already preparing to head home for the day, were stunned, especially since the new twelve-story headquarters was not yet complete. Chung mobilized a team of workers to finish the new office before morning.[67] Such stunts, and his vast economic power, led the Korean press to nickname Chung "King Chairman." By the 1990s, Hyundai companies produced cars, trucks, ships, semiconductors, electronics, and heavy equipment, and operated shipping lines, department stores, a fund management firm, and a brokerage. Chung staged an unsuccessful run at Korea's presidency in 1992, and, in the years before his 2001 death, he indulged in a personal bid to resolve the confrontation between North and South Korea, even herding cattle from his own ranch across the heavily armed border as a peace offering. If Park Chung Hee was Korea's CEO, then Chung was the chief operating officer, executing the president's grand plans that others scoffed were impossible. "Everyone acknowledges that while others ruled South Korea, Chung Ju Yung built it," David Sanger of the *New York Times* once said.[68]

Chung was born in 1915 in the village of Asan when Korea was still a Japanese colony.* His early years were marked by destitution. Chung's father slaved away for fifteen to sixteen hours a day on his four-acre plot, growing rice and vegetables, but still the family often went hungry. Their daily meals consisted of a morning bowl of oatmeal and an evening bowl of bean porridge. "My parents both worked hard from early morning until late into the night, but they were always poor," he recalled. With only one set of simple clothing, Chung was usually infested with lice. His grandmother hung his outfit outside in the bitter cold during the winter to scare off the

* Asan is now in North Korea.

vermin. These painful memories were Chung's main motivation as a businessman. "I was driven to accomplish things because of the poverty I experienced as a child," Chung once said.

In 1931, Chung finished primary school, and, aside from some Confucian teaching from his strict grandfather, that was all the education he got. Yet the back-breaking labor of his father's life was not for him. An avid reader, he devoured biographies of famous figures. (Napoleon and Abraham Lincoln were major inspirations.) At local marketplaces, he saw the wealthy men of the area and determined he would be one of them. "I decided to go somewhere where I could eat all the rice I wanted," he said. After three failed attempts to run away from home, he made his way to Seoul in 1934, where he worked odd jobs—as a construction worker, a handyman at a starch factory, and eventually a delivery boy for a rice company. That last job provided three meals and a half sack of rice each day. His work ethic convinced the ill shop owner to hand over the business to Chung. It was his first time as a manager.

Chung then borrowed money to buy an auto-repair garage. He knew nothing about cars, but in typical Chung style, he figured he would learn on the job. After getting tossed out of business during World War II, he reopened at the war's end and called the new garage Hyundai Auto Service. Chung chose the name because it means "modern" in Korean. In 1947, Chung, watching the frenetic construction work being undertaken by the rich American military force stationed in the country, founded the Hyundai Civil Works Company, which became the base for his eventual empire. During the Korean War, Chung completed small construction jobs for both the Korean and U.S. militaries. His big break came in December 1952, when U.S. President-elect Dwight Eisenhower traveled to Korea. Eisenhower intended to visit an army cemetery, which, in the middle of winter, was covered in dead, unkempt grass. Worried officers called in Chung to see if he could figure out how to make the cemetery look its best. Chung ingeniously bought thirty truckloads of barley—which stayed green amid the cold—and planted it among the graves. A thankful U.S. Army paid him three times the promised fee. "From then on, all construction projects for the 8th Army were mine," he said. After the Korean War, Chung took on bigger and bigger projects, including the construction of bridges across the Han River. A tyrant even then, Chung called his project managers at all hours, set unreasonable deadlines, and showed up unannounced for inspection tours. By 1960, Hyundai was the largest construction firm in Korea.

Chung first worked with Park Chung Hee shortly after the new government came to power. Chung was invited to the regular export-promotion meetings Park held with senior civil servants and top businessmen. He also took early advantage of Park's economic policies. Using government loans, he opened a cement plant in 1964 to support his growing construction business. Chung rose to prominence due to his role in Park's cross-country expressway. Park summoned Chung in 1967 to his Blue House office—their first one-on-one meeting—to ask for Chung's expert opinion of the project and his estimate of the cost. Chung spent the next three weeks studying the expressway plans and flying over the route for a first-hand look. When Chung returned to Park, he proposed altering the highway's route to circumvent, rather than tunnel through, mountains, allowing the road to be built more quickly and cheaply.[69] Chung's estimate of the cost was only 40 percent of the price calculated by the Ministry of Construction.[70] Park was skeptical at first, but Chung's confidence won him over. He told Chung to take the lead in forming a consortium to build the highway, with Hyundai responsible for a large share.

During the construction, Park and Chung forged their close relationship. Hyundai's crews worked around the clock to meet the president's deadlines; Chung lived on the construction site, sleeping in an old jeep. "We worked so hard that we didn't even notice the seasons changing," Chung later said.[71] Park had finally met someone who could match his own capacity for work. One story describes how Park dropped in on Chung's construction site unannounced in a helicopter early one morning, only to discover Chung already awake and exhorting his workers on at the roadside.[72] Chung made only a tiny profit on the project,[73] but he earned Park's trust. Chung became Park's regular Thursday night dinner partner at the Blue House; the two, informally dressed without ties, would talk for hours over Korean rice wine.[74]

Simultaneously with the highway marathon, Chung was taking Hyundai into a new business—automobiles. Park's second five-year plan included tax incentives and tariff reductions for local car assembly, and Chung, remembering his days in his auto-repair shop, could not resist. He used a government loan to buy land in the village of Ulsan, build an assembly plant, and launch Hyundai Motor in 1967. It would be the first step in a fruitful relationship between Chung and Ulsan. The fishing village would become the base of Hyundai's industrial enterprises and develop into one of Korea's most important cities, thanks almost entirely to Chung and his investments. Hyundai Motor first began assembling a Ford model; then, in 1973, Chung inked a deal with Japan's Mitsubishi Motors to license auto technology. With the help of a former president of British Leland, Hyundai developed Korea's first homemade car, the subcompact Pony, which rolled off the Ulsan assembly line in 1976.[75]

Chung, though, truly made his mark in shipbuilding. Inspired to enter the industry in 1970 when his construction firm was looking to build port facilities in the Middle East, Chung approached Japan's Mitsubishi Heavy Industries in search of technical assistance. After long negotiations, Mitsubishi was willing to offer only a highly restrictive arrangement that Chung worried would throttle his efforts. Chung instead signed an agreement with a British firm for technical support and went in search of financing. Park's government, eager to see Chung succeed, put up some of the money, but he required an additional $40 million to launch his shipbuilding company. Not surprisingly, banks in Switzerland, France, and Britain rejected Chung. Neither Hyundai nor any other Korean company had ever built a ship of the size Chung envisioned. During a meeting with a skeptical executive at Barclays, Chung tried every argument he could to sway the bank's position.

"Don't you know," Chung pleaded, "that the person who thinks a job is possible is the one who is going to get it done?"[76] Park was furious with Chung's failure and demanded he try harder. "If you only want to do what's easy," Park supposedly threatened, "then you'll get no more help from me."[77]

Chung came back at Barclays through the back door. In a meeting with Greek shipping magnate George Livanos, he wrangled an order for two oil tankers. That commitment finally got Barclays and a consortium of European banks to release a $50 million loan. The last remaining challenge was producing the tankers. Livanos required ships built to an existing design, which Chung acquired. He began welding the first ship together in 1972 while still building the dry dock around it. Chung, as usual, demanded a superhuman pace. Workers often spent seventeen hours a day on the job; Chung paced the docks and rallied them on with visions of a prosperous future. "You'll have a TV and a refrigerator in five years," he promised them. "And a car in fifteen." At this point, though, Hyundai's inexperience began to show as engineers struggled with the ship design. "We didn't even know how to read the blueprints," recalls one welder. When the two halves of the ship were brought together to be merged into the completed vessel, engineers found to their horror that the internal fittings did not match up, requiring a time-consuming process of adjustment. In 1974, after nearly two years of relentless work, the first tanker was ready for launch. No one in the company was certain it would float, and the entire staff collected anxiously on the dockside. As it slipped into the bay and sailed effortlessly away from the shore, they erupted into riotous cheers. Hyundai was in the shipbuilding business. Within a decade, Chung would be the largest shipbuilder in the world.[78]

· · · ·

HYUNDAI'S SHIPBUILDING SUCCESS is considered, by some economists, proof positive of the power of Park's version of the Asian model. Economists Leroy Jones and Sakong Il believe that "without the personal urging of President Park it is virtually certain that the project would have been shelved" and "without efficient and energetic bureaucratic support the project could not have been completed on time."[79] Others are not convinced. The World Bank believes that Park's entire heavy industrialization program failed to transform the structure of the economy away from labor-intensive sectors as he had desired. Even more, the perquisites granted to companies in favored sectors burdened state finances and generated large losses in the banking sector. By 1980, the costs of the Big Push were a key contributor to an economic slowdown and many of the support programs for Park's favored industries were eliminated or scaled back.[80] As in the case of Japan, the impact of MITI-style industrial policy is mixed at best.

Politically, Park himself became a burden on Korea as he grew more and more repressive through the 1970s. In 1972, he shocked the country by announcing the imposition of martial law. Then he introduced a new constitution ending direct presidential elections and effectively enshrining Park as president for life. The growing oppression sparked public protest. The chief thorn in Park's side was Kim Dae Jung, an outspoken democracy advocate with strong ties to students and the working class. In the 1971 presidential election, Kim came close to unseating Park,[81] which only heightened Park's paranoia. Kim became a marked man. In August 1973, as Kim departed from a lunch meeting at a Tokyo hotel, three men in dark suits pushed him into a nearby room, beat and anesthetized him, dragged him to a car, sped off to a nearby port, and placed him on a ship bound for Korea, with weights attached to his arms and legs. Protests from an outraged Tokyo and sharp warnings of severe consequences from the U.S. ambassador in Seoul quite likely saved Kim's life. Five days after his abduction, Kim was released near his Seoul home and put under house arrest.[82] By the late 1970s, Park was under siege. Student protests grew and workers launched more militant strikes.[83] Park tenaciously clung to power.

The end came unexpectedly. On October 26, 1979, Park dined at a safe house near his office with Kim Jae Kyu, who, as director of the KCIA, was Park's spy chief, as well as two of the president's aides. A famous model and a well-known singer knelt and poured glasses of Chivas Regal as the men ate around a traditional low Korean table. Park and one aide, Cha Chi Chol, the head of presidential security, began berating Kim for failing to quell the protests intensifying in the southeast. Cha was especially harsh, criticizing Kim for being too soft. Kim left the dinner, went up to his office on the second floor of the building and got his .38 Smith & Wesson pistol. When he returned to the dining room, Kim opened fire, first at Cha, then at Park. When his gun jammed, he took another from a KCIA officer nearby and fired at the two again. Park slumped forward in a pool of blood. "Are you all right, Your Excellency?" asked one of the women. "I am all right," Park responded. Those were his final words.[84]

. . . .

THE GREAT NATION builder was gone, ironically a victim not of his northern enemies, but of the instrument of his own repression. Kim Jae Kyu was later found guilty of murder and executed. At his trial, he claimed that he assassinated Park in order to restore democracy.[85] If that was true—which is unlikely—his plan failed. Another dictator soon emerged to take Park's place, Chun Doo Hwan.

The economic model Park set in place continued to thrive after his death. South Korea became one of the original Asian Tigers. "The poverty and aimlessness that marked our life at one time have been replaced by a new confidence and determination to bring about an affluent society," Park wrote shortly before he was killed. "As I reflect on the past thirty years of our generation which walked over a path so strewn with thorns, I cannot but be moved at the shining contrast that today presents." Korea, he believed, was poised "to knock on the doors of a new historical era."[86] He did not live to see that new era himself.

CHAPTER THREE

MINISTER MENTOR'S ASIAN VALUES

By nature and experience, we were not enamored of theories. What we were interested in were real solutions to our problems. —LEE KUAN YEW

Lee Kuan Yew was exhausted, but he still could not sleep. He tossed and turned, unable to calm his mind. Lee had good reason to worry. The next day—August 9, 1965—he would become the first prime minister of a brand-new country, the city-state of Singapore.

Lee took on this task with trepidation. Unlike Nehru, Park, or most other post-colonial leaders, who saw their freedom as an opportunity to achieve national greatness, Lee doubted the viability of tiny Singapore as an independent state. For the previous two years, Singapore, once a British colony, had been part of a federation with neighboring Malaysia. The partnership, Lee believed, was crucial to Singapore's survival. But the match proved ill-fated. His relations with the federal government in Kuala Lumpur grew so acrimonious that it became impossible for the union to continue. Furious last-ditch negotiations over the separation wore Lee down, and the weight of the responsibilities that lay ahead overwhelmed him. Throughout that night, he woke every hour or so, reached for his notepad, and added more entries onto his lengthy to-do list.

At 10 a.m., Singapore declared independence. Lee was too busy to read the proclamation before it was released to the world. Two hours later, Lee appeared at a press conference at Singapore's television station. He took a few questions and then recounted the dramatic events of the previous days. The end of the federation with Malaysia would be regarded as "a moment of anguish," Lee told the journalists. "All of my life I have believed in merger and the unity of these two territories," Lee continued. "It's a people connected by geography, economics, and ties of kinship." Then he paused. Tears welled in his eyes. "Would you mind if we stop for a while?" he plaintively asked. It took him twenty minutes to regain enough composure to continue the conference. "Among Chinese it is unbecoming to exhibit such a lack of manliness," Lee later wrote. "But I could not help myself."

Despite his feeble emotional state, Lee launched himself into building his new country. His first priority was defense. That morning, he gave a letter to the Indian deputy commissioner asking if New Delhi would send officers to train a Singaporean army. Not only was Lee concerned about the island's hostile neighbors, but he also doubted the loyalty of his own people. Singapore's population was composed mainly of immigrants from China with small communities of Indians and local Malays. None of them had any concept of a Singaporean identity. Uncertain of even his own ministers, Lee required that each of them sign the separation agreement as proof of their commitment to the new government. Lee spent most of his first day huddled with his closest aide and colleague, Goh Keng Swee, an old friend from college, discussing the country's future course. "We were in a daze," Lee wrote, "not yet adjusted to the new realities and fearful of the imponderables ahead."[1]

Lee's attention quickly turned to the Singapore economy, which he called his "biggest headache." Since its founding by Great Britain in 1819, Singapore had been the center point for trade in the region. With the end of empire came the end of Singapore's main occupation. Nationalist Malaysia wanted to develop its own commerce, and due to a political dispute, Indonesia was cutting off its usual trade with Singapore. "I used to see our godowns* filled with rubber sheets, pepper, copra, and rattan and workers laboriously cleaning and grading them for export," Lee wrote. "There would be no more imports of such raw materials from Malaysia and Indonesia." Something had to be done. Unemployment was 14 percent and rising. Singapore had no natural resources to export, and its population of two million was too minuscule to support much industry on its own. "We inherited the island without its hinterland," Lee lamented, "a heart without a body." The stark realities left Lee despondent. "We faced tremendous odds with an improbable chance of survival," Lee believed.

If Singapore was to endure, Lee resolved, it would need a unique approach to economic development. "We had to create a new kind of economy, try new methods and schemes never tried before anywhere else in the world, because there was no other country like Singapore," he wrote later. "I concluded an island city-state in Southeast Asia could not be ordinary if it was to survive. We had to make extraordinary efforts to become a tightly knit, rugged, and adaptable people who could do things better and cheaper than our neighbors. . . . We had to be different."[2]

No one would accuse the Singapore that Lee built of being anything else. Singapore's transformation from down-and-out tropical outpost to vibrant metropolis of international stature is one of the great tales of the Miracle. The island today is one of the world's busiest ports, a major regional finance hub, and a globally recognized center for stem-cell research. The constant factor throughout Singapore's entire story has been the combative Lee, who guided his nation with expansive vision and indomitable will. Lee, like his island, has been uplifted from the insecure local official of 1965 into Asia's greatest statesman, a man who possesses far more influence on the world stage than his micro-nation should warrant. His wisdom and insights are sought out by everyone from American presidents to African politicians. Former U.S.

---

* A godown is a warehouse.

President George H. W. Bush called Lee "one of the brightest, ablest men I have ever met," while former U.K. Prime Minister Margaret Thatcher, after reading "every speech" of Lee's, proclaimed that "he was never wrong."[3]

Lee himself is a complicated cocktail of contrasting characteristics. He has shown himself wise and petty, open-minded and myopic, tough and finicky. He is a socialist who fostered one of Asia's most vibrant capitalist societies and a self-styled devotee of multiculturalism who preaches Chinese superiority. The paradoxes continue with the physical man as well. Though born in the sultry tropics, the sensitive Lee cannot tolerate its heat and humidity, and he says a "turning point" in his life came when he first installed an air-conditioner in his bedroom.[4] This fussiness extends to every aspect of his life. "He is incapable of doing anything slovenly or carelessly," wrote Alex Josey, a journalist and Lee chronicler, "whether it is putting on a highly polished shoe, or reaching an important decision." Perhaps Lee's single most dominating trait is his computer-like pragmatism. Josey says that Lee "is by nature and by reasoning an attacker of problems, not a student of the abstract."[5] During his decades in politics, Lee has displayed an extraordinary ability to ditch policies and invent new ones, based solely on the results he is striving to achieve. *Time* magazine once described Lee's "basic personality" as "sharp intelligence allied with an unsentimental, almost clinical rationality and supreme confidence in his own judgment."[6] Yet even though Lee can be remarkably generous to his citizens—Singapore has undertaken the most successful public housing program in history—he also possesses an equally remarkable arrogance, and has shown a die-hard belief that only he knows what is best. As one British diplomat once said, Lee is "the most brilliant man around, albeit just a bit of a thug."[7]

Though Lee adopted some aspects of the "Asian model" of development—primarily a heavy role of the state in the economy—his version had crucial differences. One distinction concerns the relationship between local private enterprise and the state. Unlike in Japan and Korea, Singapore's bureaucrats did not focus as much on nurturing Singaporean firms run by local entrepreneurs. When Lee and his team wished to enter into a new business, the state often undertook the venture directly. In this regard, Lee's intervention in the economy was arguably greater than either MITI's or Park's. In fact, Singapore was probably the most carefully crafted and highly engineered of all of the newly industrialized states of Asia.

Lee's most important deviation from the "Asian model" as practiced in Japan and Korea was his use of foreign investment to generate rapid growth. Lee was willing to accept a level of foreign influence in the economy that a xenophobic nationalist like Park would never have stomached. Lee turned the government into a foreign investment promotion machine that aggressively pursued international companies. Through this process Lee and his economic team "picked winners" like professional Japanese MITI men, but they did so through "targeting" certain types of multinationals that could create the largest number of jobs, import new technologies, train Singaporeans in advanced technical and management skills, and produce exports. In this way, Singapore replaced the activities of the *chaebols* in Korea or the *keiretsu* in Japan with multinational corporations. It was an ingenious plan, and one that shows the transformative power of foreign investment in making poor countries rich.

In following this path, Lee linked the future of his tiny country to the forces of globalization to a greater degree than either Japan or Korea. Singapore hooked onto the emerging concept of offshoring, in which multinational corporations transfer operations from their home economies to foreign countries, usually in search of lower costs. The beginning of Singapore's Miracle coincided with the technological innovation—better communication systems and faster, more reliable transportation—that made offshoring less costly and risky. Lee's strategy therefore was based on a paradox. The government both intervened in the economy and integrated into international markets, making

Singapore simultaneously more state-driven yet more exposed to shifts in the global economy than either Japan or Korea. Lee took the interplay of the state and market inherent in the "Asian model" to new levels of complexity.

Singapore has received a tremendous amount of attention from policymakers and economists who have studied whether Lee's model can be transferred to other countries. Lee believes it can. The basic building blocks of development, Lee contends, are straightforward. The starting point, he argues, is an environment of meritocracy. "It is important to establish a system in which the more a person educates himself, trains himself, develops skills and contributes to the economy, the more he is rewarded," says Lee. He also takes an extreme view on the power of markets, more so than Asia's other export-oriented leaders. "Never believe you can go against market forces," Lee explains. "If you try, then nothing will happen."[8]

Here, however, we run into the first of many contradictions in Lee's economic philosophy. While he preaches the universality of development, he is simultaneously the chief proponent of the contentious argument that culture and economic success are linked. Lee believes that the Miracle was an Asian phenomenon based on certain aspects of Asian, and specifically Confucian, culture, which cannot be easily transplanted around the globe. He argues that economic or policy-focused explanations of the Miracle leave out this crucial cultural factor. Certain societies, Lee believes, are inherently more capable of rapid development than others. Confucian and Confucian-influenced societies possess a devotion to education and savings, a spirit of self-sacrifice, and a societal cohesion based on common social norms, and these "Asian values," Lee believes, laid the groundwork for the Miracle. Other developing countries "will not succeed in the same way as East Asia did because certain driving forces will be absent. If you have a culture that doesn't place much value in learning and scholarship and hard work and thrift and deferment of present enjoyment for future gain, the going will be much slower," Lee told journalist Fareed Zakaria in a 1994 interview.[9]

Lee creates the most controversy, however, with the tight-fisted fashion in which he has governed Singapore, and the complex "Asian values" argument he uses to justify it. Singapore's economic development has come with a price—the limitation of civil liberties and human rights. The Singaporean state intervenes in the personal lives of its citizens to a degree that would be unacceptable in the West. Officially, Singapore is a parliamentary democracy with regular elections, which Lee's People's Action Party has won since 1959. In reality, Singapore is a one-party state. Lee and the PAP leadership use government power to stamp out opposition, as well as much public debate. A favorite tactic of government leaders is filing defamation lawsuits against opposition politicians who criticize them. These suits, commented the U.S. State Department, "had a stifling effect on the full expression of political opinion and disadvantaged the political opposition."[10] The press, both foreign and domestic, comes under similar pressure. In its 2008 press freedom index, Reporters Without Borders ranked Singapore 144th out of 173 countries, languishing behind the authoritarian regimes of Sudan and Kazakhstan.[11] Singapore has faced its greatest international criticism over its use of capital punishment. A 2005 United Nations report revealed that Singapore has "by far" the highest rate of executions on a per capita basis of any country in the world—nearly twice that of Saudi Arabia, which has the second-highest rate.[12] Those who escape the executioner are often sentenced to caning. Lee feels little guilt for imposing such treatment. "Between being loved and being feared, I have always believed Machiavelli was right," he once said. "If nobody is afraid of me, I'm meaningless."[13] In a conversation with Chris Patten, the last British governor of Hong Kong, Lee said that he eradicated Singapore's problem with triad organized crime syndicates by tossing several hundred people in prison. Patten was taken aback. "Several hundred?" Patten asked. "Were they really all triads?" "Probably," Lee responded.[14]

Lee, like Park, sees his method of governing as a necessary ingredient in Singapore's Miracle. "With a few exceptions, democracy has not brought good government to new developing countries," Lee explained in a 1992 speech in Tokyo. "Democracy has not led to development because the governments did not establish the stability and discipline necessary for development." Lee, however, goes much further than Park. Democracy like that practiced in the United States, he argues, is a bad fit with the culture and history of Asian societies. Asians, he contends, prefer to be governed based on "Asian values"—a desire for order, a loyalty to family and community, and an acceptance of hierarchy. Lee says that, as an Asian, he expects government to be "honest, effective and efficient in protecting its people, and allowing opportunities for all to advance themselves in a stable and orderly society, where they can live a good life."[15] In this way, Lee implies, Asians favor the rights of the greater community over individual rights, and they therefore prefer a government that preserves social stability over personal liberties. "In Eastern societies, the main objective is to have a well-ordered society so that everyone can enjoy freedom to the maximum," he wrote.[16] Lee goes so far as to dismiss the fundamental tenets of Western democracy as misguided. "It is assumed that all men and women are equal or should be equal," Lee said in his Tokyo speech. "But is equality realistic? If it is not, to insist on equality must lead to regression. . . . The weakness of democracy is that the assumption that all men are equal and capable of equal contribution to the common good is flawed."[17] Democracy, as it is understood in America, is therefore *not* universal, nor is it a requirement for a market-based economy. Any effort to make it such is cultural imperialism, an attempt by the West to impose its value system on the rest of the world. "America should not foist its system indiscriminately on other societies where it would not work," Lee wrote.[18] As Michael Barr, a professor of international relations, wrote in his study of Lee Kuan Yew, "Lee is at the forefront of both practical and theoretical efforts to reconcile undemocratic, illiberal elitism with the requirements of a prosperous capitalist state operating in the global economy."[19]

For many in the West, Lee's "Asian values" argument is simply a fancy concoction to legitimize and perpetuate authoritarian regimes in Asia—including his own. "Asian values . . . were increasingly summoned in aid in recent years as a sort of all-purpose justification for whatever Asian governments were doing or wished to do," blasted Chris Patten. "Old men who wanted to stay in power, . . . old regimes that feared the verdict of the ballot box— all could pull down the curtain between East and West and claim that whatever they were doing was blessed by an ancient culture and legitimized by the inscrutable riddles of the East."[20] Lee dismisses such criticism as the West's cultural arrogance, but other Asians have been infuriated by Lee's ideas, the most passionate of whom is Kim Dae Jung, the South Korean democracy activist. In a 1994 article in the journal *Foreign Affairs*, Kim argues that "Lee's view of Asian cultures is not only unsupportable but self-serving." Contrary to Lee's assertions, Kim contends, democratic ideals have been part of Asian political systems long before they took root in Europe and therefore are, in fact, a natural outgrowth of Asian values, not an imposition from the West. "Asia should lose no time in firmly establishing democracy and strengthening human rights," Kim wrote. "The biggest obstacle is not its cultural heritage but the resistance of authoritarian rulers and their apologists."[21]

Such attacks have had little impact in Singapore. More than four decades after Singapore's independence, Lee remains unchallenged. Though he retired from the prime minister post in 1990 after thirty-one years of uninterrupted rule, he has not fully retired from governing. Today he holds the enigmatic title of "Minister Mentor," while his son, Hsien Loong, has served as prime minister since 2004. Lee and his family have thus achieved a level of control in Singapore unmatched anywhere else in non-Communist Asia.

Yet in 1965, on that first independence day, all of this success and controversy was beyond Lee's wildest imagination. That evening, Lee put off sleep once again and whacked 150 golf balls from a practice tee outside his official residence, which made him feel better. Yet Lee was still racked by doubt and worry, and his sleeping problems became so severe that on one occasion he held a meeting with the British high commissioner while in bed. "There are books to teach you how to build a house, how to repair engines, how to write a book. But I have not seen a book on how to build a nation out of a disparate collection of immigrants . . . or how to make a living for its people when its former economic role as the entrepot of the region is becoming defunct," Lee wrote. "On that 9th day of August 1965, I had started out with great trepidation on a journey along an unmarked road to an unknown destination."[22]

. . . .

FOR A MAN who professes the virtues of Confucianism, Lee shows no filial piety. He was born on September 16, 1923, in a large two-story bungalow in Singapore to a sixteen-year-old mother and a father, Lee Chin Koon, who Lee once snarled had "little to show for himself." Chin Koon grew up with enough money to splurge at Singapore's ritziest department stores, but when the family fortune was lost during the Great Depression, Chin Koon, with limited formal education, ended up a mere shopkeeper for the Shell Oil company. The elitist Lee found his father's failings unacceptable.

He felt similarly about his family's Anglophile tendencies. The British ruled Singapore at that time, and his grandfather decided to give Lee the Christian name "Harry." Few Chinese took English names and the added "Harry" made Lee a target of teasing in school. But Lee still excelled and earned admission to a prestigious secondary school, the Raffles Institution, named after Singapore's founder, Stamford Raffles. Ironically, the discipline-obsessed Lee was a troublemaker as a youngster. "There was a mischievous, playful streak in me," Lee wrote in his memoirs. "Too often, I was caught not paying attention in class, scribbling notes to fellow students, or mimicking some teacher's strange mannerisms." On one occasion, such antics got him into serious trouble. The school had a rule that any student who was late three times in one term would receive three lashes of a cane. Lee was always a late riser—"an owl more than a lark," he later wrote—and he broke that rule in 1938. The principal administered the lashes, perhaps a foreshadowing of Lee's use of this same punishment on his own populace. "I have never understood why Western educationists are so much against corporal punishment," Lee wrote. "It did my fellow students and me no harm."

Lee planned to study in England, but when World War II broke out, he took a scholarship at local Raffles College instead. His studies there, too, were interrupted by the war, and Lee joined a volunteer military medical unit. On the last day of January 1942, with the Japanese advancing toward the city, Lee and a fellow student were on duty on the parapet of a Raffles College administrative building when they were rocked by a tremendous explosion. Stunned, Lee blurted out: "That's the end of the British Empire." His off-the-cuff remark was not entirely incorrect. The explosion was the sound of the British blowing up the causeway that linked Singapore to the Malay Peninsula. Singapore was under siege, and surrendered in February 1942.

The British defeat—one of the most embarrassing the empire ever suffered—altered Lee's view of the world. Since the founding of Singapore, "the white man's supremacy had been unquestioned," Lee wrote. "The superior status of the British in government and society was simply a fact of life." However, with the Japanese victories, "British colonial society was shattered, and with it all the assumptions of the Englishman's superiority," Lee believed.[23] The British defeat was a seminal moment in Lee's life. "The fundamental thing that made him go into politics," Maurice Baker, a college friend, said of Lee, "was the fact that the Japanese defeated the British in thirty days or so. . . . I remember him saying: 'We must not let this happen again. We must defend ourselves and look after ourselves. Let us get control of the country and run it ourselves.' "[24]

With the war's end and the return of the British, Lee enrolled at Cambridge to study law. Lee became politically active, participating in an informal study group of students from Malaya and Singapore called the Malayan Forum.[25] During a speech at one session, Lee told his fellow students that they should pursue the end of British rule. "Our duty is clear," he said, "to bring home to even the most diehard imperialist that his is an untenable position."[26] Upon his return to Singapore in late 1950, however, he discovered the local Communist Party had become the leading political force on the island.[27] Lee determined to prevent Singapore from falling into its hands. Like Park, Lee, though left-leaning in his younger years, also found Communism detestable. "I rejected it because it was coercive," he once said, "it used methods which I disapproved of. . . . A chap disagrees and you stab him and kill him. There is no give and take."[28]

Lee began building a political base while representing the city's unions in labor disputes. After a few victories, Lee became a champion of Singapore's working class. By 1953, he collected an assortment of leftists into meetings in the stifling heat of the basement of his home to discuss the formation of a new political party. These sessions led to the founding of the PAP in 1954. Over the next five years, Lee's PAP managed to outmaneuver its opponents in a complex series of alliances and negotiations with the British authorities, rival political movements, and even the Communists. Lee's rise coincided with Great Britain's withdrawal from empire. The British allowed Singapore a great degree of self-rule, and Lee's PAP won a spectacular victory in legislative elections in 1959.[29] Lee became prime minister.

In 1961, Tunku* Abdul Rahman, the prime minister of the Federation of Malaya—newly independent from British rule—offered Lee's Singapore an opportunity to forge a union. Lee believed the merger would provide economic benefits by making tiny Singapore part of a wider market, and in 1963, the two joined with other British colonies on the island of Borneo, to form the state of

---

* The word "Tunku" is a Malay title roughly translated as "prince."

Malaysia. The union was doomed from the start. The chief aim of the Tunku, a Malay nationalist, was to uplift the backward Malay community. He saw the new Malaysia as a vehicle to promote Malay dominance. Lee, on the other hand, considered Malaysia a modern state that should pursue equality of opportunity for all of its communities.[30] This progressive position left Lee frustrated at his treatment by the Malaysian government. Relations between Lee and the Tunku deteriorated, and Lee reluctantly accepted that the federation was finished. He agreed to negotiations for separation in 1965. Singapore was on its own.

. . . .

IN THE EARLY days of Singapore's independence, Lee floundered about for a solution to the country's economic problems. He asked the finance minister to send a delegation to Africa to drum up trade, but the results were not encouraging. It was clear Singapore could not depend on its traditional trading businesses anymore. The city would have to follow the same path as South Korea. "All of us in the cabinet knew that the only way to survive was to industrialize," Lee wrote.[31]

Industrialization was made even more imperative by the continued influence of the Communists in Singapore. As in South Korea, the Communist threat motivated the government to achieve rapid economic growth. In Park's case, the fight was against an external foe, Communist North Korea; in Lee's Singapore, the war was internal, but the challenge was the same. If Lee did not strengthen the economy, deliver jobs and better welfare, and thereby bolster support for the PAP administration, the Communists could topple his regime. "If over the next decade the Communists begin to outstrip the non-Communist states, Asians are going to ask themselves: 'What's all this free society mean? Does it mean that politicians are free to loot and plunder, that people are free to be hungry and ill-fed and ill-educated?'" Lee said in 1965.[32]

To Lee's great benefit, he had a strong ally in this contest, his old college friend, Goh Keng Swee. Lee describes Goh as "my alter ego." "We were two different personalities but we shared certain common perspectives, common values, on what we thought should be done," Lee says. "Without him to help me on the economic side and on the organizational side, I don't think we would be half as developed" as the country is today.[33] Those who worked with Goh found his broad intellect intimidating, yet he also had a reputation for acting as a father figure and mentor for many civil servants. Goh was born in the town of Melaka, now in Malaysia, in 1918. When he was a baby, his family relocated to Singapore, where he spent part of his childhood on a rubber plantation. Even at an early age, Goh possessed a fascination with economic development. In college in 1939, as president of the Economics Club, he delivered an address on the reconstruction of Germany. Like Lee, Goh studied in the United Kingdom—at the London School of Economics—and the two were active in the Malayan Forum, which Goh helped found.[34] Lee named Goh his first finance minister after the PAP won the 1959 elections, and from then on he held a series of top government posts for the next twenty-five years. Less flamboyant than Lee, Goh was the technocrat of the two, the hands-on, nuts-and-bolts policymaker behind Singapore's Miracle.

Though Goh spoke often of the power of free enterprise, he did not trust market forces to develop Singapore quickly enough on their own. Like MITI's Sahashi, he believed the state had to intervene to produce the right results. Colonial-era laissez-faire policies "had led Singapore to a dead end," Goh once wrote, "with little economic growth, massive unemployment, wretched housing, and inadequate education. We *had* to try a more activist and interventionist approach." Heavily influenced by European socialism, Goh expected the government to start and own important companies and ensure the betterment of its citizens, especially through the provision of public housing. In fact, Goh once stated that "the most important single factor in determining the rate of economic progress in an LDC [less developed country] is the government."[35]

Goh wasted no time getting directly involved in Singapore's

industrialization. In 1960, he asked the United Nations (UN) to send a delegation of experts to Singapore to consult the government on a program to develop industry. Goh was specifically interested in advisors from other small states that had built influential economies, like Belgium and the Netherlands. The UN asked Dutch economist Albert Winsemius to lead the study team.

At first, Winsemius was wary about accepting the position. He called another UN official, I. F. Tang, who had fled China when Mao took over in 1949, and said he had heard at a dinner with oil executives that Singapore might go Communist. "Who told you so?" Tang asked. "It's not true." Two weeks later, Winsemius, still dubious, agreed to take the offer—on the condition that Tang join him. The two arrived in Singapore near the end of 1960. Lee hosted them at a dinner soon after their arrival. "I don't smell any communists in there," an impressed Winsemius commented afterward.[36] Winsemius would remain an economic advisor to Lee for over two decades.

The choice of Winsemius was lucky for Lee. The Dutchman had a much different ideological background than many economists of the day. Prior to earning his doctorate in economics, Winsemius had been a cheese salesman,[37] leading him to once quip that "it is more difficult to sell cheese than to run an economy."[38] This frontline business know-how, combined with his experience of the postwar reconstruction of Europe, gave Winsemius a market-oriented and practical outlook on economic development that ran counter to the conventional anti-trade, pro-state philosophies popular among development experts during that era. Winsemius's knowledge of the international business scene was invaluable to Lee. Lee praised Winsemius as "a practical, hard-headed businessman" who made "many contributions that were to be crucial in Singapore's development."[39]

Singapore's pitiful state took Winsemius and Tang aback. "We had not quite expected the severity of Singapore's problems," Tang later wrote. Of special concern was the frightening degree of Communist influence. The country's "future was literally hang-

ing in the balance, suspended by opposing ideological winds,"
Tang wrote. "The running joke was that a factory would be set
up on Monday and all sorts of banners screaming 'Exploitation of
Workers' would be hung up by Friday."[40]

Nevertheless, the team began crafting an industrial blueprint
for Singapore. Winsemius recommended the government form a
single agency to attract and assist private investors. The Netherlands had experimented with a similar organization, which had
proven highly successful. Lee agreed and formed the Economic
Development Board, or EDB, in 1961.[41] The EDB would become
the engine of Singapore's Miracle, an efficient and inventive task
force that coordinated among various government ministries and
departments to make foreign investment as smooth and attractive as possible. To back up the EDB, Goh developed an industrial park for new factories on a stretch of wasteland in Jurong
in the island's southwest with water, power, and port facilities and
transportation links.

Companies, though, did not come knocking. Investors, Winsemius warned, considered Singapore "a lemon, not a Rolls
Royce." Government officials encouraged local businessmen to set
up factories to make vegetable oil, cosmetics, mosquito coils, hair
cream, and even mothballs. The EDB formed joint ventures to
recycle paper products and make ceramics, but both failed due to
a lack of management experience. Locals derided the near-empty
Jurong estate as "Goh's Folly." Even Lee admitted his program
had "an unpromising start."[42]

Goh tried to make the best of the situation. When asked years
later if he held any doubts about Jurong's success, he simply responded: "When you have so many things to resolve, you do not
worry about whether the thing will succeed or not." Goh staged
public relations tricks to create an impression that Singapore was
a hot destination for new investment. He attended every factory
launch, no matter how small the facility. Sometimes he generated
multiple publicity events off a single investment by holding ceremonies at various stages of a factory's development—one at the

groundbreaking, another at the beginning of construction, and another at the start of production. His staff made sure journalists and photographers were always present. The packed schedule of such events, combined with intense stress, took a toll on Goh's health. Whisky was a common feature at these ceremonies and Goh's alcohol consumption led to liver ailments. His wife tried to convince him to switch to Chinese tea, but Goh, afraid to scare off potential investors, refused.

The state stepped into the industrialization effort directly. In 1962, Goh began building a steel mill in Jurong, which became National Iron & Steel Mills.[43] The government also invested in shipbuilding and a shipping line, and founded an airline and a state development bank.[44] Singapore's economic prospects, however, did not improve enough to lift Lee out of the doldrums. During a 1968 trip to London, a senior executive at retailer Marks & Spencer, Marcus Sieff, visited Lee at his hotel. Sieff had seen Lee on the BBC and he came with a business proposition. The nimble fingers of Singapore's Chinese would be well suited to making high-value lures and fishhooks for trout fishing, Sieff noted, and Marks & Spencer would be willing to market them. "I must have looked forlorn on television for him to have taken the time to see me," Lee wrote. "I thanked him but nothing came of it."[45]

. . . .

LEE, HOWEVER, WAS formulating a strategic vision that would finally spark Singapore's Miracle. The inspiration, oddly enough, came not from Japan or Asia's other high-growth countries, but from Israel. Lee was impressed by how the Jewish state built a thriving economy in the face of a full boycott from its Arab neighbors by linking itself to the United States and Europe. Lee believed Singapore should pursue a similar strategy—to "leapfrog the region," as he put it. That strategy required a shift in industrialization. The island's attempts to develop industry before its separation from Malaysia were based on a kind of import-substitution—producing goods for the larger population of the federation. Singapore's independence rendered this plan useless. In its place, Lee adopted a Japan-style export-led program, aimed at selling into the giant markets of the industrialized countries. Unlike Japan and Korea, however, Singapore could not develop its own companies to export to the West quickly enough. "Had we waited for our traders to learn to be industrialists we would have starved," Lee wrote.[46] The answer, then, was to find other people to create the companies and markets for Singapore.

This line of thinking led Lee to pursue foreign investment. The world's giant multinationals (MNCs), Lee figured, could provide exactly the capital, jobs, and training Singapore needed. These MNCs would bring ready-made markets for the goods produced in Singapore. The factories these MNCs built would export to their home countries and other industrialized nations. "We were getting companies from highly developed industrial societies with state-of-the-art technologies," Lee explains. "They were going to bring to us second or third generation technologies, but that was good enough for us, and they were bringing us management skills which we didn't have."[47] Lee was especially interested in wooing American MNCs, which he called Singapore's "best hope." American MNCs could create more jobs with larger investments and provide better technology than investments from other countries.[48] A two-month sabbatical at Harvard University in 1968 convinced Lee this strategy was promising. He spent his time there discussing the global economy with business leaders and economists. American companies, he found, "were on the expansion, they were in a dynamic mode, going abroad. The economy was in full steam. I saw that they were looking for ways to cut costs and expand their business, widen markets, and bring back products to America and sell to the rest of the world," Lee says. "I suddenly saw this was perhaps an answer to my problems."[49] Of special influence, professor Ray Vernon woke Lee up to the power of low wages in the global, free-market economy. These wages, Vernon explained, could be used to attract investment from Corporate America, which was willing to capitalize on such opportunities much more rapidly than Lee had ever believed possible. Vernon "dispelled my previous belief that industries changed gradually and seldom moved from an advanced country to a less-developed one," Lee wrote. "Reliable and cheap air and sea transport made it possible to move industries into new countries."[50] In other words, Lee came to understand the tremendous potential economic benefits of offshoring, both for his tiny nation and for the global economy.

At the time, this kind of thinking was radical. Many development economists and leaders of postcolonial countries considered MNCs—and especially American MNCs—the devil's spawn. They were the standard-bearers of neocolonialism, ruthless exploiters of the resources and labor of poor nations which would condemn a developing economy like Singapore's to perpetual servitude to the West. Lee, however, did not agree. In building Singapore's Miracle, he was guided not by ideology or textbooks, but simple pragmatism. He was perfectly willing to go against convention—if he thought his method could work. "By nature and experience, we were not enamored of theories. What we were interested in were real solutions to our problems and not to prove somebody's theory right or wrong," Lee says. "All we had was our labor and our location and our skills, and if [the MNCs] can turn that into a profit, and make a living for us, good luck to them." In this way, Lee differed from Korea's Park and Japan's nation-building bureaucrats, whose priority was to create world-class corporations of their own. "Japan's paradigm was to learn from Europe and America and re-create in Japanese fashion what they saw there," Lee says. "We had no such ambition. We were prepared to learn from everybody. Just get us there, never mind if it is not an original Singaporean product." The mix of ideas and policies that generated Singapore's Miracle, Lee believes, became a new model for development. "In the process, we produced a new doctrine," Lee says. "We had not reinvented the wheel, but picked up ideas from many sources and put the pieces together to produce something useful for ourselves and the world."[51]

The truly hard part came next—convincing American companies to bet their money on Singapore. A big part of that responsibility fell onto the inexperienced shoulders of a young but persistent former English teacher.

. . . .

CHAN CHIN BOCK arrived at John F. Kennedy Airport in New York City on a bitter cold day in January 1968. He was sent by the EDB to open its first overseas office in New York to promote Singapore as an investment destination. It was a daunting task. "I didn't know anything about how to do this job," he says. "No one knew what to do." As he trudged through the New York snow, the possibility of failing his country chilled him even more than the freezing temperatures. "The prospect of having to set up home, live alone by myself, and worse still, convince hard-headed American executives that Singapore was the best place for them to put their money . . . sent a shiver through my almost frozen body," he later wrote.

A typical Singaporean government official of that time, Chan was not an economist, nor did he have any special training to help him in his mission. His route to the EDB began with a misplaced pair of sunglasses. Chan had been working as the communications manager for the local operation of Ford Motor when he met S. Dhanabalan, an EDB staffer. Dhanabalan had come to Ford's offices for a meeting with its manager, and left his sunglasses sitting on a conference table. Chan returned them to Dhanabalan, who then mentioned to Chan that the EDB needed to hire a liaison to work with potential investors. Interested in the challenge, Chan joined the EDB in 1964.

As Lee's vision for the economy became clearer, so did the EDB's role in bringing it to life. The EDB became the command

center in Singapore's effort to industrialize through foreign investment. Winsemius suggested that the EDB open an office in New
York to act as a contact point for potential American investors.
The Netherlands had wooed American companies the same way.
Chan, with his Ford experience, was tapped to open it. "Nobody
else had even the slightest inkling of how an American MNC
works or thinks," he says. He immediately ordered a heavy suit
and a thick wool sports jacket from his favorite tailor. It was the
first cold-weather clothing he ever owned.

Once in New York, Chan worked from a one-room office on
Fifth Avenue with a Cuban immigrant as his secretary and sole
staff member. With no contacts in the United States, he began cold-
calling company headquarters seeking meetings.[52] Some CEOs he
met did not even know where Singapore was. He had to point out the
island as a speck on a globe.[53] But slowly, Chan formed a network.
He scheduled lunch meetings with senior executives almost daily,
and even if they were not rushing to invest in Singapore, they still
shared their thoughts on how American corporations were changing and what options Singapore might have. Chan took advantage
of what he called the "open door" spirit of American business.

Lee was an important ally in Chan's efforts. Whenever Lee visited the United States, Chan put him in front of senior U.S. executives, often over lunch. Chan met the participants in advance to
inform them about Singapore and gauge their interest in investing.
Winsemius briefed Lee on what these executives wanted to hear.
"They looked for political, economic, and financial stability and
sound labor relations to make sure that there would be no disruption in production that supplied their customers and subsidiaries
around the world," Lee wrote. The quick-witted Lee was always
a hit. "Word got around that I was worth listening to, and the
numbers swelled," Lee boasted. Hundreds of businessmen sometimes showed for Lee's speeches.[54] Lee staged an equally impressive performance for those executives who investigated Singapore
in person. He made sure that the roadways along the usual route
a visiting CEO would travel in Singapore—from the airport to

the main hotels to his office—were carefully landscaped. The government complex that housed Lee's office, called the Istana, was a showpiece, a gated oasis of green lawns and woodland with a nine-hole golf course right in the center of the city. "Without a word being said, [CEOs] would know that Singaporeans were competent, disciplined, and reliable," Lee wrote.[55] Many CEOs got an audience with Lee himself. Lee says his message to them was straightforward: "We are a society that is determined to make things work. When we invite you to invest, we are going to help you to make your investment successful."[56]

The effort began to pay off in the months after Chan arrived in New York. Chan learned during his informal lunches that the semiconductor industry could be a potential target for Singapore. Under extreme pressure from low-cost Japanese competitors American chip makers were looking to cut their own expenses. Chan employed an agent in California to visit chip outfits and lobby them to consider Singapore as a base for new facilities.

Chan's big break came unexpectedly. On a flight from Taipei to Hong Kong, I. F. Tang happened to be sitting next to Mark Shepherd, president of Texas Instruments (TI). Shepherd explained that he was in Taiwan examining a possible investment in a chip assembly plant there. Tang, taking advantage of his captive audience, pitched Singapore as an alternative. Upon landing in Singapore, Tang had the EDB shoot off a telegram to Chan telling him to expect a phone call from TI. When it came, Chan was ordered to drop everything and do whatever it took to get the company to invest.

The call came through and Chan flew to Dallas, TI's home city. Whisked into a meeting with Shepherd and other executives, Chan gave his best pitch. He stressed Singapore's English-language skills, low labor costs, and tax incentives, and argued that the country's small size would allow the government to organize what TI needed quickly. Speed was on Shepherd's mind. The executives told Chan that TI wanted the operation up, running, and exporting within fifty days of the decision to invest. Could

Singapore make that happen? Chan was stunned. It was a commitment he could not make, but he promised Shepherd: "We will try our best." After the meeting, Chan warned his EDB colleagues in Singapore about the fifty-day deadline in a telegram. "You must get your act together," Chan says he told them.[57]

Shepherd decided to investigate Singapore in person. When he arrived in September 1968, the EDB was ready. Shepherd had flown in from Taipei and was in a grumpy mood. The proposed site for TI's factory was still just rice paddies. The EDB had a chance to outmaneuver the Taiwanese. Shepherd was shown a ready-made factory building, developed by the government, which could quickly be converted into TI's assembly plant.[58]

Shepherd was convinced. TI opened its plant in Singapore in 1969, as did two other major chip firms, National and Fairchild, making semiconductors a major export for the island. "The future began to look promising for the first time since Singapore became independent," Chan later wrote. The do-whatever-it-takes spirit shown in wooing TI became a regular feature of Singapore's investment promotion drive. In 1969, Dutch electronics giant Philips planned to build a factory for the machines and tools it used in its production sites in Asia. Taiwan was already short-listed for the investment, but the EDB wanted the factory as well. Philips would add a big European name to its list of investors and bring in an operation that used skilled workers. The EDB was tipped off by a Philips's local employee that a vice president was planning an overnight stop in Singapore on his way to Taiwan. The EDB staffers went to work. When the executive landed at the airport, the EDB convinced him to take a look at Singapore as a possible location. Its officers brought the vice president to a training center the EDB had founded to teach Singaporeans metal-industry skills. The Philips executive was so impressed that he decided to invest in Singapore instead of Taiwan. Chan, meanwhile, continued to hustle in the United States. Between 1968 and 1970, he went on a nationwide campaign to attract investment from General Electric, flying around the country to visit the chiefs of the conglomerate's far-flung divisions. He secured ten GE investments in those three years, and by 1972, the U.S. multinational was the largest foreign investor in Singapore, employing thirteen thousand people.[59]

. . . .

LEE FINALLY ALLOWED himself to relax. Growth had reached Miracle heights, and the economy weathered the oil shock and the other disruptions of the early 1970s. His Communist opponents were defanged. The onetime labor activist feared the Communist-leaning unions would scare off potential investors. Using the fragile state of the economy as an excuse, he had launched a relentless crackdown on labor unrest. "In newly independent Singapore, on its own and highly vulnerable, the government could not allow any union to jeopardize Singapore's survival," he wrote. To break a 1967 cleaning workers strike, Lee arrested the union's leaders and sacked the strikers. At a 1968 union conference, he warned that he would treat a dockworkers strike as "high treason." Lee's PAP passed new laws beginning in 1968 that curtailed worker benefits and gave more power to companies to hire and fire. By 1969, Singapore had no strikes at all.[60]

The crucial factor behind Lee's success was the foreign investment pouring into the country. The Jurong industrial estate that had been mocked as "folly" was a laughingstock no more. By late 1972, the estate housed 417 plants employing 48,000 people, with another 74 being built or planned.[61] Much of the investment that would come to Singapore was in high tech—computer peripherals, disk drives, semiconductors, and other IT equipment. "We welcomed everyone," Lee wrote, "but when we found a big investor with potential for growth, we went out of our way to help it get started."[62] As a result, Singapore compressed the development pattern engineered in Japan and South Korea—that transition from low-wage, low-tech, labor-intensive industries into more capital-intensive, high-skill industries. "Instead of doing textiles and garments and slowly climbing up the technology ladder, we moved into a whole lot of IT items which were very high tech at the time," Lee explains.[63]

Singapore received an amazing share of the foreign direct investment heading into Asia.

FOREIGN DIRECT INVESTMENT INTO SINGAPORE (US$ MILLIONS)

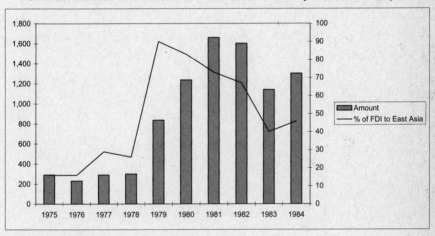

Source: World Bank.

And the foreign money drove Singapore's Miracle.

ROLE OF FOREIGN FIRMS OWNED OR CONTROLLED IN SINGAPORE'S MANUFACTURING SECTOR

	1968	1975	1980	1990
% of total output	46	71	74	76
% of workers	26	52	58	59
% of direct exports	NA	84	85	86
% of capital expenditure	43	65	75	71

Source: Kwong et al. *Industrial Development in Singapore, Taiwan, and South Korea.*

How Lee attracted all of this investment is perhaps the most important lesson of the Singapore story. Lee's goal was "to create a First World oasis in a Third World region." If Singapore could develop top-rate security, infrastructure, telecommunications, education, transportation, and health services, it could attract engineers, managers, and entrepreneurs who wanted to do business in the region. Singapore differentiated itself from other emerging countries by creating a climate that bolstered the confidence of foreign investors. "We had one simple guiding principle for survival," Lee wrote, "that Singapore had to be . . . better organized, and more efficient than others in the region. If we were only as good as our neighbors, there was no reason for businesses to be based here."[64]

CHAPTER FOUR

THE EARLY DAYS OF SUPERMAN

The most important enjoyment for me is to work hard and make more profit. —LI KA-SHING

The Hassenfelds were worried they would run out of heads. Rhode Island–based toymaker Hasbro, founded and managed by the Hassenfeld family, ordered the plastic heads to its popular G.I. Joe dolls from a manufacturer named Cheung Kong in far-off Hong Kong. The proprietor, Li Ka-shing, an immigrant industrialist from China, had his expensive molding machine churning out the round dollops of skull-shaped plastic as quickly as possible. Still, G.I. Joes were so hot in 1967 that Hasbro feared the supply might fall short, leaving the firm with stacks of headless G.I. Joe bodies it could not sell.

With rising concern, Stephen Hassenfeld, one of Hasbro's family-managers, phoned Li from the United States and urged him to purchase a second molding machine to ensure Cheung Kong could fill Hasbro's orders. Though willing to make the large investment, Li realized adding more equipment would not solve Hasbro's immediate problem. Ordering and installing such a complex piece of machinery would take another three to four months. Hasbro could not wait that long.

Hassenfeld's conversation with Li did little to calm the

American's nerves. Hong Kong at that moment was in an unusually unstable state, with leftist-inspired riots, caused by political unrest in neighboring China, sweeping across the city. As the two chatted, a huge explosion shook Li's office. A bomb, in a box marked "Compatriots Beware," had exploded only 20 feet from Cheung Kong's factory. Hassenfeld heard the blast through the phone receiver. "What was that?" he asked. "It was a bomb," Li answered flatly. He attempted to defuse the tension with humor. "But we are still working," Li continued, "so you should give us a medal instead of rushing us for the order."

The only way to ease Hassenfeld's mind, Li realized, was to get Hasbro the heads it needed. Though Li had no formal training as an engineer, he had by that point been working with plastics machines for two decades. He knew his way around a factory. After reading through some industry magazines and conducting other research, Li became convinced he had discovered a way to modify his current machine to double its output. He brought his idea to a senior engineer Hasbro had sent to Li's plant to monitor production. Li said he was "99% sure" the adjustments would work. But there was a catch. He would have to shut down the machine for eight hours to make the changes. The engineer was, in Li's words, "hopping mad." "I have 30 years' experience and I haven't thought of a way to do this," the engineer lectured. Li suggested that he relax in his hotel while the modifications were completed and come back the next morning. Instead, the infuriated engineer phoned his boss in the United States, waking him up in the middle of the night, to complain about Li's plan.

Li, fully confident, managed to sweet-talk Hasbro into giving him a chance. He switched off the machine and, after six hours of tinkering, finished his fixes. When he started it up again, the machine pumped out heads at twice the speed, just as he had predicted. The next day, the surprised yet pleased engineer returned to the factory and worked with Li to make further modifications, which doubled output again. Hasbro would not run short of G.I. Joe heads.[1]

This type of creativity and reliability made Li, and the thousands of small industrialists across East Asia just like him, crucial players in the more and more globalized system of industrial production. Beginning as far back as the 1950s, American firms in a wide range of consumer industries began enlisting companies in Asia to manufacture components or entire products for sale in the United States. Once produced, the goods were often marked with well-known American brand names before they were sold to American consumers; the foreign industrialists remained anonymous. In some cases, the American buyers were importers or retailers ordering new, cheap products from Asia to market at home. In other cases, American manufacturers hired Asian industrialists to produce their products, or parts of their products, rather than doing it themselves in the United States. This process became known as "offshore outsourcing." Over the decades, these practices caused more and more production to shift to Asia, which has been an integral engine of the region's rising wealth to the present day. Outsourcing also integrated Asia into the global trading system so tightly that it forever linked the economies of East and West. Li was not just a simple supplier to Hasbro. He was indispensable to the toymaker's success.

Li's relationship with the Hassenfelds grew so close, in fact, that they became almost one big family. Li was especially fond of young Alan Hassenfeld, Stephen's brother, who was first dispatched to Hong Kong in 1968, even before he graduated from college, to work with the company's Asian suppliers. Li took Alan under his wing, inviting him out for afternoon boating trips on weekends with his two sons, Victor and Richard, teaching him how to use plastic-molding machines, and sharing lunchtime bowls of noodles while squatting in the corner of Li's factory. Li, no matter how busy, insisted on welcoming Alan at Hong Kong's airport and escorting him on the ferries to Hong Kong Island every time he flew into town. Alan says that Li, or "KS" as he calls him, "had a great effect on my life" and "became like a father figure to me."[2]

The rapport between Li and Alan was unusually intimate, but their business relationship was typical. Hasbro began hiring Asian firms to manufacture toys beginning in the early 1960s. The company bought from Japan at first; the early products were inflatable toys and dolls' clothing. Then Hasbro had toys made in Hong Kong, South Korea, and Taiwan. By the 1970s, roughly a quarter of Hasbro's toys were produced by Asian manufacturers. Alan spent eight months of the year in the early 1970s monitoring Hasbro's suppliers around the region from a room at Hong Kong's Hilton Hotel. He posted telexes on the walls around his bed to track orders.[3] The toy industry was only one in which production shifted to Asia on a wide scale at an early stage. Others included textiles, apparel, shoes, and consumer electronics. Over the decades, American firms in more and more advanced industries had their products made by Asian manufacturers, including computers and other high-tech electronics gear.

The main reason for this shift of work was cost. The labor-intensive nature of businesses like toys and apparel made wage rates an important element of the competitiveness of a product. With a significantly higher level of development, the United States simply could not compete with a poor, populous Asia on labor costs. A factory worker in Hong Kong in 1970 earned only 33 cents an hour—a tenth of what an American manufacturing worker pocketed. (Wages in Singapore and Korea were even lower.)[4] As a result, the savings American firms enjoyed by outsourcing to Asia were irresistible. The cost of manufacturing a G.I. Joe head in the United States in the 1970s was roughly seven times greater than in Hong Kong, even after taking into account shipping costs.[5]

Asia became a primary global production base not only because of cheap labor. The developing world of the 1960s and 1970s had lots of hungry people willing to work for a pittance, yet manufacturing industries did not shift to places like Africa or the Middle East to the same degree as they did to Asia. The difference was the economic policies pursued by Asian governments. The stable economic environments and pro-business regulatory schemes set in place in Hong Kong, South Korea, Taiwan, and Singapore fostered an investment climate much more comforting and welcoming to foreign businessmen than elsewhere in the developing world. Improved telecommunication systems and faster and more reliable transportation links made the process of shifting production to Asia easier, cheaper, and less risky. Asian manufacturers like Cheung Kong also developed great expertise in an array of production processes that made them efficient and extra competitive. American toymakers, for example, never developed the capability to paint a G.I. Joe head or apply the hair mechanically.

The movement of production to Asia had widespread benefits. The American firms saved money, enlarged profits, and freed funds for new investments. They passed on the cost savings gained from Asia-based production to American consumers in the form of lower prices, which allowed Americans to enjoy a higher quality of life. In Asia, the increased production created exports and higher incomes. The factories that sprouted up in Hong Kong and its neighbors generated new employment for Asians. Many of these factory workers were lured away from their farms and brought into the industrialized economy for the first time. The work was miserably hard and in some cases unhealthy. They slaved for long hours, bent over sewing machines or screwing together TV sets in assembly lines, but the wages they earned were far greater than what they could get out of their rice paddies. The factories became beacons of hope for a better life, and, like California gold mines, compelled the poor to leave rural hamlets for the region's shining new industrial zones.

By the 1990s, however, the massive shift of manufacturing to low-cost Asia—and specifically the outsourcing of production to Asia by American firms—had become the most contentious economic issue between the United States and Asia. As more and more factories like Li's Cheung Kong opened around Asia, more and more factories shuttered their doors in the United States. With the plants went the employment they provided. Americans complain

that Asia is "stealing" their jobs as entire sectors have been almost
wiped out by Asian competition. In 1990, for example, nearly a
million Americans worked in apparel manufacturing; today, that
number has sunk under 200,000. The Hassenfelds tried to maintain as much production in the United States as economically
feasible, but they, too, eventually conceded to financial reality. In
1998, they shut Hasbro's main toy factory in Rhode Island (though
some products, like board games, are still made in America).[6] The
steady advancement of the Miracle has threatened employment
in more and more sectors of the American economy, raising cries
from politicians, labor unionists, and anti-trade activists to curtail
America's economic relationship with Asia.

In Asia, on the other hand, the Miracle was made possible by
the manufacture of low-end consumer goods for export to the
United States and Europe. Rapid growth in every country that
experienced the Miracle was jump-started by this movement of
production to Asia. Hong Kong's development was almost entirely driven by this shift in global manufacturing. In 1950, Hong
Kong, then still a part of the British Empire, was mainly a center
of finance and trade and possessed minimal manufacturing. By
1975, however, Hong Kong exported $3.5 billion's worth of ap-
parel, toys, textiles, and electronics. A large group of small industrialists like Li set up shop in the colony in the years following
World War II and began to export their wares to the United States
and Europe soon thereafter.

Through this process, the private sector drove Hong Kong's
Miracle almost entirely on its own. There were no Shigeru Sa-
hashis "picking winners," no "Asian model"–style cooperation
between government and business. Though the British governor
and his small team of civil servants did assist the local business
community—by, for example, developing public land as industrial estates,[7] as in Singapore—their main contribution was smart
policymaking. The same stable, efficient, open, and corruption-
free economic environment that attracted businessmen like Alan
Hassenfeld also permitted entrepreneurs like Li to build their

companies. These new firms then took advantage of the ever-freer global trading system to export around the globe. Hong Kong became a Tiger because of free markets, free trade, and the forces of globalization, not government intervention. Economist Milton Friedman proclaimed Hong Kong the "best example" of a contemporary society relying "primarily on voluntary exchange through the market to organize their economic activity."[8]

The history of Hong Kong's Miracle, therefore, raises serious questions about the validity of the "Asian model" of development. Hong Kong shows that countries can experience the same rapid growth without state-directed financing or overbearing bureaucrats by employing a combination of good governance and open markets. Despite all the attention and praise given to Japan's MITI model of development, Hong Kong's success suggests that the key ingredient in the Miracle was simple, old-fashioned capitalism. Even countries in which the state dominated the development effort, like South Korea, government policies were linked to the competitive advantages of their economies within the global economy. Following this line of analysis, the heavy-handed bureaucrats of Japan and Korea were unnecessary to the achievement of the Miracle, or their function has been greatly exaggerated.

Yet we cannot yet dismiss the "Asian model" entirely. Economies with a greater state role developed *differently* than Hong Kong. The nature of Hong Kong's economy, with its many small industrialists backed by strong finance and trading firms, has remained more or less in place through the decades. Japan and South Korea, on the other hand, changed the nature of their economies by building heavy and high-tech industries to a greater degree than Hong Kong. There are no POSCOs or Hyundais in Hong Kong. Proponents of the "Asian model" proclaim that the difference was the use of industrial policy. Growth was only one goal of the "Asian model"; another was to alter the entire *structure* of the economy into higher value industries. This crucial transformation, the argument goes, may never have happened, or would not have happened as quickly or successfully, in a purely free-market system. The case of Hong Kong shows that could be the case. The debate over the "Asian model," therefore, continues.

. . . .

LI KA-SHING WAS one of those hard-nosed entrepreneurs who capitalized on Hong Kong's liberal economic regime and sparked the colony's Miracle. By the time he and Alan Hassenfeld slurped noodles together, Li was laying the foundations of a fortune far greater than those of other local industrialists. According to *Forbes* magazine, Li is the eleventh-richest man in the world, with a net worth estimated at $26.5 billion. He did not get that rich off of G.I. Joe heads. Li was savvy enough to bet the money he made in plastics on the future of the Hong Kong economy, mainly through timely purchases of local property and other assets, before expanding internationally. Today, Li's chief company, conglomerate Hutchison Whampoa, controls advanced mobile phone networks in Europe and Asia and operates more ports around the world than any other company. At home in Hong Kong, Li is omnipresent. He owns supermarkets, drugstores, and wine shops; builds apartments; and operates the local power utility. The companies under his control command about 15 percent of the capitalization of the Hong Kong stock market. An associate once commented that Li is so powerful in Hong Kong that "he can almost rewrite history."[9] Along the way, Li developed a reputation for possessing a magical ability to find the perfect deal. Journalist Louis Kraar wrote in *Fortune* that Li "combines the instincts of a gambler with the calculations of an actuary."[10] The locals nicknamed him "Superman."

Yet like many other Chinese tycoons, Li tries to maintain a relatively modest lifestyle, at least in public. He shares a two-story home in Hong Kong with his elder son, Victor. Li has one floor to himself, while Victor, his wife, and three daughters reside on the other.[11] When Kraar met him in the early 1990s, Li was clad in the standard dark business suit and plain tie of the Asian manager. He pointed out that his Citizen electronic wristwatch cost only $50. Kraar thought that Li looked "like an amiable, intelligent bank clerk." He expounds a business philosophy that is equally simple. "If you keep a good reputation, work hard, be nice to people, keep your promises, your business will be much easier," he once said.[12] Li has generally heeded his own advice. He is well known in Hong Kong for his diligence and relentless work schedule. "The most important enjoyment for me," Li said, "is to work hard and make more profit."[13] However, as his fortune and power have grown, so has public resentment toward him. His unparalleled influence in Hong Kong has made him a target of the city's toiling middle classes, who gripe that just about anywhere they spend their hard-earned wages, a percentage ends up in Li's coffers.

Yet when Li first entered the business world, he was just like most of the territory's Chinese—unknown and poor, with apparently few prospects. One scribe calls his rags-to-riches tale a "real-life fairy story."[14] Li was born at the worst of times, in a China in turmoil, on July 29, 1928. By the late 1930s, Japan's imperial army was ravaging its way across the country, and his hometown, Chaozhou in Guangdong province, came under attack. Classes in the school where his father, Yun-jing, was headmaster were suspended. Fearing for the safety of the family, he fled with his wife and three children in 1940 to Hong Kong, then still controlled by the British.

The family moved into a partitioned room, and both Li and his father went to work at a watch factory owned by Li's uncle—Yun-jing in the finance department, Li as a young apprentice. In 1941, the Japanese caused trouble for the Lis once again. Japanese troops conquered Hong Kong, the economy withered, and the family struggled to make ends meet. Li's mother and siblings returned to Chaozhou. Soon thereafter, Yun-jing contracted tuberculosis and convalesced at a public hospital. Li cared for him as best he could—he even purchased used medical texts to teach

himself the proper treatment—but his father's condition worsened.[15] "You must have the strength of character," Yun-jing told
Li on his deathbed, according to one account. "Then you can rise
as tall as the sky."[16] Li assured his father that the family would
enjoy better times in the future. Yun-jing died in 1943, leaving Li,
only fourteen, alone in Hong Kong and the chief breadwinner for
the family.

Li excelled at his uncle's watch factory. He first served as a
stock keeper, who managed the inventories of watches and wrist-
bands. At seventeen, he was promoted to a salesman of plastic
belts.[17] "People were working eight hours a day," Li later recalled,
"but I worked sixteen hours. . . . It was really full, nonstop work.
During the day I worked in the office to bring in business, to sell.
After office hours I worked in the factory to see that the orders
were taken care of and we'd give good delivery."[18] He was so successful that he was named the plant manager a year later, and
the general manager of the operation the year after that, at only
nineteen years old.

By 1950, Li was ready to branch out on his own. He took his
life savings of $1,750 and borrowed another $7,000 from family
and friends to invest in his own plastics factory. He named the operation Cheung Kong,[19] which means "long river," a reference to
China's mightiest waterway, the Yangtze (Chang Jiang). The name
was not only a signal of Li's ambitions, but also, to Li, a lesson on
how to ensure the success of his start-up. "In Chinese we have a
saying: If you want to be successful, whatever your business or position, you need to accept different opinions and different people,"
Li once explained. "Why did the Yangtze become a long river? It's
because it can accept smaller rivers and become big." He started out
manufacturing basic household items like plastic soap containers
and combs,[20] but after conducting some research, he discovered the
growing popularity of Italian-made plastic flowers in both North
America and Europe and shifted into producing his own.[21] It was
a wise decision.

In 1957, a foreign businessman wandered into Li's factory. As it turned out, he was a representative of an American importer called Joseph Markovits, Inc. The businessman had heard—erroneously—that Cheung Kong was the biggest plastics manufacturer in Hong Kong and he was interested in placing an order for plastic flowers. "I was puzzled," Li explains, "because my factory was only mid-size at the time, hardly the largest in Hong Kong. I wondered who would mislead him in such a way." As the agent kept talking, Li figured it out.

About a year earlier, Li had manufactured a batch of plastic toys for a local trading firm, but shortly before the crates were set to ship, the African buyer fell into financial trouble and refused to take the goods. The trading firm offered to compensate Li for the toys, but Li told its managers not to worry. Cheung Kong would find new customers for the toys on its own. "I casually asked him to simply refer more business to me in the future," Li says. Then he forgot about the matter.

The traders, however, did not. They responded to Li's generosity with some of their own, referring the American importer to Li with their highest recommendation. The American company placed an order for six months' worth of Li's plastic flowers. A short time later, the head of Joseph Markovits, Nicholas Marsh, flew to Hong Kong to meet Li. It proved to be one of Li's most important business relationships, and Li and Marsh became lifelong friends.[22]

With large orders from Marsh and other foreign businessmen, Li greatly expanded Cheung Kong's manufacturing capability. "I lived and breathed plastic flowers for ten years," Li recalls, "and all day long all I could think of was how to make them look more life-like and how to be more creative." He designed a process that could mold long-stem plastic roses in one piece—eliminating the need for employees to sew the petals and stem together—and developed a dual-injection system that could make flowers with two colors.[23] Li became known as "The King of Plastic Flowers."

. . . .

LI WAS ONLY one of many Chinese immigrants who were transforming the Hong Kong economy. The city became a rare safe
haven for Chinese refugees fleeing chaos in China, especially after
World War II, when the civil war between the Nationalists and
Communists ravaged the country. Hong Kong's population was
only 600,000 in 1945; five years later, it had surged to 2.5 million. Most were poor laborers and farmers; others rich businessmen, many of them from Shanghai, who feared for their lives as
Mao's Communists took control. Both groups were instrumental
in Hong Kong's Miracle. The rich invested what capital and assets
they could get out of China into new industrial enterprises. The
poor became factory laborers.[24] They called Hong Kong the "Adventurous Paradise."[25]

One of these wealthy immigrants, H. C. Ting, manufactured
batteries and flashlights in Shanghai as the civil war heated up.
Ting at first refused to flee, but he also worried about the future,
and as a precaution set up a small plastic-molding business in
Hong Kong in 1946 to make parts for flashlights. It proved a smart
investment. With the political uncertainty in China rising, Ting
flew to Hong Kong in 1948. The Communists later purchased his
Shanghai factory, and Ting, worried about those he left behind,
gave most of the money he received to his former employees. He
started over again in Hong Kong.

Ting's new enterprise, Kader Industrial Company, began in
similar fashion to Cheung Kong—making simple plastic household items. By the mid-1950s, Kader had developed the capability to produce molds to make plastic goods and started
manufacturing toys.[26]

Kader's business was helped along by a growing network of
industrialists and traders that arose among the new factories in
Hong Kong. One of the most influential was Fung Hon-chu. The
manager of a trading firm called Li & Fung, he was also a Chi-

nese immigrant. Originally based in the southern metropolis of Guangzhou, Li & Fung moved its headquarters to Hong Kong in 1937 and shut down its China operations in 1949. At first, Fung exported traditional Chinese wares like porcelain, firecrackers, and bamboo products to the West. But by 1950, this business had begun to dry up. The quality of goods coming over the border from Communist China deteriorated and the demand for these old-fashioned products in the United States and Europe dwindled. Fung had to find a new way to make a living.

He found the solution in Hong Kong's nascent industrial sector. Fung joined his fellow immigrants in setting up small factories, which manufactured wooden bowls, metal utensils, and even plastic flowers. He also connected with other new Hong Kong outfits to export their textiles and plastics to the United States. As Li & Fung's business expanded through the 1950s, Fung received more and more orders that his own factories were too small to fill, so he contracted other manufacturers to produce the goods for him. Li & Fung eventually transformed into a full-time "sourcing" agent. Such a firm does not manufacture anything itself but takes orders from overseas companies, locates the right factories to fill the orders, and exports the end products to its clients.[27] Under Fung Hon-chu's two sons, the firm would come to play a key role in altering the process of manufacturing itself.

In this role as sourcing agent, Fung Hon-chu approached Ting at Kader with new export opportunities. He brought models of plastic toys to Kader and asked Ting to manufacture them for clients in the West. Kader quickly became a major toy exporter to the United States and Europe. American toy company Ideal was an important early customer. As the business advanced, Kader began designing toys jointly with its U.S. clients. By the 1980s, Kader was producing many children's favorites, including the popular Cabbage Patch Kids.[28]

The relationships among businessmen like Ting and Fung built the colony into a major manufacturing center by the 1970s. Many, like Ting, stuck with their original businesses and grew bigger and richer. Li Ka-shing, however, set his sights on a much grander target.

. . . .

WILLIAM PURVES STRODE between the noisy plastics machines in Cheung Kong's factory in 1970 on his way to Li's office. He found Li ensconced in a glassed-in cubicle cluttered with empty teacups, scattered papers, and a spittoon. Purves was a British senior manager (and later chairman) of the Hongkong & Shanghai Banking Corporation, now better known as HSBC. Back then, the institution was simply called "the Bank" in Hong Kong. Purves invited Li to become one of the bank's clients. This was an unusual opportunity for a Chinese businessman. A bastion of British colonialism in Hong Kong at that time, the Bank did not extend such offers lightly. Now the Bank wanted to strengthen its ties to Hong Kong's increasingly wealthy Chinese entrepreneurs. Li had already begun to rise above the rest of his fellow immigrant industrialists. Through a series of aggressive investments and smart deals, Li was becoming a major Hong Kong property baron. Purves's offer would solidify Li's growing influence and gain him an entry into the highest circles of the Hong Kong business community. With the interests of both men in concert, the agreement was automatic. "We knew we'd got the account," Purves later recalled, "because Li himself came down to the car to see us off."[29]

Li had entered the property business somewhat by accident. In 1958, his plastics business was growing quickly, but he still leased his factory space. This arrangement became an irritating problem. His landlord refused to sign more than a two-year lease, which allowed him to increase Li's rent payments with wallet-straining regularity. Li instead decided to build his own factory on his own property. At the same time, he also constructed his first residential apartment building. "I firmly believed that property would be one of the best businesses in the future," he once declared.[30] "I could see that the supply of land in Hong Kong was limited, whereas population was unlimited."[31] His property holdings grew steadily, especially in the late 1960s. The same leftist riots that made the Hassenfelds nervous scared off many investors in the city, but Li remained confident and bought up the best properties at bargain prices.[32] By the late 1960s, Li was already making more money off his property business than plastics,[33] and by the 1970s, property became his main preoccupation. In 1981, he shut his plastics operation completely.

By then, the high-society contacts the bank brought Li proved invaluable. In 1979, HSBC decided to sell its 22-percent stake in Hutchison Whampoa, which, due to its shareholding structure, was a controlling stake. Hutchison was one of the old British trading houses, called *hongs*, that dominated the local economy. In the 1970s, Hutchison fell on hard times and required a rescue by the bank. After shoring up the hong's finances, the bank wanted to find a new owner. It turned to Li.

He jumped at the chance. Li had been eyeing the hongs' property portfolios and other assets.[34] The bank, Li once explained, "could not sell Hutchison to just anybody, just for money. It had to make sure the new owner had the kind of quality needed to lead Hutchison. I think the bank knew me quite well, and knew I could do it."[35] On New Year's Day 1980, Li took control of Hutchison. He left no doubt about who was in charge. "After gaining control," Li explained, "I immediately told the management team that I didn't care about the chairmanship, but wanted to head the executive board and to make the final decisions for each company in Hutchison. I didn't care how things might look from the outside. I wanted genuine control."[36]

Li's acquisition of Hutchison was a seminal moment in Hong Kong's economic history. He became the first Chinese to run a British hong, and he gained control of many of the businesses that would become mainstays of his empire, such as ports and retail chains. The British elite in Hong Kong, who had always worked hard at keeping the commanding heights of Hong Kong's economy in their own hands, were appalled at what the bank had wrought. Now, one of the city's proudest establishments was under the thumb of a plastic flower salesman. The bank, however, was simply acknowledging reality. Li's ascendency made clear the changing nature of the Hong Kong economy. The old British trading class was on its way out. The aggressive Chinese industrialists were the up-and-coming power. The Miracle and its impact could no longer be denied.

CHAPTER FIVE

A TALE OF DUCK EGGS AND DRAGON DREAMS

The Chinese, having missed the first Industrial Revolution . . .
could not afford to miss the opportunity again. —STAN SHIH

Stan Shih learned the bad news from a friend in accounting. The Lin family, who controlled Qualitron, the firm where Shih worked, was funneling bank loans out from the electronics maker to support another family enterprise, a troubled textile company. In 1976, Qualitron was one of Taiwan's fastest-growing companies, but it was racking up debt it could not pay back. Bankruptcy threatened the whole operation, Shih realized. As a senior research and development (R&D) engineer, he decided to try to save the firm himself.

Shih scheduled a meeting with Vincent Lin, the family member in charge at Qualitron, and pleaded with him to stop transferring funds from the firm.[1] Lin refused to listen. "This is none of your business," he shot back, "this is a family matter."[2] But Shih did not give up that easily. He approached two other companies in secret and pressed them to invest in Qualitron, but to no avail. Shih conceded that Qualitron was doomed. He would have to find work elsewhere.

That proved a challenge. Though Taiwan's economy was booming, Shih's expectations were difficult to match. At only thirty-one years old, he was already something of a star in Taiwan's budding electronics industry. Shih designed Taiwan's first homegrown, handheld calculator and the world's first pen with an embedded LED clock. Shih wanted to continue his original research and delve into new technologies, but in those days Qualitron was one of the few firms in Taiwan that invested heavily in R&D. Most companies were low-tech operations that merely assembled TV sets, radios, and other simple items. "I'm a pioneer," Shih says. Other companies "didn't give me a platform for new developments."[3]

Those "new developments" involved a technology that had become an obsession—microprocessors. Though today these specialized chips appear in everything from cars to refrigerators, in the mid-1970s they were the new frontier in electronics. Shih had learned about microprocessors at a seminar in Los Angeles in 1974 held by Rockwell International, an early developer of the technology. When he returned to Taiwan, he ordered Qualitron's engineers to find out everything they could about the promising new chips.[4] Just as Morita saw the transistor as a breakthrough in electronics two decades before, Shih believed the microprocessor "would be another turning point in industrial development history."[5] As Qualitron faded, however, so did Shih's hopes of working with microprocessors. He resolved that he had only one option: to start his own business.[6]

Shih's decision was a crucial moment for Taiwan. His start-up developed into Acer, the world's third-largest computer maker and Taiwan's best-known company. Shih himself became the patriarch of Taiwan's powerful electronics industry. His example inspired the island's aggressive, nimble entrepreneurs, who, as in Hong Kong, are responsible for making Taiwan indispensable to the global economy. Shih also left his indelible mark on the entire global personal computer, or PC, industry. He pioneered a method of manufacturing computers that became standard for most PC companies; it was nicknamed the "fast-food model." Shih learned to make PCs the way Burger King slaps together hamburgers—

matching production to incoming customer orders, and carefully managing the supply of components so the most updated parts can be utilized.[7] The system slashed costs and increased the speed at which the latest technologies could be brought to store shelves. Shih is "a big reason why your PC costs $1,000, not $10,000," Paul Otellini, CEO of Intel, once commented. He "saw how marrying cheap chips with efficient manufacturing could spread computing power to the masses."[8]

The tale of Shih and Acer demonstrates a key, and often over-looked, factor in the Miracle—the uncanny ability of Asian economies to play catch-up in technology with the West. Taiwan constructed a world-class electronics industry in a remarkably short period of time that has become central to the global manufacturing of IT products. By 2005, Taiwan companies churned out about 80 percent of all personal digital assistants, or PDAs, more than 70 percent of the notebook PCs and two-thirds of the flat-panel computer monitors. This "catch-up" was present in all of the "early movers" and across various industries, from Korea's rapid advancement in shipbuilding to Sony's innovations in consumer electronics. As Shih says, "We demonstrated that we can develop advanced technology compared to the global market."[9]

How did Asia "catch up"? Proponents of the "Asian model" credit government action, and Taiwan provides evidence that they might be right. Though Taiwan's technocrats did not adopt the "Asian model" wholesale, as in South Korea, they played a much more instrumental role in guiding the island's development than the British civil servants of Hong Kong. This disparity in the role of the government in Taiwan and Hong Kong provides a rare opportunity to examine the impact of the "Asian model" on the advancement of industry.

In many ways, the economies of Taiwan and Hong Kong are similar. Both are composed of a large number of small firms, often started by entrepreneurs. Both were heavily dependent on exports and got much of their business through outsourcing from foreign firms. They each also developed a strong consumer electronics industry at roughly the same time. But over the years, the two sectors diverged. Taiwan firms advanced into products with a higher level of technology and closed the gap with their American competitors much more quickly than Hong Kong's. Companies in Taiwan are also better skilled at product design and R&D. Hong Kong electronics firms, on the other hand, remained to a greater degree in their original business model, based more on low-cost labor and manufacturing flexibility than higher levels of technological capability. One key difference was government policy. Taiwan's technocrats put in place myriad policies that helped the island's electronics companies develop and market advanced products. The story of Acer shows how the interaction between resourceful entrepreneurs like Shih and inventive technocrats propelled Taiwan's economy toward high technology. In Hong Kong, the more passive civil servants implemented policies that were generally pro-business but did not aid specific industries. The added assistance of the state in Taiwan could account for the advancement of its electronics sector over Hong Kong's. The proponents of the "Asian model" believe that state action accelerated not just the growth of the many Asian economies that adopted it but also contributed to a shift in their *structure* to high-value-added, more technologically intensive industries. In the case of Taiwan's electronics industry, that appears to be true.[10]

Yet once again, it is wise to be wary of giving the government too much credit. Though Taiwan's technocrats created the conditions for technology catch-up, businessmen like Shih did the hard work. Even the officials who designed Taiwan's policy saw their role as merely supportive. Li Kuo-ting, one of Taiwan's leading policymakers, said in 1980 that "the government played a key part" in Taiwan's Miracle, but he quickly added that "the sustained rapid growth of production and exports during the past two decades was made possible mostly through the efforts of the private sector."[11]

Shih appears an unlikely centerpiece of this complex story. With his oversized eyeglasses and grandfatherly, soft-spoken manner, Shih resembles a high-school chemistry teacher more than a high-powered entrepreneur. His wife, Carolyn, once wrote that Shih "is not obsessed with fine food or clothes. He eats whatever is available and buys his clothes on discount."[12] He still enjoys a rousing game of Ping-Pong, a habit he picked up in college.[13] K. Y. Lee, CEO of BenQ, a Taiwan electronics manufacturer, and one of Acer's first employees, describes Shih as honest and sincere, "like a person you feel so much warmth from in the countryside, that if you don't know the route to your destination, you ask and he gives you a very warm welcome and tries to do whatever he can to support you." Yet, throughout his career, Shih has displayed an almost mystical ability to identify and capitalize on new trends in computing and to nurture the industry's latest technologies. As Lee says, Shih "spends almost all his time thinking about business."[14] "Creating new value is the value of my life," Shih says.[15]

Shih used this simple philosophy to launch Acer (then called Multitech) in 1976. Shih convinced three other Qualitron researchers to join his start-up and they scraped together $25,000 as investment capital.[16] Shih's 40 percent share came mostly from a chunk of money his mother had given him, which he had kept as savings.[17] Carolyn, a bit surprised by Shih's venture, remembers, "I never thought he would start his own business. He was shy and not good in social interaction, nor did he have any ambition while he was in school."[18] Yet Carolyn supported her husband and became an Acer co-founder. She had done some bookkeeping for her father's company, so she came on to handle the finances. "They didn't have enough money to hire a financial guy," she says.[19] Carolyn was named "Chairman of the Board," the responsibilities of which included mopping the front stairs of the office.[20] The group, eleven in all, crammed into a 1,200-square-foot apartment converted into an office and research lab to begin what Shih calls "collective entrepreneurship."[21] Shih and Carolyn lived in a small apartment in a building next door with their three young children. As money was short, Carolyn took no salary at all for two years.[22]

Yet at the time, money did not matter to the young engineers at Acer, like K. Y. Lee. He first met Shih when he applied for work at Qualitron. Called into Shih's office for an interview, Shih broke into an extended lecture on the wonders of the microprocessor. Lee was sold on the technology and Shih. He joined Qualitron, then a few months after Shih formed Acer, Shih invited Lee into its R&D department. The salary Shih offered, at about $125 a month, was half what Lee could have earned elsewhere, but, like Shih, Lee wanted "a non-stereotype job" that was "something more innovative." Acer, he believed, was the future.[23]

Despite his firm's humble beginnings, Shih, too, had a vision of the future, something he called a "dragon dream." Not only would Acer become a major success, but it would uplift Taiwan and Chinese society with it. "When we were young, teachers always talked about how great the Chinese are, but not today," Shih says. "The dragon dream was to make sure the Chinese contributed more to global society, to make sure we weren't behind."[24] The microprocessor was the answer. "The Chinese, having missed the first Industrial Revolution which resulted in the weakening of the country, could not afford to miss the opportunity again."[25] And why not think big? In the Taiwan of the 1970s, anything seemed possible. The island had already embarked on the Miracle.

. . . .

"THE PAST YEAR has been the darkest and bleakest in my life," Chiang Kai-shek, the leader of China's Nationalist government, scribbled into his diary on October 31, 1949, his sixty-second birthday. The civil war he was fighting with Mao Zedong's Communists for control of China was going badly. Nationalist armies suffered a series of catastrophic defeats and were being pushed to the far reaches of the country. The Americans, his chief allies, had abandoned him. President Franklin Delano Roosevelt once saw Chiang as a key ally in the war against Japan and a pillar of the postwar world order. But by the late 1940s, Washington was fed up with Chiang's corrupt, autocratic regime and military mismanagement. "Vinegar" Joseph Stilwell, an American officer assigned by Washington to be the Allies' chief of staff in China during World War II, once told Roosevelt that Chiang was "a vacillating, tricky, undependable old scoundrel." After Roosevelt's death, President Harry Truman, who feared Chiang's war was a lost cause, limited aid to the Nationalists. "They're all thieves, every damn one of them," Truman once complained. Chiang, meanwhile, still hoped he could resurrect his fortunes. "I have suffered ignominy and defeat," Chiang wrote in his diary. "However, I should not be worried, angry, nor should I be conceited. . . . Danger and difficulty lie ahead. I must heighten my vigilance so that I can revive China and re-establish the republic."

It was not to be. On December 1, the base of Chiang's wartime headquarters, Chongqing, fell to the Communists. The Nationalists decided to flee the mainland and set up a new seat of government on the island of Taiwan. On December 10, Chiang arrived at the airstrip at Chengdu, the capital of Sichuan province in China's southwest, and boarded a DC-4 for Taiwan. Dense clouds made it impossible for the pilot to navigate by features on the ground. He charted much of the journey by instinct. Chiang landed safely, and he and his son, Ching-kuo, rested at a hotel at one of the island's most scenic locales, Sun Moon Lake. As the remaining Nationalist armies surrendered to Mao's forces, or died in a last-ditch attempt at resistance, Chiang, by one account, rented a boat and went fishing. "If I can continue my ambition and carry it out," Chiang wrote on Christmas Day, "I should become aware that the new undertaking and history should begin from today."[26]

Those words proved prescient, but not in the way Chiang envisioned. Chiang's sojourn in Taiwan was supposed to be temporary, an opportunity to regroup, rearm, and launch a new war to reclaim all of China. That hope was pure fantasy by the time he went fishing on Sun Moon Lake. His truncated forces had little hope against the Red Army, and Washington, fearful such an invasion could turn the Cold War hot, kept him on a tight leash. Instead, Chiang stayed on his small island and lorded over his new state as dictator for more than twenty-five years. The Nationalists started something they had had little opportunity to do in the past—manage a government in relative peace.

They proved quite good at it. The economy was a top priority from the start. About 1.6 million refugees clambered across the Taiwan Strait to escape the Communists, including hundreds of thousands of Nationalist soldiers, all of whom had to be resettled. Inflation raged and food was scarce. Based on past performance, the Nationalists were ill equipped to cope with problems of such magnitude. While in China, Chiang, with little background in economics, had mismanaged the areas of China under his control to the brink of financial collapse. But he had learned his lesson. The immense corruption of his officials and the suffering of the Chinese poor under his rule drove millions toward the egalitarian ideology of Mao's Communists and undermined his army's fighting capability and spirit. In Taiwan, Chiang, much like Park Chung Hee, knew the success of his rule would depend on economic progress. He kept himself out of economic policymaking and left it to a team of technocrats.

The prototype of these professionals was Li Kuo-ting, whom Shih describes as "a visionary." Li was born in 1910 in Nanjing in China. His father manufactured hookahs. Feeling the early stirrings of nationalism, Li chose to be a physicist, believing that China's weakness vis-à-vis the West was due to its backwardness in science. Awarded a scholarship, he went to Cambridge in 1934, but when the Sino-Japanese war broke out three years later, Li, flush with anti-Japanese fervor, discontinued his studies and rushed home. During the war, he repaired antiaircraft equipment and automobiles for the Nationalist forces, then became a manager at a steel mill, and, after the Japanese surrender, an executive at shipbuilding companies in Shanghai and Taiwan. His success as an executive at these state enterprises led to his career as a technocrat. In 1953, he was appointed to the Industrial Development Commission of the new Nationalist government in Taiwan, which was charged with creating a modern economy on the small island.[27] For the next four decades, from a variety of posts, Li, with a select team of like-minded public servants, guided the economy with pragmatism and guile, ditching strategies and deftly adopting new ones as Taiwan's economy changed and advanced, much like Lee Kuan Yew in Singapore. Much of Li's relentless fortitude came from religion. A devout Christian, he read the Bible daily and knelt with his wife each night by their bedside for a lengthy prayer.[28]

Li was typical of many of Taiwan's top policymakers in that he did not have a true background in economics. At times, the island's economic team appeared to have no clear, long-term plan of action. "We did not set out in the early 1950s with anything like what I would call a comprehensive strategy," Li later wrote. Taiwan's economic team, like Lee and his aides in Singapore, usually shunned strong attachments to any economic theories. "Ideology is fine, but a lot of good is lost and damage done by means justified by dogmatic ends that are then never achieved," Li wrote.[29]

One philosophy to which they attempted to adhere was that of Sun Yat-sen, the founding father of the Nationalists. A revolutionary hero whose followers contributed to the collapse of China's final dynasty in 1911, Sun, ironically, is revered by China's Nationalists and Communists, both of whom claim to be his true descendants. Sun compiled his thoughts into three principles, one of which, the "Principle of People's Livelihood," advocated a mix of restrained capitalism and state socialism as the route to prosperity. He believed that the government carried the responsibility of lifting the people out of poverty by ensuring they had proper food, clothing, and shelter. In doing so, he argued, the state would achieve overall national development. The concept of an interventionist state, charged with the task of protecting the downtrodden, was a radical departure from the aloof, insulated government of China's failed imperial dynasty. Sun's teachings, Li wrote, "provided Taiwan with more than the framework; it also charged the government with a goal: improving 'the people's livelihood.'"[30]

The Nationalists pursued that task with gusto. A core element of Sun's program was the provision of land for poor farmers to alleviate rural poverty. Beginning in 1949, the government undertook a bold policy of land reform on Taiwan. The Nationalists sold public land to tillers and redistributed plots owned by large landholders to small farmers. The number of land-owning farmers rose significantly, as did their incomes. Chen Cheng, the governor of Taiwan who championed the program, later wrote that "social stability, improved people's livelihood and economic development could take place only through land reform."[31]

Cheng was not exaggerating. The boost in rural welfare provided a ready market for manufactured goods and a source of savings for investment, setting the stage for Taiwan's next economic step—industrialization. Much like Park in Korea, Chiang and his economic team equated industry with independence and power. An industrialized economy, the Nationalists believed, was necessary to defend Taiwan against Communist China, just as Park believed development was crucial in his defense of South Korea from the North. Furthermore, Chiang wanted to turn Taiwan into a "model province" that would outshine and outperform mainland China and prove the worth of his rule over Mao's.[32]

Again, Sun Yat-sen's advice pointed the way forward. The state, he argued, should play a leading role in developing a poor country. "Goods used throughout China depend upon other countries for manufacture and transportation hither, and consequently our economic rights and interests are simply leaking away," Sun explained in a 1924 lecture. "If we want to recover these rights and interests, we must quickly employ state power to promote industry, use machinery in production, and give employment to the workers of the whole nation."[33] Taiwan's policy team took this advice to heart. The government would direct, handhold, and prod industry for the next forty years.

At first, the Nationalists employed classic import-substitution policies by fostering sectors such as fertilizers, cement, and textiles behind lofty tariff barriers. That strategy produced some strong growth in the 1950s, but the program soon ran out of steam. Taiwan's tiny domestic market could not support large-scale industry on its own, and the local economy became swamped by excess production.[34] Even more troubling for the Nationalists, the economy still depended on U.S. aid. Between 1951 and 1965, the United States gave Taiwan $4 billion, financing 40 percent of the country's imports and investment.[35] By the late 1950s, Li and his nimble cohorts took Taiwan in a new direction—toward that export-oriented growth model made famous by the Japanese. The United States was heavily involved in this shift. In 1958, U.S. Secretary of State John Foster Dulles visited Taiwan and inked an agreement with the government in which the Nationalists agreed to focus on economic development rather than military recovery of the mainland. U.S. policymakers linked continued economic aid to the adoption of pro-market reforms. One of the most outspoken advocates of a more open Taiwan economy, Wesley Haraldson, head of the China division of the U.S. Mutual Security Mission beginning in 1959, publicly berated Chiang's government for excessive military spending and a poor record on encouraging private investment. Many of Taiwan's policymakers were irked by Haraldson's attacks, but in the end, Li and his colleagues took much of his advice. Starting in the late 1950s, the government introduced a wide range of pro-export reforms that created a new currency system and provided tax incentives and low-interest loans for exporters.[36] Taiwan began to take on aspects of the "Asian model," and these steps set the stage for Taiwan's Miracle.

The most important innovation introduced by Taiwan's policymakers was the concept of the export-processing zone, or EPZ—a feature that figures prominently later in this story. Policymakers defined specific areas that had their own administration and regulation geared for the facilitation of exporters. Companies that set up in the zone received perquisites such as duty-free imports of raw materials and streamlined investment procedures. In return, they had to export 100 percent of their production. The domestic market, which was far more heavily regulated, remained protected. To prevent smuggling, the government surrounded EPZs with walls, watchtowers, and police guards. In this way, the EPZs were an experiment in liberal capitalism, a crucible of progressive policy in a state-driven economy. Though today the EPZ sounds simple and logical, at the time, the concept was radical. "There was a sincerely held concern that Taiwan was yielding sovereignty in the zones to foreign investors in the name of trade and investment," Li recalled. The EPZ was originally formulated by Taiwan's more liberal technocrats in 1956, but the first zone, located by Kaohsiung Harbor in the south, did not open until a full decade later. It was an instant hit. Within two years, 128 firms had approval to open factories in the zone, exceeding the government's expectations. Two more EPZs launched later.[37]

The EPZs were part of a campaign to attract foreign investment in manufacturing, and multinationals played an important role in developing Taiwan's electronics industry at this early stage. RCA, Zenith, Philips, and Texas Instruments were among the early investors.[38] Between 1963 and 1972, Taiwan's exports increased ninefold.[39] Taiwan, South Korea, Hong Kong, and Singapore became known as the four Asian Tigers, or, in economist-speak, the NIEs, or newly industrialized economies.

Yet by the late 1960s, Li Kuo-ting and his colleagues, their antennae tuned to change, realized that Taiwan needed to alter course yet again. Rising wages were making the labor-intensive export industries, like textiles, less competitive, and the technocrats saw the need to shift into more complex production to support higher wages. Technology seemed to be the answer. Li Kuo-ting and his technocrats began to direct their energy toward developing Taiwan's technology industries. Their effort encouraged "Asian model"–style cooperation between government and business. "We hope, through the coordinated efforts of government, industry, and the educational system, to create a climate in which science and technology can naturally flourish, with growing benefits to high-technology enterprises and all society," Li once said.[40] Stan Shih was setting up shop in that tiny apartment in Taipei at just the right moment.

. . . .

STAN SHIH LIVED through Taiwan's tumultuous creation in relative peace. He was born on December 18, 1944, in one of the island's oldest and more prosperous townships, Lukang, in Taiwan's midwestern region. Back then, the island was, like Korea, a Japanese colony. (Control of the island returned to the Chinese after Japan's defeat in World War II.) Shih's father was a well-respected incense maker, but he fell ill with a recurring high fever in 1947 and died early the next year. Shih was only three. According to one story, as his father lay in a semidelirious, feverish state, he would ask Shih's mother, known by her pet name Ah-Shiu, about her hopes for their son. "I want him to be a businessman, a big businessman, known from north to south over all of Taiwan!" he would tell her.[41]

Ah-Shiu had to provide for her son by herself. She opened a small store from which she sold a wide range of items—stationery, lottery tickets, watermelon seeds, and, especially, duck eggs. They were far from wealthy—Shih recalls hardly ever wearing shoes—but Ah-Shiu made sure her son always had a little more pocket money than the other children in Lukang. While in most families, any income would be broken up among numerous children, Shih says he "got 100 percent of a small pie."

He learned business basics from his mother. Many other merchants at the time rigged scales or fudged weight measurements, but Ah-Shiu made sure to treat her customers fairly. "When you're doing business, you have more knowledge than your customer, but you should be honest," Shih lectures.[42] He also picked up some tips he would use later as a PC entrepreneur. He noted that the duck eggs made the most profit even though they had a narrower margin than his mom's other main item, stationery. The perishable eggs sold in larger quantities at a faster rate.[43] Shih would come to realize the "perishable" nature of computer technology and the need to get new machines onto store shelves and into consumers' hands with great speed.

Shih required all of his mother's fortitude in his quest to build Acer. From the earliest days of the company, Shih had more ambitious goals than many of his fellow Taiwan businessmen. He wanted to design and manufacture his own products under his own brand, while most others, much like Li's Cheung Kong, took orders from U.S. companies and produced the goods in anonymity. At its inception, however, Shih's young Acer did not have the capital to manufacture anything at all. Instead, Acer distributed microprocessors from U.S. chip firm ZiLOG in Taiwan.[44] To build a market, beginning in 1978 Shih set up training centers where engineers could take a fifty-hour seminar on how to use microprocessors to control everything from traffic lights to machinery. In four years, his centers trained about three thousand local experts in this new technology. Most important, Shih's team of researchers got intense experience in product development. Shih turned Acer into an R&D lab focused on creating microprocessor-based electronics products for larger Taiwan technology companies to commercialize. The R&D staff "worked diligently day and night . . . with very limited resources," Shih remembers. "When screwdrivers were not enough, coins were used as replacements; when the pliers broke, their teeth were substitutes." The team scored some hits, its biggest being the first cathode-ray tube computer terminal developed in Taiwan.[45]

By 1980, these businesses had generated enough capital for Shih to market his inventions on his own. The first item was called the Heavenly Dragon Chinese computer. Shih took an ordinary computer and inserted a card developed by Acer that allowed a Chinese speaker to input information in Chinese characters. Computers at that time operated primarily in English, presenting a tremendous stumbling block for most Chinese. The Chinese-language systems that had been invented were of limited use, since they would not run readily available software. The problem with developing a Chinese-language system that could be used on any computer was the complexity of the characters, which took up far too much memory to be cost-effective. With the help of a computer scientist, Shih's R&D team overcame these hurdles. Acer's product could operate with English-language software but allow a user to communicate with the machine in Chinese characters. That gave Chinese speakers access to widely available software for the first time.[46]

Shih's big break, however, came a year later, when his company designed and produced its own minicomputer, called the Microprofessor. The portable machine could play simple games and do basic word processing. Later generations competed with the famous Apple IIe. An instant hit, the Microprofessor gave Shih his first major international sales. Marketed as an "entertainment/educational" computer, it became one of the first computers to appeal to the home market. The Microprofessor, Acer boasted, was a computer "that anyone can use, from seven to 70 years old."[47]

By this point, support from the Taiwan government became crucial for Acer. Li and his fellow technocrats had been busy devising all kinds of ways to help the island's technology entrepreneurs. From the beginning, the technocrats linked their efforts to the needs of businessmen competing in a global market. "It is my belief," Li said in a 1978 address, "that no technology can be a viable one if its products do not have a market large enough to support itself."[48] One of the most important government contributions was the founding of the Industrial Technology Research Institute, or ITRI, in 1973. The brilliance of this laboratory was that it was not an academic think tank but a collection of engineers focused on providing Taiwan with new technologies that could be easily turned into products for export. Much of the technology it researched was licensed and imported from American firms and then disseminated to the private sector in Taiwan. The other major government contribution was the Hsinchu Science-Based

Industrial Park, supported by Li and opened in 1980. Expanding on the concept of the EPZ, the park encouraged technology companies with financial incentives—such as cheap land—and an "incubator" effect. With so many technology outfits in one place, the government hoped that the managers and engineers would learn from one another, much like what has happened in Silicon Valley.

Taiwan's technocrats and entrepreneurs successfully shifted the economy into higher-technology products.

PERCENT OF MANUFACTURING BY SECTOR

	1951	1961	1971	1981	1991
Food	29	25	11	10	8
Textiles	15	11	12	9	7
Electronic equip & appliances	0.6	2	10	11	16

Source: Jomo, K. S. *Manufacturing Competitiveness in Asia.*

Aside from Li, the other policymaker who played an invaluable role at this time was Sun Yun-suan, minister of economic affairs and premier from 1969 to 1984. Sun, an engineer, first rose to prominence in the mid-1940s, when he repaired Taiwan's power stations—which had been bombed out during World War II—in only three months. He drafted green university cadets as staffers and pillaged old parts from damaged machines to cobble together working generators. An impressed World Bank enlisted him to run Nigeria's power company in the mid-1960s. In Taiwan, he championed the creation of ITRI and pushed through early investment in semiconductor research and manufacturing. "The people who can get things done in my country," he once said, "are all my people."[49] Despite his immense responsibilities, Sun remained something of a quiet family man. Each night, Sun watched TV soap operas with his family before retiring to bed with a stack of documents "to do his serious thinking," according to his son, Joseph. He strove to keep his work and family life as separate as possible. Dinner-table questions about economic policy were politely dodged. "You'll read about it in the newspaper tomorrow," he would say.[50]

Shih took full advantage of Sun and Li's tech-friendly policies. Soon after Hsinchu's founding, Shih opened his first factory inside the park. It was an unimpressive affair—a two-story building built by the park authorities totaling about thirty-six hundred square feet. With so little space, Shih could do little more than place desks end-to-end as an assembly line.[51] Shih made his Microprofessors in the factory.[52]

It did not stay small for long, thanks to Shih's talent for divining the future—and a heavy dose of help from ITRI. In 1982, Shih returned from a Comdex computer industry trade show in Las Vegas convinced that Acer had to head in an entirely different direction. The machine that got special attention at the show—especially from Shih—was the first fully IBM-compatible computer, introduced by Compaq. That computer, Shih thought, pointed to a shift in the entire industry. A dizzying array of competing computing systems, from Wang Labs, Digital Equipment, Hewlett-Packard, and others, had been put on the market. None of these systems were compatible with each other—or with Acer's own Microprofessors—and Shih realized this situation could not continue. With computers becoming more widely available, the industry would have to move toward a standard. "This brought me much enlightenment that the compatibility of computers is very important," he says. Shih determined to make IBM-compatible machines as well.[53]

Shih's decision was a major shift for a company that had been bent on designing products on its own. He proceeded with caution. A new version of the Microprofessor was in development, and instead of ditching it, Shih chose to produce that machine and pursue an IBM-compatible computer at the same time. His research team, however, was too small to complete both tasks. Any attempt at an IBM-compatible PC would require delays.

He took an unusual step. Shin hired ITRI to develop an IBM

system for him,[54] for a $375,000 fee. ITRI readied a prototype within one year.[55] Despite problems caused by government interference—Taiwan's intrusive policymakers insisted Shih had to share this new technology with the rest of the industry[56]—Acer had its first IBM-compatible PC on the market by late 1983.

The launch set Shih on the path toward becoming a major figure in the computer industry. Over the next two years, Acer's sales more than tripled to $165 million.[57] That still was not enough for Shih. By the mid-1980s, Acer was just one of many manufacturers of IBM-compatible computers, known as "clones." American, South Korean, and even other Taiwanese companies were churning them out. Many of these cloners, especially those made in Taiwan, had miserable reputations for ripping off IBM designs and manufacturing their machines in sweatshops. The sorry image perturbed Shih, who said he felt "a personal responsibility to change it."[58] Acer had to differentiate itself somehow.

The best way, Shih figured, was to outpace other cloners in technology. In that way, Acer could sell its own products in major markets like the United States on an equal footing with American brands. "We want to go from the periphery to the core," Shih said in 1987.[59] "We want to use [the] Taiwanese cost structure but offer international, first-class products, services, and image. We want to be a multinational company from Taiwan."[60]

Shih, as it turned out, had an advantage. In 1984, he made a $1 million investment to start a small research firm in Silicon Valley called Suntek to study new computer technologies in the United States. A year later, he dispatched an R&D team from Taipei that began work with an advanced chip from Intel, the 386,[61] which was the basis for a significantly faster personal computer than Acer, or anyone else, produced at the time. The researchers returned to Taipei and undertook the tedious task of piecing together the circuitry for a 386 computer with individual chips.[62]

By 1986, Shih had his biggest breakthrough yet. Acer became the second computer maker in the world to produce a PC with a 386 chip, behind only industry giant Compaq. Acer even beat out a startled IBM. Shih believes it was Acer's most important turning point.[63] "To catch up to the U.S. in technology was always my goal," Shih says.[64]

Orders quickly began to pour in from the United States for Acer's new machines—too quickly, in fact, for Acer to handle. An especially large order came from the U.S. firm Unisys. For Shih to fill it, he would need to expand his factories. Again, Li Kuo-ting came to the rescue. Li and Shih had met soon after Acer's founding at an electronics fair, and Li kept an eye on Shih's progress. When the Unisys order came through, Shih called Li to ask for his help. Li worked the phones, calling bank chairmen in Taipei and urging them to lend to Shih. The loans, not surprisingly, materialized, Shih built new manufacturing capacity, and Unisys got its PCs.[65] Unisys was so impressed that it licensed the 386 PC technology from Acer—the first time an American firm completed such an agreement with a Taiwanese company.[66]

Shih says that his 386 PC "broke the perception that Acer was an IBM follower."[67] In a mere decade since Shih and his tiny staff had crammed into their tiny office, Acer had caught up to the most powerful firms in the industry. Taiwan could rightly claim to be a true competitor in technology. By 1988, Acer was churning out a PC every twenty seconds, half of them under the Acer brand while the rest were manufactured for major companies like Philips, Siemens, and Canon for sale under their names. Acer was being called "a national treasure" and Shih "the Steve Jobs of Taiwan." Shih, who continued to pour money into R&D, promised even greater feats. "This is just a start," he told the *New York Times* in 1988.[68]

Taiwan's technocrats agreed. Li and his friends wanted to push Taiwan even higher up the technology ladder.

. . . .

MORRIS CHANG[69] WAS out of work. Chang had resigned from his job as chief operating officer of the U.S. tech firm General Instrument in 1985, disappointed with its indecisive management.

With such an impressive résumé, he had no shortage of options. The China-born Chang, with an electrical engineering doctorate from Stanford, had spent twenty-five years at Texas Instruments, including six years in charge of its semiconductor division. Within days of his resignation, his phone began to ring with offers.

One call stood out from the rest. It was from the chairman of ITRI. Would Chang be interested in moving to Taiwan to become ITRI's new president? An attempt by ITRI to lure top-notch technical talent to Taiwan was not unusual. ITRI and the Taiwan government had a long-standing goal of attracting Chinese-born scientists and engineers—and their skills and knowledge—into the island's technology sector. Chang, however, was surprised by the call. He had never lived in Taiwan before. Born in Zhejiang province in China in 1931, Chang survived the Japanese and civil wars by fleeing from place to place and then, in 1949, immigrated to the United States. His first visit to Taiwan was in 1968, when he was an executive at Texas Instruments. It was not a very positive experience. He thought of Taiwan at that time as "the boondocks." Dispatched to start the process of building a chip assembly plant in Taiwan, Chang ran into bureaucratic hassles and the investment was put on hold. (The same investment Chan Chin Bock stole for Singapore.) Eventually, the ever-present Li stepped in, found the company some land, and promised to uphold the company's intellectual property rights. Texas Instruments built its factory in 1969.

Still, Chang was curious enough to fly to Taiwan to visit ITRI. Li gave Chang the hard sell. High tech, Li proselytized, was the best way to ensure that Taiwan's economy continued to prosper. Taiwan needed him; his fellow Chinese needed him. Li "felt I was a man who had a missionary zeal," Chang says. The pitch worked. In August, after thirty-six years in the United States, Chang uprooted himself and moved to Taiwan.

He was not allowed to settle in before Li threw him into an unexpected and complex project. About two weeks after his arrival, Li called Chang to his office. The government, Li said, had been approached for money by three small chip-design firms founded by Chinese in the United States. Li thought supporting these firms might accelerate technology in Taiwan. Which one should he choose? Chang was skeptical of all of them and of the investment plan itself. It was impossible to determine which firm would succeed. Li suggested that maybe they should form one company that could help out all of these research firms. "Look, why don't you think seriously about it," he said to Chang. "Think about how you want to start a company." Chang returned to his ITRI office. The phone rang a few hours later. Li had already gone ahead and arranged for Chang to present his plans to the premier. Chang had to come up with something, and quickly.

But what? Chang believed that the chip industry was changing rapidly enough that Taiwan might just have an opportunity. During the early days of semiconductors, the large manufacturers conducted most of their own research. By the 1980s, however, a host of small outfits had popped up, many of them in Silicon Valley, which designed chips but had no fabrication facilities of their own. Called "fabless" chip companies, they had to hire a manufacturer—often a Japanese company—to produce their chips for them, an often uncomfortable relationship. Those manufacturers were also competitors of the "fabless" firms, who worried about the safety of their proprietary technology. "I sat for a couple of nights and I was really thinking," Chang said. "Then suddenly, it was like something just struck me."[70] Why not start a company that only manufactured chips, that had no design capability of its own? Then these "fabless" design firms would have a factory ready to make their chips without having to turn to a competitor. Chang's chip firm would survive on outsourcing. He pitched the idea at his meeting with the premier. The presentation, he says, "was one of the best I made in my life." The government was sold immediately.

Chang spent the next year lining up the $220 million he needed to build a chip factory. The government put up half the money itself.[71] Chang tried to convince Texas Instruments and Intel to invest, but both companies rejected the idea. It sounded like too risky a proposition. Could such a business be stable, or would chip firms just hire Chang's firm on the irregular occasions when they needed some extra manufacturing capacity? Eventually, he convinced Philips to invest. He approached over two dozen local companies to squeeze them for the rest.

In 1987, Chang's company, Taiwan Semiconductor Manufacturing Company, opened its doors—the first independent chip foundry in the world. Chang took 120 engineers and researchers from ITRI, who had worked on the institute's pilot chip project, as TSMC's first employees.[72] He used his contacts in the United States to attract business from Intel, Motorola, and Texas Instruments. (Stan Shih at Acer was also an early customer.) Just as Chang had suspected, those "fabless" chip companies came to Taiwan in droves. Once again, the Taiwan government had engineered a way to keep the island's Miracle on its blistering pace.

. . . .

THE MIRACLE THAT Stan Shih, Li Kuo-ting, and Sun Yun-suan brought about in Taiwan came to have far-reaching consequences, beyond technology industries, beyond the island itself. For across the Taiwan Strait, Taiwan's Communist enemies were keeping an eye on their renegade province and absorbing some of the ideas that launched its Miracle. The Nationalists would, in a way, come to take over the mainland, but not in the way Chiang Kai-shek could ever have imagined.

CHAPTER SIX

TO GET RICH IS GLORIOUS

It does not matter if it is a yellow cat or a black cat,
as long as it catches mice. — DENG XIAOPING

Deng Xiaoping needed to make a bold statement. In late 1978, Deng, already seventy-four years old, was embroiled in a power struggle for supreme control of China. Mao Zedong, the patriarch of China's Communist movement, had died two years earlier, setting off a contest between divergent factions within the party with different visions of China's future. Some cadres remained loyal to the dictates of Mao, with his focus on the traditional ideological tenets of Communism. Deng and his allies, however, wanted to take China in a new direction, one that concentrated less on politics and more on rejuvenating a moribund nation. While Japan and the Tigers experienced their Miracles, China remained mired in its own self-imposed quagmire of political upheaval and endemic poverty, cut off from the rest of the world. Deng wanted change.

A perfect opportunity to force that change came in December. A crucial assembly of the Communist Party's leadership—the Third Plenum of the Eleventh Party Congress—was scheduled that month. Deng intended to use it to solidify his power. He was slated to deliver a major address at a party conference just ahead of the plenum that could set its agenda. It would prove to be the most important speech he ever made.

Even Deng's colleagues, however, had difficulty surmising how forcefully the old Communist would confront Mao's loyalists. Deng had already rejected a first draft of the speech written for him by a senior party official as too focused on "class struggle" and too soft on reform. "Look for someone to rewrite it," Deng told Hu Yaobang, a devoted supporter who would later serve as general secretary of the party.

On December 1, Hu summoned Ruan Ming, a professor at the party's school for cadres, to his room at a military hostel and asked him to help prepare a new draft. Ruan was taken aback. Merely a middle-ranking party member, Ruan was surprised that Hu would entrust him with a task of national importance. "I was still unsure whether I could write the kind of powerful speech that was needed at the time," he later confessed. Ruan had little time for indecision. A speech of such magnitude usually required several months to finalize. Ruan had only a few days.

Ruan's head swam in possible themes for Deng's speech. The atmosphere within the party after Mao's death was turbulent, with conflicting ideas about Marxism, democracy, economic policy, and reform swirling together. Ruan had his own ideas about where China should head, ideas he had held since he first became a Communist in the 1940s. Back then, as a teenager in Shanghai disgruntled with Chiang Kai-shek's inept rule, he began attending meetings of the Communist Party. At the time, Mao spoke about building democracy in China—the same democracy as Lincoln and Roosevelt, Ruan believed. He joined the Communist cause, but the democracy he sought never materialized. China under Mao became a pernicious dictatorship. Yet Ruan still held out hope for a more liberal China. Did Deng feel the same way? "I was a little confused," Ruan wrote, "since I didn't really understand Deng's train of thought."

The next day, Deng made himself clear. He called Hu's new speechwriters—eight in all—to Beijing's government complex near Tiananmen Square to outline his views. Ruan found the diminutive Deng in an excitable mood. As he outlined his views, Ruan realized that Deng intended to end the terror of the hardliners and challenge China's strict adherence to Mao's revolutionary ideology. "Since everybody is still afraid to speak out because of their lingering fears, we are unable to come up with decent ideas. What we should fear most is the masses refusing to speak up," Deng told them. "Thus in order to develop the economy, we must have democratic elections, democratic management, and democratic oversight."

Inspired, Ruan and the other writers produced a draft of a new speech in one day. Ruan even included some of his thoughts about greater political openness. After three quick revisions, it was ready.[1] On December 13, 1978, Deng stood before the party's top leaders and delivered the address. China was never the same again.

Deng's speech was a clarion call for reform. What China needed, Deng argued, was a fresh outlook, in politics, ideology, and, most of all, economics. The Communist Party, he told its leadership, should focus on economic development and improving the well-being of the masses, not waste its energy on political squabbles and pointless ideological conflicts. The time had come to bring China into the industrialized world. "Let us advance courageously to change the backward condition of our country and turn it into a modern and powerful socialist state," Deng pronounced. To achieve this goal, Deng said the party's "primary task" was to "emancipate our minds," to overcome ideological orthodoxy and open up to new thinking that could help the nation. "To make revolution and build socialism," Deng said, "we need large numbers of pathbreakers who dare to think, explore new ways and generate new ideas. Otherwise, we won't be able to rid our country of poverty and backwardness or to catch up with—still less surpass—the advanced countries."

Deftly employing Mao's own words to justify his position, Deng advocated a fundamental break with Maoism. He had come to see Maoist economic theory as a miserable failure. For thirty years the government had pursued Mao's economic program but the country's development remained stunted. "We must learn to manage the economy by economic means," Deng said in his speech. The people could not be inspired to build a thriving economy on political slogans alone, Deng said. What they required was the encouragement of an old-fashioned and un-Communist concept—money. "Revolution takes place on the basis of the need for material benefit," Deng said. "It would be idealism to emphasize the spirit of sacrifice to the neglect of material benefit." The Maoist devotion to egalitarianism, Deng argued, was misguided. Allowing those who excel to reap the benefits would spur faster economic development. "I think we should allow some regions and enterprises and some workers and peasants to earn more and enjoy more benefits sooner than others, in accordance with their hard work and greater contributions to society," Deng told the party. "This will help the whole national economy to advance wave upon wave and help the people . . . to become prosperous in a comparatively short period." It would be crucial to dismantle elements of the state planning system to unleash the entrepreneurial spirit of the nation. "Just imagine the additional wealth that could be created if all the people in China's hundreds of thousands of enterprises and millions of production teams put their minds to work," Deng said.[2]

Deng's speech was one of the most important turning points of the Miracle. It helped discredit the leftists, and by the end of the congress, Deng was clearly China's new ruler. Over the next decade, he implemented a wide array of reforms that reversed much of Mao's program. Deng called his new system "socialism with Chinese characteristics." Many would recognize it as purebred capitalism. The soul of Deng's new China was symbolized by one 1980s party slogan: "To Get Rich Is Glorious."

This switch from Mao to market was unprecedented. Deng infused a Communist political and economic system with the financial discipline and creative forces of the free market to a degree unmatched anywhere in the Soviet world. Deng's policies transformed China into the rising giant of the global economy, a budding superpower and the main contender for international influence with the United States—all in a mere twenty years. His reforms fundamentally altered the way in which the global economy works by making China the manufacturing center for everything from PCs to Barbie dolls. In the process, China has challenged the competitiveness of the industrialized world—including America—more than any other emerging country of the past century, creating a global scramble for control of trade, natural resources, and investment. At home, the consequences of Deng's reforms have been no less dramatic. China's 1.3 billion people have seen greater wealth and opportunity than at any other period in the country's modern history. China's ascent is the most globe-altering outcome of the Miracle.

No other leader of the Miracle has had a bigger impact on the welfare of a larger number of people than Deng. His persistence and political genius were indispensable to China's quest for economic greatness. Yet on the surface, Deng appears the most unlikely of reformers. His daughter Maomao describes Deng as "an introvert and a man of few words."[3] Deng had little formal education and did not consider himself a scholar. He once boasted that he never bothered to read Marx's *Das Kapital*.[4] Even at the height of his power, he played down his influence. "I am quite insignificant," he told a journalist in 1980.[5] However, he possessed wide-ranging experience, a brilliance for administration, and a formidable memory. Mao once called him a "living encyclopedia."[6] He could be hot-tempered, sharp-tongued, and blunt in presenting his views. Lee Kuan Yew called Deng "a five-footer but a giant among men."[7]

Deng, too, might seem fundamentally different from Asia's other nation-builders. In many ways, he looks like the Communist menace both Park Chung Hee and Lee Kuan Yew were committed to resist. Taiwan's Chiang Kai-shek fought him on the battlefield during the Chinese civil war. However, Deng, in many key ways, was not that dissimilar from his anti-Communist counterparts. He was a nationalist determined to raise China to its proper place in the world. To achieve that end, Deng, like Park, Lee, and Taiwan's technocrats, was a pragmatist willing to forgo ideology and adopt policies that would solve problems and produce results. "It does not matter if it is a yellow cat or a black cat," he remarked, "as long as it catches mice."[8] In this way, Deng was engaged in an ideological contest with Communism like the Miracle's other champions, except that his struggle took place *within his own regime*. Deng tussled with more radical Communists in his own government as he pressed for policies that they believed flouted doctrine and copied China's capitalist enemies.

The policies Deng implemented in many aspects were not all that divergent from those utilized by other Asian leaders. Deng succeeded in achieving rapid growth by linking the Chinese economy to the international marketplace and thereby benefiting from the forces of globalization. Much like Hong Kong and Singapore, China capitalized on the growing trends of outsourcing and offshoring. Its cheap labor and political stability were irresistible to foreign investors seeking a low-cost environment for the basic manufacturing of consumer goods like toys and textiles. As did

In an amazingly short period of time, China turned itself into an economic juggernaut, built on foreign investment and exports.

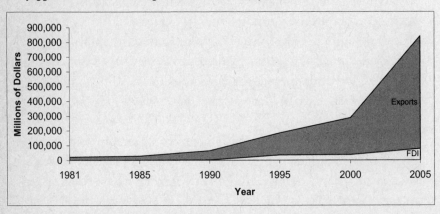

Source: World Bank, Asian Development Bank.

its neighbors, China jump-started its Miracle with exports, especially to the United States.

On the other hand, the story of China shifts the focus of the Miracle away from the "Asian model." While Japan, South Korea, Singapore, and Taiwan adopted some aspects of the model with governments that intervened in the economy, "late movers" like China tended to achieve rapid growth more like Hong Kong. China entered the Miracle by *removing* government influence from its economy—by decentralizing economic decision making, limiting the power of planners, opening up to foreign investment, and tying its economic future to international trade. The story of China's development, however, does not mean that the model was irrelevant. Deng was not *creating* a system for the first time, as in Korea, Taiwan, and Singapore. He was replacing an existing, state-dominated economic system that did not work with one based more on the market. The story of China helps *prioritize* the Miracle's causes. Recall that MITI-style industrial policy combined state action with market forces. The case of China and the other "late movers" further tips the scales away from government action and toward the power of globalization in the international market economy as the Miracle's key cause.

It would be a mistake, though, to give Deng full credit for China's Miracle. Deng provided the vision and impetus for reform, but he possessed only vague notions about economics and often did not design specific policies himself. Economist Barry Naughton has gone so far as to state that Deng "has never said anything original about economics or economic policy, and rarely displays any particular insight into the functioning of the economy."[9] Reforms were usually suggested or implemented by other party officials, often at a provincial or local level. Two of the most influential of Deng's lieutenants were Zhao Ziyang and Hu Yaobang. Zhao, a party secretary in the late 1980s, was perhaps China's most inventive and persistent economic tinkerer. He had a greater impact on the reform movement than any other official aside from Deng himself. While party chief in the province of Sichuan, Zhao was an early proponent of the decollectivization of agriculture and reform of state enterprises. He blended into international circles better than most of his colleagues. The only senior Communist to confess a love of the bourgeois game of golf, he was said to play in the same way he approached reform—always aggressively swinging for the green.[10] Journalist Harrison Salisbury described Zhao as "a no-nonsense pragmatist who looks and talks like a corporate board chairman."[11] Hu Yaobang was one of China's more active advocates of freedom of expression and political reform. He had a penchant for speaking off the cuff and a reputation for reacting emotionally. "I am not a man of iron," he once said. "I am a man of passion, of flesh and blood." His remarks often made him the target of conservative attacks. In 1984, he roiled his opponents by recommending Chinese give up chopsticks and the habit of eating from communal platters. "We should prepare more knives and forks, buy more plates and sit around the table to eat Chinese food in the Western style, that is, each from his own plate," Hu said. "By doing so we can avoid contagious diseases."[12] Of all China's top leaders, he may have had the least regard for Mao's legacy. When asked which of Mao's ideas could assist China's efforts to modernize, he supposedly responded: "I think, none."[13]

Despite the creativity and support of cadres like Zhao and Hu, Deng's reform efforts were far from smooth. Deng at times pressed reforms with great haste and daring, while at other moments, he slowed or even blocked change. "Sometimes he acted with a clear mind; at other times he appeared befuddled, driving both forward and backward in the huge cart of China's reform," wrote Ruan.[14] Deng's apparent inconsistency was caused by the unstable nature of his reform coalition. While Deng collected a wide range of support within the Communist Party for change, not everyone agreed on what form that change should take. Some feared China's opening to the world would allow corrupting influences to seep into society that could threaten Communist rule. Others thought Deng was ditching Communism altogether. "Some people are worried that China will turn capitalist," Deng admitted in 1985. "We cannot say that they are worried for nothing."[15] He was unable to ignore the more conservative elements of his party, and these internal policy debates and power struggles often played themselves out in the nature and pace of reform. However, there was one constant throughout the entire reform process: If Deng threw his weight behind a policy, it happened. Naughton called Deng "the political godfather of economic reform."[16]

. . . .

WHY DID DENG, a lifelong Communist, reject large swaths of Maoist doctrine and turn China toward the international capitalist economy? It is one of the most important questions of the Miracle.

The starting point for any explanation is China's pitiful condition in the late 1970s. Under Mao, China's planners, like those in the Soviet Union, favored the development of heavy industry but produced few benefits for the average citizen. Between 1952 and 1980, the gross output of industry and agriculture grew ninefold but average individual income only doubled.[17] As in the Soviet Union, consumer goods were always scarce. There was a prevailing sense among China's leaders that the economy was in crisis, and unless something drastic was done to improve human welfare, the survival of the regime itself was at risk. For Deng, reform was the only answer, the only sure way to preserve the existing Communist government. "We haven't made reforms in time," Deng said in his Third Plenum speech. The country's "socialist cause will be doomed if we don't make them now."[18] His thinking, in this regard, resembles Park's, Lee's, and Chiang's— economic growth became his primary tool to fortify an unstable regime.

Deng also utilized reform to build support for himself. His contest for control of China forced him to take a pro-reform position to differentiate himself from his chief opponent, Hua Guofeng. As the standard-bearer of Mao's legacy, Hua was considered his chosen successor. If Deng were to unseat Hua, he needed to offer China an alternative course. He provided an enticing vision of a stronger, economically vibrant nation created by a bold program of reform. Deng capitalized on China's feeble economic state to undermine Hua and his hard-line allies.[19] Deng—like Park and, ironically, Chiang, when they founded dictatorial regimes in Korea and Taiwan—linked his right to rule with economic growth and improvements in living standards. Deng's "claim to legitimacy thus rested squarely on his ability to 'deliver the goods,'" wrote political scientist Joseph Fewsmith. "His position in the political order virtually demanded breaking precedent and producing high growth rates."[20]

The Miracle elsewhere in Asia also influenced Deng. He saw during visits to other Asian nations in the late 1970s how far behind China had fallen. After a 1978 tour of Japanese carmaker Nissan, Deng exclaimed: "Today I have learnt what modernization is like."[21] While in Singapore, Deng remarked that he "discovered how the country used foreign capital."[22] Chinese leaders were often shocked by the rapid advancement of their country's neighbors. "One Sunday we went out to a busy street," wrote a senior cadre in a report on a 1978 trip to Japan. "Of all the women we saw, no two wore the same style of clothes. The female workers accompanying us also changed clothes every day."[23] The disparity irked Deng, who felt his country's feebleness embarrassed a civilization as advanced as China's. "It is not enough just to say we are poor, and actually, we are very poor," he told Zambian president Kenneth Kaunda in 1980. "Such a status quo is far from being commensurate with the standing of a great nation such as ours."[24] Much like Park, Lee, and Chiang, Deng feared his nation would remain a victim of aggressive foreign powers, as it had been during the final century of the decrepit Qing Dynasty, unless it strengthened its economy. "Backwardness will leave us vulnerable to bullying," he told Japanese Prime Minister Masayoshi Ohira in 1979.[25] It was therefore imperative, Deng believed, to launch a massive undertaking to expand and modernize the economy and raise the standard of living of China's oppressed masses. Mimicking Japan's famous "income-doubling" promise, Deng approved of a goal set by Hu in 1982 of quadrupling the country's industrial and agricultural output by the end of the twentieth century.[26] To achieve such a goal, Deng was convinced the party could not simply tinker with the existing economic system. China, he believed, needed "to carry out major reforms in the various branches of the economy with respect to their structure and organization as well as to their technology."[27] The modernization of China required "a great new revolution," Deng said in 1979.[28]

The scope of Deng's reforms has led to the widespread view that he rejected Communism for capitalism, but that is not the case. Deng "considered himself a very loyal disciple of Marx," contends Ruan Ming. "He considered his policies totally different than capitalism."[29] Deng believed he was using the tools of capitalism—modern technology, professional corporate management, foreign trade—to strengthen China's socialist economy. "Of course, we do not want capitalism," Deng declared in 1979, "but neither do we want to be poor under socialism." Deng was convinced that a socialist system, modernized with carefully selected practices from capitalism, could generate even better results than a purely capitalist one. This socialist system, Deng hoped, would prepare the way for China's eventual entry into textbook communism, in keeping with Marxist theory that a society passes through several stages of development before reaching communism. Deng contended that China was at an early stage on this march toward communism. The underdeveloped state of the economy demanded that China follow the principle "to each according to his work," he said, instead of the standard Marxist belief of "from each according to his ability, to each according to his needs."[30]

The key to Deng's economic vision was the role of markets. His more conservative colleagues considered a state-planned Communist economy and a free-market capitalist system as antagonistic; Deng believed that elements of both could be mixed. "It is wrong to maintain that a market economy exists only in capitalist society and that there is only [a] 'capitalist' market economy," Deng contended. "Why can't we develop a market economy under socialism? Developing a market economy does not mean practicing capitalism."[31] Deng looked to create something new—an economy that meshed Communist ideas with free-market practices. "We must integrate the universal truth of Marxism with the concrete realities of China, blaze a path of our own and build a socialism with Chinese characteristics," Deng told the party in 1982.[32] He was embarking on a great experiment, one that, at the time, had an uncertain future.

. . . .

DENG'S REFORMS DID not come to him out of the blue. The ideas Deng expressed in the late 1970s had been percolating in his head for some time—in certain cases, for decades. They were the result of nearly sixty years of practical experience in the Communist Party.

Deng was born on August 21, 1904, in a village called Baifang, located in the far western province of Sichuan. His daughter Maomao describes the place as "poor and remote." The family home was simple, with wooden walls and a tile roof. Deng's family raised aggressive geese to act as house guards.[33] Yet Deng was better off than most in China's countryside. His father was a small landowner, who in his later years rented out his land and worked for the government. Deng always had enough to eat and a comfortable bed.[34] Able to focus on his studies, he excelled. While living in the metropolis of Chongqing, Deng's father noticed a newspaper advertisement for a new school preparing Chinese students for study in France. The program's goal was to teach young Chinese new skills from the West to help the nation modernize. He asked Deng to enroll.

After graduating in 1920, Deng departed for France by steamer, arrived in Marseilles in a bowler hat and pointed shoes, and began studying at a school in Normandy. However, after a short time, the organization funding the program ran out of money. Deng was forced to drop out and find work.[35] His first job was in the steel-rolling workshop of France's giant Schneider & Cie Iron and Steel Complex. Deng pulled hot steel plates and rods through the factory's machinery with long pincers, often in temperatures that topped 100 degrees Fahrenheit. Merely sixteen at the time, Deng could not handle this dangerous and exhausting work. He quit in less than a month. Deng "personally experienced the plight of the working class," Maomao wrote. "The oppression and exploitation by capitalists, the insults and abuse by foremen, and the miserable life greatly shocked his naïve heart." Deng said later that he "got an initial feel for the evils of the capitalist society."[36]

Over the next several years, Deng worked as a fireman on a locomotive, as a kitchen hand, and other odd jobs.[37] He also assembled waterproof overshoes in a rubber factory[38]—just the type of light assembly work Deng's reforms would later provide for millions of Chinese. He never earned enough, though, to return to school. "One could hardly live on the wages, let alone go to school for study," Deng later recalled. "Thus, all those dreams of 'saving the country by industrial development,' 'learning some skills,' etc., came to nothing."[39] Instead, his intellectual curiosity and patriotism drew him toward Communism. Deng began attending meetings organized by Chinese and French Communists. Several young Chinese living in France at that time would become senior leaders of the Chinese Communist movement. The most famous of them was Zhou Enlai,[40] later a highly respected premier of Mao's China. In 1923, Deng began working for Zhou in a Paris-based organization of Chinese Communists, and the two grew close. "I have always looked upon him as my elder brother," Deng once said.[41] Deng worked in the cramped party "office"—a small hotel room that served double duty as Zhou's residence. Deng helped edit and print copies of the local party's magazine, *Red Light*, which earned him the nickname "Doctor of Duplication." Life was rough for Deng. Cash-strapped, he often could afford little more than bread or noodles to sustain himself. For a big splurge, he would buy croissants and milk. Yet despite his hardship, his faith in revolution only strengthened, and he formally joined the Chinese Communist Party in 1924.[42]

Deng's years in France left an indelible mark on him. He retained many of the "bourgeois" habits he adopted there—including a love of French wine and cheese, coffee and soccer, and, of course, croissants.[43] Deng's experience in France also contributed to his different outlook on China's economic development and relations with the outside world. These differences would become apparent as Deng's career in the Communist government progressed.

After a brief stint studying in Moscow, Deng returned to China in 1926 and participated in all of the defining moments in the Communist Party's early history. He survived the horrific mid-1930s Long March, during which the enfeebled Communists trekked six thousand miles through China's interior in flight from a then ascendant Chiang. Deng fought against the Japanese in World War II and then in the civil war against Chiang's Nationalists. After the Communists' victory, Deng appeared the devoted adherent to Mao's leftist economic policies. As an official in his home province of Sichuan in the early 1950s, Deng pursued the party's land reform program so aggressively that he even dispossessed his own family.[44] He also supported Mao's 1958 "Great Leap Forward." This quintessential Maoist mass movement pushed peasants to increase crop output and start small industrial enterprises. The symbol of the Leap became the mini-blast furnace, used to make a crude steel. Hundreds of thousands of them popped up throughout the countryside. Giant communes formed in rural regions, often comprising thousands of families.

The Leap, however, proved a catastrophe—and a turning point for Deng. The dislocation caused by collectivization, misguided agricultural policies, and poor central planning led to a drastic reduction of food production. By the end of 1961, some 30 million people had died from starvation. In 1960, Mao woke up to the crisis and allowed a small group of leaders, including Deng, then general secretary of the party, to step in and stem the damage. By late 1961, this team had drafted new policies that reversed many of the more egregious practices of the Leap. These policies stripped communes of much of their power, allowed farmers to tend private plots, and abolished equalized salaries in enterprises and communes.[45]

The Leap seems to have influenced Deng's economic thinking. By the early 1960s he had become less ideological and more pragmatic. He came to realize that economic development could not be generated by political exhortation and ideological conviction alone. "We have had too many movements, launching a movement for each and every undertaking," he complained in a July 1962 speech. "It seems that they have not worked out successfully." Deng therefore argued that it might be necessary to withdraw temporarily from some traditional Communist practices for the good of the economy. "At present, it looks as though neither industry nor agriculture can advance without first taking one step back."[46]

Deng's efforts helped to resurrect China's economy by the mid-1960s, but they also contributed to a rift between him and Mao. In 1966, Mao again brought upheaval to China through another mass movement—the Cultural Revolution. Mao believed the party leadership was not pressing forward quickly enough to bring about a communist society. He organized China's youth into squads called Red Guards who ferreted out teachers, intellectuals, government officials, and other authority figures deemed ideologically suspect. Mao also cynically used this movement to reassert his authority over the party. Those Mao believed were drifting from his control were prime targets of his new revolution.

Deng neared the top of the list. He came under attack from the party's radicals for his economic policies after the Leap, including his effort to decollectivize agriculture. Mao found Deng's increasingly independent role in policymaking insulting. "Deng Xiaoping has not consulted me about anything," Mao complained. "I do

object to being treated like a dead ancestor." At a party conference in late 1966, Mao ordered Deng to make a "self-criticism."
Under tremendous pressure, Deng capitulated. Calling himself a
"petty intellectual," he told the party he represented a "false bourgeois line" of thought. His "confession" only worsened matters.
In 1967, Red Guards denounced him as a "capitalist roader" and
held "struggle meetings" at his Beijing home; at one session, students forced Deng to kneel before them with his arms extended
behind his back in what was called the "airplane position." Deng
fell out of public view for six years.[47] His family presumed he
was dead.[48]

Deng was in internal exile. In 1969, after two years locked in
his house, he and his wife were secretly ushered out of Beijing
and held in part of a house in rural Jiangxi province. For several
hours each day, he was escorted to a nearby tractor repair center
and put to work. His political career, however, was far from over.
Mao, realizing his Cultural Revolution had left the government in
shambles, needed Deng's administrative expertise. In 1973, Mao
invited him back to Beijing. By 1975, Deng had recovered all of his
former powers and was recognized as a possible successor to Mao
himself.[49]

Deng had also restarted his efforts at rebuilding the Chinese
economy. In March 1975, he told party secretaries that "our country's overall interest" was "to build an independent and relatively
comprehensive industrial and economic system by 1980" and
"turn China into a powerful socialist country with modern agriculture, industry, national defense and science and technology by
the end of this century." He criticized the party's obsession with
politics to the neglect of the economy. "I am told that some comrades nowadays only dare to make revolution but not to promote
production," he complained. "This is utterly wrong."[50]

Deng went too far. Mao again questioned his revolutionary
zeal while his growing authority irked the radicals, led by Mao's
wife, Jiang Qing, who called Deng the "old king of counterrevolu-
tion." After protests erupted in April 1976 in Tiananmen Square,

Jiang and her cohorts pinned the blame on Deng. Mao ordered the party to strip Deng of his posts. This time, however, Deng was prepared. He secretly flew to Guangzhou, where he was protected by local supporters. These months were rough on the already elderly Deng. On one occasion, his allies kept him hidden inside a closed, steamy paddy wagon while traveling through Guangdong province.[51]

Deng got another political life after Mao died in September 1976. Hua Guofeng arrested Jiang and her allies, and party members called for Deng's rehabilitation. In August 1977, Deng was restored as the third-ranking member of the government. Over the next several years, the crafty Deng outmaneuvered Hua to place his supporters in key posts in the party and government.[52] By late 1978, Deng's reform coalition was poised to change China and the world economy.

· · · ·

AS DENG REASSERTED his authority in Beijing, the destitute masses of China launched the reform process without him. In the winter of 1978, a local Communist Party secretary in the province of Anhui in central China visited the farmers of the Shannan Commune in Feixi County, one of the country's poorest regions. The hungry peasants told him that they wanted to return to "the old ways," which meant independent family farming. They had become sick and tired of the giant communes, in which the peasants suffered constant political interference and little hope of improved livelihoods. The communes had been a complete failure. A 1980 study showed that a full quarter of China's farmers had an annual per capita income of a measly $33. The farmers were desperate for change.

The local party official did not know how to respond to the peasants' demands, so he said nothing. The farmers took his silence as tacit approval and went about dismantling their commune. Its production leaders parceled plots of land to each adult farmer and allowed him to till it independently. In return, every farmer was obligated to give a portion of the wheat he produced to the collective. If the farmer harvested grain above that quota, he could sell it or eat it.

This production process is called the "household responsibility system" in China, a fancy name for family farming. Under this system, the land is still owned by the state, as required by Communist doctrine. However, the household system allows for a greater degree of freedom for the farmers, and, most important, much more incentive to work than the egalitarian communes. Each farmer is permitted to till an allotted plot. The state then enters into a contractual arrangement with the farmer in which it purchases a set amount of his output at a set price. Any surplus the farmer grows, he keeps. The household responsibility system was controversial at the time. Mao himself had prohibited it. Fearing punishment, the farmers at Shannan Commune tried to keep their reforms secret, but inevitably word got out. Within a few months, the system spread throughout Feixi's communes and into neighboring counties. Without explicit permission from the Communist Party, the farmers knew they were taking a big risk. In nearby Fengyang County, the eighteen families of the Xiaogang Production Team took an oath before adopting the household responsibility system in which they pledged "to raise the children of village cadres until they are 18 years of age" if any of them "came to grief." The farmers drew up this promise into a formal document and signed it with their fingerprints.[53]

Fortunately for the bold peasants of Anhui, the man in charge in the province, party secretary Wan Li, was one of China's most open-minded and aggressive economic reformers. A devoted protégé of Deng's, Wan Li was acutely sensitive to China's poverty. He once spent several days with Beijing's "money-cart drivers," who had the unenviable task of collecting the city's human waste, in order to better understand the lives of the poor.[54] These sympathies made him no fan of the communes, which he derided as "labor camps." He experimented with agricultural reform to avert a looming humanitarian catastrophe. A severe drought hit Anhui and other parts of central China in 1978, and the terrible conditions it created gave Wan Li more leeway to take the initiative.[55] When party officials complained to him about the spread of the household responsibility system in the province, Wan Li threw his support behind the peasants and gave his approval to cadres in Feixi to proceed.

He kicked over a hornet's nest. Wan Li faced furious opposition from conservatives who believed he was undermining Mao's legacy—and socialism itself. In December 1978, Beijing outright banned the household system. Opponents of Anhui's reforms managed to get a story on the front page of the *People's Daily* the following March that warned the household system would "dampen enthusiasm, hamper production, and adversely effect agricultural modernization."[56] As Wan Li put it, the "struggle was very sharp." He did not flinch, however, using similar arguments to Deng's to stand his ground. "Any method that can mobilize the enthusiasm of the masses is permissible," Wan Li said after touring Fengyang County in January 1979. "Anything that can increase production, make greater contributions to the state, . . . increase the masses' income, and improve their standard of living is a good method. . . . In fact, individual farming is nothing to get excited about."[57] Wan Li's persistence and defiance made him a popular figure among Anhui's peasantry. "Eating rice is your plan?" went one local rhyme. "Wan Li is your man."[58]

There was a limit to how far Wan Li could go without approval from Beijing. Deng was sympathetic to his cause—the Anhui reforms fit neatly with his ideas of spurring economic development with material incentives—but he remained cautious, realizing the tinderbox nature of the issue and fearing a political backlash against his still-fragile coalition. Deng, however, did not put a stop to Wan Li's efforts either. He left Wan Li alone to test the political waters.[59]

Meanwhile, Wan Li launched a lobbying effort to push the center toward his way of thinking. In mid-1979, an Anhui provincial official, Guo Chongyi, was sent to Beijing carrying a report showing that areas that adopted the household responsibility system had increased grain production one and a half times in just one year. Anhui's reforms were so controversial, however, that many Beijing officials feared even meeting Guo. The report eventually got to Hu Yaobang, who was so impressed that he gave his personal endorsement to the reform experiment—the first specific approval from Beijing.

Resistance slowly melted away. In March 1980, Wan Li met Deng and gave him the hard sell on his reforms. Deng, obviously pleased, promoted Wan Li to vice-premier and put him in charge of national agricultural policy one month later. Finally, in May, Deng endorsed household farming practices.[60] Referring specifically to the Anhui experiments, Deng told party leaders that the household system "has proved quite effective and changed things rapidly for the better." Deng also countered criticism that the system was a step backward for socialism. "Some comrades are worried that this practice may have an adverse effect on the collective economy. I think their fears are unwarranted," Deng said. Agriculture, he argued, needed to be strengthened so that China's socialism could move forward. "It is certain that as long as production expands . . . lower forms of collectivization in the countryside will develop into higher forms and the collective economy will acquire a firmer basis," Deng said. "The key task is to expand the productive forces and thereby create conditions for the further development of collectivization."[61]

With Deng's support, the central government issued a document permitting the household system in January 1982. That was the watershed. Six months later, nearly three-fourths of the country's rural production teams had implemented the household system.[62] Farm production soared. Deng and Wan Li had managed in a matter of a few years to effectively dismantle Mao's communes and improve the rural economy and the lives of the long-suffering peasants. In late 1983, Wan Li told a work conference that the household responsibility system "is not an expedient measure to solve the problem of providing the people with enough food and clothing; it is a reform of fundamental importance involving the entire rural economic system, and it is of immeasurable significance in building socialism with distinctive Chinese features."[63] It was the start of China's transformation.

. . . .

THE REFORMS IN the countryside were spectacular in nature, but would only get China so far. To truly modernize his nation with any rapidity, Deng needed two crucial ingredients—money and technology. China had neither. In an odd way, therefore, Deng's China, with one billion people, faced a similar problem to Lee Kuan Yew's Singapore with a mere two million. Deng's solution resembled Lee's. He would turn to the global economy and tap into the knowledge and wealth of the West. "China made contributions to the world down through the ages," Deng said in 1978. "Now it is time for us to learn from the advanced countries."

Deng advocated a greater opening to the outside world than a reclusive China had allowed in centuries. He blamed Mao's xenophobia for keeping China mired in poverty. "For a certain period of time, learning advanced science and technology from the developed countries was criticized as 'blindly worshiping foreign things,'" Deng said. "We have come to understand how stupid this argument is. . . . China cannot develop by closing its door."[64] If China remained isolated, Deng believed, the country would never catch up to the industrialized countries. "The world is advancing. If we do not develop our technology, we cannot catch up with the developed countries, let alone surpass them, and we shall be trailing behind at a snail's pace," Deng lectured local party officials in September 1978.[65]

Deng, like Lee, was also too impatient to wait for China's own enterprises to revitalize themselves. Deng took the same route as Lee: He welcomed foreign investment. This thinking was radical, nearly heretical, in 1970s China. With foreign investment would come dangerous bourgeois ideas and exploitative capitalists. Deng believed the risk was worth it. Global capital could finance China's development and bring in new management know-how and technologies with which the country could construct more competitive, modern industries.

Deng was influenced by the Tigers in regard to foreign investment. After his 1979 journey to Singapore, Deng told a party conference how foreign investment in the island nation brought high salaries to workers and greater revenues for the government, and stimulated Singapore's overall economy. "I think that in studying financial and economic questions, we should concentrate on and take advantage of expertise in using foreign capital," Deng told the cadres. "If this is not done, it will be a great pity." Deng, once again tearing a page from Lee's plan, wanted China to jump into the widening competition among Asian nations for foreign capital by making itself as attractive as possible to investors. "Foreign entrepreneurs invest here in order to make a profit, so we should ensure that they can make more profits from investments in China than they can make through investments in other countries," Deng said.[66]

To make his policy successful, Deng needed the United States, the world's largest economy and main source of advanced technology. China could not thrive without access to the American market and money from U.S. firms. Relations between the two countries had improved since Richard Nixon's surprise visit to Beijing in 1972, and Deng normalized relations with the United States in January 1979. Later that month, Deng traveled to the United States as part of a major charm offensive to remake China's image with wary Americans still consumed in the Cold War. In Texas, he dined on barbecued ribs and attended a rodeo, winning a whoop from the crowd when the diminutive Deng donned a ten-gallon hat. "At times," noted *Newsweek*, Deng "acted as though he were running for office." The Carter administration was equally eager to impress. The president hosted Deng at a gala ceremony at the Kennedy Center in Washington, which included performances by John Denver, the National Children's Choir (which sang in Chinese), and, much to Deng's delight, the Harlem Globetrotters. Yet the true highlight of Deng's visit was a meeting with Carter at the White House. Deng, puffing on his favorite Panda cigarettes, deftly handled sensitive issues to defuse possible tension. When Carter pressed him on human rights concerns over Chinese restrictions on emigration, Deng joked that one-billion-strong China could "send you 10 million immigrants right away." (Carter politely declined the offer.) After the session, as he walked Deng to his limousine, a buoyant Carter called the summit "one of the most historic events in our nation's history."[67]

Deng caught Carter at the right moment. Some policymakers in Washington hoped economic ties between China and America could exacerbate a split between the Soviet Union and China and help the United States in its global struggle against Moscow. In early 1980, the United States granted China most-favored-nation status. This step was a crucial turning point. Without such preferred access to the giant U.S. consumer market, any attempt by China to attract foreign investment and develop a modern export sector would have been impossible. Deng's new friendship with the United States allowed China to adopt the export-led growth model that had worked so brilliantly for Japan and the Tigers.

The hard part came next. How could Communist China, so long hostile to the capitalist world, convince foreign companies to invest? The solution came, once again, not from the mandarins in Beijing but the provinces. In the autumn of 1978, Ye Fei, the minister of transport, met in Hong Kong with officials of the China Merchants' Steam Navigation Company, or CMSN, which was owned by the Chinese government but based in Hong Kong. Ye had just returned from an overseas trip, and he had heard about the concept of an "export processing zone," like the EPZs opened by Li Kuo-ting in Taiwan. He was excited at the prospect of introducing them into China and implored CMSN to undertake such a project. CMSN devised a plan to develop a ship-breaking operation in an industrial zone in Guangdong province. Cheap Chinese labor would dismantle the ships and the scrap metal would be sold to burgeoning Hong Kong to earn foreign exchange. The firm's chief, a well-connected Communist war hero named Yuan Geng, took the proposal to the party's leadership, and in January 1979, Beijing authorized CMSN to develop its zone in Shekou across the border from Hong Kong. This authorization was quite likely the first time modern China set aside a geographic area as a potential home for foreign investment.[68]

This unusual policy decision was a first step in a process that changed not only China but also the entire world economy—the introduction of the special economic zone, or SEZ, in China. Shortly after the formation of the CMSN industrial zone, Deng got involved in the issue personally. In April 1979, he met with two senior Guangdong party secretaries who raised the idea of setting up SEZs. Deng agreed immediately.[69] "We can carve out a patch of land and call it a special zone," he told them. He placed the responsibility mainly on their shoulders. "The Center doesn't have any money, though, and wants you people to do it by yourselves." he instructed them.[70] Soon after that meeting, a special work team headed by Gu Mu, a vice-premier of the State Council, was dispatched by Beijing to investigate the possibility of setting up SEZs on the Chinese coast. Based on this study, the State Council in July 1979 permitted the formation of four zones—three in Guangdong province at Shenzhen, Zhuhai, and Shantou, and one in Fujian province at Xiamen.[71]

The SEZs resembled Taiwan's EPZs. They were designed to encourage trade and attract foreign investment with looser regulation and tax incentives—the same tools utilized by Singapore and Taiwan to draw in Western corporations. The Singapore model was especially influential—Goh Keng Swee, Lee's chief economic expert, was an advisor to China's SEZs. The zones heralded Communist China's entry into the global economy.[72]

At the beginning, however, the SEZ experiment was limited. Inside the zone, foreign firms could build and operate manufacturing operations with relative ease. Outside the zones, China remained a Communist, state-dominated, closed economy. China could thus experiment with foreign trade and foreign-owned enterprises and attract investment and technology while protecting the vast majority of the economy from any possible destabilization the outsiders might cause. It was as if two entirely different Chinas were glued together.

This situation, however, did not last long. Though the wall between these two Chinas was impenetrable early in the reform process, as Deng's reforms progressed, the overall Chinese economy began to adopt many of the policies introduced in the SEZs. Shenzhen, for example, was one of the first places in China to experiment with incentive-based pay systems, freer land use, and a reduction of government bureaucratic interference in corporate management—practices that would soon become widespread throughout China.[73] These zones, therefore, became the guiding light for market reform in China, and a key cause of the country's Miracle.

The locations of the first four SEZs were brilliantly selected. Three of them were placed directly across from a Tiger. Shenzhen shared a border with bustling Hong Kong, while Xiamen and Shantou are across the strait separating the mainland from Taiwan. (Zhuhai was located at the border with the Portuguese colony of Macau, another potential source of foreign finance.) The timing was also auspicious. China opened its SEZs just as Hong Kong, Taiwan, and the other Tigers were coming under serious pressure. As their economies advanced, wages and other costs of doing business increased. The higher costs ate away at the competitiveness of many of the labor-intensive industries that had sparked their Miracles—such as apparel, toys, and electronics assembly. Companies in these countries were looking for ways to cut costs to maintain profitability. China hoped they would find the answer within the SEZs. Labor in mainland China was significantly cheaper than in the Tigers. The average monthly wage in Shenzhen was about one-sixth that in Hong Kong in the mid-1980s, and in all of China, it was on average less that one-tenth.[74] Companies could move their operations into the SEZs or build additional factories, tap into China's vast pool of cheap labor, and regain their competitive edge. The appeal of the SEZs was almost irresistible.

The Tings at Hong Kong toymaker Kader Industrial thought so. H. C. Ting's son Kenneth began experimenting with manufacturing in China as early as 1980. He contracted a factory in Guangdong to produce plastic motorcycles for Kader. The plant was attached to a school, and the teachers worked the assembly lines to earn extra cash after class. He built a factory of his own in 1982 at Shekou (which became part of the Shenzhen SEZ). Doing business in China at that time was difficult and primitive. As the first factory in the area, Kader was surrounded by rice paddies. Ting tapped into the Hong Kong electricity grid to power the operation and used a microwave phone to communicate with his Hong Kong headquarters. With no easy road links, Ting spent two hours on a boat from Hong Kong to get to the plant.[75] Ting, though, had little choice but to take his chances in the SEZ. With costs rising at home, he had few other options.

Ting persevered—as did many others. Beginning in the early 1980s, thousands of factories began sprouting out of the rice paddies of the SEZs. The SEZs led the way to what became China's great export boom. Manufacturers from Hong Kong and Taiwan moved much more quickly into China than more risk-averse firms from America or Europe. By drawing on the resources of the newly industrialized Asian countries, China built its Miracle on the success of other Miracles. Asia began to develop itself.

The emergence of the SEZs also contributed to another fundamental change in the global economy—the concept of "borderless manufacturing." In this process, different components are acquired from various countries around the world, brought together in one place, and assembled. Among the pioneers of this complex system were the Fungs of Hong Kong's Li & Fung. Hon-chu's sons, Victor and William, were confronted with a problem when factories began to uproot from Hong Kong and move to China in the early 1980s. The skill and technology level was so low in China that certain parts of the production process could not be completed to the standards the Fungs' customers in the West demanded. Their solution was to split manufacturing into stages. The Fungs shipped designs for shirts and toys to factories in Shenzhen, where Chinese workers assembled the goods, then brought them back into Hong Kong for testing and packaging before shipping them to the United States. Over the years, this process expanded to encompass many other countries in the region. Components were manufactured and purchased in South Korea, Taiwan, Japan, and elsewhere, then shipped into China for final assembly. The Fungs had hit on the "idea that you can take work apart and allocate it to other parts of the world," Victor says.[76] This scheme altered the method by which consumer goods were made—enhancing efficiency, cutting costs, and making many products more affordable.

The SEZs became one of Deng's major accomplishments, yet the rapid pace of social change within the zones and their high visibility also made them a primary target of those Communist leaders who opposed his program. The more conservative members of Deng's coalition were still wary of foreign investors and distrustful of the impact they could have on the country. "Foreign capitalists are still capitalists," Chen Yun, one of the most powerful party conservatives, said in 1980.[77] Opponents also compared the SEZs to the hated "concessions" offered to the European powers in the nineteenth century. By pandering to foreign investors, they contended, the modern SEZs represented a similar embarrassing loss of sovereignty. One party official complained that "nothing in Shenzhen is socialist except for its five-starred red flag."[78]

Deng also worried about the side effects of the SEZs. Though he was willing to push the envelope on economic change, he was much more cautious on political and social issues. In an October 1983 speech to the party's Central Committee, Deng insisted that "it is right for us to carry out the economic policy of opening to the outside world," but added that the party must "firmly combat all corrupting bourgeois influences."[79] Deng's criticisms allowed the conservatives to launch a late 1983 campaign against the "spiritual

pollution" trickling in from abroad. The movement targeted everything from the miniskirts favored by young women to aggressive
sale promotions in retail shops. Hu and Zhao were beside themselves. They realized Deng's opponents were trying to undermine
the entire economic reform program by attacking the SEZs. By
early 1984, Deng, too, saw he had gone too far. One account has
it that Deng's son, Pufang, warned his father that the antipollution
campaign could ruin the reform effort and weaken Deng's position.
Deng quickly reversed course and squashed the campaign.[80]

He also resumed the offensive on reform. In January and February 1984, Deng visited all the SEZs. Upon returning to Beijing,
he made a spirited defense of the SEZ experiment. He told the
party's Central Committee how impressed he was by the productivity he witnessed in Shenzhen. "It doesn't take long to erect a tall
building; the workers complete a story in a couple of days," Deng
said. "Their high efficiency" is due "to a fair system of rewards
and penalties." He remained firm in his belief that the SEZs were
crucial to the modernization of China. "As the base for our open
policy, these zones will not only benefit our economy and train
people but enhance our nation's influence in the world," Deng
said. He proposed expanding the policies of the SEZs to other
areas of China. "We shall allow some areas to become rich first;
egalitarianism will not work. This is a cardinal policy," Deng
said.[81] In July, fourteen coastal cities, including the metropolises
of Shanghai and Guangzhou, were opened to foreign investment.
The days of China's isolation were over.

· · · ·

IN 1984, THE reformers were ascendant. Hu made sure the
People's Daily was filled with commentaries praising the new policies. One revived an old slogan from the Cultural Revolution and
put it to use to support market reform: "Boldly smash the old and
create the new." Other papers followed suit. Another stated that a
goal of reform was to "enable people to get rich."[82]

Taking advantage of this precious momentum, the reformers took their most significant steps in another crucial, but also controversial, area of policy: corporate reform. Deng had set out to overhaul China's giant state enterprises upon returning to power. Angered by the pitifully poor productivity of China's factories, he wanted to instill a greater spirit of professionalism in them. "Our present economic management is marked by overstaffing, organizational overlapping, complicated procedures and extremely low efficiency," he grumbled in his 1978 Third Plenum speech. "Everything is often drowned in empty political talk." The problem, Deng diagnosed, was that the state-dominated system did not encourage managers and workers to excel or hold them accountable for their performance. "Right now a big problem in enterprises and institutions across the country . . . is that nobody takes responsibility," Deng complained. "In theory, there is collective responsibility. In fact, this means that no one is responsible."

Deng determined the central planning system was at fault. As in the Soviet Union, the planners decided which factories made how much of which products. Chinese enterprises were run more by the party and its political calculations than the executives supposedly in charge. As a result, corporate managers had little incentive or authority to do anything to make their factories more efficient. The solution was to transfer decision-making power in state enterprises from the government bureaucracy to corporate management. Deng suggested in his Third Plenum speech that "we must extend the authority of the managerial personnel" and "select personnel wisely and assign duties according to ability." In simple terms, Deng wanted Chinese companies to be run in a more independent, professional—and capitalist—fashion.[83]

As in agriculture, much of the initiative on corporate reform came from the provinces. Zhao Ziyang was the most aggressive trailblazer when he was party secretary in Sichuan. His inspiration came from the Communist countries of Eastern Europe. On an official visit there in 1977, he was impressed by systems of corporate self-management in countries such as Yugoslavia. The next year, Zhao began experimenting with practices aimed at giving greater autonomy to state enterprises in his province. In usual Chinese Communist practice, enterprises did not have clearly defined and independent accounts—the revenues and profits went to the state, and the planners handed back funds for operation. Zhao, in a series of steps, allowed enterprises to take full responsibility over their own finances. Instead of forwarding their profits to government coffers, managers could keep them and pay the state a tax. The retained profits were used for investment and pay incentives, which linked the company's performance to employee compensation. The results were astounding. The enterprises allowed to enter the program saw massive increases in production and profits. The central government was simultaneously conducting its own experiments with the reform of state companies. Various methods of management autonomy were being tested in thousands of state enterprises across the country.[84]

But Zhao and Deng ran into a wall—the central planners. Zhao's efforts undermined the entire idea of central planning. The reformers believed the country would be better off with less planning, which, they argued, ignored the needs of customers and the costs of manufacturing, led to the oversupply or shortage of key products, and therefore wasted scarce resources. Devotees like Chen Yun, however, saw Deng's corporate policies as too fundamental an attack on the Communist concept of a state-dominated economy. Enterprise reform also met resistance from the bureaucracy. Any gain of authority by factory managers meant a loss of influence for the government and party officials who had controlled them. By mid-1981, the conservatives had all but put a halt to the type of corporate experimentation pursued by Zhao.[85]

The hard-liners in the bureaucracy, however, could not hold back reform indefinitely. Reform in China began to take on a life of its own. The more sectors of the economy were privatized or set free from government control, the harder it became for the state-dominated sectors to remain trapped in the old system. As the SEZs progressed, the number and influence of foreign-invested firms grew. Small-scale Chinese private enterprises also began to flourish as Deng's reforms encouraged the Chinese to pursue their own businesses. These private companies were far more competitive and efficient than those run by the government and its central plan. China's state sector was getting left behind.

The reformers slowly regained the upper hand, until Deng rejected the conservatives' economic thinking altogether. The biggest breakthrough came in October 1984, in a document called the Decision on Reform of the Economic Structure. Enterprise managers were given unprecedented control over production, marketing and pricing of products, the use of retained profits, as well as the hiring and firing of staff. The document was a devastating blow for the central planners and a watershed for Deng.[86] The reforms not only curtailed government interference in corporate management, they also started unwinding the overbearing control of the plan. The *Wall Street Journal* said the document "is laced with enough free-market, supply-and-demand, anti-welfare, get-the-government-off-our-backs rhetoric to sound at times like an old Ronald Reagan campaign speech."[87] Corporate China was being let free from the handcuffs of the government, to rise (or fall) on its own. It marked one of Deng's biggest steps yet toward a market economy.

. . . .

POLITICAL REFORM UNDER Deng trailed economic reform. When Deng spoke of democracy—which he did repeatedly—he did not mean the democracy of Lincoln, as Ruan Ming had hoped. Deng wished to encourage a more open debate within the party but he never intended to extend that right to the general public. He definitely would not allow anything to undermine the authority of the party itself. If the reforms strayed too far into the realms of politics or society, he squashed them. Deng feared reform in China would take the course of reform in the Soviet Union, which ended in the chaotic collapse of the Communist regime.[88] The views of Singapore's Lee Kuan Yew and Deng Xiaoping again converge. Both have strived to create open economies with closed political systems.

Those party officials who failed to understand Deng's position on the sanctity of Communist rule paid the price, no matter how senior or how close to Deng they might have been. In 1987, Hu Yaobang was removed from the post of general secretary of the party after conservatives attacked his permissive attitude toward free expression and blamed him for student protests in late 1986. Zhao Ziyang was removed as well as a result of the massacre on Tiananmen Square in June 1989—the defining political event of the Deng period.

The dramatic events began with the death of Hu in April 1989. Student admirers of Hu's liberalism collected on Tiananmen Square to lay wreaths and pay their respects. The students soon started making demands on the government for reforms, including greater freedom of speech, more democratic practices in the government, and a clampdown on corruption. By mid-May, one million people were marching in the streets of Beijing—not just students, but workers, journalists, and many others. Some three thousand students held a hunger strike on the square that won tremendous public sympathy. The protests were very much a product of Deng's reforms. The students, too, were misled by Deng's talk of democracy. A sudden economic downturn and rising inflation, which ate away at the income gains of the 1980s, exacerbated the unrest.

Matters came to a head on the morning of May 17 at a meeting of the Standing Committee of the Politburo at Deng's home. Deng laid out his view on the crisis. "Of course we want to build socialist democracy, but we can't possibly do it in a hurry, and still less do we want that Western-style stuff," Deng told the party leaders. "If our one billion people jumped into multiparty elections, we'd get chaos." Deng considered the unrest on Tiananmen Square not just a simple student protest but an attempt to upset Communist rule. "Our adversaries are not in fact those students but people with ulterior motives," he said. Order must be restored, Deng believed, to preserve China's economic successes. "If we don't turn things around, if we let them go on like this," Deng said, "all our gains will evaporate, and China will take a historic step backward." Deng then dropped a bombshell. He said that after thinking "long and hard" about the situation, he favored calling in the army and declaring martial law in Beijing. Quelling the turmoil, he said, was "the unshirkable duty of the Party."

Zhao was dismayed. "It will be hard for me to carry out this plan," he told Deng. When the meeting resumed later that day (without Deng), Zhao explained his reasoning. "To impose martial law will not help calm things down or solve problems. It will only make things more complicated and more sharply confrontational," Zhao said. He feared that a harsh response would undermine the party's authority. "One more big political mistake might well cost us all our remaining legitimacy," he warned. Zhao offered his resignation at the end of the session. "I cannot continue to serve," he admitted.

Zhao's protests had little impact. The next day, Deng and other party elders insisted on martial law. After another long Standing Committee session that dragged on into the early morning of May 19, Zhao appeared on Tiananmen Square at 4 a.m. Bleary-eyed, emotional, and exhausted, he spoke to the students through a bullhorn. "We have come too late," he told them. He implored the students to end their hunger strike and clear the square while they could do so peacefully. "I have to ask you to think carefully about the future," he said.

It was Zhao's final public act as general secretary of the party. Deng was furious, and Zhao was suspended from his duties. On June 4, tanks and troops chased the protestors from the square. Estimates of the number killed vary widely, with some reaching three thousand, but the toll was more likely several hundred. The incident permanently tarnished Deng's reputation.

In defending his actions before the party leadership later that month, Zhao got at the root cause of his disagreement with Deng.

Zhao believed that economic and political reform could not be separated from one another, that Deng's attempt to build an open economy without political change was doomed to fail. "I used to call myself 'a reformer in economics and a conservative in politics,'" Zhao said. "But my thinking has changed in recent years. I now feel that political reform has to be a priority; if it is not made a priority, then not only will economic problems get harder to handle, but all kinds of social and political problems will only get worse."[89] Zhao's defense failed to save him. He spent the remaining sixteen years of his life hidden from public view under house arrest.

The economic reforms progressed, however, and China's economy continued to grow and strengthen. So far, Zhao's position that political and economic reform are inexorably connected has been proven wrong. China has built a thriving market economy without significant political reform. Whether this situation can persist as China becomes richer is the biggest question facing the country.

CHAPTER SEVEN

THE FATHER OF DEVELOPMENT
AND HIS MAFIA

Development is a fierce struggle. —SUHARTO

The death threats kept coming. Each day, Ali Wardhana received a new batch of hate mail from irate civil servants decrying his recent reforms. Hundreds of them arrived, for weeks on end, some with thinly veiled threats that his life was in danger. "I know when you leave in the evening," some warned. "I know the route you take to your house," others menaced. Wardhana was unperturbed. He had no intention of backing down to a bunch of bureaucrats he considered incompetent and crooked. Wardhana did not even bother to enlist bodyguards or police protection. "I left it to God," Wardhana says.[1]

The kerfuffle was over a 1985 decision to dramatically overhaul Indonesia's customs service. The organization was so corrupt that the country's economic policymakers saw it as a restraint on trade. Wardhana, then the coordinating minister for the economy—a sort of deputy prime minister with oversight over all economic policy—was in the midst of a major reform effort to liberalize the economy and boost exports. The customs service was in the way. Radius Prawiro, finance minister at the time, wrote that customs was a "law unto itself."[2]

The scheme Wardhana and his team devised was daring and

brilliant. He planned to shut down much of the customs service and replace it with a Swiss firm that would inspect cargo and collect duties on goods entering Indonesia at the ports of origin, not in Indonesia itself. That would end the endless haggling over duties and outright extortion commonplace at Indonesia's ports. It would also render many of the customs officials redundant.[3] The plan would create an inevitable uproar.

Before implementing his plan, Wardhana needed the approval of Indonesia's president, Suharto.* Though Wardhana had already been one of the president's top economic advisors for nearly two decades, he could never be sure how the enigmatic Suharto would react to a new policy initiative. Suharto was no economist—a former general, he had gained power in a military coup—and he sometimes had trouble choosing between the differing policy recommendations offered by his various advisors and cabinet ministers. He also had a cryptic method of communicating his wishes—a traditional Javanese way of guiding people through careful hints to avoid direct confrontation. In the words of his official biographer, a smile from him could mean "yes," "no," "maybe," or "never."[4]

Still, Suharto, like Deng, Park, and the other leaders of the Miracle, had long understood the value of economic development for knitting the fragmented country together and legitimatizing his own rule. "Development is a fierce struggle," Suharto once wrote. "At home I think about it; in the office I act upon it. Even when I am at leisure, I am always pondering new means and ways."[5] Suharto had also grown to trust that Wardhana and the other members of his hypereducated team of economic ministers would counsel him wisely. This group had been together more or less since the beginning of Suharto's rule in 1966. Since several key members, including Wardhana, had received doctorates in economics from the University of California at Berkeley, they became known as "the Berkeley Mafia." When Wardhana approached him to talk policy, Suharto listened. After Wardhana

---

* Suharto, like many Indonesians, has only one name. His name is also spelled Soeharto.

laid out his customs plan, an impressed Suharto asked if the country could hire a foreign company to replace the equally useless internal tax administration as well. Politely, Wardhana said that would not be possible.[6]

With Suharto's blessing, Wardhana went after the customs service with a vengeance. He sacked the director-general of the service, and Radius assumed the job on top of his finance minister duties. Two months later, the Swiss company was brought on and about half of the customs officers were placed on indefinite leave.[7] Then the hate mail started pouring in.

It was another stunning victory for the Mafia, one of the many that set Indonesia on its Miracle. The relationship between Suharto and the Mafia produced a remarkable record of economic progress. In the early 1970s, about 60 percent of Indonesia's population—or 70 million people—lived in abject poverty. By 1990, that figure had fallen to 27 million, or only 15 percent of the total populace.[8] In 1984, the country became self-sufficient in rice for the first time in its history, an accomplishment Suharto considered among his greatest achievements, one, he proclaimed, that was "the result of a vast undertaking by all of the people."[9] Indonesia's economic ascent was also among the Miracle's most unlikely success stories, ranking with South Korea's. In the mid-1960s, Radius estimates that Indonesia was the least industrialized of the world's large developing countries.[10] Its huge population—with 235 million citizens today, Indonesia is the world's fourth most populous country—and widely disparate ethnic, religious, and linguistic groups spread over a tremendous distance made the development of Indonesia a far stiffer challenge than the more controlled environments in Singapore, Taiwan, or Korea. Indonesia became the leader in a second wave of entrants to the Miracle that also included Thailand and Malaysia. The convention in Indonesia that selected the nation's president once voted to award Suharto the title of "Father of Development."[11]

Yet the Mafia deserves the lion's share of the credit. This group of economists held most of the country's top economic posts from the mid-1960s until the late 1980s. Some remained Suharto's economic advisors into the next decade, an amazing record of longevity and consistency. Though of diverse social backgrounds, the Mafia's common education and close personal ties gave its members a unified perspective on economics and development—a belief in free markets and private enterprise, a focus on poverty alleviation, and, like Taiwan's technocrats, a pragmatic flexibility in shaping and altering policy. "Intellectually, we grew in a common climate," says Emil Salim, a Berkeley alum and core Mafia member.[12]

The members of the Mafia could not have differed more from their patron, Suharto. The economists were urbane, English-speaking, outward-looking, and skilled; the president, a onetime poor farm boy, was autocratic, traditional, quiet, and intelligent, but not well educated. Even as president, Suharto maintained many aspects of his former village life. He rose each day before 5:30 in the morning as "is routine for a farmer or soldier," he said, and enjoyed resting in the afternoon while smoking his distinctly Indonesian clove-laced *kretek* cigarettes, sometimes rolled in a corn husk. His favorite food remained the simple local dish of vegetables cooked in coconut milk, prepared by his wife.[13] Singapore's Lee Kuan Yew once described him as a "careful, thoughtful man" who "speaks calmly and softly," maintained a "somewhat taciturn expression," and "did not set out to impress people with his oratory or his medals." But Lee felt that Suharto was "clearly a tough-minded man who would brook no opposition to what he set out to do."[14]

This unlikely tandem of old-fashioned general and high-powered Berkeley PhD's formed an indissoluble relationship. The Mafia found Suharto open-minded and willing to make difficult and potentially unpopular decisions. "He was a humble man," explains Salim, "knowing that 'I'm from the village and I don't have the formal education.' But he asked the right questions."[15] When the Mafia first began advising Suharto, he behaved like an eager student, showing up at meetings with a ledger and large ballpoint pen. "He wrote down everything we said," recalls Wardhana. "He was trying to learn, to understand, what economics is all about."[16] The bond between Suharto and the Mafia was based on mutual respect, and, even more, strong personal friendship. Suharto invited the Mafia members to his holiday retreat on Monkey Island off the coast of Java along with his own children. "It's not like boss and employee. You're part of the family," says Salim. "We're like friends, fighting a battle together. He relied on you, you relied on him."[17]

The Mafia's unofficial don—"the head of the village," in Salim's words[18]—was Widjojo Nitisastro, who spent much of his career in charge of the government's economic planning board. A brilliant economist, humble and unassuming, Widjojo, according to Wardhana, was "the driving force" behind the policymakers, who prodded them to put their knowledge of economic theory to practical use. Widjojo taught them that "it isn't enough to just be a good teacher. We also have to think of how to increase the welfare of the population and develop the nation," says Wardhana. "He didn't want us to be in an ivory tower."[19] Endlessly patient, Widjojo had the most intimate bond with Suharto of any of the technocrats, and also the highest degree of influence over the president. A careful strategist, he would send colleagues to Suharto to confront him on touchy issues to preserve his own relationship with the president.[20] As Salim says, quoting a famous Javanese phrase, Widjojo was a master of "how to be victorious without defeating."[21] Widjojo's economic beliefs were primarily pro-market. Unlike many economists in the developing world, he doubted the ability of the state to run companies. His focus was much more on village development and human welfare—the schools, water systems, and market roads that the Suharto government built in abundance. "Throughout his career, he deliberately kept a low profile and yet if there is anyone who deserves the title of 'architect of Indonesia's economic development,' it is Widjojo," Radius wrote.[22]

Widjojo and the Mafia played a role in Indonesia similar to Deng's in China. Both reversed leftist, state-led economic programs that had failed and redirected their giant populations toward the international marketplace. Indonesia, also like China, then benefited tremendously from the economic booms of the "early movers." As costs rose in Japan, South Korea, Taiwan, and Hong Kong, their companies began to seek out lower-cost environments for basic manufacturing. They moved parts of their operations into Indonesia, in the same way as they shifted production into China's SEZs.

The Miracle in Indonesia shared many of the same elements of those in the rest of Asia, especially China, Hong Kong, and Singapore. Indonesia's spectacular record was a result of export-led growth and foreign investment. Yet the Miracle in Indonesia eventually proved to be the most fragile in Asia as well. At the heart of the problem was Suharto himself, who strayed from key principles that had created the Miracle in other Asian countries.

One problem created by Suharto was a lack of consensus on policy direction within his government, a crucial element in the success of the "early movers." The Mafia represented only one view on development within the Suharto regime—the market-driven, outward-looking philosophy. Another group pressed for more inward-looking, state-driven strategies. They have been called the "nationalists." The Mafia and the nationalists fought it out with a third faction—the "cronies." This clique of businessmen pressed the president for special favors, such as monopoly rights on trade and production, which distorted markets, impaired Indonesia's competitiveness, and ran counter to the Mafia's efforts to open the economy.[23] "Everybody was fighting for Suharto's attention," explains Salim. "It was a battle of ideas."[24] Sometimes the Mafia commanded Suharto's thinking and the economy headed toward the international marketplace; at other times, the Mafia lost out to other competing groups, and economic policy changed course. Suharto, unlike Deng, never utilized his political power to impose a clear direction on these squabbling factions. The perpetual conflict cultivated something of a siege mentality in the Mafia, a belief that they were fighting a life-and-death struggle for the future of the nation. "There were a lot of people who were against us," Wardhana says.[25]

The story of Indonesia also goes some way toward debunking the theory that authoritarian rule is a crucial prerequisite to rapid development. Though Suharto's grip on political power allowed the government to make quick, clean decisions, as in Park's Korea and Chiang's Taiwan, he often did not make the right decisions. Suharto held only vague ideas on the direction of economic policy and he would pick and choose among competing policy menus like he was loading up a plate at a smorgasbord. Since he was an autocrat, however, there was no way to implement policy without him. The result was often the introduction of contradictory policies or dramatic shifts in policy direction based entirely on Suharto's preference for one faction over another. The different themes that brought development to Asia—state-led initiatives, the embrace of market forces and globalization, and personal connections between government and business—fought for dominance instead of working together. In his personalized rule, furthermore, Suharto sometimes favored the interests of his family and friends over the good of the nation. In this way, Suharto's one-man reign was as much a detriment as a benefit to overall development.

. . . .

IN SUHARTO'S EARLY years, he never seemed destined to command such power and responsibility. His journey began inauspiciously on June 8, 1921, the day he was born in an isolated village called Kemusuk on the island of Java to a poor, unhappy couple. Suharto's father, an irrigation officer, and his young wife quarreled over his gambling habit; the two eventually divorced. Still, his father's hopes for the newborn were encapsulated in the name he gave him: Suharto means "better wealth."[26]

His mother was too ill to breast-feed, so she entrusted the care of the infant Suharto to his great-aunt when he was only a month old. The next several years were among the happiest of

Suharto's life. He would often accompany his great-uncle when he went to labor in the rice fields. "Sometimes he carried me on his back while working the land, and when I grew, let me ride the plough," Suharto later recalled. "It was great fun, moments that I will always treasure, when I would sit on the plough and spur the buffalo on, steering them left or right. I would leap into the paddy field, playing in the water, getting covered in mud." He also caught eels in the paddies, which remained a favorite food his entire life. When he was four and "hadn't even begun to wear trousers," Suharto's mother returned to take him back, and after that, he spent the remainder of his childhood passed among different family members. He ended up attending school in the large city of Yogyakarta, where he, like other poor students, sported the bare feet of the countryside.

After he graduated in 1939 from secondary school, his family could not afford the expenses for further education. He spent a short, unhappy stint as a bank clerk, which ended when he tore the traditional Javanese sarong he was required to wear on a bicycle spring and he did not have the money to replace it. "My future seemed bleak," he later wrote. The deprivation he faced in his youth was a major influence on the economic policies he favored as president. "This is why a great feeling and wish arose in me to help people avoid hardship," he wrote. "I know how it is; I've gone through it."[27]

With few other options, Suharto enlisted in the Dutch army and enrolled in a cadet school. In the middle of his studies, World War II broke out, Japan invaded the Dutch colonies, and the European colonialists surrendered. Again unemployed, he rejoined a reconstituted national army under the Japanese. Suharto grew to detest his Japanese overlords (though he remained a devotee of their food his whole life). The officers treated the local recruits with cruelty, and Japan's oppressive rule "only increased within us, the youth of Indonesia, the burning desire to defend our own country."[28]

Suharto would soon get his chance. An Indonesian independence movement was taking shape, led by a larger-than-life firebrand, Sukarno. One of the developing world's strongest anticolonial voices, Sukarno became a mythical figure to the average Indonesian. Hundreds of thousands would wait to catch a glimpse of the man they called "Brother Karno" whenever he toured the country.[29] The collapse of the Japanese empire gave the movement a chance to take power. On August 17, 1945—two days after Japan's surrender—Sukarno stood outside his home in Jakarta and, in a simple ceremony, read out a two-sentence proclamation announcing the independence of the Republic of Indonesia. Suharto played no role in the nationalist movement, but when he learned of Sukarno's proclamation, he vowed to protect the republic. He collected other military officers in a defense unit later absorbed into a new national army. His services were needed. The Dutch, ignoring Sukarno's proclamation, returned to reclaim their colony. The national army and Dutch forces fought on and off until December 1949, when the Dutch, pressured by Washington, conceded and recognized Indonesia's independence.[30] Suharto performed well during the conflict and rose up the ranks of the military, as he continued to do throughout the 1950s. By 1965, he was among the most senior generals in the army.

The catalyst for Suharto's move into political power came while he was asleep. For several years, a political contest for influence within Sukarno's regime had simmered between the military and the expanding Communist Party. On the night of September 30, 1965, the maneuvering broke into open warfare. Left-leaning junior officers ordered a clandestine assault on the army's top brass and executed six of their superiors while their troops claimed key parts of Jakarta. Roused from bed at 4:30 a.m. by a television cameraman who reported hearing gunshots in the city center, Suharto donned his uniform and drove to his headquarters in his Toyota jeep. Familiar with the revolt's leadership, who called themselves the 30 September Movement, Suharto suspected that they were part of a Communist plot to take control of the nation. "If we don't fight them," he told a meeting of military brass, "we'll die a futile death anyway."[31] With loyal troops, he launched attacks to retake the national communications centers and overrun the rebels' headquarters at a nearby airbase. By the next morning, the Movement had melted away, leaving Suharto in charge of the capital. Though the exact role of the Communists in the failed coup has never been established, the army and its civilian supporters, at the encouragement of Suharto, moved against the Communist Party in an orgy of violence. Over the next several months, an estimated 500,000 suspected leftists were killed in a slaughter the CIA called "one of the worst mass murders of the 20th century."[32] "I felt that my primary duty was to destroy" the Communists, Suharto later wrote, "to smash their resistance everywhere."[33]

The destruction of the Communists left Sukarno severely weakened and touched off a duel for power between the president and Suharto. Suharto moved cautiously against the still-popular president. During one meeting, Sukarno asked Suharto: "Just what are you going to do with me?" A deferential Suharto answered: "I was taught . . . to show respect for people we hold in high esteem."[34] In January 1966, when Sukarno, attempting to stem a rapid economic decline, raised fuel prices and devalued the national currency, large student protests erupted demanding drastic changes in Sukarno's regime. On March 11, the military decided to act. Students surrounded the presidential palace while Sukarno calmly presided over a cabinet meeting in slippers. He was handed a note. The palace, it said, was surrounded, not just by students, but also soldiers. Sukarno, in a near panic, left the cabinet session and fled by helicopter to his other presidential mansion in the mountain town of Bogor, south of Jakarta.[35]

That same day, three generals took a helicopter to Bogor to meet Sukarno, praying along the way. They had just visited Suharto at home, where he was resting throughout the dramatic events with a bad flu. Suharto asked the three men to pass on his "kind regards" to Sukarno and "convey that if he trusted me, I would handle the situation."[36] When the generals met Sukarno, he criticized them for allowing the demonstrations to continue and asked what could be done. After an awkward silence, one of the generals, Amir Machmud, said that Sukarno should "give in easily" and govern with Suharto. The generals wrote up a draft order that gave Suharto the power to restore order and security in the country. Sukarno read it carefully. "In the name of Allah," he said and signed the order.[37]

That signature unceremoniously ended the Sukarno era. Though he lingered on as official president for two more years, he had effectively transferred presidential authority to Suharto, whose administration called itself the New Order.

. . . .

WHEN SUHARTO STEPPED into power, he inherited a bankrupt economy. Sukarno and his leftist supporters had taken the country toward socialism and away from the international economy. The government nationalized the assets of most foreign investors, doled out subsidies on basic goods such as rice and petrol, favored state enterprises, and, in the process, built up monstrous budget deficits. The country's foreign debt burden swelled, at first on loans from Western countries, then increasingly from the Communist bloc. The tilt away from capitalism was rooted in Sukarno's anticolonial fervor. In a country that had fought a vicious war for freedom against a European power, joining a Western-dominated, free-market system was distasteful. By 1965, however, the economy had slammed into a wall. Inflation ran at 650 percent, foreign reserves evaporated, and the central bank defaulted on a letter of credit. "Although Indonesia had recently been freed from the bondage of colonialism, through its own policies the country was slipping back to pre-colonial economic conditions of several centuries earlier," Radius wrote.[38]

At this crucial moment, Widjojo and the Mafia took control of policymaking. The team was well prepared. While at Berkeley, the Indonesian group met weekly beginning in the late 1950s to discuss possible development strategies for their home country,[39] and they had written papers on everything from balancing the budget to improving transport systems.[40] Highly influenced by their classical economics training at Berkeley, they also tried to merge these laissez-faire ideas with economic concepts rooted in Indonesian culture. One was *gotong royong*, which means "mutual assistance." A basic element of Indonesian village life, *gotong royong* describes how a rural community comes together to help its members, especially those in need. Such concepts provided "a 'homegrown' ideological basis for guiding economic policy that was socially responsible, solicitous of the welfare of each individual, and generally compatible with free-market economics," Radius wrote. The rapid industrialization in Japan, South Korea, and the other original Tigers also influenced the Mafia, especially their success in using exports to drive growth, though they believed Indonesia was too large and poor to adopt their neighbors' policy programs in full.[41] The methods that created Indonesia's Miracle resemble those of China, Hong Kong, and Singapore rather than of Japan and South Korea. Trade and foreign investment were the dominant factors, not a MITI-style industrial policy.

The Mafia put its theory into practice as soon as Suharto gained power. After returning from Berkeley in the early 1960s, several Mafia members, including Widjojo, Salim, and Wardhana, were asked to teach economics at an army command school, where they met many of the generals who became prominent in the New Order. Suharto, too, was briefly a student at the school, though most of the Mafia members did not get to know him well at the time. That changed at a conference held by the New Order in Bandung in August 1966. The generals invited the Mafia to present its ideas on the economy to the new national leadership.[42] Suharto, impressed with its common purpose,[43] soon collected the Mafia into an advisory team for economic policy that consulted him directly.[44] Suharto put it to work resurrecting the Indonesian economy.

The Mafia drew up a plan to break with the past. Socialism,

state enterprise, and nationalistic policies were out; free markets and foreign investment were in. The first priority was suppressing inflation, which required curtailing government spending. The team realized such cutbacks would contract demand and send the economy into a possible recession, inflicting further suffering. It devised a scheme to maintain, and even accelerate, overall economic growth while fighting inflation at the same time by reducing certain types of spending drastically, mainly that of the government, while directing the banking sector to maintain credit to selected industries that could drive new growth. The central bank lent to commercial banks at below-market interest rates to stimulate investment. The goal, explains Radius, was to "create purchasing power from almost nothing." The slate of policies was "unorthodox and radical," Radius says. "To some, this idea was preposterous. To the economic planners, however, stabilization without growth was tantamount to finishing fourth in the Olympics—no medals, no parades, just a glorious achievement perceived as a failure. . . . No one—not even the economic team—knew whether the measures would work."[45]

The Mafia had to sell the plan to Suharto. He had no problem with the shift away from socialism. He later blamed the disorder of the Sukarno years on the country's deteriorating economic conditions. "The decline of the social and economic life of the community that we experienced all along was due to the absence of economic development," Suharto wrote. Economic growth, he realized, would go a long way toward fostering loyalty to the New Order regime and strengthening the nation itself. "The New Order had to give top priority to economic development, and with economic progress, nation-building in a broad sense could be enhanced," he wrote.[46] Perhaps most of all, Suharto, like Park, Chiang, and Lee, figured that improvements in the welfare of the country's giant population would assist him in his fight against the hated Communists. Suharto "always put his interest in the community, in the people, in the farms," says Bob Hasan, a long-time friend of Suharto. "Otherwise, if you're poor, everyone leans

Communist."[47] Radius wrote that "the New Order staked its existence on its ability to build the Indonesian economy. If it failed in this effort, its credibility and the basic platform on which it was founded would have been destroyed."[48]

Yet some of the specific measures the Mafia suggested were politically dangerous for the new regime. The most sensitive was a proposed reduction of subsidies on consumer goods. The government spent so much to cap the cost of petrol, says Wardhana, that the "price was even cheaper than a glass of ice water." Cutting subsidies was crucial to bring the budget in control, but could also spark public anger, even unrest. The Mafia pressed its case. Wardhana says the team told Suharto: "You have to do this: Otherwise, the economy would be in the doldrums."[49]

In the end, Suharto approved the Mafia's plans. "The economic team couldn't do it alone," explains Wardhana. "You had to have a very strong man behind [the policies]." Suharto "made it possible to undertake those unpopular measures."[50] In October 1966, the first elements of the stabilization plan were put in place. The technocrats used this concrete program to convince the country's foreign creditors to restructure its onerous debt burden. The Mafia backed up these efforts with a new investment law in 1967 that welcomed back foreign investors. The government even restored some assets that had been nationalized under Sukarno to their original foreign owners.

The Mafia's controversial scheme worked. By 1969, inflation had fallen under 10 percent, but the economy also returned to growth. GDP advanced a robust 5.8 percent a year between 1966 and 1970.[51] These early steps, says Wardhana, were "the beginning of successful economic policy." Suharto and his Mafia had set Indonesia on the path to the Miracle.

· · · ·

FOR THE NEXT two decades, the Mafia maintained a viselike grip on the country's top economic posts. Ali Wardhana was finance minister from 1968 to 1983, then spent another five years as coordinating minister for the economy. The portfolios of trade, industry, and the environment as well as the governorship of the central bank and the top post at the planning board were almost always in the hands of a Mafia member or its protégés. The Mafia seemed as entrenched as Suharto and the New Order itself.

Yet the Mafia never had full control over economic policy. That power Suharto held. And he was often lured off course by people who disagreed with the Mafia's free-market route to growth. The most influential was Bacharuddin Jusuf (B.J.) Habibie, the chief of the nationalist faction. Habibie and Suharto first met in 1950. Suharto was participating in an army operation to quell a rebellion on the eastern island of Sulawesi, and the Habibies lived across the road from where his brigade was camped. Habibie's mother was originally from Java, and she would entertain the soldiers by telling them stories in Javanese. "The atmosphere at the Habibie house made us really feel at home," Suharto later wrote. Merely a teenager at the time,[52] Habibie went on to become Indonesia's most prominent engineer. He set off for Germany in 1955 to attend the Rheinisch-Westfälische Technische Hochschule Aachen, where he got a doctorate in aeronautical engineering. He then joined a German aircraft manufacturer that later merged into Messerschmitt-Bölkow-Blohm. The talented Habibie achieved important breakthroughs in aircraft design and rose to be the firm's vice president and director for technology application. His experience in the aircraft industry in Germany, during a period when that country was experiencing its own type of economic miracle, influenced Habibie's ideas on development. He made a link between technology and growth that he carried with him to Indonesia.[53]

Suharto stayed in touch with Habibie throughout this period. In 1970, the two met during Suharto's state visit to Germany, and the president told Habibie to "broaden his knowledge and experience in areas that might be of benefit to his own country and people."[54] Three years later, Suharto sent a note to Habibie saying that the time was ripe for his return. One month later, in January 1974, he moved home.[55] Suharto told Habibie: "You can do whatever you want [in Indonesia] short of fomenting a revolution."[56]

Habibie's economic message came in direct conflict with the Mafia's. Widjojo, Wardhana, and their colleagues wanted to hitch Indonesia to the world economy and capitalize on the forces of globalization. Habibie thought the Mafia's strategy lacked an industrial policy. By following the Mafia, Indonesia would grow based on its cheap labor and other natural advantages, but Habibie saw this process eventually running out of steam. For Indonesia to continue to develop, the country needed to adopt high technology and "pick winners," that is, target strategic industries, MITI-style, which would build new comparative advantages in Indonesia. Habibie wanted to re-create the industrial development programs of Korea's Park, though with an even heavier state role. He believed the private sector was incapable of long-term investment. The state would have to take the lead. The engineers and specialists trained in these government enterprises would then span out across the economy and spark new high-tech ventures. "Promoting value-added manufacturing and high-technology industries won't bring high growth in the short run . . . but in the long run national interest will have been well served because national economic development will no longer be determined by the international division of labor," he said in a 1993 speech.[57] Habibie wanted to adopt elements of the "Asian model" to shift the structure of Indonesia's economy into high technology.

Suharto installed Habibie at the state oil company Pertamina as the chief of its advanced technology division upon his return.[58] After Pertamina defaulted on massive foreign debts and needed a Mafia-organized rescue, Suharto promoted Habibie to minister for research and technology in 1978. Habibie developed and managed a government-owned empire of ten firms in armaments, telecommunications, steel, and heavy equipment—all backed by nearly limitless government funds. He also commanded a planning commission for high-technology industries that competed with the planning board controlled by the Mafia.[59] Widjojo, Wardhana, and their compatriots opposed Habibie's plans and used their formidable influence to block his program. They believed the high-tech industries favored by Habibie were far too advanced for a country just beginning to feed itself, nor were they comfortable with the state taking the primary role in building these new industries.[60]

The Mafia's message began to fall on Suharto's deaf ears. Part of the reason was the intimate personal relationship Habibie forged with Suharto, one that easily rivaled, and most likely surpassed, the connection he had with Widjojo and the Mafia. "He regards me as his own parent," Suharto once wrote of Habibie.[61] Habibie also knew how to sell his ideas to his patron. He was a brilliant speaker who could mesmerize Suharto with his technical expertise while still appearing humble before the autocrat. Habibie "is not a man who thinks he knows best," Suharto wrote. "Whenever he reports to me, he spends hours with me only because he wants to understand what I think of the matters he puts forward; what my philosophy is."[62]

The real secret of Habibie's success was his shared penchant for megaprojects with Suharto. Much like Park, Suharto had a fascination with heavy industry. Part of this interest came from his military background—like Park, he thought steel mills were good for national defense. Even more, he equated an industrialized Indonesia with a unified and peaceful Indonesia. Suharto wrote, "[Indonesia] must be viewed as one national entity," and "this requires the development of our own strategic industries in order to free ourselves from dependence on foreign sources."[63] Suharto became increasingly partial to Habibie's view of development. Compared to Habibie's plans, the Mafia's philosophy of market-oriented growth and small-scale private enterprise seemed neither sexy nor sustainable. "History has shown that only by the command of science and technology can a nation advance,"[64]

Suharto wrote. "Abundant natural resources alone are not sufficient to bring our nation into a high standard of living and an
extensive welfare program," he continued. The development of
Habibie-style industries "stems from our awareness of the serious
problems and weaknesses we would have in the future if we were
to remain constantly dependent upon the science and technology of other nations."[65] Emil Salim believes Suharto was thinking
about his legacy, one that could be made grander by homegrown
arms factories than palm oil plants. "Great leaders all suffer the
same thing," he says. "They want to be remembered eternally."
Habibie's plan "satisfies your ego."[66]

No other project better symbolizes Habibie's influence than
Indonesia's attempts to develop its own airplane, an idea generated during a meeting between Habibie and Suharto shortly after
Habibie's return from Germany. Habibie suggested he employ
his expertise in aerospace and start an aircraft firm. Suharto approved the plan on the spot.[67] Pertamina parented the project at
first, but after its financial debacle, a new state company, Nur-
tanio Aircraft Industry, later renamed IPTN, formed in 1976,
with Habibie as its chief. Habibie decided to skip intermediate
steps into the industry, like component manufacturing, opting
for full-on assembly of planes instead. At first, Habibie secured
licenses to assemble planes and helicopters designed by three European firms (including his former employer, Messerschmitt). In
1979, he inked a joint venture with a Spanish company to design,
develop, and manufacture an Indonesian plane, a forty-seater
called the CN-235. The first one rolled off IPTN's assembly line
in 1983.[68] Suharto was enthralled with Habibie's airplanes. By the
mid-1990s, he expected IPTN to have forty thousand employees.
"Is there any other government industry that can do the same?"
Suharto asked. "There is none." He made it a national priority
to purchase Habibie's planes to support his budding firm. "It is
our duty to buy our own products, even though they may not be
perfect," he wrote.[69]

. . . .

WHILE CONTENDING WITH Habibie, the Mafia also battled the "cronies." This small coterie of business leaders, almost exclusively from the country's Chinese minority, built massive empires based to a great degree on their personal access to Suharto. In return, Suharto called on them for financial favors. Suharto's family entered into business deals with the cronies as well. They generated inefficiencies that perturbed the Mafia and, eventually, threatened the very existence of the New Order.

The prototype crony was Mohamad "Bob" Hasan. Born to a Chinese family, Hasan converted to Islam at a young age and became the "adopted" foster son of a senior general who happened to be Suharto's commanding officer in central Java in the mid-1950s.[70] Hasan spent this period, as he says, "learning about business." At the time, the army controlled large swaths of the local economy, and Hasan helped the area's military officers undertake business ventures.[71] Suharto and Hasan engaged in a controversial smuggling operation in which they illegally shipped sugar to Singapore in return for fertilizers, military equipment, and other supplies.[72] The two became fast friends. No other businessman in Indonesia enjoyed such a rapport with Suharto. They played golf together two or three times a week for the entire New Order era.[73] Hasan, in the words of journalist Raphael Pura, was "a presidential crony who can make even other cronies uneasy."[74]

Hasan's break came in 1972 when he got an opportunity to enter the timber industry. He was on a flight to Singapore with a government official when they were approached by another passenger, an executive at Georgia Pacific. The American firm wanted to develop a forestry concession in Indonesia and was looking for a local partner to help manage the business. Could they recommend anyone? the executive asked. The official pointed to Hasan.

Hasan flew to Georgia Pacific headquarters, then in Portland, Oregon, for discussions with senior management. Hasan signed on, and was given a 10 percent equity stake in Georgia Pacific's Indonesian unit, which Hasan was allowed to pay for from future dividends. He received his first piece of the timber business for nothing. This seemingly minor event would have tremendous implications for the Indonesian economy and the New Order regime.

The joint venture had a concession for a large tract of forest on Indonesian Borneo. Hasan had much greater plans for the industry. He became dismayed that Indonesia had no timber processing businesses of its own. Timber firms simply shipped raw logs overseas to Singapore, South Korea, or Taiwan to be manufactured into plywood boards and other products. He felt that, as a result, Indonesia was losing much of the potential value from its timber exports.

Hasan says he began discussing the matter with Suharto. Restricting exports of raw logs, Hasan recommended, would create incentives for companies like Georgia Pacific to invest in local timber-processing facilities.[75] Beginning in the late 1970s, the government began adopting such policies, first raising export taxes on logs, then, in 1981, imposing a phased ban on the export of logs entirely. The result was a massive wave of timber investment. Between 1978 and 1985, plywood production capacity increased eightfold. Meanwhile, Hasan expanded his own business interests with investments in new factories and concessions—on occasion, he partnered with members of the Suharto family. In 1983, Georgia Pacific pulled out of Indonesia as part of a shift in strategy. Hasan secured the multinational's shares for himself, paying for them with future plywood shipments, and took full control of the large operation.

The real source of Hasan's wealth and power, however, was his dominance over the plywood industry's business organization, the Indonesian Wood Panel Producers Association, known by its Indonesian acronym, Apkindo. In the early 1980s, amid a global economic downturn, plywood prices declined, competition among the many new Indonesian producers intensified, and Hasan and the government worried about the industry's health. Beginning in the mid-1980s, the state gave Hasan, Apkindo's chair, a wide-ranging mandate through a series of policy decisions to transform the association into a cartel to minimize competition and stabilize prices. Hasan set up a commission to study different export markets and determine proper prices, then organized the plywood producers into marketing boards and allocated export quotas among the many firms. The system became so strict that Hasan and Apkindo had power over how much plywood each firm could export to key markets. Apkindo priced its plywood very aggressively, undercutting competitors and running them out of business. As a result, the cartel turned Indonesia into the dominant producer in the global plywood trade. In 1980, Indonesia accounted for only 7 percent of world plywood exports; by 1991, that share had grown to 79 percent. Hasan tightened his personal grip on the industry by setting up trading firms for different export markets that were given monopoly rights by Apkindo to import Indonesian plywood. By one estimate, more than half of all tropical plywood exports in the world passed through Hasan's hands. In a detailed study of Hasan and Apkindo, Christopher Barr contends that Hasan effectively placed himself between Indonesia's plywood producers and the global market, and in the process "secured very substantial profits for himself, the Suharto family, and military interests with whom he is aligned."[76] Perhaps Hasan himself put it best during one of history's most bizarre rounds of golf, featuring Hasan, Suharto, and Hollywood action star Sylvester Stallone. "I told Rambo," Hasan later recounted, " 'I'm King of the Jungle.' "[77]

Hasan denies that he ever had any role controlling Indonesia's timber industry. Apkindo, he claims, was not a cartel, but just offered guidance to the local exporters. Nor, he says, did he control a network of firms with monopoly marketing rights for Indonesian plywood. Suharto, he also says, never intervened to award him forestry concessions. "I was just trying to develop the local industry," Hasan says.[78]

Whatever the true extent of Hasan's influence over the timber industry, Suharto's relationship with businessmen like Hasan took a toll on the New Order's popularity and legitimacy. Throughout large sectors of the Indonesian economy, a small group of businessmen with close ties to the Suharto regime were able to capitalize on their connections to create massive business empires. The cronies became symbols of the regime's lack of transparency, corruption, and nepotism. The story of Hasan and his fellow cronies begs an important question about how the Miracle manifested itself in different countries. Government favoritism toward certain businessmen or corporations was a standard feature of the Miracle, and especially the "Asian model." MITI had its favorite *keiretsu*, Park his Chung Ju Yungs. Governments across the region gave companies that pursued priority projects cheap credit and other perquisites. So what made Suharto's chosen ones "cronies" and these other darlings "entrepreneurs"? *Why were some government-business relationships considered positive for the economy and others negative?*

The differences between the role of the "cronies" in Indonesia compared to state-backed businessmen elsewhere were crucial to the course of the country's development. First, many of the favors granted to the cronies were monopoly rights on trade, distribution, and production of goods important to the economy. In some cases, the cronies used these privileges to build successful enterprises. However, these monopolies often allowed the cronies to reap massive profits above what open competition would have created. The way in which Hasan sat himself on top of the plywood trade is a perfect example. The cronies' activities often added costs and inefficiencies into the economy, making Indonesia less competitive. Second, Suharto allowed the cronies to expand their economic clout whether or not they were successful in building internationally competitive industries or forwarding the overall betterment of the economy. Park may have protected companies he considered core to his industrialization program, but he also held Chung and the other *chaebols* to often lofty standards. If they did not perform up to snuff, he pulled the plug on them. One indispensable factor behind the success of the "Asian model" was the government's insistence on performance. Suharto did not impose this strict discipline.

The most important difference with Indonesia's cronies, however, was that they included members of Suharto's own family. As the New Order aged, so did Suharto's six children, and at least some of them began to pursue their own business ventures, many of which were linked to government projects or companies. Like the other cronies, the Suharto family received special licenses, monopoly rights, choice contracts from government firms, and other sweetheart deals. At various times, Suharto family members controlled, with partners, soymeal production, tin plate supply, and plastic materials imports. They also held stakes in insurance, sugar, plywood, toll road, milk powder, baby food, television broadcasting, and cooking oil ventures. The most notorious of the Suharto children was Tommy, the youngest son. After dropping out of school in the United States, he formed a company called Humpuss in 1984 with an older brother, Sigit.[79] At first he got lucrative petrochemical distribution deals from the state oil company Pertamina. Later, Tommy and Bob Hasan teamed up to acquire a charter airline from the military that they turned into the first privately owned carrier in the country. His most controversial, and destructive, venture came in 1990 when he wrangled control of the clove industry. An important commodity for Indonesians, cloves are the key ingredient in their beloved *kretek* cigarettes. The idea was to buy up all of the country's cloves and then sell them to the cigarette manufacturers at inflated prices, allowing Tommy and his partners to pocket the profits. Tommy, together with some local traders, secured a monopoly from the government on the distribution of cloves. He promised to pay clove farmers significantly more for their crop and thereby painted himself as the defender of the poor against the big cigarette makers. In need of finance, Tommy appealed to his father to pressure a recalcitrant central bank to allocate money.

The scheme was doomed from the start. The cigarette producers used their existing stocks of cloves to avoid the excessive prices charged by Tommy. Meanwhile, the higher clove prices enticed farmers to grow more and supply increased. By 1992, Tommy's monopoly had failed. His stocks rose to the point where Tommy stopped buying new cloves, leaving the farmers with large harvests and no place to sell them.[80]

Despite the controversy over his business activities, Tommy remained unrepentant. In 1992, he admitted to the *Asian Wall Street Journal* that being a Suharto made it "easier for me to make an appointment or discuss the business with ministers or government officials," but he considered this "normal" for a person of stature anywhere in the world. "I don't rob or steal something from the government," Tommy said, "so why should I feel worried or embarrassed?"[81]

One of the enduring mysteries of Suharto's reign is his willingness to condone—and often encourage—his children's economic exploits even as they undermined his political support. Suharto biographer R. E. Elson speculates that Suharto wished that his children could enjoy happier—and wealthier—lives than he had as a poor youngster in rural Java, or that he failed to recognize how his political dominance was responsible for his children's success.[82] Suharto was always extra considerate about his family's needs. When he first became president, he chose not to move into the presidential mansion, the Merdeka Palace, and instead remained in his home in downtown Jakarta, hoping his children could in this way have greater freedom. What is clear, however, is that Suharto either was fully deluded about the nature of his children's activities or thought he could snow the public. "None of my children has been pampered. Not one," he boldly wrote in his autobiography. "On the contrary, they take a low profile and do not feel or act as if they are children of a President."[83]

. . . .

THE MAFIA TRIED to fight back. Wardhana recalls Suharto asking him to grant a tax holiday for a hotel development project being undertaken by one of his sons. "I said no," Wardhana said. Suharto "was angry, but he cannot do anything."[84] Because of their long relationship with Suharto, the Mafia was not afraid to confront the president. Emil Salim says the technocrats would meet with Suharto, usually in a group, and outline for him the economic damage being done by a certain monopoly or special license. Suharto would always listen, but all too often he would stand by his friends, saying of the favors, "I deem it necessary."[85]

Despite such impediments, the Mafia found a way to dominate much of the economic policy of the 1980s. The reason was that the economy was once again headed for trouble. The cause was oil. Indonesia was East Asia's sole member of the Organization of the Petroleum Exporting Countries, or OPEC, and the country experienced a windfall with the oil boom of the 1970s. Radius wrote that Indonesians saw the oil as "a fountain of gold."[86] The flood of foreign exchange led to an attempt at "Indonesianization" of the economy. The government forced many foreign investors to forge joint ventures with Indonesians to do business in the country, and barred them from some sectors entirely. A maze of licenses, non-tariff barriers, and prohibitions restricted trade. Such inward-looking policies did not create many problems as long as oil prices stayed high, but by the early 1980s, crude prices began to decline. Indonesia was heading for yet another crisis.

The Mafia divined the solution. It was sweeping in scope and highly controversial. As in the late 1960s, it proposed another, major reorientation of the economy toward the free market— deregulation of trade and investment and a smaller government role in the economy. The Mafia "recognized that the state could no longer serve as the dominant generator of economic growth," Radius wrote.[87] The goal was to boost non-oil exports and re-create a more hospitable environment for foreign investors in order to replace the hard currency lost from reduced oil prices. The plan would integrate Indonesia into the world economy more than ever before.

In order to proceed, the Mafia needed to win over Suharto. In a series of meetings around 1983, the team presented its plans to Suharto, and told him bluntly of the consequences of not adopting them. "In the past, you can do [certain policies] because we had a lot of oil revenues. But you can't do these again, you can't afford the same policies," Ali Wardhana says the team told Suharto. "You have to give the market a free hand to operate."[88] The team's recommendations presented Suharto with some tough choices. Some of the Mafia's prescriptions would quite likely undermine the business interests of some of the president's close associates. The Mafia, however, kept preaching its message. Suharto "was fully aware of the seriousness of the economic situation" and "it took him not too long to make the decision," says Wardhana.[89] In the end, Suharto gave his approval.

The result, wrote Radius, was a "paradigm shift."[90] Starting in 1983, the Mafia deregulated Indonesia's financial sector to strengthen the banks and capital markets. Then, beginning in the mid-1980s, it embarked on an intensive campaign of trade and investment reform. Exporters were allowed to bypass import monopolies on raw materials.[91] The Mafia even scored some victories against the cronies, abolishing the costly plastics import monopoly in which two of Suharto's sons were partners.[92] In a bid to attract more international capital, the Mafia also raised ceilings on foreign ownership in local operations, especially in export industries, granted foreign firms tax breaks and access to special credit schemes, and lifted restrictions on foreign investment in specific sectors.[93] "The deregulation movement," Radius wrote, "took on an aura that was both revolutionary and almost mystical."[94]

The reforms worked wonders. Non-oil exports soared by 650 percent between 1985 and 1996.[95] Foreign investment was twenty-four times greater in 1996 than a decade earlier.[96] The Mafia's free-market thinking was proven correct once again.

The Mafia, however, did not receive many thanks. Its liberalization drive proved to be its swan song. In a new cabinet formed in 1993, many technocrats were replaced, including Radius, and they surrendered several of their traditional posts to Habibie's

The great triumph of the Mafia was shifting the Indonesian economy away from its dependence on oil exports.

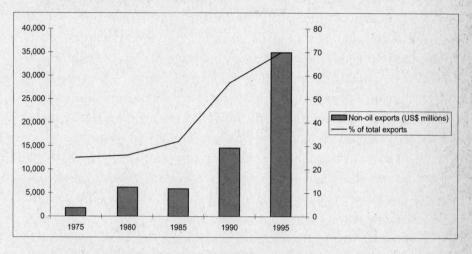

Source: Radius Prawiro, *Indonesia's Struggle for Economic Development,* p. 356.

supporters.[97] The nationalists and cronies finally had the upper hand.

Habibie's influence expanded. In November 1994, he unveiled Indonesia's first airplane designed entirely in-house, the seventy-seat N-250. After it was rolled out of its hangar in Bandung covered in dry-ice mist, a proud Suharto broke a traditional clay jug over its nose and christened it "Gatotkoco," after a mythical Javanese flying warrior. Habibie's ambitions for IPTN continued to grow. He plotted to open an airplane factory in the United States[98] and pledged $2 billion to develop a 130-seat jetliner.[99]

Much like his conciliatory treatment of the cronies, Suharto never demanded that Habibie produce profits or top-quality products. The finances of Habibie's airplane venture, though opaque, were most likely poor.[100] Nor were Habibie's companies forced to compete on an international scale, as Park had insisted with his *chaebols*. With few exports, Habibie relied heavily on local, and especially state-linked, customers.[101] Suharto protected Habibie against all criticism. In 1994, finance minister and Mafia protégé Mar'ie Muhammad tried to limit funding for Habibie's airplane company;

Suharto simply diverted state funds from a reforestation project.[102]
When a local magazine criticized a Habibie-led deal to purchase
old East German warships in 1994, Suharto shut it down.[103]

The cronies, too, ran amok. In 1996, the government granted
Tommy the right to develop a national car called the Timor. His
chief competition in the bidding was an older brother, Bambang.[104]
The actions of Habibie, Tommy, and the other cronies led to two
Indonesian economies running in parallel—one organized by the
Mafia and based on a strong link to the international economy,
rule of law, and sound fundamental economic practices, while the
other was centered on heavy state resources, private connections,
and the personal rule of Suharto. The two economies were natural antagonists. The deregulation, competition, and foreign investment favored by the Mafia ate away at the special privileges of
the cronies and the protection of state enterprises. As the cronies
pressed Suharto to preserve their positions, they hamstrung the
technocrats' efforts to reform the economy. It was a vicious and
self-destructive cycle, one that would soon prove catastrophic.

CHAPTER EIGHT

MR. THUNDER'S
AMERICAN DREAM

The government couldn't tell me what to do. —Soichiro Honda

What do you think of the cake?" Soichiro Honda asked his bewildered executives. Honda, founder of the Japanese car company that bears his name, had only a few minutes earlier entered his suite at the Ritz-Carlton Hotel in Detroit to find a cake waiting for him. The hotel baker had crafted the dessert to look like Japanese sushi. At first Honda's handlers were a bit startled. They had meticulously planned Honda's October 1989 visit to the United States; the company's Ohio factory even manufactured two cars specifically for Honda's use. The unscheduled cake was thus a surprise. Honda cut off a slice, nibbled on it, and ordered all of the executives with him to collect in his suite for a taste of their own.

As the staff ate the cake, Honda could not stop talking about it. "What do you think of the cake?" he asked them repeatedly. "How is it?" They all thought the cake was pleasant, but no one could figure out why Honda was so focused on it and, in their confusion, stood awkwardly cramped together in silence. Honda, sitting in a chair, began to shout, "Did you taste it? How is it?" The flavor of the cake, he continued, "was very well-balanced. It's not too sweet. The person who made this sushi cake must have thought about me, how old I am, that I'm Japanese. I'm 82 years old, so it has to be soft because my teeth aren't good."

As Honda went on and on, the executives had not the slightest clue what he was trying to tell them. Yet the prescient patriarch, a legend at home in Japan, was delivering an important message to his executives: Do not disregard your competition. Honda and the other major Japanese carmakers might have had America's Big Three—General Motors, Ford, and Chrysler—pinned against the ropes in 1989, but their American managers, like the baker of the sushi cake, could adapt to the demands of the marketplace just as well as any Japanese firm. "You guys think that you have surpassed the Americans," he scolded. "You guys have become too arrogant. Look at this cake. The person who made this cake definitely put his feet into my shoes." Honda then ordered Shin Tanaka, the chief of the company's Detroit office, to find the baker. When the pastry chef, a twenty-something American—to Honda, a boy— showed up at the suite, he became emotional. "Never underestimate America," he warned.[1]

Had the old man lost his marbles? That year, the company's sedan, the Accord, would become the best-selling car in America. It would hold that title for three consecutive years. Honda himself had just attended his induction ceremony into the Automotive Hall of Fame, the first Japanese so honored. (Honda was so overwhelmed by his selection that he told his wife: "I didn't think we could get this far."[2]) Honda's success was only part of a general advance by Japanese carmakers in the United States. Their market share rose steadily throughout the 1980s, and by 1990 reached a record 28 percent. Meanwhile, the Big Three seemed incapable of matching the Japanese in either quality or price. The two countries were heading in opposite directions. Japanese carmakers built eight factories in the United States in the 1980s.[3] Meanwhile, between 1987 and 1990, General Motors and Chrysler shuttered ten.[4] Soichiro Honda had surmised correctly that his management team believed in its own invincibility. "There was a sentiment among the Honda executives in the United States that Detroit was gone," admits Tanaka.[5]

That attitude was not limited to the auto industry. Across the spectrum of the global economy, Japanese companies appeared to be catching up to, and even overtaking, their American and European competitors. Japan was coming to dominate industries as diverse as semiconductors, motorcycles, and pianos. The advantage Japanese firms had over their competition was real and serious. They could manufacture new products more quickly and efficiently. In shipbuilding, Japan, which held the largest global market share, was making vessels 20 to 30 percent more cheaply than European outfits. Japanese steelmakers had invested in larger, more modern facilities than their American competitors. By the late 1970s, Japan had fourteen of the world's twenty-two largest modern blast furnaces; the United States, none.[6] Japanese companies also seemed to be way ahead in identifying consumer trends and inventing the hottest products. This was the era of Akio Morita's Walkman, a portable cassette player that altered the way Americans listened to music. Back in Japan, the economy's spectacular global success spawned an even more spectacular surge in asset prices—in fact, one of the most dramatic in history. By the end of 1989, Japanese shares represented a spellbinding 42 percent of the value of all stocks globally, compared to only 15 percent in 1980. Property prices followed to equally dizzying heights. The value of land in Japan in 1990 was four times that of all property in the United States.[7]

Japan's economic boom contributed to a simultaneous collapse of confidence in the United States about its own future. Compared to Japan, America seemed to have lost its economic vibrancy and sense of national purpose. Its major corporations appeared prostrate and uncompetitive, and its government overburdened and incapable of tackling the major problems facing the economy and society—unemployment, budget and trade deficits, rising crime, and deteriorating educational standards. Everywhere the average American looked, Japan seemed to be taking full advantage of American weaknesses. In 1987, the U.S. trade deficit—to many, the most obvious measure of America's competitive position in the world economy—had reached $151 billion, nearly 40 percent of which was with Japan.[8] Such statistics fueled the arguments of "declinists" who believed that America was rapidly losing its hegemonic status to countries with greater energy and new perspectives—like Japan. One of the most famous of these theorists was economic historian Paul Kennedy. In his 1987 book *The Rise and Fall of the Great Powers*, Kennedy contended that the United States in the 1980s was undergoing a relative decline in economic strength and thus suffered from "imperial overstretch," in which the country's strategic commitments around the world outweighed its actual capability to meet them. The era of American hegemony would inevitably fade into the history books, just like the empires of Spain and Great Britain.[9]

To some observers, the solution to America's many problems could be found in a rising Asia. Japan seemed to have reinvented the basic laws of economics. Its government-managed "Asian model" appeared better equipped to create an internationally competitive economy, absorb external shocks, and handle sticky issues like the restructuring of declining industries. The hyperefficient production methods developed at major Japanese companies like Honda were thought to give them an insurmountable advantage over their American competitors. The way for America to regain its vigor, some advocated, was to adopt the business practices and economic policies invented by this rising juggernaut. The United States needed its own Meiji Restoration. Ezra Vogel took this view in an influential 1979 book whose title said it all, *Japan as Number One*. "It is readily demonstrable that in many areas Japanese institutions are coping with the same problems we confront, more successfully than we are," Vogel wrote. "Could we not profit by showing the same eagerness to learn from the East that Japan has shown in learning from the West?"[10]

Yet to many Americans, Japan was simply a threat to their jobs and pride. They lashed out in a burst of anti-Japanese sentiment and protectionist fervor. In a July 1989 poll, Americans felt that Japanese economic might was a greater menace to the country than Soviet military power—by a factor of three to one.[11] Bookshelves and newspapers filled with apocalyptic visions of America as a future economic colony of Japan. The United States "is fast losing control of vital parts of its economic body" to the Japanese, wrote Robert Kearns, a journalist turned economic researcher, in a sensational 1992 book entitled *Zaibatsu America*. The lives of future Americans, he claimed, would be spent working in Japanese companies and adapting to their foreign ways, while suffering from a declining standard of living. "At stake," Kearns warned, "is nothing less than America's economic sovereignty."[12] The fear of the Japanese worked its way into American popular culture. In 1992, novelist Michael Crichton wrote the controversial *Rising Sun*, a murder mystery about a prostitute killed in the slick offices of a powerful Japanese corporation in Los Angeles. The book (and later the movie) captured American unease with growing Japanese influence in the country. "Japanese corporations in America feel the way we would feel doing business in Nigeria: they think they're surrounded by savages," lectures one character.[13]

The ascent of Japan awoke Americans to how the Miracle was changing the dynamics of the global economy. After the collapse of the Sovet Union and the Communist Bloc, rising Asian economic might became the single most important factor shaping the global balance of power, both economic and political. In that regard, Japan was surely Number One, the first Asian nation to burst on the world scene and demonstrate the globe-altering consequences of the Miracle. Japan would not be the last.

In no one industry did the threat from Japan hit harder—especially on the American psyche—than in automobiles. And no one company symbolized the dramatic shift in global economic fortunes between Japan and the United States better than the improbable carmaker built by Soichiro Honda.

. . . .

CARS FASCINATED HONDA at six years old, when a Ford Model T came rambling through his hometown, a village that has since become part of the city of Hamamatsu. It was the first car Honda had ever seen, and he chased after it. "Every time that Ford car stopped, it left a little bit of an oil slick underneath," Honda later reminisced. "I smelled that oil slick, I enjoyed it thoroughly."[14]

Honda got his chance to work with cars at age fifteen. He saw an advertisement in his favorite magazine, World of Wheels, in which an auto repair shop, Art Shokai, announced it was looking for new staff. Honda's father, a blacksmith who later owned a bicycle shop, took the teenager to Tokyo, where Honda became an apprentice mechanic. Though he spent the first six months on the job babysitting the shopowner's young child, he eventually got his hands on auto engines. Six years later, he opened his own Art Shokai branch in Hamamatsu.

From this inauspicious beginning, Honda rose to become the most successful automobile entrepreneur of the last sixty years. Combining bravery in business with engineering genius and a fearsome temper that earned him the nickname "Mr. Thunder," the hardheaded Honda drove his company into an industry of giants. He lived his life with equal recklessness and bravado. In his early years, he raced cars,[15] threw lavish parties, and cavorted with geishas.[16] His irreverent exploits became legendary. In 1950, a foreign businessman visiting Honda's headquarters got blind drunk at a rowdy party Honda held in his honor. While vomiting, the businessman lost his false teeth down a primitive toilet. Upon hearing of the incident the following day, Honda stripped off his clothes, descended into the toilet, and recovered the teeth. That night, he entertained his guest at another geisha bash by placing the dentures in his mouth and dancing around the room. Somehow, Honda turned this nausea-inducing tale into a management lesson. "The man holding the top position," Honda said of the incident, "has the responsibility to be always prepared to do things that are most repulsive to others."[17]

Never the stereotyped stuffed-suit Japanese manager, Honda was sharp-tongued, irreverent, and witty. Toshikata Amino, later a senior executive in Honda Motor's American subsidiary, got a taste of Honda's biting sense of humor the first time they met, on a stairwell at the company's headquarters in 1974. Honda was about to embark on an overseas trip, and Amino, a nervous young employee, stammered that Honda's willingness to try many different types of food would help him on his journey. "Thank you," Honda responded, "but don't say that my stomach is like a pig's!"[18] Even at home, he behaved differently than most Japanese. He embedded a television set in the ceiling above his bed so he could watch the morning news broadcast without sitting up; before the era of remote controls, Honda pieced together his own device with components from a local hardware store to turn the TV on and off.[19] "Honda's life," Sony's Masaru Ibuka wrote of his longtime friend, "teaches us the possibility of making one's dreams a reality."[20]

The saga of Honda also further undermines the arguments of those Japan experts who attribute Japan's Miracle primarily to the guidance of bureaucrats. Whereas Sony may not have been heavily and directly supported by the government, Honda's relationship with Japan's bureaucrats was outright hostile. He even fought them over car paint. The transportation ministry banned automakers from using red and white as colors for their passenger cars, reserving these shades for emergency vehicles like fire engines. Honda loved everything red—he often wore red shirts instead of the standard white shirt–dark suit uniform of Japanese business—and he raged against this policy. "I'm aware of no other industrial nation in the world," Honda wrote in a newspaper essay, "in which the state monopolizes the use of colors." Honda, with some hard lobbying, got the rule changed, and his first sports car—unveiled in 1962—was painted the brightest red his engineers could find.[21] His relationship with MITI was no better. Honda's entire car operation brazenly flouted MITI directives. "Probably I would have been even more successful had we not had MITI," Honda said later in life. "MITI was not capable of making automobiles. I was."[22] The example of Honda does not dismiss the role of industrial policy in Japan's Miracle—clearly, Honda's case was exceptional—but it does provide dramatic evidence that MITI's importance can be overblown. Honda's story lends more proof that the power of capitalist competition and open markets are more important for achieving economic development than the industrial policy that is the centerpiece of the "Asian model."

Honda also undermines many other stereotypes of Japanese corporate culture. In a business community obsessed with prestigious degrees and social pedigree, Honda broke the mold by never completing a university education. He made a point of hiring engineers with the mediocre grades or second-rate university backgrounds Toyota would summarily reject. "A ticket to a movie theater will get you into a theater, but you cannot even see a movie with a diploma," he once said.[23] Once inside Honda, these employees experienced not the placid, consensus-based management glorified by many Japan experts, but a corporate tyranny worthy of Korea's Chung Ju Yung, the Hyundai founder. Honda managers recount stories of frequent abuse, even violence. Hideo Sugiura, a senior engineer, recalled one occasion when Honda hit him twice in front of thirty of his subordinates because a bolt, by Honda's specifications, was protruding by three millimeters. According to Tadashi Kume, at one time the company's president, the executives could determine Honda's mood by the position of the hat on his head. If it was pushed back, he was in good spirits; if pulled low on his forehead, he was in a foul mood. In that case, "everyone began to hide the rulers and wrenches that were lying around," Kume explained. "This was because when he got mad, he blindly reached for anything lying around, and started throwing whatever was in reach randomly at people; it was dangerous!"[24]

Honda's aggressive nature proved a great advantage as a businessman. He first attempted to build his own vehicle in 1946, during the dark days after World War II. The transport systems in the country were damaged and fuel was scarce, which made getting from place to place inconvenient. Honda saw a need for a new simple form of transport. He collected small engines once used to power military radios, which had been abandoned as scrap, made a few simple adjustments, and attached them to bicycles to create a primitive motorized bike. For fuel he used pine resin instead of scarce petrol, and for a "tank," an ordinary water bottle. The ungainly machines had little power, but Honda still managed to sell about five hundred of them. In 1948, he founded the Honda Motor Company with money from his father, who sold a prized patch of timberland to raise the cash, and began work on a full-fledged motorcycle. When the prototype was completed in 1949, someone remarked that it was "like a dream" to see the machine come together. Inspired, Honda named the bike the Dream.[25]

In 1950, Honda, backed by fresh investment, bought an old sewing machine factory, converted it to motorcycle production, and began churning out Dreams. But the bike was not the smash Honda expected. The main problem, Honda determined, was the tiny engine. He headed back to his lab, and he and his engineers designed a much more powerful engine for the Dream. The redesigned bike was tested in 1951 by an engineer, who zoomed up a nearby mountain in a downpour. Honda, trailing behind in a Buick, was thrilled. "This is the first time I have felt happy being behind someone else," Honda joked. The new Dream was Honda's first hit.[26]

Like Sony's Akio Morita, Honda quickly maneuvered his fledgling firm to take on the world's top motorcycle makers. He issued a proclamation to his employees in 1954, promising that Honda would enter the Tourist Trophy Race on the Isle of Man, one of the world's most prestigious motorcycle contests. This decision proved to be a major turning point for Honda. Winning races, first with motorcycles and later Formula One racers,

became a main motivating force behind the company's technological advancements. "The greatest purpose of Honda Motor," he
told the staff, "is to raise the honor of Japanese manufacturing."
Entering the Tourist Trophy required a major technical leap for
Honda—he needed to triple the power of his engines. Honda embarked on a trip through Europe to collect the necessary parts.
With suitcases so stuffed he could not close them, he tried to
board his flight back to Japan in Rome, but he was told by the
airline's agents that he had exceeded his weight limit. Honda flew
a rage. "How about that fat woman there?" he yelled. "She's much
heavier than me!" Honda got his parts on the flight.

By 1959, Honda Motor was the world's largest producer of motorcycles. Two years later, he won his first Tourist Trophy.[27] But
that was not enough for Honda. In the early 1960s, Honda, the
smell of Model T oil still fresh in his mind, decided to enter the automobile business. He faced a ferocious adversary—MITI. "Monster" Shigeru Sahashi had hatched a plan in 1961 to consolidate
Japan's automakers into three giant groups to try to strengthen
the industry to compete with Detroit's Big Three. New entrants to
the business were unwelcome. Honda was furious, as usual, and
refused to back down. The result was a colossal confrontation.
"I deluged [Sahashi] with complaints," Honda later recounted, "I
had the right to manufacture automobiles. . . . We were free to do
exactly what we wanted. . . . I shouted at him angrily, saying that
if MITI wanted us to merge, then they should buy our shares and
propose it at our shareholders' meeting. After all, we were a public
company. The government couldn't tell me what to do."

Sahashi was unmoved, but so was Honda. In January 1962,
Honda sent an order down to the R&D team: Proceed at full
steam to develop an automobile. He intended to get a car on the
market before Sahashi's plan took effect, presenting MITI with a
fait accompli. Honda put his engineers on a grueling schedule. He
wanted to unveil the new model at a large meeting of dealers and
employees slated for June 5. The night before, his team was still
placing the final touches onto two models, both small sports cars.

The next day, Honda personally took the steering wheel of one model, the S360, and zipped in front of the crowds.[28] Later, Sahashi's plot to reorganize Japan's auto industry faced tremendous opposition and was abandoned. Mr. Thunder had defeated the Monster.

· · · ·

MUCH LIKE SONY'S Morita, Honda thought of conquering world markets soon after founding his business. "No one can claim to be number one in Japan by selling only in Japan," Honda wrote to his employees in a 1952 company newsletter.[29] America fascinated Honda. Henry Ford was one of his heroes, and the idea of carving out a presence in the United States was a priority. If Honda could make it there, he figured, he could make it anywhere.[30] In 1959, he formed the American Honda Motor Company.

Its first president was a marketing executive named Kihachiro Kawashima. He rented an $80 apartment in Los Angeles, with one bed for himself and two assistants, and an old warehouse in a rundown part of the city to store the crates of motorcycles. The early going was slow. After six months, Kawashima had sold only two hundred bikes. Even worse, customers complained of leaky engines and faulty clutches. Unlike in Japan, Americans rode their bikes at higher speeds and longer distances on the country's open roads. The Japanese designs could not handle the punishment. "Our reputation in America was practically destroyed before we could get started," Kawashima said.

Yet Kawashima soon had a brainstorm that turned around the company's fortunes. He ran errands on a Honda Supercub, a model so lightweight that no one at the company thought it would sell in the United States. Americans, the company believed, preferred large, powerful bikes, like those produced by Harley-Davidson, and the Supercub, in Kawashima's words, "was not macho." Yet bystanders kept asking Kawashima about his Supercub, and he changed his mind on the potential market. Motorcycles at that time were sold out of greasy garages to the tattoo-and-leather set. Those bikers would not buy a Supercub, but what about everyone else? Kawashima launched a marketing campaign under the slogan "You Meet the Nicest People on a Honda," which showed ordinary, middle-class folks riding their Hondas, and marketed them through bicycle shops, hardware stores, even college bookstores. The strategy drew new types of customers to motorcycles, and the Supercub proved a smash. By 1964, Honda Motor dominated nearly 50 percent of the U.S. motorcycle market.[31]

The success with motorcycles encouraged the company to export cars from Japan to America. In 1973, the company launched the Civic in the United States. Sales were an uninspiring 32,575 units the first year.[32] Honda's standing in the American market rose dramatically soon after, thanks to legislation that other carmakers decried. In 1970, the U.S. government, responding to growing environmental concerns, passed the Clean Air Act, which set strict limitations on the levels of pollutants emitted by car engines. The new standards had to be met by 1975. The Big Three howled it was impossible to meet such strict requirements by the imposed deadline. Soichiro Honda, however, saw the act as an opportunity. "Now's the chance for Honda to take over the world marketplace," Honda told his engineers. "Every manufacturer is facing the exact same problem. We're all at the same starting line. . . . This is a rare chance. . . . When it comes to developing new technologies, we can't lose."[33] Honda formed a team of engineers to tackle the problem, which tried out all kinds of adaptations to the combustion engine. Honda himself was often one of the tinkerers.

By 1971, Honda's engineers had determined that the best course was to use a different mix of gasoline and oxygen in the combustion chamber. A combination with more oxygen—or a "lean" mixture—would produce fewer emissions and theoretically meet the U.S. standards. But there was a catch. The combustion process would be hard to ignite and might not burn consistently. Honda's team solved the problem by attaching a small second combustion chamber onto the engine with its own source of fuel. In the small chamber, the engine used a gasoline-rich mixture, which would ensure ignition; meanwhile, in the main chamber, the mixture was heavier on oxygen. This two-chamber format reduced the use of gasoline and created a clean burning temperature that reduced emissions. In 1972, Honda submitted a prototype to the Environmental Protection Agency for approval. It easily met the new emission standards. The Big Three were stunned. Not only had their protests against the Clear Air Act been exposed as nonsense, they also had been outmaneuvered by a tiny industry upstart—and a Japanese one no less.

The engine, called a Compound Vortex Controlled Combustion engine, or CVCC, set a new standard. Ford eventually licensed the technology. Honda first introduced the CVCC in the United States in a Civic in 1975. Thanks to the engine's "lean" gasoline mixture, the car got more miles to the gallon than any other on American roads, a big plus for consumers still suffering sticker shock from the first oil crisis two years earlier. In 1976, Honda sold more than 130,000 Civics in America. The CVCC catapulted Honda to the front ranks of the automobile industry and gave added prestige and legitimacy to Japanese carmakers in general. As automotive journalist Richard Johnson wrote: "Nothing would ever be the same again."[34]

. . . .

ONE MORNING IN April 1976, James Duerk read a tiny story in the *Columbus Citizen-Journal* reporting that an unnamed Japanese carmaker was considering building a plant in the United States. Duerk, the director of development for the state of Ohio, was always on the lookout for such opportunities. Investment from Japan could provide new jobs in the state. That morning, he walked into the office of Ohio Governor James Rhodes and showed him the clipping. "Perhaps we ought to go to Japan in the next few weeks and check this out," Duerk suggested. Rhodes read the report and said: "We'll go tomorrow."

Unsure which company was planning the investment, Rhodes and Duerk met with executives at Toyota, Nissan, and Honda, and made a pitch for them to locate the plant in Ohio. In a reversal of what Chan Chin Bock had done for Singapore, Duerk was cold-calling Asian companies looking for foreign investment to create jobs and income in the United States.

Though none of the carmakers revealed their plans, Duerk suspected Honda was the company of the *Citizen-Journal* press report. He was right. Honda's managers first broached the idea of a U.S. manufacturing presence in 1974. To outsiders, the plan appeared another reckless Honda maneuver. Honda was still a small fish in the auto industry. Splurging on a major operation outside of Japan seemed foolhardy. Honda's management did not see it that way. The company's business in the United States was growing rapidly, while its factories in Japan were running flat out. Honda Motor needed a new factory somewhere. It might as well be in America. Honda believed that building its products in the country where they were sold kept the firm close to the customer.

Still, nothing came of the Ohioans' jaunt to Japan until the following January, when Shige Yoshida, a vice president at Honda in California, traveled to Columbus, where he met Rhodes and Duerk in a downtown hotel to maintain confidentiality. Yoshida asked a ton of questions and the two tried their best to answer them. Later in the year, Honda Motor sent teams to scout out possible locations for its factory; a site near a state-owned auto-testing track, one of the best in the world, appealed to the Honda men. Even more attractive, the Ohio government promised $2.5 million in direct aid to improve roads and utilities in the area. Honda Motor purchased a 260-acre stretch of farmland just outside the town of Marysville. A formal agreement with the state was inked in October 1977. The Japanese were coming to small-town America.

Honda Motor edged in slowly by first building a motorcycle factory, which started production in 1979. Encouraged by the results, the company broke ground one year later on a $250 million auto plant. Civics began rolling off the line in 1982.[35] It was the first Japanese car plant in America, and once again, Honda's aggressiveness paid off. In 1981, pressure from Washington coerced the Japanese government to restrict exports of passenger cars to the United States. MITI allocated a quota to each manufacturer. All of the Japanese auto firms found their growth in America hamstrung by politics—except Honda, which already had a plant in the works. Soon all of Honda's compatriots would build their own American factories.

One big question still remained: Could the Japanese, with their unique corporate culture, successfully build cars in America? The Big Three could not wait to find out the answer.

. . . .

SECRECY WAS A top priority. In March 1982, Eiji Toyoda,* then the president of Toyota and a member of its founding family, traveled to New York to dine with Roger Smith, chairman of General Motors, the largest carmaker in the world.[36] The matter these two giants of the auto industry intended to discuss was potentially explosive.

Much like Duerk's trip to Tokyo, the dinner symbolized the shifting balance of power between the United States and Asia. Previously, such business meetings between Asian and American firms usually entailed the inexperienced Asian executive trying to buy technology or gain expertise from leading American companies. Eiji Toyoda himself had once been in that very position. In 1950, Toyoda visited Dearborn, Michigan, to spend six weeks educating himself on the auto business at Ford. He marveled at Ford's factories, which at that time were the model for manufacturing efficiency. "I spent most of my time simply wandering around, observing and asking people working there all sorts of questions," Toyoda recalled. When he returned to Japan, Toyoda's colleagues

---

* *The Toyodas chose to spell their company name as "Toyota" instead of "Toyoda" since they believed it sounded more modern.*

frequently asked him—how long will it take Toyota to catch up to Ford? Toyoda could not give them much hope. "To tell the truth, there was no way of knowing," he later wrote. "I was certainly not presumptuously downplaying Ford's tremendous lead." Ford smashed out eight thousand vehicles a day; Toyota only forty.[37]

However, as Smith and Toyoda sat down together thirty-two years later, the tables had turned. Toyota, already the third-largest auto company in the world, was, like Honda, eating up U.S. market share. GM's line-up of gas-guzzlers was out of touch with post-oil-shock consumer preferences for smaller, more fuel-efficient cars[38] like Toyota's Corolla and Honda's Civic. But GM could not match the Japanese in price or quality on small cars. Smith needed Toyoda more than Toyoda needed Smith.

As dinner began, Toyoda found Smith charming. By the end of the meal, they had outlined a new partnership. Smith and Toyoda agreed to manufacture cars together. In the final arrangement, Toyota would produce Corolla-class cars at a mothballed GM factory in Fremont, California; GM would sell the cars through its Chevrolet dealerships.[39] Both sides got what they wanted. Amid rising protectionism, Toyota realized the need for a U.S. production base and saw the joint project as a less risky option than Honda's go-it-alone project in Marysville. GM would get an inside look into how Toyota manufactured cars so efficiently. Smith was going inside the belly of the beast to learn its secrets and eventually use them against his Japanese teachers in the global contest for dominance of the auto industry. The joint venture was named the New United Motor Manufacturing Inc., or Nummi for short—appropriately pronounced "new-me."[40]

The manufacturing process GM sought was called the Toyota Production System, which became more generically known as "lean" manufacturing. Though perfected at Toyota, Honda and the other major Japanese carmakers adopted similar techniques. Eiji Toyoda and his production guru, Taiichi Ohno, were the central figures in the system's development. By the time of Toyoda's dinner with Smith, the process they pioneered gave Japanese car-makers an insurmountable edge over the Americans.

Toyota's experiments in new forms of manufacturing began back in the 1950s. Ohno was shocked at how much more productive American factories were than Japan's. He thought it impossible that Americans had an innate ability that made the Japanese ill-equipped to match them. "Could an American really exert ten times more physical effort?" Ohno asked rhetorically. "Surely, Japanese people were wasting something. If we could eliminate the waste, productivity should rise by a factor of ten." This launched a lifelong quest to eradicate waste, or *muda* in Japanese. "My own efforts to build the Toyota production system block by block," Ohno wrote, "were . . . based on the strong need to discover a new production method that would eliminate waste and help us catch up with America."[41]

The system he created was an outgrowth of Toyoda's discoveries at Ford, but the two realized the impossibility of re-creating Ford's production methods in Japan. Ford's system, based on massive manufacturing of large numbers of vehicles, was ill suited to Japan's tiny market in the 1950s. Furthermore, Japan did not have the foreign currency to purchase the required advanced machinery from abroad. The equipment Toyota could afford had to be put to best use. The system Ohno devised based on these realities was surprisingly simple, but it nonetheless represented a revolution in manufacturing.

Through trial and error, Ohno found ways of slicing the time needed to perform certain tasks, allowing machinery to be used more effectively. For example, the process of changing the heavy molds, called dies, used to stamp out different steel auto parts in giant pressing machines usually took a full day at U.S. auto plants in the 1950s. Ohno, with fewer machines to stamp out a wide variety of parts, could not afford that loss of time. He installed special rollers to move the dies in and out of position. By the late 1950s, Toyota could change a die in only three minutes. Such tricks were introduced up the entire assembly line.

Ohno broke his staff into teams, each with a team leader, which was assigned a certain job to complete in the assembly line. Unlike in the United States, where each worker did only one task, members of the team often had to learn several. The workers were also expected to be quality-control inspectors. Rather than leaving problems like faulty parts to special quality officers down the line, as in Ford's factories, Ohno taught his staff to report and fix errors on the spot. A cord hung above every workstation that anyone could pull to halt the entire production line when a problem needed solving. As a result, flaws were found immediately and car quality improved significantly. Ohno also encouraged his workers to make recommendations as to how the production process could be made even more efficient. This practice was known as *kaizen*, or "continuous improvement."

The most glaring symbol of *muda* was inventories. U.S. factories stored heaps of components at great cost. Ohno did away with them by making it possible for parts to be delivered—both to the factory by suppliers and within the factory to the assembly line—only as needed. This innovation was called the "just-in-time" production system.[42] "There is no waste in business more terrible than overproduction" and ending it requires "a revolution of consciousness," Ohno wrote. "Industrial society must develop the courage, or rather the common sense, to procure only what is needed when it is needed and in the amount needed."[43]

These production techniques demanded a tremendous amount of discipline and consistency from managers, workers, and suppliers. There were no safety nets—no extra inventories in case some part ran out, no extra workers around to help with emergencies, no large teams of quality-control experts to check cars. But the system improved labor productivity, sliced costs, and bolstered quality control. One study that proved the superiority of Ohno's production methods over those of the Big Three compared GM's Framingham assembly plant with Toyota's Takaoka factory in Japan in 1986. The GM facility required thirty-one hours of labor to build one car; Toyota's only sixteen. The car produced by Toyota also had only one-third of the defects. The GM plant kept two weeks' worth of components; Toyota's only two hours.[44] Ohno had not only found a way to catch up to America but had also left the Big Three behind.

. . . .

THE KEY QUESTION remained: Could Japanese production techniques be transplanted to American soil? Honda management was already dealing with this complex issue. The man tapped to merge the two cultures was a quirky, effusive engineer named Shoichiro Irimajiri, known to his American colleagues simply as "Mr. Iri." Irimajiri took his task of adapting to America very seriously. While posted in Marysville, he mastered English, gave up smoking, took up golf and jogging, and developed an unhealthy penchant for McDonald's.[45] It was his open-mindedness that made Irimajiri capable of not only solidifying Honda's presence in America, but also beginning the process of making Japanese firms acceptable to Americans in general. "In Japan, the symbol of Honda was still Soichiro Honda," wrote Japanese journalist Masaaki Sato, "but in America it was 'Mr. Iri.' "[46]

Irimajiri was a top-quality engineering grad, hailing from the prestigious University of Tokyo. An aeronautical engineer, he had heard of Honda's interest in building an airplane and decided to sign on in 1963. Assigned to the auto-racing team to work on Formula One engines, he had his inevitable run-in with an irate Soichiro Honda. After a racer lost the 1965 British Grand Prix, its engine was shipped back to Japan and Honda supervised its inspection. He found a fault in a burned piston and demanded to know who designed it. Irimajiri stepped forward. He tried to explain the reasoning behind his redesign—arguing it was based on sound data—but Honda turned into an "angry fireball," in Irimajiri's description. "You fool!" Honda yelled. "I hate college graduates! They use only their heads." Honda ordered Irimajiri to apologize to everyone in the company who had worked on the ill-conceived piston. Honda stood by his side for each embarrassing apology.[47]

Irimajiri survived the incident and was later part of the team that developed the CVCC. He arrived in Marysville in 1984.

Irimajiri's predecessor had already put in place as much of Honda's Toyota-style production system as he could. The workers were broken into teams as in Japan and given extensive training, some of it in Japanese factories. The egalitarian office environment was also decidedly Japanese. The perquisites senior managers enjoyed at GM and other U.S. carmakers—the secluded office suites, preferential parking spaces, and exclusive dining rooms—were eliminated. Most of the managers sat with everyone else in large, open rows of desks. Everyone in the company, from Irimajiri to shop-floor workers, wore the same uniform.[48] Honda Motor had also started implementing its "just-in-time" supply system to the United States, but with difficulty. With few suppliers based in the United States at the beginning, many components shipped all the way from Japan. Honda partially solved the problem by investing in joint ventures with parts suppliers to build plants close to Marysville.[49] But the biggest issue facing Honda's U.S. operation was quality. It was widely believed among auto executives at the time that the American assembly-line worker was lazy, resistant to change, and thus one important cause of the Big Three's woes. "We had been seeing some deterioration of the Detroit industry," says Irimajiri. "The big question was: Can we make high-quality products with those people?"[50]

When Irimajiri arrived at Marysville, he found that the precision, "lean" manufacturing system imported from Japan was not functioning. The staff—or "associates" in Honda lingo—was not taking independent action or engaging in the process of *kaizen* in the same way as Honda's workers in Japan. "The Japanese people were the teachers, the American people were the students," Irimajiri explains. "The structure had to be changed. The associates had to become people who could work by themselves, depending on their experience and knowledge."[51]

Irimajiri started that process while fixing a rattling noise in the dashboard of Marysville-built Accord sedans. The issue was more

important than it sounds. Honda Motor could not allow customers
to think the cars built at Marsyville were deficient in quality compared to those imported from Japan. Otherwise, the entire program
of shifting production to the United States would be jeopardized.
Irimajiri ordered the quality data to be sent to the work teams involved so they could repair the problem themselves. Nothing happened. His American workers were not accustomed to taking the
initiative in problem-solving as were their counterparts in Japan.
Irimajiri ordered every "associate" assembling the dashboards to
place his employee number on each one he completed. That did the
trick. With greater personal accountability, the unwanted noises
vanished, and Irimajiri learned an important lesson. His more individualistic Americans needed more individual encouragement than
workers in Japan. He began offering awards to workers who made
the most valuable innovations, and walked through the factory to
talk to the workers about improving the plant's operation.[52] Irimajiri also hired a former lawyer, Scott Whitlock, to run the plant
while his Japanese managers slid to the background.[53]

His methods worked. By 1985, the Marysville plant was the
showpiece of American automobile manufacturing, with a productivity level that could compete with its progenitors back in
Japan. In a clear example of Marysville's astounding efficiency,
an entirely redesigned 1986 Accord started production just as the
last 1985 model was rolling off the end of the same assembly line.
The Big Three required two to three months to engineer a similar
model change.[54] Marysville became a living, breathing example
of how superior Japanese production techniques could be implemented in the United States.

Irimajiri generously threw the plant open for anyone to visit
and study. His most eager student was Chrysler, which conducted
a major study of Honda's production methods. A willing teacher,
Irimajiri met with Chrysler researchers and even offered feedback
on their final report. He was not worried about lending a hand to
his competition. Chrysler "couldn't do anything like us because
their fundamental philosophy was different," Irimajiri believed.[55]

He appeared to be correct. Despite the mounting evidence of the superiority of the "lean" manufacturing system, the Big Three struggled to introduce the concepts into their factories. Was it really possible for America to learn from Japan?

. . . .

SOME AMERICANS THOUGHT their country's future might depend on it. The quest for Japan's economic secrets became an American phenomenon. Researchers dissected Japanese management and production systems to uncover the secrets behind corporate Japan's exceptional productivity. They found American companies at fault in everything from their treatment of workers to the closed-door design of their offices to even their focus on profitability and shareholder value. The soul-searching, however, went much further than the CEO's office. The ascent of Japan led Americans to question their values, culture, and national ideology. An article by Richard Tanner Johnson and William Ouchi in the *Harvard Business Review* in 1974, for example, concluded that America's apparent inability to compete with the Japanese was rooted in the nation's very history. The frontier spirit of the United States, a legacy of the Wild West, had created a free-spirited individualism, the article claimed, that was a poor match for the more collective and cooperative culture of the Japanese when managing the modern enterprise. "It is possible that Japanese methods are more suitable for crowded organizational life than the Western approach," the article declared. "Perhaps some of our deep-seated American values are inappropriate for these times."[56]

The answer to America's problems, some Asia experts determined, was to adopt the economic, political, and cultural norms of Japan. Many of those enamored with Japan believed the Asian nation had formed a more advanced society that was better adept at handling the challenges of the modern world than the United States and was well worth copying. The chief proponent of this view was Ezra Vogel. "By the 1970s, . . . institutions that once served our country effectively have often been found wanting and have been strained almost to the breaking point," Vogel wrote in *Japan as Number One*. "The pace of economic change has accelerated . . . but America's institutions are not strong enough to guide these developments or to respond effectively to the problems of its declining economic competitiveness." Japan, on the other hand, "has developed solutions for many of these problems that America, with its more individualistic and legalistic history, might never have invented."

The United States, Vogel contended, should especially adopt elements of Japan's "Asian model." The key to Japan's competitive edge, he believed, was its dedicated, highly skilled bureaucracy. The MITI men, in his estimation, were almost superhuman—a class of supreme beings who made the correct decisions for a complex economy without any hint of favoritism, corruption, or collusion. Vogel suggested that the United States create its own elite corps of bureaucrats and implement a MITI-style industrial policy in which these professionals would play a greater role in guiding American business. Antitrust legislation, he wrote, should be softened to permit "Asian model"–style cooperation between government and business. Vogel shared the belief with "Monster" Sahashi that laissez-faire economics was ill suited for the demands of modern economic competition. "The United States government . . . can no longer afford not to give more positive guidance . . . if our country is to continue to provide world leadership and an optimal quality of life for its own citizens," Vogel argued.[57]

Even Americans not as infatuated with Japan advocated adopting Japanese methods. Many leaders in government and business saw Japan's "Asian model" as inherently aggressive and unfair. The Japanese government, the thinking went, subsidized its major industries and blocked off foreign competition in ways that gave Japanese companies an undue edge. The United States had to respond in kind or suffer the consequences. Clyde Prestowitz, the former U.S. trade negotiator, argued that Americans were disadvantaged in their battle with Japan by their very economic ideology. The U.S. government must see the economy as a matter of national security and deal with the economic challenge from Japan in the same way it confronted the nuclear threat from the Soviet Union. The free market could not defend the U.S. economy from a country that played by a different set of rules. If the United States did not adopt a version of the "Asian model," the consequences for American global power would be disastrous, Prestowitz argued. "In my view, the easy assumptions and tranquilizing bromides underpinning much American economic and strategic thinking are faulty and have contributed immeasurably to the U.S. decline," Prestowitz wrote in 1988.[58]

One of the chief proponents of this view was Lee Iacocca, the outspoken CEO of Chrysler. Iacocca believed he was competing not just against Honda and Toyota but all of Japan Inc., that network of government, business, and finance that gave Japanese firms benefits Chrysler did not receive in the United States. He wrote that "our economic struggle with the Japanese is critical to our future" but that Americans are "playing with one hand tied behind our back." He argued that "we're being played for suckers" if we did not "replace free trade with fair trade" and match Japanese protection and industrial policy in America. "Otherwise," he warned, "within a few years our economic arsenal is going to consist of little more than drive-in banks, hamburger joints, and videogame arcades." Washington had to take a tougher stance against this Asian upstart, Iacocca determined. "It's time for our government to call the kid in after class and ask him to explain his behavior," Iacocca wrote.[59]

Washington came close to taking Iacocca's advice. Trade disputes began erupting with Japan in the 1960s, and as the U.S. trade deficit ballooned through the 1980s, so did calls by American industry for protection and action. Irate businessmen and government officials accused Japan's bureaucrats of nefarious schemes to keep American products out of Japan, including irrational product standards, overbearing testing requirements, and Byzantine regulations. Repeated promises to liberalize Japanese trade regulations often came to naught or had little impact. The nationalistic spirit of Sahashi still loomed large. The two countries sparred over Japanese import restrictions on American beef, oranges, telecommunications equipment, baseball bats, and cigarettes. The Japanese government sometimes turned to unusual measures to deflect American criticism. In 1985, Japan's Prime Minister Yasuhiro Nakasone appeared on national television and urged every Japanese to buy $100 of imported goods; if the public did what he asked, "foreign countries would be happy," he said.[60] Such steps proved little more than publicity stunts. Equally unfair practices were employed to promote Japanese exports in the United States, the American business community contended. There was a widespread belief in the early 1980s that the Japanese government stage-managed the value of the yen to keep it artificially cheap in order to give Japanese exports a price advantage in the U.S. market.

The uproar grew so loud that even the promarket administration of President Ronald Reagan was forced to turn protectionist. In 1987, Reagan imposed financial penalties on certain imported Japanese electronics products in a dispute over semiconductors. The U.S. government believed Japanese firms were selling chips in the United States below production cost to drive out American competitors. The move turned U.S.-Japan relations frosty. TV commentators in Japan described the mood with the term *kaisen zen-ya*, which translates to "on the brink of war," a phrase used in Japan during the period just before Pearl Harbor.[61]

The view from Japan was different. To many Japanese, the source of the trade imbalance and weakened position of American industry was due to America's own faults, not aggressive Japanese behavior. One of the most outspoken on this issue was Sony chief Akio Morita. The problem, as he saw it, was that American firms did not make products that their own people, or consumers elsewhere in the world, wished to purchase. "There are few things in the U.S. that Japanese want to buy, but there are a lot of things in Japan that Americans want to buy," he wrote. "The problem arises in that American politicians fail to understand this simple

fact. It could never be the case that we are selling too much; . . .
the [trade] imbalance arises as a result of commercial transactions
based on preferences."[62]

It is hard to argue with Morita's position, but such views made
little impact on an increasingly panicky and emotional America.
Morita himself was in the middle of the maelstrom.

. . . .

A DISAPPOINTED AKIO Morita sipped his green tea. Earlier
that day in August 1989, Sony's eight-man Executive Committee had decided to abandon negotiations to purchase Hollywood
film studio Columbia Pictures. The asking price was too steep,
and they realized they did not have the experience to manage the
studio. Yet the decision was a major let-down for Morita. Pre-
sciently divining the importance "content" would come to play
in the economy, he believed Sony needed an entertainment business to support its consumer electronics operation. As he dined
with the executives after the meeting, Morita placed his cup of tea
on the table and said: "It's really too bad. I've always dreamed of
owning a Hollywood film studio." That was all it took for Sony
to shift gears. Morita held almost godlike status inside Sony and
what Morita wanted, Morita got. By the next morning, the Columbia deal was back on. Price was no longer a concern.[63]

The $3.4 billion acquisition, finalized in September 1989, hit
America like an atomic bomb. It was one thing for Japan to sell
TV sets and compact cars in America; it was another to purchase
beloved companies seen as integral elements not only of the Amer-
ican economy but also of America's economic self-confidence. If
Japan was buying its way into Hollywood, what was next? What
would be left for America? *What could stop Japan?* Richard
Goodwin, a onetime assistant special counsel to President John
Kennedy, blasted the Columbia deal—and most foreign investment in the United States in general—as part of "the continuing

saga of American decline." "By the time we reach the 50th anniversary of Pearl Harbor in 1991," Goodwin wrote, "our 'partners' will have achieved with money what our 'enemies' could not do with weapons—substantial control over the lives and destinies of the American people." Goodwin advocated prohibiting foreign acquisitions of American companies which he deemed "constitute the framework of economic and political activity," like media, transportation, and finance. "If we don't act, and soon," Goodwin warned, "if we choose to stand by as if we were helpless, then we will be accomplices in our own defeat—the defeat of the powerful dream that is America."[64]

Less than a month later, Japan delivered another jolt to the American economic psyche. A unit of the giant Mitsubishi group acquired a controlling stake in the real estate company that owned famed Rockefeller Center. The deal, part of a Japanese shopping spree of American real estate, fueled fears that Japan was "buying up" America. The Rockefeller Center grab touched a sensitive nerve. The complex is home to American icons like Radio City Music Hall and the New York City Christmas tree, and the deal sparked anger and bewilderment. The talk show *Late Night with David Letterman* featured three Japanese with briefcases who handed the announcer Bill Wendell fistfuls of cash to buy the buildings in the replica New York skyline behind Letterman's desk. One woman sold politically incorrect T-shirts that read "Welcome to Wokafellar Center" to tourists visiting for the Christmas holidays. A visitor waiting to see the *Donohue* show at NBC studios at Rockefeller Center bitterly told the *New York Times* that "certain things are sacred. Radio City, the tree. What are they going to do, have a bonsai now?"[65]

There was an occasional voice of reason. An editorial in the *Christian Science Monitor* titled "Will the Rockettes Wear Kimonos?" sharply countered Japan's critics by pointing out that European investors had greater holdings in the United States than the Japanese but never experienced such hostility. "Americans have to be alert that they aren't raising the cry against Japan's economic 'invaders' for racial reasons," the editorial scolded. Americans, it continued, would have to become accustomed to a new global economy in which the United States was no longer the sole economic force. "Americans thought the globalization of business and finance was a fine thing, when it was almost exclusively their game," the editors wrote. "Now the shoe is on the other foot."[66] In Tokyo, Akio Morita felt the sting of racism in America's outcry as well. At a dinner with foreign journalists, he noted that Australian-born Rupert Murdoch had earlier purchased another Hollywood studio, 20th Century–Fox, and no uproar ensued.[67]

Morita, a longtime friend of America, would usually have held great moral authority on such issues, but by the time of the Columbia purchase, much of his standing in the United States had eroded. He had become a symbol of the new "aggressive" Japanese. Earlier in 1989, a controversial book of essays written by Morita and a jingoistic politician, Shintaro Ishihara, was published that, in American eyes, encapsulated the true feelings of Japan. It was entitled *The Japan That Can Say "No."* In it, Morita critiqued the problems facing American business and the Japan-U.S. relationship. He identified a preference for short-term profits over long-term business interests as a primary weakness of the American businessman. "Americans today," he criticized, "make money by 'handling' money and shuffling it around instead of creating and producing goods with some actual value. . . . We are focusing on business ten years in advance, while you seem to be concerned only with profits ten minutes from now." As a result, the "American economy . . . is an economy without substance," he said.[68]

By September, just as the Columbia deal was coming to fruition, informal English translations of the book caused a stir in Washington. Amid the fallout, Morita tried to distance himself from Ishihara and he removed his portions of the text in later editions.[69] But the damage was done. Columnist James Flanigan wrote that he feared Morita's comments would give ammunition to Japan's critics in Washington and possibly lead to anti-Japanese policies.

"Which is unfortunate," Flanigan wrote, "because America and Japan, with a lot more to cooperate on than to quarrel about, need to build trust and reduce suspicion. Sadly, Akio Morita, who was always seen as part of the solution in that regard, now appears to be part of the problem."[70]

Yet only weeks after the Columbia purchase, the fortunes of Japan and America would undergo a dramatic and unexpected reversal. Morita should have heeded the words of Soichiro Honda and the lessons of the sushi cake: *"You guys have become too arrogant!"*

. . . .

ON CHRISTMAS DAY 1989, the Bank of Japan raised its benchmark interest rate by half a percentage point. Under normal circumstances, such a decision would have been noticed primarily by bankers. But not this time. Nine months later, the Nikkei stock market index had fallen by nearly half,[71] and by 2001, it had shed 70 percent of its value. Land prices followed suit, sinking 80 percent between the end of 1989 and 2002.[72] With the inflated asset prices went Japan's famous inflated growth. Between 1992 and

JAPAN'S LOST DECADE

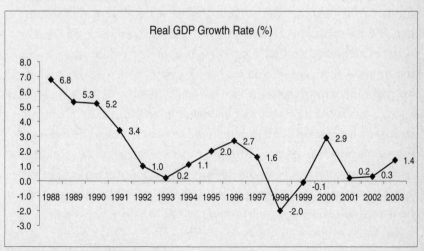

Source: International Monetary Fund.

2003, growth averaged less than 1 percent a year. The Miracle had come to a screeching halt. In its place, Japan experienced what became known as the Lost Decade.[73]

What went wrong? In the heady days of the 1980s, when Japan seemed destined to conquer the global economy, the country had become convinced that the Miracle would never end. The result of such thinking—that economies always grow, property prices and stocks always rise—created an exuberance that proved irrational. Japan's conviction in its own invincibility had caused a rise in asset prices that endangered the economy. The Miracle had spun out of control.

The starting point of the problem was land. Greatly valued on the crowded islands, land prices escalated through the 1980s. Based on these inflated values, Japanese banks were willing to lend to property owners, both corporate and private, in larger and larger amounts. Some of the money borrowed was invested in new factories and other assets; some was used to speculate on land and stocks. Property and share prices pushed each other to loftier and loftier, and less and less rational, heights. Japan entered the Bubble Economy.

Japan's supposedly infallible bureaucrats, meanwhile, pursued policies that only added fuel to the fire. Throughout the late 1980s, the Bank of Japan kept interest rates low, which only encouraged further lending and asset price inflation. This policy was formulated to counter concerns over the value of the yen. In 1985, Washington, pressured by the escalating U.S. trade deficit, convinced the finance ministers of the major industrialized nations, including Japan, to coordinate to weaken the dollar. The pact became known as the Plaza Accord. Two years later, the value of the yen had doubled against the dollar and Japan's financial mandarins fretted the strong yen would hamper an export-oriented economy. A more expensive yen made Japanese products pricier, and thus less competitive, in international markets. The solution, the bureaucrats believed, was to stimulate the domestic economy to pick up the slack. Their loose monetary policy generated the necessary funds to keep Japan's manufacturing firms expanding both at home and around the world.

Japan's bureaucrats, however, were playing a treacherous game. Banks were swelling their loan portfolios based not on a borrower's ability to pay, but on the inflated values of assets. If the Bubble burst, the entire financial sector would be at risk. Eventually, the government got nervous about the Bubble, but by then it was too late. In 1989, the central bank began rapidly hiking interest rates to cool down asset prices. The trigger proved to be the Christmas Day rate hike. As the third such action that same year, the bureaucrats were sending a signal that the level of asset prices worried them. The movers and shakers of the economy had taken their cues from the bureaucracy for decades. They did so again.

As the stock market slid, it brought everything down with it. Banks, which had used the artificially valued shares as part of their capital, curtailed lending and demanded repayment of loans to keep themselves solvent. Companies had borrowed far more than they should have and could not pay. Suddenly everyone needed real cash, leading to further declines in stocks and real estate prices. Bankruptcies escalated. By the late 1990s, the banking sector was crushed under some $600 billion of bad loans—the equivalent of more than 15 percent of Japan's GDP. Banks, securities firms, and other financial institutions folded. As the crisis dragged through the decade, a desperate Bank of Japan set its benchmark interest rate to zero in 1999—allowing banks to borrow effectively for nothing—but that, too, failed to restart growth. Companies had built too many factories with too much debt and had little incentive to borrow any more.

The failures of Japan in the 1990s sent economists into a frantic debate over what went wrong. Many found the answer in the "Asian model." The very institutions and practices that had so recently been praised as the causes of Japan's Miracle were now blamed for Japan's collapse. The role of the state in the economy that seemed to give Japan its competitive edge became the source of its problems. The system and society that experts like Vogel deemed superior to those of the West were now considered backward and incapable of adjusting to the modern world. The "Asian model" became a target of ridicule and derision. "The much-celebrated government model is wrong; in fact, it explains Japan's failures more than its successes," concluded Michael Porter and Hirotaka Takeuchi in 1999.[74] It was one of the most sudden analytical reversals in the history of economic theory.

The "Asian model" always had serious weaknesses that economists and analysts ignored in the glow of rapid growth. At the center of the trouble was MITI and its industrial policy. Lured by government incentives, companies tended to overinvest in targeted sectors, which created excess capacity. A steadfast determination to expand exports at all costs led corporate management to sacrifice return on investment for greater production. The result was a corporate sector short on profits, buried in debt, and trapped in bureaucratic regulation. While Japan's economy roared ahead, these problems were considered mere trifles; in fact, those enamored by the "Asian model" considered them virtues. Japan's system "focused . . . on an ultimate purpose," Japan-loving journalist James Fallows wrote. "The purpose was not anything as limited or strictly financial as 'maximizing profit' or 'increasing shareholder value.' "[75]

This disregard for profitability and the interests of shareholders, however, allowed Japanese firms to make the risky, speculative investments that created the Bubble Economy. The "Asian model" succeeded in helping Japan catch up to the West, as Fallows argued, but as the economy advanced and became more complex, the flaws introduced by the model became more dangerous. Just as Deng Xiaoping had seen happen in China, the intrusion of government skewed the incentive structure of Japan's economy, leading its players to make uneconomic decisions. Banks granted loans based on ministry fiat or historic corporate connections without the rigorous credit analysis that would have ensured their health. Companies, shielded from the usual demands of shareholders and bankers, pumped up production and built unneeded factories. The close relationship between government and business, so praised by Vogel, created clubby networks that protected their own interests at the expense of the country's. A series of corruption scandals broke in the early 1990s that exposed the true nature of these cozy ties. Securities firms covered the stock-market losses of major clients, and bankers issued billions of dollars of fake certificates of deposit for use as phony collateral.[76]

To solve its problems, critics contended, Japan needed a good dose of the American-style, laissez-faire free market that had been deemed archaic in the 1980s. Companies and banks, economists lectured, had to be exposed to true competition at home. They needed to make profits, not just products. The government, with its dense web of controls and regulation, had to get out of the way and allow the economic freedom demanded by the new era of globalization. America no longer needed to learn from Japan; Japan needed to learn from America.

Yet the entrenched ideological beliefs of the "Asian model" proved difficult to uproot. Its bureaucrats, bankers, and businessmen were reluctant to institute reforms that would either dilute their power or undermine the chummy ties forged by Japan Inc. The symbol of Japan's paralysis was the "zombie" company. These firms were so indebted that they should have gone bankrupt, but their close ties to bankers and the government kept them afloat. The "Asian model" had become Japan's albatross. Even Chalmers Johnson, one of the great proponents of the model, lost patience with what it had become. "Japan has complacently continued to protect its structurally corrupt and sometimes gangster-ridden firms and has made only gestures toward holding anyone responsible," he boomed in 1997.[77]

Japan sunk into a malaise. Just as Americans had done in the 1980s, Japanese in the 1990s began to question the institutions and social mores that had seemed invincible only a few years before. "The national traits that were once seen as the secret of Japan's economic success—stability, consensus, and homogeneity—appear to contribute powerfully to the sense of drift," wrote international relations professor Masaru Tamamoto in 2000. " 'Japan, Inc.' was out of business."[78]

. . . .

THOSE WHO HAD doubted the superiority of Japan's system could not contain their glee. "Japan's bureaucratic bust amounts to one more trauma for those who want to believe that mandarins can outperform markets," wrote Paul Gigot in the *Wall Street Journal* in 1997. "The debate that's been settled is the one over the superiority of the Japanese model of bureaucratic-led economic growth. The bureaucrats lost."[79]

There can be little doubt that the flaws of Japan's model came back to haunt the economy. Many of these weaknesses were created by government intervention. *But does the Lost Decade prove that the "Asian model" was a failure?* Can we finally resolve the debate over whether government action or free enterprise caused the Miracle? The only way to do that for certain is travel back in time to 1950, manage the Japanese economy minus MITI's industrial policy, and see what happened. Either way, the proponents of the "Asian model" most likely exaggerated the role of government and downplayed that of private enterprise. The laws of economics are not so easily rewritten.

However, it is equally impossible to deny that certain sectors in the Japanese economy—though perhaps small in number—did become global powerhouses under government direction. The same was true in other economies in Asia that adopted Japanese methods. As with Taiwan's electronics sector and the stories of Acer founder Stan Shih and chip magnate Morris Chang, government assistance can help a developing economy catch up with industrialized nations in technology and propel the economy into more advanced production.

How, then, can we explain Japan's transformation from world-beater to world basket case? Economies change, and economic policy must change with them. The Japanese model that contributed to the Miracle may have functioned well when countries were poor and striving to become rich, but once they got there, the model began to hamper, not help, development. Government intervention and "Japan Inc." ties came to constrain corporate behavior and enshrine outdated economic thinking. Instead of moving to the industries of the future—information technology and services—Japan remained locked in the build-factories-and-export-at-all-costs mentality of the 1950s, a strategy that could no longer produce the same results in Japan's advanced economy. MITI's bureaucrats, infected by the spirit of "Monster" Sahashi, clung to their powers for too long. Ezra Vogel came around to this point of view. "When the Japanese were catching up, those virtues and the structures they created served them well," Vogel wrote in his follow-up treatise, *Is Japan Still Number One?* "But now they have caught up and must adapt to a new stage of globalization. . . .These structures have needed revision which the Japanese have been slow in making."[80]

In American eyes, the Lost Decade stemmed the threat from the East. Though certain Japanese companies continued to advance, especially carmakers like Toyota and Honda, Japan as a whole no longer appeared a relentless juggernaut destined for global hegemony. Meanwhile, it was America that proved surprisingly adept at economic and corporate management in the 1990s as the economy excelled in the businesses of the New Economy. Even manufacturing industries many believed doomed, such as automobiles and semiconductors, staged a comeback.

The great threat from the Miracle receded. But not for long.

CHAPTER NINE

THE MAN IN THE BLUE TURBAN

Let the whole world hear it loud and clear.
India is now wide awake. —MANMOHAN SINGH

I n July 1991, Manmohan Singh, India's newly appointed finance minister, called the top civil servants from the country's economic-related ministries into an unusual conference to deliver an important message.[1] He had big plans for India's economy, controversial plans. The bureaucrats assembled before him controlled the government's vast machinery and held the power to thwart his efforts if they wished. He had no intention of allowing that to happen.

Clad in his trademark powder-blue turban, Singh, in his usual soft, calm voice, reminded them of the severity of India's economic predicament. The country was facing its worst economic crisis as an independent nation. With a pathetic $1.2 billion in foreign currency reserves[2]—enough to cover debt payments and imports for only two weeks—a default on India's mountain of international debt seemed imminent.

To Singh, that was an unacceptable embarrassment. Staving off a default was "an issue of India's honor," he said in an interview at the time.[3] He was devising a response to the country's crisis that was bold and far-sighted. India, he determined, was in trouble not because of a simple, temporary cash crunch. The seeds of the crisis were buried deep in the structure of the economy itself. India had for too long kept its industries fettered by a web of regulation and isolated from the world. The result was an economy that was out-of-date and uncompetitive. Solving the crisis would, in Singh's view, entail fundamental reform of the orientation, direction, and even ideological underpinning of the economy. It was a daunting prospect. India had been committed to a development strategy of state control and central planning since its independence. To implement his reform agenda, Singh would have to confront the country's political establishment and reverse decades of economic policy.

Singh showed no fear in his meeting with the civil servants. He stressed to them that immediate and drastic action was necessary to rescue India from catastrophe. "I have the prime minister's mandate to think big," he told the bureaucrats. "The world must know that India has changed." Then he bluntly made his position clear. If any of them felt uncomfortable with his reform program, they should come forward and inform him immediately. Singh would transfer them to new jobs. He ended the meeting with a simple plea: "I need your help."

That meeting was only one in a series of rapid-fire events in that sweltering summer of 1991 that changed the course of India's future. Singh's serene yet steely resolve steered India not only through its financial crisis, but also onto the path of the Miracle. He embarked on a revolutionary program of economic reform that ranks as the most influential in recent times, save perhaps for Deng Xiaoping's in China. Singh's program, much like Deng's, ended economic isolationism in India and embraced globalization for the first time. He opened markets, unfettered the private sector, welcomed foreign investors, and unleashed India's entrepreneurial spirit. Kamal Nath, a minister of commerce and industry, went so far as to write that "India's modern age began in 1991."[4]

Singh's effort was long overdue. While the rest of Asia latched

India finally joins the Miracle after decades of wasted opportunity under the License Raj.

INDIA'S AVERAGE REAL GDP GROWTH RATE (%) FOR FISCAL YEARS ENDING MARCH 31

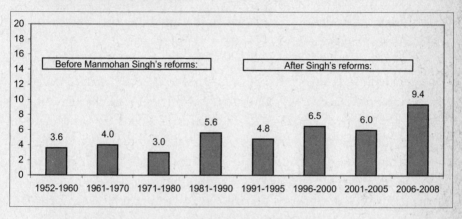

Source: India Ministry of Statistics and Program Implementation.

onto the forces of globalization, India stood aside, wedded to a nearly autarkic economic agenda. India's economic performance had been mediocre at best compared to the super-growth economies of East Asia. From the 1950s to the 1970s, gross domestic product grew only 3.5 percent per year, which one economist dubbed the "Hindu rate of growth." To some economists and businessmen, India became proof positive that democracies are ill equipped to match the rapid growth achieved under authoritarian governments. India's democratic traditions, the argument went, made it impossible for policymakers to maintain a safe distance from the immediate needs of electoral politics. Thus the government could not muster the will or provide the stability needed to ensure the high levels of investment necessary for economic growth. Even some Indian observers held to this position. Noting the success of Southeast Asia under dictatorial regimes, Indian diplomat and author Shashi Tharoor wrote that his country "put the political cart before the economic horse."[5]

India's recent success has finally put to rest this misguided thinking. Though India, as the one true Asian democracy to experience the Miracle,* is an exception, its record of economic growth since Singh's reforms can rival any attained by East Asia's authoritarian regimes. "To attribute the Far Eastern nations' success to their authoritarian politics and India's [relative] failure to her democratic politics," economist Jagdish Bhagwati declared, "is simply a non sequitur."[6]

With a country's political system removed from the equation, the fundamental reason why some countries prosper and others stagnate can emerge. There is one common element present throughout the entire story of the Miracle: the power of globalization. Every Miracle country took advantage of free trade and the new technologies that allowed production and services to transfer around the globe. They may have utilized a different mix of policies to attach themselves to these history-altering forces—from the heavy hand of Park Chung Hee to the mild-mannered market reform of Manmohan Singh, and from the complex state intervention of "Monster" Sahashi to the bare-bones capitalism of Hong Kong entrepreneur Li Ka-shing—but the rapid growth in every case was due to the transformative impact of the global economy. International market forces imposed a discipline that caused resources to be invested rationally and efficiently, opening up opportunities for growth that would not otherwise have existed. There is no reason to assume that an authoritarian government can connect to the global marketplace any better than a democracy.

Democracies, however, do suffer from one major weakness. As the case of India shows, the free-wheeling nature of democracy

---

* Some readers may disagree that India is the only democracy in our story. It is true that Japan has experienced free and fair elections since the American occupation, but during the high-growth period the government was dominated by one party, the Liberal Democrats, and the opposition exerted almost no influence over policymaking. Malaysia, too, holds relatively open elections, but there as well Mahathir's UMNO has always dominated the government and policy. In India, the Indian National Congress held power for the first thirty-two years in postindependence India, but, interestingly, the reform period that ushered in India's high-growth era came about in a far more fractured political environment, in which Congress ruled as a minority government and was often out of power. It is on this basis that I justify my statement that India is the only true democracy to implement the correct policy mix to join the Miracle.

makes it far more complicated to forge the political consensus necessary to implement the policies to achieve rapid growth. Such consensus has been another crucial factor behind the Miracle in every other country, no matter the type of government. In dictatorships, this "consensus" is often achieved by force or by limiting the number of entrants to the political process. In India's democracy, Singh could not employ riot police and spy agencies to "align" the nation. He had to endure a far more excruciating process of political maneuvering and lobbying to sell his ideas to the country's wide array of potential dissenters. At every step Singh took, he faced an aggressive opposition, a critical free press, and resistance from labor, farmers, businessmen, bureaucrats, and other special interest groups. Singh often did not have the support of his own political party, the Indian National Congress, which had been the architect of India's state-led economic system. Many of its members believed Singh was betraying the ideals on which the nation was built. His reforms were thought to favor foreign interests and India's own wealthy to the detriment of the poor. Congress members routinely tried to undermine Singh's efforts and attacked him publicly. Most important, Singh and his colleagues had to contend with the real risk of falling from power in a fresh election—a threat no one else in our story faced. As a result, Singh had to convince people of the worth of his policies on a larger scale and with much greater guile, perseverance, and compromise than any other policymaker of the Miracle.

India's path to the Miracle, therefore, has been far more convoluted than elsewhere in Asia. A constant complaint of businessmen and investors, both foreign and domestic, is that India's reforms, despite their obvious success, never seem to go far enough. Policies that Singh first broached in the early 1990s were still being debated years later, and some important reforms, for instance, the privatization of inefficient state enterprises, have made minimal progress. The halting nature of India's reforms has led many businessmen and economists to whine that India's democratic traditions hold the nation back. Singh, despite the difficulties India's politics created for him, defends the power of democracy with as much reason and passion as Singapore's Lee Kuan Yew argues for his tight-fisted "Asian values" regime. Though he concedes that in the short run authoritarian governments can make policy decisions with greater efficiency, he feels that over time the democratic process builds a stronger consensus behind economic policies and thus creates more sustainable economic growth. "It may seem to be moving slowly in the short run, but I have every reason to believe that this slow and steady will win the race," Singh explained in 2004.[7]

The tumultuous and confrontational nature of India's democracy, however, has tarnished Singh's reputation as a reformer. On one level, Singh is feted as a national hero, the man who brought greater prosperity and economic opportunity to India than anyone else in centuries. The high esteem he enjoys with the public carried him into the post of prime minister in 2004. At the same time, many Indians are also frustrated with Singh. The more reform-minded believe Singh has not taken full advantage of his unmatched moral authority and obvious brilliance to push forward even more wide-ranging reforms. His failure to achieve parts of his agenda has fostered a public perception that he is weak and vacillating. The Indian newsmagazine *Outlook* described Singh as a "meek and humble economist," an "ineffectual technocrat," and a "faceless bureaucrat"—all in one 2004 article.[8] His detractors believe Singh lacks the fire and conviction shown by other leaders of the Miracle to a degree that hampers his ability to bring his vision for India to fruition. Playwright Gurcharan Das concluded that Singh "is a man of great integrity" but "not a passionate reformer."[9] Singh's perceived weakness has left some Indian observers longing for a more forceful leader to manage India's reforms. Journalist Prem Shankar Jha lamented that India "had no Deng Xiaoping to steer it through periods of doubt and indecision."[10] Singh, therefore, does not benefit from the undying appreciation lavished on other, more controversial figures of the Miracle—like Park and Deng—even though there are no Tiananmen Squares or torture squads soiling his record.

Singh certainly does not present the image of a hard-boiled reformer. His former cabinet secretary, B. K. Chaturvedi, describes

Singh as "the most courteous man I have ever met."[11] A devoted Sikh, Singh sets aside time each morning for prayer, no matter how busy his schedule. Lacking the bravado of a Deng or Lee, Singh seems to revel instead in self-deprecation. "I have no head for figures," he says when discussing economic policies.[12] He is equally humble about his role in India's economic revival. "I'm a small person put in this big chair," he told Charlie Rose in a 2006 interview. "I think whatever I've done, I hope I've earned a foot-note in India's long and tortuous history."[13]

Historians will devote far more attention to Singh and his reforms than that mere footnote. In his five years as finance minister, from 1991 to 1996, Singh unleashed the creative power and productivity of the nation's one billion people and let loose India's aggressive industrialists onto the world stage as never before. Just like Li Ka-shing or Stan Shih, these businessmen in turn used India's comparative advantages—skilled, cheap labor matched with sound technology—to create globally competitive companies. "There were lots of doubting Thomases, there were lots of people who were sharpening their knives hoping that I would fail," Singh once said. "But we persisted."[14] His motivation was at its heart similar to all of the other Miracle leaders—an undying nationalism mixed with visceral horror at the pitiful state of the Indian people. Singh wished to bring to reality the dream of Jawaharlal Nehru, India's first prime minister, "to wipe every tear from every eye" once and for all. The vision that inspired India's economic reform, Singh once said, was "a new India, an India where there will be no poverty, the freedom from poverty, ignorance, and disease." The path to achieve this goal was through "India becoming a major global player in the world economy."[15]

. . . .

SINGH HAS ACHIEVED that goal. The emergence of India has generated nearly as much excitement, attention—and concern—as China's. India is perceived in the United States and Europe as the other great threat to the existing economic order. With similar projected futures, India and China have been bunched together in the discourse among economists and businessmen simply as "Chindia."

China and India are in many ways two of a kind. They are home to the world's largest populations—with 2.4 billion people combined, or a full third of the globe's total. Both are two of history's oldest, most advanced, and most influential civilizations. China's Confucian teachings, ornate linguistic characters, and equally complex architectural styles spread throughout East Asia and remain entrenched today; India's religious legacy (Hinduism and Buddhism) has left its mark from Afghanistan to Japan. Its artistic influences can be seen throughout Southeast Asia, in, for example, the impressive temples of Angkor in Cambodia. In modern times, China and India consciously chose for decades to sit out the amazing economic reformation taking place around them until crises forced their leaders to ditch their failed models of development and undertake a long process of fundamental reform. The seeds of their economic lifelessness were also similar, even though the economies themselves diverged greatly in structure. China's Communist system left little room for private enterprise; the state owned and controlled nearly everything. India's resembled the "mixed" socialist-leaning systems of Europe. The state played a much larger role in the economy than in the United States and dominated key sectors like energy, transportation, and telecommunications. Unlike China, however, India's private sector—from industrial moguls to independent farmers—accounted for the majority of the nation's output. In the end, both systems created the same woeful problems. They suppressed initiative, misused scarce resources, and perpetuated poverty.

The cause of these failures was also the same—excessive government control. The Indian government micromanaged the economy through a dizzying array of regulations called the License Raj. Under this tangled system, private companies needed government permission to conduct nearly every aspect of business—to invest in new operations, expand factory capacity, introduce new products, import equipment, and lay off workers. The License Raj shifted the decision-making power in the economy from corporate management to the bureaucracy. The results were similar to those created by China's Soviet-style central planning regime—uncompetitive companies and excessive political interference in corporate boardrooms. Both countries also distrusted the global capitalist system and cut themselves off from the world economy with insurmountable restrictions on trade and foreign investment that created a huge gap in technology with the industrialized countries.

Despite their obvious failure to produce growth and development, both nations perpetuated the status quo due to strong ideological beliefs that proved resistant to change. India's program was based on the ideas of Jawaharlal Nehru. Together with Mahatma Gandhi, he led the country's freedom movement against British rule, and his economic beliefs were shaped by that political struggle. Like many leaders in the developing world of the 1950s, Nehru saw Western colonialism as a natural outgrowth of international capitalism. This conclusion was not unreasonable. The British conquest of India began in the late eighteenth century as a commercial enterprise led not by the Crown but by a trading monopoly, the British East India Company. This painful history instilled in India's future leaders a distrust of foreign companies, international trade, and, to a certain degree, private enterprise itself. The profit motive was seen as lowly and dangerous. Private businessmen could not be trusted to act in the best interests of the nation overall. The state needed to keep them in line and protect the poor. Nehru's thinking was reinforced by the growing global power of the Soviet Union in the 1950s, whose statist system appeared to produce rapid industrialization and national self-sufficiency without capitalism. Nehru and the economists surrounding him—much like Mao in China—believed government central planning could produce better economic results, allocate national resources more efficiently, and uplift the poor more rapidly than free markets. Only the state, Nehru believed, could eradicate the poverty that so moved him. Nehru created a system decidedly antiglobalization in nature. Nehru's ideas were much more mainstream in development circles in the 1950s than those of Lee Kuan Yew in Singapore, Park Chung Hee in Korea, and the other Miracle leaders. Import substitution, a bias against exports, heavy interference by the state, and protectionism were all popular concepts of the day.

Indian policymakers took these ideas into an extreme direction—to the License Raj. The controls were deemed necessary to prevent the monopolization of industries by large industrial houses, nurture small-scale companies, and ensure balanced development throughout the nation. The bureaucratic nightmare that resulted, however, achieved none of these goals. The limitations imposed on investment and production kept both large and small companies at inefficient levels of production. An overcooked focus on heavy industry led to meager job creation. Domestic companies, protected from both local and foreign competition, had little incentive to invest in new technology or updated facilities, and, like Chinese state enterprises, made shoddy, out-of-date products with bloated staffs. The symbol of the Indian economy became a clunky sedan called the Ambassador. The gas-guzzler remained little changed from its original 1948 British design, yet consumers, with few other options, often waited years for their ordered cars to arrive. Singh considered the vintage vehicle "a measure of the lost opportunities as a consequence of being stuck at a very old-style model" of economic development. Doing business in India ended up having little to do with ingenuity and management expertise and more on navigating through the Indian bureaucracy and wooing the goodwill of the civil servants who dished out licenses. That often degenerated into bribery. Singh complained that the controls "became instruments of corruption. They became instruments of delay. They became instruments of uncertainty, and the economy simply could not get a clear sense of direction."[16]

The results of Nehru's economic system were the opposite of what he intended. Instead of helping the poor, the License Raj trapped hundreds of millions in poverty by restricting private enterprise and job growth. It was becoming apparent to some in India as far back as the 1970s that its economic system was not achieving its goals, and the government began a halting liberalization program in the mid-1980s. The effort, though, was short-lived, hamstrung by political opposition. India slid further and further into economic oblivion. By 1990, South Korea, with a fraction of India's population, was already exporting four times more manufactured goods to the major industrialized countries. Due to its "maze of Kafkaesque controls," complained Bhagwati, "India's model of development had turned out to be the one that couldn't."[17]

Facing similar problems, Singh pursued similar policies as Deng in China. India's government, Singh believed, had to support, not suppress, entrepreneurship. State control had sapped the initiative of Indian businessmen and workers to excel. The License Raj had to go. "I've come to the conclusion that equity does not mean filing of more regulation of private enterprise. That in the long run, equity and poverty can be dealt with only in the framework of an expanding economy," Singh explained in 2004. "And that means that those who create wealth must be given all possible encouragement."[18] Singh also blamed his country's problems on its isolation from the international economy. Opening up to trade and investment, Singh believed, would "cut short the process of modernizing our economy."[19] That meant implementing policies that would have horrified Nehru, such as lifting restrictions on foreign companies. Singh, like Deng and the other leaders of the Miracle, realized that India's future was linked to the global economy. "The people of India want our industry to produce quality goods to compete with multinationals not only within our own country but also abroad," Singh once explained. "India can do it. . . . But if you believe you can isolate yourself from the rest of the world—I think we made that mistake in the 17th and 18th and 19th centuries when the rest of the world was showing great industrial revolution. . . . If today we make that mistake, history will never forgive us."[20]

. . . .

THERE IS ANOTHER major similarity between Singh and Deng—both were products of the systems they overturned. Singh was born on September 26, 1932, in the poor village of Gah in the northwestern region of Punjab, then part of British India. At independence in 1947, the region was partitioned into Hindu-dominated India and Muslim Pakistan. Nearly 18 million people uprooted themselves and crossed the border between the new states. The young Singh was one of them. Then living in Peshawar, on the Pakistan side of the border, Singh, like many Sikhs, fled to India in June 1947, two months before independence. In 1948, once Singh's father, a dried-fruit seller, joined him in India, the family settled in the northern India town of Amritsar,[21] the center of the Sikh religion and home to its most revered shrine, the Golden Temple.

Singh was moved to study economics from an early age. "Right from the beginning, as a thinking student of 15 . . . I was troubled by the grim poverty that I saw around me," Singh explained. He was heavily influenced by a popular book called *Our India*, written by a politician, Minoo Masani.[22] The treatise is a simple economics text written for children that provides a semisocialist prescription for India's poverty. "It concluded India happens to be a rich country inhabited by very poor people," Singh said.[23] Singh excelled academically and won scholarships to study at Oxford and Cambridge, where he prophetically was awarded the Adam Smith prize. In the 1970s and 1980s, he held several posts in the Indian government, including governor of the central bank.

Yet, much like Deng, Singh always held misgivings about his government's economic policies. As far back as 1964, in his book *India's Export Trends and the Prospects for Self-Sustained Growth*, Singh warned that the economy's antiexport orientation would hamper development. Singh wrote of "a feeling of dissatisfaction regarding the attitudes towards export promotion prevailing in India."[24] In 1971, as a government advisor, Singh wrote a paper for the recently elected administration of Prime Minister Indira Gandhi (Nehru's daughter) entitled "What to Do with Victory." The paper warned that the License Raj would strangle growth and increase inequality. Yet during his decades of government service, Singh, like Deng, had little influence on India's economic course. "I have lived within the system and . . . I have not been successful in changing the system's thinking earlier," Singh once admitted. The reason, he said, was that he did not possess the political power to implement his ideas. "I have spoken my mind freely and frankly" Singh said in 1991. "But I've also served as a faithful civil servant. Even if I have been overruled, I have carried out the orders of my political masters."[25]

As the decades of poor economic performance wore on, Singh became more exasperated with India's backwardness. Like Deng, he began comparing his country to the rest of Asia. In 1987, Singh departed India for Geneva to become secretary-general of the South Commission, which produced an international study of the development of poor countries. In that post, he traveled to South Korea and Taiwan, where he saw the impact of the Miracle firsthand and realized just how far India had fallen behind.[26] These travels, he later said, were eye-opening. "I got the message that India has to wake up."[27] Concurrent with this revelation came the collapse of the Soviet Union and its final demise as a development model for India. The Soviets' ruin "was telling proof that a command-type of economy was not as secure as we had thought," Singh said.[28]

Singh realized the entire Indian economic system needed an overhaul. What India required, he determined, were policies more akin to those pursued in the rest of Asia. "There are opportunities, and countries of East Asia have taken advantage of those opportunities of the [global] trading system," Singh said. "India has to do the same thing, taking advantage of these opportunities to realize its destiny."[29] By the time he became finance minister, Singh had become convinced that reform could no longer wait a moment more. "I used to be in favour of gradual change," he said in 1991. "But I look around the world and realize that time is not on our side. This country will be marginalized if we don't move forward at a breathtaking pace."[30]

A series of dramatic and unexpected events gave Singh his opportunity.

· · · ·

RAJIV GANDHI, NEHRU'S grandson, stood on a red welcoming carpet surrounded by supporters at a rally in the town of Sriperumbudur in the southern state of Tamil Nadu in May 1991, campaigning to bring his Indian National Congress party back to power. Ten thousand people had collected for his hastily scheduled visit. With minimal security, women from the crowd pressed forward to hand him garlands of flowers. One of those women carried much more—a girdle hidden under her clothing with sticks of plastic explosive. As she bowed with the rest of his fawning fans, she detonated the bomb. The explosion ripped through Gandhi's torso. The suicide bomber's head was thrown, her face fully intact, twelve feet from the blast.[31]

The attack was a revenge killing by Sri Lankan Tamil separatists for Gandhi's interference in their civil war with the island's government while he was India's prime minister in the 1980s. A stunned India mourned. Yet even such a devastating attack on the country's premier political family could not stop India's democratic process. The election went on. Sympathy for Gandhi ran so high that Congress won the most seats in parliament, yet without the youthful Gandhi, the party was leaderless and lost. A few elders tried to convince Gandhi's Italian-born wife, Sonia, to step in and replace her husband, but she demurred. India could ill afford this political uncertainty. The country's economic crisis was worsening by the day, and only strong-willed and popular leadership could tackle it. India, it appeared, would have no such good fortune. Congress's political mandarins compromised and chose an unthreatening, long-serving functionary to become India's new prime minister—P. V. Narasimha Rao.

Rao seemed an especially poor choice to rule India at that crucial moment. Only days away from his seventieth birthday, Rao had four months earlier considered retiring from politics to write books. Though brilliant—he spoke fourteen languages—Rao had little popular support and often appeared dour and detached. As a senior Congress minister and policymaker since the 1970s, Rao, much more than Singh, was truly a creation of the existing system. Few believed he had the will to change it. Worst of all, Rao was considered hesitant and vacillating. ("He couldn't decide whether to have coffee or tea at a meeting," quipped one colleague.)[32] Political analysts in India had already written him off by his first days in office. *India Today*, a respected newsmagazine, commented that Rao was "a man propelled to the center stage . . . by fate, drama, fortune, and happenstance rather than drive, vision, or ambition." Rao's government, furthermore, appeared equally weak. Though the largest party in parliament, Congress did not hold an absolute majority. *India Today*'s conclusion was bleak: "No one expects miracles."[33]

India needed one. The previous government, which lasted a mere seven months, had taken some emergency steps to stem the foreign currency shortage—it negotiated a $1.8 billion loan package from the International Monetary Fund in January—but did almost nothing to solve India's underlying problems. At one point, the country's access to international capital markets had become so constrained that some debt had to rolled over every twenty-four hours. As much as $2 billion was borrowed overnight each day to avert a default. Rao himself was daunted by the tasks he faced. On June 20, the night before he was sworn in as prime minister, Rao was briefed by Deepak Nayyar, the government's economic advisor, about the crisis. Nayyar was blunt. The situation was so desperate that the previous administration had used twenty tons of gold confiscated from smugglers to raise $200 million from the Union Bank of Switzerland. In

India, gold is a prized asset. Its abuse as collateral for foreign loans was shocking. (Rao, however, would soon be forced to match the scheme, shipping forty-seven tons from India's central bank gold reserve to London to secure another $400 million loan from the Bank of England and Bank of Japan.)[34] Major reforms to India's foreign exchange regime and government budget were needed to prevent bankruptcy. Rao was taken aback. "Are we in such a mess?" he asked Nayyar. "Do we really need to do all this?"[35]

Everyone, though, had underestimated Rao. The morning after Nayyar's briefing, Rao had already recovered his balance and began talking boldly of reform.[36] One day later, Rao appeared on national television, telling the nation that big changes were on the way. "We have to take some very tough decisions," he said. "There are no soft options left."[37] Rao became the political backbone of the reform effort, keeping a close grip on the entire process, working with a small group of ministers and aides, and protecting them as best he could from their opponents both outside of and within the Congress party. In some cases, Rao took the lead on reform himself. Singh later confessed that "without [Rao's] active support and help, I could do nothing."[38]

Rao chose Manmohan Singh as his partner. He knew that his finance minister would become the focal point of the reforms, and therefore could not be a politician. He needed a Li Kuo-ting, the Taiwan technocrat, or an Ali Wardhana, of Indonesia's Berkeley Mafia, an impartial economics czar, without political connections or ambitions, to push through the hard measures needed. India's situation was so dire that Singh's friends counseled him to steer clear. Within six months, they predicted, he would find himself discredited and kicked out of his ministry, a scapegoat for the government's failures. Singh, however, was not a man to shirk what he believed was his duty. "I had trepidation," Singh later said of his decision to accept the post. "If I fail, that's of no great consequence. And who fails if India wins?"[39]

Singh's first priority was shoring up the nation's finances to avert a default. Severe cost-cutting to reduce the federal budget deficit was unavoidable—and mandated by the IMF as a condition for its loans—but Singh worried about the fallout. A sharp reduction in government spending could send the struggling economy into a severe downturn that would hurt the lower classes. He determined to find a different way. "Above all, we must not adopt an adjustment path which imposes undue burdens on the poor," he said in an interview at the time. "What we need is growth-oriented adjustment, adjustment with a human face. We must not perpetuate stagnation."[40] The answer, Singh determined, was to pair retrenchment with reform to spur economic growth. "We could, in a traditional way, tighten our belt, and we did that, tighten and tighten," Singh later explained. "But persistence on that path would have led to more misery, more unemployment. Stabilization plus a credible structural adjustment program would shorten the period of misery."[41] Thus Singh viewed India's economic crisis as a chance to push through long-overdue reforms that could place the country on a more rapid growth trajectory. He made this position clear to Rao in a briefing after taking office. "We are on the verge of collapse," he said he told the prime minister. "It is possible that we will still collapse, but there is a chance that if we take bold measures, we may turn around." The crisis presented, he said, "an opportunity to build a new India, to do things which many people before us have thought and said should be done, but somehow were never done."[42]

Singh at the time had only a general idea of the direction he wished to take. The reforms began as an emergency response to the crisis and took on greater coherence as the process went on. "We didn't sit down and draw up a blueprint" for reform, confesses Palaniappan Chidambaram, then minister of state for commerce and a key Singh ally. "We did some reforms and we moved on to the next stage. The blueprint came after the reforms started."[43] The crisis-induced nature of the program made the task of implementing reforms more difficult. "We did not have the time to ensure proper sequencing of reform and this complicated my job," Singh later admitted.[44]

Singh's first major move came July 1. He met with a small group of top officials—Rao, Nayyar, the governor of the central bank, and the secretary of the finance ministry. Singh wanted to devalue the local currency, the rupee, the exchange rate of which was at the time controlled by the government. This issue was far more sensitive than it might sound. Not only would a weaker rupee hurt certain special interests in the country—it would increase the cost of important imports like oil—a decrease in the rupee's value was considered a sign of national weakness. Singh was adamant. He believed a devaluation was "critical to restore confidence in the Indian economy." A weaker currency would start to attract foreign money back into the country, begin the process of promoting exports, and indicate to international investors that India was serious about addressing its problems. There was some debate over how to proceed. Nayyar was not opposed to the idea in principle but thought Singh's plans unnecessarily dramatic. In the end, though, they pressed ahead.[45]

There were, however, serious political concerns. When Rao consulted Ramaswamy Venkataraman, India's president, about the devaluation, Venkataraman complained that Rao's government was still a minority administration that had not yet received a vote of confidence from parliament. Venkataraman feared Singh's rupee devaluation too drastic a step to take. Singh refused to back down, telling Rao that "we had to act immediately and if we waited till Parliament met we would have nothing to say in our defense in dealing with the crisis." Singh pointed out the severe consequences of inaction. "I would have to declare the country a defaulter on its debt obligations," he told Rao. In the end, Rao gave Singh the green light, but they decided to act with caution. Instead of one big cut, as Singh preferred, they devalued the rupee in two steps[46]— 9 percent on July 1 and 11 percent two days later.

The devaluation was a mere warm-up to much more fundamental change. After the second devaluation on July 3, Singh told Chidambaram that he planned to abolish export subsidies provided by the government to Indian industry. Not only did Singh consider the subsidies unnecessary after the devaluation of the

rupee—which made Indian exports cheaper for foreign buyers—
the expensive program also drained the national coffers, a luxury
the strained budget could no longer afford. Chidambaram approved of Singh's plan in principle, but he had political concerns.
"It is difficult for me to start my tenure by withdrawing a scheme,"
he told Singh. Chidambaram discussed the matter with the chief
secretary at the commerce ministry, Montek Singh Ahluwalia.
A longtime friend of Singh and former World Bank economist,
Ahluwalia was another reform-minded civil servant who had been
stymied by political weakness and bureaucratic inertia. Having
advocated for liberalization since the 1980s, he had penned an influential paper on economic reform for then Prime Minister Rajiv
Gandhi in 1989. Though Gandhi approved of his ideas, the report
had gotten shelved due to an upcoming election. Ahluwalia recommended to Chidambaram that they replace export subsidies
with a more comprehensive program of trade liberalization, thus
handing Indian industry a beneficial reform in return for canceling
the subsidies. The idea appealed to Chidambaram. Like Singh, he
viewed the crisis as a golden opportunity to force change. A Harvard MBA, Chidambaram had practiced corporate law in India
and witnessed firsthand the disastrous consequences of the License Raj. "I was clear in my mind that trade controls had to go,"
he says. The License Raj was "clearly suppressing anyone who had
entrepreneurial talent or skills."

Later that day, Chidambaram and Ahluwalia brought up their
liberalization plan during a meeting with Singh, who agreed in-
stantly. But there was a catch. Singh was insistent on announcing
the elimination of subsidies that evening. With the rupee devalued, Singh did not want to wait to eliminate the costly subsidies.
Chidambaram had only a few hours to finalize his new program.

Chidambaram sat down with Ahluwalia and spent the afternoon deleting large sections of the License Raj on trade. They
abolished the need for some seventy-five hundred licenses given
each year to exporters and importers in only a few hours. Yet
Chidambaram and Ahluwalia realized a new regulatory system

would be needed to replace what was being dismantled. Some new framework was required to allocate hard currency in the economy, but with the country already starved of foreign exchange, they were wary of immediately instituting a full free-market system. Ahluwalia mentioned an idea that had been bouncing about the ministries for some time—"exim scrip." Under this system, exporters could in effect keep a portion of their foreign exchange earnings in the form of this scrip—a kind of currency substitute. The exporters could then use the scrip to get foreign exchange to import goods or sell them to other companies that needed imports. Importers would then no longer require government licenses. They just had to buy the scrip on the open market. A reform of great consequence, the trading of scrip would in effect create a market-determined value for India's currency.

By the early evening, Chidambaram and Ahluwalia had their scheme drafted. Overjoyed with the new program, Singh signed the document immediately. Singh, Chidambaram, and Ahluwalia headed to Rao's office to get his approval. Chidambaram briefly outlined the basics of the plan. Rao turned to Singh. "Do you agree with all this?" Rao asked. Singh said he did. Rao, without hesitation, signed the document.[47] With that, Rao, Singh, Chidambaram, and Ahluwalia wiped clean decades of controls imposed under the License Raj.

More would come, and quickly. Rao personally took charge of an effort to end the License Raj on industry. His chief secretary, A. N. Varma, was a key ally. Another reform-minded civil servant, Varma, while previously serving in the industry ministry, had pressed for deregulation of corporate India. His effort, like Ahluwalia's, had gone nowhere. Rao and Varma drew up an aggressive proposal to end licensing on a wide range of industries and allow greater scope for foreign investors. Singh lobbied for the plan within the government and squashed opposition to the changes inside his own ministry.[48] When Rao presented his plan to the cabinet in a mid-July meeting, however, a heated debate ensued: Singh and Chidambaram came to Rao's support but other members lashed back that Rao was undermining Nehru's legacy. The proposal did not have enough support in the cabinet to pass, forcing Rao to backtrack. He asked Chidambaram to rewrite sections of the proposal to make it more palatable politically.[49]

Chidambaram tried so desperately to cover the true drama of the industrial reforms that he even started the policy statement, released on July 24, with Nehru's name. The government's purpose in introducing its new policy, the document insisted, was to forward the "goals and objectives set out for the nation by Pandit* Nehru on the eve of Independence," "build a modern, democratic, socialist, prosperous and forward-looking India," and "continue to follow the policy of self-reliance." Beyond these catchphrases, Rao's plan eradicated much of Nehru's economic program. The new policy aimed "to unshackle the Indian industrial economy from the cobwebs of unnecessary bureaucratic control." The licensing system was abolished in all but eighteen industries, which were deemed sensitive for defense or environmental reasons. Special restrictions on the expansion of India's large industrial conglomerates were eliminated as well. Foreign investors were permitted to own majority stakes in their local operations; in thirty-four industries, approval of such investments was automatic.[50] Kamal Nath called this document "revolutionary."[51] The License Raj, after resisting economic reality for decades, was dying a rapid death indeed.

The same day the new industrial policy was announced, Singh stood before parliament and delivered his budget for the year. He set India on the course toward financial stability by slashing government spending, in part by cutting a politically sensitive subsidy on fertilizers. The speech was much more than a budgetary document. Singh made a rousing call for change, for a new India. "The crisis in the economy is both acute and deep. We have not experienced anything similar in the history of independent India," he told the lawmakers. "There is no time to lose." He made clear

---

* Pandit *is a respectful title used in India for a learned man.*

to the lawmakers the dramatic change that was necessary in order for India to move forward. "The massive social and economic reforms needed to remove the scourge of poverty, ignorance and disease can succeed only if backed by a spirit of high idealism, self sacrifice and dedication. The grave economic crisis now facing our country requires determined action on the part of Government," Singh said. "We are fully prepared for that role."[52]

. . . .

SINGH KEPT HIS his promises. The pace at which Singh, Rao, and Chidambaram brought about fundamental reform in the first months of their administration was startling. Singh and Nayyar often roused Rao at 3 a.m. in the morning to get his approval on time-sensitive steps. With few available moments even to eat, Nayyar would sneak bites of a sandwich in the corner of a conference room while Singh announced new policies.[53] In these early days of reform, Singh's efforts witnessed much greater acclaim than criticism. J. R. D. Tata, the patriarch of the Tata Group of companies, India's largest industrial house, declared in the *Times of India*: "Let the world now say: 'A new tiger has emerged in Asia—a tiger uncaged.'"[54]

Still, it was only a matter of days before reactionary forces gathered around Singh like famished vultures. Opposition politicians accused Singh of selling out to the IMF. Illustrating one July 1991 article in *India Today* was a cartoon portraying Singh as an evil scientist cooking up a "stew" of reforms in a fiery cauldron. A self-satisfied, well-dressed foreigner representing the IMF sat waiting to gorge himself at a dinner table, while in the background half-naked peasants looked on with broken bowls begging for scraps.[55] One Communist Party lawmaker accused Singh of attempting to "liquidate the policy of self-reliance."[56] Singh met with opposition leaders to explain his position and outline his plans.[57] His efforts bought him little time.

Singh's first contest came in late July soon after his budget speech. His cut in fertilizer subsidies, which raised prices by some 40 percent, generated ire in the countryside. Antireformists capitalized on the policy to accuse Singh of burdening India's poor. This accusation was false—Singh compensated farmers with an increase in the state's crop procurement prices and boosted development funds for especially impoverished rural areas[58]—but facts mattered little in the charged environment. Protests by farmers broke out in several parts of the country. In the southern state of Andhra Pradesh, farmers looted fertilizer delivery trucks and stores. Two farmers were killed when police opened fire on an unruly mob. On August 4, Singh met with Congress party members, hoping to win their support for his price hike. Instead, they attacked him. Singh "does not comprehend politics," complained one Congress lawmaker. "What can he do for us?"

The confrontation forced Rao to call a meeting of Congress's senior leadership to find a solution. Singh refused to back down. Reducing the fertilizer subsidy, he argued, was a crucial part of his plan to restore fiscal balance. The party elders were convinced that the new government could not survive unless it reversed the price hike. In the end, Singh was badgered into a compromise. The next day, he returned to parliament and announced that fertilizer prices would increase only 30 percent.[59] The political defeat was ominous.

Yet over the next two years the reforms continued. The License Raj on trade was generally abolished by early 1992. The state sector was pared down. Industries like aviation, telecommunications, and power generation, once reserved for state companies, were opened to private investors. Tariffs were reduced. Foreign investors could buy shares on the stock market, and regulations controlling share listings by Indian companies were removed. Interest rates were deregulated. To signal India's new attitude toward multinationals, a few headline-grabbing investments— from Coca-Cola, Ford, and General Electric, among others— were approved immediately. The rupee floated freely after a series of interim steps (and became fully convertible on India's current account in 1994). The crisis that had sparked the reform effort faded into history as hard currency returned to India's coffers. By March 1994, reserves had recovered to $15 billion.[60]

Singh implemented change amid heavy opposition through an ingenious strategy. With few dramatic pronouncements of wide-ranging measures, especially after the first few weeks of his tenure, Singh presented his program in miniature doses. A new reform was announced to the public every week or so. This approach concealed the sweeping nature of the reforms and made it difficult for the opposition to organize itself against any individual policy. He also kept the opposition off balance by mixing together new policies that were popular among certain special interests with those that were not. Yet Singh could not escape India's political realities for-ever. As the crisis of 1991 drifted into the distance and the economy regained its footing, politics once again rose to the forefront.

Singh's most dangerous political opponent was the Hindu re-vivalist Bharatiya Janata Party, or BJP. At the beginning of the Rao government, the BJP was already a major opposition party, and over the next several years, it would rise to become the Con-gress's chief rival to national power, in part by exploiting dis-content over Singh's reforms. The BJP professed its resistance to foreign investment and argued India should pursue a more nation-alistic, South Korea–style economic program that depended on local resources, not foreign money, for growth. Ironically, the BJP co-opted Mahatma Gandhi's cherished concept of *swadeshi*—or "self-reliance"—and used it against Gandhi's own Congress party. Singh, the BJP contended, was contravening *swadeshi* by opening up India to the international economy. The BJP focused its at-tacks on eight "fast-track" power plant projects the Rao govern-ment had signed with foreign companies to solve India's persistent electricity shortages. One project got special attention: the Dabhol plant in the state of Maharashtra, which was being built by Amer-ican power company Enron. The BJP accused Enron of inflating its capital costs to milk more money out of the Indian govern-ment. Though the BJP had no evidence to support this claim, the issue was a political headline-grabber, and when the BJP and its allies took control of the Maharashtra state government in 1995, it canceled the project. The BJP simultaneously forged an alliance with some powerful industrialists who were angered by Singh's reforms. Though India's business community welcomed the end of the License Raj, it also believed it was being treated unfairly. The country was rapidly opening to foreign multinationals but domestic reforms in key areas of the economy—especially its restrictive labor laws—were trailing behind, making it difficult for Indian firms to compete. Congress was at the same time getting bombarded by leftist parties, especially the still-active Communists, which argued that Singh's reforms were threatening jobs and imposing further hardships on the poor.[61] Singh was getting painted into a corner.

Singh fought back. In a 1996 speech, he called for the country to come together in the cause of development and defended his program. "We cannot afford to fritter away the vast energies of our nation in senseless communal strife or caste and class wars," Singh said. "Nor can we allow the national commitment to Swadeshi to be misused by the forces of obscurantism to perpetuate economic backwardness and prevent India from occupying her rightful place in the world."[62] But Singh's problem was that the attacks were not only coming from outside Rao's administration. The Congress party was becoming increasingly alarmed by the political consequences of Singh's reforms. A turning point came in 1994 when Congress lost elections for two important state governments that it usually dominated. Congress leaders blamed Singh's reforms. As the enemies of change grew in number and power, Singh's program slowed to a crawl.[63]

In 1996, Rao's government, despite its tremendous economic successes, met an inglorious end. Congress got booted from power in general elections and a coalition of rival parties took its place. Singh's program failed to attract voters preoccupied with communal conflicts and other noneconomic issues, nor had reform impressed the masses of rural poor who dominate Indian elections.

Though growth had picked up by the time of the elections, the impact had not yet trickled down to the lower classes. Rao retired to his writing and never returned to politics. Singh entered the opposition and continued to press for economic reform.

In 2004, Congress returned to power as the lead party in a coalition government. Singh became prime minister. Expectations ran high that the liberator of the Indian economy would let loose another rampage of new reforms, but Singh found himself hamstrung at every turn. His coalition partners—the Communists—howled in protest at every attempt at liberalization. A frustrated and weary Singh sometimes appeared to sink into despondency that overwhelmed his will to fight for change.

Yet Singh's legacy is assured. Most of the same politicians who once attacked him for selling out the nation, burdening the poor, and rejecting Nehru's legacy have come to adopt his ideas. The reforms continued, albeit at a slower pace, no matter which party governed in New Delhi. There is no more serious talk in India of reverting to Nehruvian socialism or isolationism. The most significant achievement of Rao, Singh, and their colleagues was shifting the entire economic discourse within India to support policies that produce rapid growth. Despite all of his conflicts and setbacks, Singh managed to build the consensus needed to enact the proper policy framework for development. Singh not only brought India its Miracle but also made certain the country would not deviate from the path that created it. As Shashi Tharoor wrote, "The bogey of the East India Company has finally been laid to rest."[64]

Perhaps Singh will never again match the glories he achieved in that heady summer of 1991, but the vision he expressed at that time will endure nevertheless. "As Victor Hugo once said, 'no power on earth can stop an idea whose time has come,'" Singh told India's parliament in July 1991. "I suggest . . . that the emergence of India as a major economic power in the world happens to be one such idea. Let the whole world hear it loud and clear. India is now wide awake. We shall prevail. We shall overcome."[65]

CHAPTER TEN

A DOSE OF DR. M'S
TOUGH MEDICINE

I don't care what people think. I wanted to help develop this country. —MAHATHIR MOHAMAD

Mahaleel Ariff's nerves were frayed. Mahaleel had been vice chairman of Malaysian carmaker Proton for only a few days in April 1996 when he was summoned to brief Prime Minister Mahathir Mohamad on the firm's future. As a newcomer to the car manufacturing business—Mahaleel had been an oil executive—he put himself on a crash course to learn the ins and outs of Proton's operations. It was a stressful few days, especially since what he discovered about the car company was not encouraging. Mahaleel harbored doubts about Proton's ability to survive.

This news was not what Mahathir wanted to hear. Proton was Mahathir's baby, an enterprise that he had nurtured since its birth as the ultimate symbol of a modern, industrialized Malaysia. Proton had thrived, a great degree due to government support, such as high tariffs that kept foreign competition to a minimum. The hard-headed former doctor, the most dominant political figure in Malaysia's history, expected his small Southeast Asian nation to excel. Defeatism was never welcome.

Mahaleel, however, figured he could not shield Mahathir from the hard truth. So he calmed his nerves as he entered Mahathir's office and began his briefing with as much confidence as he could muster. The problem with Proton, Mahaleel told Mahathir, was that it still was not a truly independent carmaker. Though Proton had been manufacturing cars under its own name since 1985, it relied on its Japanese partner, Mitsubishi, for many components as well as engineering and design. This situation, Mahaleel believed, could not persist. Mahaleel delivered his verdict: "You can continue to do the same way you're doing it and then you will die," he says he told Mahathir. "Or you can create your own products and your own technology and then you have a chance, but it will be very difficult."

Mahathir sat silently through the entire forty-five-minute presentation. Mahaleel girded himself for the worst. Finally, Mahathir asked him: "Which option do you recommend?" "The second," Mahaleel answered. He wanted Proton to develop its own cars. Mahathir then gave Mahaleel his marching orders: produce a 100 percent Proton-designed car by the year 2000.

Mahaleel was stunned. The company, he believed, possessed only about 20 percent of the technology and know-how necessary to design a vehicle itself. He thought the three-and-a-half-year deadline could not possibly be met. "Sir," he responded. "Do you realize we don't know how to start?" Mahathir said nothing; he only gave Mahaleel a wry smile.

The next three years, Mahaleel says, were "a nightmare." Mahaleel and his engineers feverishly worked toward Mahathir's goal, helped along by an important infusion of technology from Proton's 1996 purchase of the U.K.'s Lotus. Mahathir acted as a shadow CEO, incessantly studying financial reports, visiting the factory, and demanding new briefings. Mahaleel spoke at length with Mahathir on everything from the craftsmanship of the Lexus to the possibility of hydrogen-powered cars. In the end, Mahathir got what he wanted. In 2000, Proton introduced its first purely Malaysian car, the Waja sedan.[1]

If the manner in which Mahathir press-ganged Mahaleel feels familiar, it should. During his twenty-two years as Malaysia's prime minister, Mahathir reigned over the tropical nation much like Park Chung Hee had over South Korea. A virulent nationalist, Mahathir was as hell-bent as Park on transforming his agrarian country into an industrial powerhouse. He tried many of the same tactics. The saga of the Mahathir era in Malaysia is the prime example of how the "late movers" in the Miracle strove to copy the policies of the "early movers." Mahathir makes no secret of trying to adopt practices from Japan and South Korea. Even after Japan entered its Lost Decade, the influence of the "Asian model" endured across the continent. In fact, Mahathir used the term "Malaysia Inc." to describe his country's economic system in an effort to re-create the close business-government ties of Japan. His goal was "to bring government and the private sector together and to regard Malaysia as a corporation where everybody has to work in order to make it a success," Mahathir once explained.[2]

Yet in no other country in Asia did the active application of the "Asian model" produce more questionable results. The goal of Mahathir, like MITI's Sahashi, Park, and Taiwan's Li Kuo-ting, was to shift the Malaysian economy away from low-end goods and natural resource exports into higher-technology industries. Like Park, Mahathir wanted steel mills and car factories. Hoping to leapfrog Malaysia into the world of high tech, Mahathir dreamed up the Multimedia Super Corridor, a 31-mile (50-kilometer) swath of land near Kuala Lumpur with top-notch information infrastructure meant to house technology start-ups, an envisioned rival to Silicon Valley in a Southeast Asian jungle. Much of Mahathir's version of the "Asian model" centered on Mahathir himself. In the same fashion as Park, he often generated or sponsored projects he personally considered key to the economy, then scrutinized their implementation in excruciating detail. *Time* magazine once dubbed him the "Master Planner."[3]

Yet unlike Park's creations, Mahathir's never quite became the global competitors he had hoped. There are no POSCOs in Malaysia; Proton has not been as successful as Hyundai Motor. What went wrong? Part of the problem was that Mahathir's projects had a much heavier state role than MITI's targeted industries or Park's *chaebol*-led enterprises, which drained away some of the discipline important in making the "Asian model" work. In that way, they resembled Habibie's misguided efforts in Indonesia. But Mahathir also provides a lesson in development all his own. One key element in all of the Miracle stories was that the leadership of each country made economic development their top priority and pursued it with an uncanny pragmatism and flexibility that allowed them to adapt policy to the needs of the moment. Mahathir felt similarly, but his pursuit of rapid growth had an additional motive that to him was no less important—to uplift the Malay community in Malaysia's multicultural society. Mahathir was part of one of modern history's greatest experiments at social engineering. The Malays were the majority ethnic group in the country, but they were also the poorest, with most business controlled by a minority of Chinese immigrants. Mahathir, and the Malaysian leaders before him, implemented all kinds of convoluted policies to try to "right" this situation by expanding the role of the Malays in the economy. Growth was a crucial part of the attempt, but the benefits from that growth were meant to be skewed in favor of one social group over others. Mahathir was not just a nationalist, like the other leaders of the Miracle, he was also a Malay activist. He sometimes made decisions that undermined the modernization of Malaysia's economy in pursuit of his communal preferences.

Despite Mahathir's failures, Malaysia still experienced the Miracle, and Mahathir is unquestionably the father of it. The credit should not go to his high-profile pet projects, copy-cat "Asian model" endeavors, or pro-Malay programs. Malaysia's rapid growth is due more to Mahathir's lesser-known efforts at promoting private enterprise and foreign investment. Despite his devotion to the Malay cause, Mahathir's boldest decisions were the ones that removed regulation and altered government policy that had been set in place to bolster the community's fortunes. Malaysia provides another case of how the forces of globalization trump the power of government in creating economic Miracles.

Mahathir's willingness to participate in a Western-dominated free-trade system was even more unusual due to his oft-stated criticism of that system. Fiery and witty, Mahathir has been called a "spokesman for Asia." He has proved fearless in defending what he perceives as the rights of the developing world. In his view, the global economy has been purposely organized to operate to the detriment of emerging nations. Globalization, he once claimed, "has been introduced, designed by the Western countries to facilitate their control of the world economy." In one address, delivered in 2003, he described Europeans as innate warmongers who practice genocide and "are ready to invent false allegations in order to go to war to kill children, old people, sick people and just anyone." Malaysia, he insisted, cannot feel safe from these untrustworthy ogres. "The world that we have to face in the new decades and centuries will see numerous attempts by the Europeans to colonize us either indirectly or directly," he continued. "If our country is not attacked, our minds, our culture, our religion and other things will become the target."[4] His most notorious comments have come against Jews, who he has described as "monsters" and "pupils of the late Doctor Goebbels." In a 2003 speech to an Islamic conference, Mahathir blasted that "Jews rule this world by proxy. They get others to fight and die for them. . . . They invented and successfully promoted socialism, Communism, human rights and democracy so that persecuting them would appear to be wrong, so they may enjoy equal rights with others."[5]

Though Mahathir can sometimes sound like the most radical of Islamic leaders, he is not. Here is where Mahathir's story takes on significance well beyond Asia and economics. The Malaysia that Mahathir created is a rare find in the Islamic world—a Muslim-dominated state with a vibrant economy and an international outlook. Mahathir may bluster against the West and criticize U.S. foreign policy, but he has also been willing to embrace Western economic ideals. Mahathir welcomed U.S. multinationals into Malaysia in a similar fashion as Lee Kuan Yew in Singapore, and hitched his country's fortunes to the trends of free trade and

offshore production championed by American government officials and business leaders. Mahathir has been able to detach his
views on international politics from the development needs of his
nation. The result has been the formation of what is quite likely
the Muslim world's most modern economy. Mahathir's Malaysia
is not perfect, of course. Relations between the Muslim Malay,
Chinese, and Indian communities remain strained. Yet compared
to large swaths of the rest of the Islamic world, Malaysia is a guiding light of stability, of modernity, of internationalism. It is interesting to ponder what the world today, with its religious conflicts
and Islamic terrorist movements, would look like if more Muslim
leaders followed Mahathir's lead, and if the West found a way of
tolerating them as they have Mahathir.

This is not to say that Mahathir is wildly popular within Malaysia. He is as divisive a figure at home as he is internationally. To
his supporters, he is the beloved "Dr. M," the architect of modern
Malaysia who provided the strong leadership necessary to guide
a fractious nation into prosperity. To his enemies, he is an egotistical autocrat whose administration was tainted by cronyism
and corruption. "Maybe they'll remember me, maybe they won't.
I don't care what people think," Mahathir says about his long
career. "But I do care about being able to do what I set out to do.
I wanted to help develop this country."[6]

. . . .

DURING HIS CHILDHOOD, Mahathir's family "lived in what
would be called a slum area today," he once wrote. He was born
December 20, 1925, in the town of Alor Setar, which is now in the
northern Malaysian state of Kedah. They lived in the poor, southern part of town in a timber house divided into rooms with fold-
ing screens. He slept huddled together in the tropical heat with
his eight brothers and sisters under mosquito nets. His father,
Mohamad Iskandar, was a schoolteacher and later a government

auditor who, Mahathir wrote, "brought up his family to be very orthodox, very disciplined." A devotee of education, he gave Mahathir lessons in mathematics and other subjects at home and sent him to the town's only English school. Islam was also a major part of his early life. Though his family "was not fanatically religious," they "did adhere very closely to the Islamic faith." His mother, who had a religious education, taught him the Koran.[7]

Even as a child, Mahathir realized that something was horribly amiss in his country. Malaya, as the territory was then called, was part of the British Empire. The British residents of Alor Setar lived in a secluded community, complete with a golf course and private clubs, and rarely fraternized with the locals.[8] Mahathir was even more upset by the disparity between Malaya's ethnic communities. In Alor Setar, the young Mahathir noticed that Chinese immigrants dominated local business and were much wealthier than the indigenous Malays, who tended to be simple rice farmers. "I noticed that the Malays were far behind the Chinese," Mahathir recalls. "I felt that this was not right. As the people of the country we should have at least an equal level of development. I felt quite humiliated that, in my own country, I was not highly regarded. I felt that something had to be done. So I became a nationalist."[9]

At that time, though, Mahathir says that he and most Malays had little confidence that they could alter their fate. "Our entire world view was that we had no capability to be independent," he wrote. "We thought that only the Europeans could run our country, and felt we had to accept their superiority." However, much like Lee Kuan Yew in Singapore, he changed his mind during World War II, when the Japanese invaded Malaya and booted the British out. "The British troops blew up bridges as they retreated and the Japanese troops shot and bayoneted British soldiers who were left behind," Mahathir remembered. The Japanese success "convinced us that there is nothing inherently superior in the Europeans. They could be defeated, they could be reduced to groveling before an Asian race. . . . Thus there was a new awakening amongst us that if we wanted to, we could be like the Japanese. We did have the ability to govern our own country and compete with the Europeans on an equal footing."

Though the Japanese invaders brutalized many of the communities they conquered, the years under the Japanese went by in relative peace for Mahathir. When his English school shut down, he sold bananas at a stall in a local market until his education-minded father forced him into a new Japanese school. But Mahathir, like many Malays, was still happy to see the return of the British after Japan's defeat, hoping it signaled a return to easier, more prosperous times.[10] It did not. The British proffered a plan to unify the disparate sultanates on the Malay Peninsula and the island of Borneo into a "Malayan Union" as a prelude to self-rule. The scheme created an uproar. Malay political leaders opposed the British intention of granting full citizenship to the region's Chinese and Indian minorities, seeing the union as a ploy to tighten British control on Malaya.[11]

Mahathir was among the outraged. Back in his reopened English school, he joined his fellow students in fomenting opposition to the union plan. A talented comrade carved potatoes into printing blocks that they lathered with Chinese ink and used to print posters. They rode their bicycles through villages to form protest groups at other schools[12] and warn villagers of the dangers of the British union plan.[13] Mahathir, never one to suffer from modesty, wrote that "I always ended up taking a leading role, and my classmates naturally accepted my self-projected leadership."[14] In 1946, he joined the United Malays National Organization, or UMNO, which later became the country's chief political party. UMNO led the charge against the Malayan Union, and the furor over the British plan was so severe that it was scrapped in favor of a looser form of federation.[15]

Despite UMNO's success, Mahathir decided to put his political career on hold. In 1947, he accepted a scholarship to study medicine at a university in Singapore.[16] Higher learning, he believed, would help his future career. "Unless I had some qualifications, I couldn't become a credible leader," he explains.[17] After graduating in 1953, he returned to Malaya and became a government doctor.[18]

Meanwhile, Malaya's quest for independence was picking up pace. A triumvirate of political parties, led by UMNO, negotiated a deal with the British that resulted in Malaya's independence on August 31, 1957.[19] Mahathir, barred from political activity as a civil servant, played no significant role in these events. But shortly before independence, Mahathir quit his government job, opened his own medical practice in Alor Setar, which he named the MAHA Clinic, and began to build a political base. While he performed minor surgery and made house calls,[20] he became well acquainted with the local Malay farmers. They came out to vote for him in 1964 when he won a seat in parliament.[21]

Mahathir made a name for himself by championing Malay causes, but his route to the top of Malaysian politics got fast-tracked, ironically, as a result of disastrous events that appeared at first to doom his career. In the 1969 national election, Mahathir lost his parliament seat in part because Chinese voters rejected him as too overtly pro-Malay. Mahathir's defeat was part of a wider decline in support for UMNO and Malaysia's prime minister and UMNO chief, Tunku Abdul Rahman.[22] The Malays, who expected rapid gains in welfare and power after independence, found the slow pace of Malaysia's development frustrating. Their resentment toward the rich Chinese grew. The simmering communal tensions exploded in May in Kuala Lumpur. Armed Chinese and Malay rioters clashed for two days, burning, looting, and fighting. Soldiers were deployed to quell the riots, and the government declared a state of emergency. Officially, 177 people died, though other estimates put the death toll higher.[23]

The race riots were the final straw for Mahathir. He led a revolt against the Tunku, claiming the prime minister pandered to the Chinese minority at the expense of his own Malays. He wrote a strongly worded letter to the Tunku demanding his resignation. Mahathir's gambit backfired. The Tunku expelled him from UMNO. "I was exiled from politics in my own country," Mahathir wrote.[24] He remained unrepentant, and summed up his views in an influential book, *The Malay Dilemma*. Published in Singapore in 1970, the book was so controversial that it was banned in Malaysia until Mahathir became prime minister eleven years later. This odd treatise details the woeful tale of how British imperialists and aggressive Chinese immigrants marginalized the placid and hapless Malays in their own country. Mahathir argues the Malays were genetically disadvantaged in economic competition with other groups due to excessive inbreeding and other outdated marriage practices that perpetuated bad genes. He called for a "revolution" to rehabilitate the Malays and give them economic rights commensurate with their majority status. His prescriptions included undertaking state development projects to provide jobs for Malays and teach them new skills, building "satellite towns" to urbanize them and instituting regulations to protect Malay shopkeepers from Chinese interlopers. Mahathir even advocated a ban on "haggling" in shops so the inexperienced Malay merchants could better compete against their more savvy Chinese counterparts. He also insisted that the Malay community had to participate in its own resurrection by reforming its culture. "There must . . . be a conscious effort to destroy the old ways and replace them with new ideas and values," he wrote. "The whole process must be planned and executed with speed and thoroughness to produce a complete and radical change in the Malays."[25]

In the early 1970s, Mahathir's political fortunes revived. The Tunku never recovered from the 1969 riots and Mahathir's revolt, and he was forced to resign in 1970. Meanwhile, Mahathir's position was enhanced by *The Malay Dilemma* and his rebellion against the Tunku. He became a living symbol of Malay nationalism. UMNO invited Mahathir back in 1972. From there, his rise to the top was swift. He won back his parliament seat in 1974 and was named minister of education. Three years later, he became minister of trade and industry, and by 1981, he was the primary choice for the country's new prime minister.

. . . .

WHEN HE TOOK the country's top job, Mahathir inherited an economic platform so strongly ingrained that it was more like a sacred ideology. Called the New Economic Policy (NEP), it aimed to correct the glaring imbalances in income between the poor Malays and the wealthier Chinese. Like a massive, nationwide affirmative action program, the NEP was devised in the wake of the 1969 race riots when a shaken government realized that much of the Malay anger stemmed from poverty. In 1970, the Malays and other indigenous peoples (called the *bumiputera* in Malay) had a monthly household income less than half that of the Chinese and controlled a mere 2.4 percent of total corporate assets.[26] The rest was owned by Chinese and Indian immigrants or foreign companies.

Under the NEP, officially launched in 1971, the government employed a wide range of policies intended to lift the Malays' position in the economy, including preferential allocations of government jobs and contracts and regulations that ensured Malay investors got 30 percent of the shares of any new venture or initial public stock offering. The policy led to heavy state intervention in the economy. When the Malays did not have the cash to buy the mandated 30 percent of a company, the government set up trusts to purchase the shares for them. The central and state governments also created development corporations that launched industrial companies and filled their staff rosters with Malays. The NEP, however, did not degenerate into nationalization or expropriation of the assets of Malaysia's minorities. Instead, the NEP put a premium on economic growth to ensure that all communities enjoyed improved livelihoods while the government reordered the economic relationships between the country's ethnic communities. "It was to be a process of leveling up, not leveling down," Mahathir explained.[27]

Mahathir was not directly involved in the formulation of the NEP—it was developed by UMNO while Mahathir was expelled from politics—though it was influenced by Mahathir's ideas in *The Malay Dilemma*. Upon his return to government, Mahathir backed the NEP's goals. He once credited the NEP with making Malaysia "one of the very few countries where a multiracial people have been able to build a prosperous nation."[28] However, he had strong reservations about its policies. The NEP, Mahathir feared, made the Malays dependent on government programs. Many Malays, Mahathir complained, "perceive the NEP as an open-ended opportunity machine, where what you want you just pick up" or "as a means to get rich quick."[29] The NEP was not enough, Mahathir determined, to ensure the Malays' economic success. "The weakness of the bumiputera in the economic field can be overcome, not by government aid, but by their own upgrading of their abilities to compete," Mahathir believed.[30] Malays "had a lackadaisical, even naïve, attitude towards money and business. A cultural reformation, involving new skills, new approaches and new values, was essential," Mahathir wrote.[31] His goal was to create the *Malayu Baru*, or New Malay, who is "sophisticated, disciplined, trustworthy and efficient," "willing to face all challenges," and who "can compete without assistance."[32]

The tools to forge the New Malay could not be found within Malaysia, Mahathir determined. He had to look elsewhere for models to follow, and he found the answers he sought in the other Asian economies that had already experienced the Miracle, such as South Korea, Taiwan, and especially Japan. The rising East, bursting with economic vibrancy, seemed a much better act to follow than the West, still recovering from the oil shocks and stagflation of the 1970s when Mahathir became prime minister. "The Western nations appeared to have lost their drive," he wrote. "It was a natural conclusion, that if we were to emulate the success of foreign nations, the most valuable role models were no longer in Europe or the United States, but rather in our own backyard." Mahathir's fascination with the Japanese, first fostered during World War II, only intensified as Japan's economy became a world power. He marveled at the Japanese devotion to quality, their insistence on self-reliance, and, most of all, their diligent work ethic. Shortly after taking office, Mahathir launched his "Look East Policy." The idea was to copy aspects of the Japanese economy that Mahathir thought might work well at home. It was primarily a propaganda campaign designed to inculcate Malaysians with the same relentless work habits and spirit of self-sacrifice that Mahathir believed underwrote the Miracle in Japan and South Korea. "We wanted Malaysians to work as hard as the Japanese," he wrote. The Malaysian worker would "set the economy on a steady course of growth and development." He exhorted Malaysian companies to adopt the tight-knit executive-worker relationships, consensus-based decision making and other management practices prevalent at Japanese firms.[33]

Mahathir also copied Japan and Korea in more concrete ways, especially their "Asian model," government-led efforts to develop industry. Like MITI's Sahashi, Mahathir believed there was no way Malaysia could ever catch up with the West without government intervention. State aid and direction was necessary, he argued, in order to shift the structure of the Malaysian economy into high-value heavy industries such as automobiles. The industrialized nations "have all the competitive advantage," Mahathir said. "They have the capital, more power, market, technology, everything. What do we have? Nothing."[34]

Mahathir introduced an "Asian model" centered to a great degree on his own personal power. Like Park, he almost single-handedly fashioned a heavy industrialization program. His main tool was the Heavy Industries Corporation of Malaysia, or HICOM, a state investment company he formed while trade minister. To maintain control of its activities, he transferred oversight of HICOM to the prime minister's office when he ascended to the country's top job. Many of HICOM's projects were joint ventures with Japanese firms, including Perwaja, a steel company forged with Nippon Steel, and carmaker Proton.[35]

The idea for a homegrown Malaysian car first occurred to Mahathir during visits to Japan in the 1960s. He marveled at the

Toyotas and Nissans on the streets of downtown Tokyo. His fertile mind imagined all of the "spin-off" benefits such an industry could spawn back in Malaysia—engineering expertise, managerial training, and marketing know-how. Learning how to build a car "will enable us to leapfrog and catch up with the developed countries," Mahathir says. When he became prime minister, he decided to make his dream a reality. Several private initiatives were discussed, but Mahathir believed Malaysian businessmen did not possess the financial muscle to get the job done on their own. The state would have to take the lead.

Mahathir decided to take charge of the project himself. His first preferred partner, Japan's Daihatsu, turned him down. Then he met with executives at the giant *keiretsu* Mitsubishi and offered them a share of the national car project. Mitsubishi, he told the executives, would gain a larger presence in the Malaysian market by participating in Mahathir's plan than marketing its own imports. In 1983, two Mitsubishi companies formed Proton with HICOM. Mahathir believes his direct involvement ensured the project's success. "We needed a kind of heavyweight to push this idea forward. If some minor officials were to propose it the automotive companies wouldn't have taken them seriously," Mahathir explains. "As prime minister, I can gain access" to the right people.[36]

Few in Malaysia shared Mahathir's enthusiasm for Proton, however. Critics lambasted the national car project and the rest of his big-ticket industrial programs as expensive luxuries with little hope of ever becoming profitable or competitive. Malaysia's domestic market, with fewer than 14 million people in 1980, could not possibly sustain a car company, they contended, and the subsidies and tariffs needed to keep it afloat would so tax the economy, and especially consumers, that it would be more efficient to import Malaysia's cars from overseas. He faced resistance even within his own cabinet. His No. 2 official, Deputy Prime Minister Musa Hitam, cautioned Mahathir that there was a "danger of the Japanese taking over if you did not know how to do it."

Mahathir brushed off his critics. Malaysia, he believed, had no chance of ever becoming an independent economic power unless it developed companies like Proton. "We are always being told that it is cheaper to buy than produce yourself," Mahathir complained. "This is, of course, the propaganda of the developed countries." He was not looking at heavy industries in purely dollars-and-cents terms. The new skills and know-how Proton would generate within the economy were worth the potential extra expense, he argued. "It is cheaper to buy a foreign car but it may be necessary for us to pay the price of having cars made more costly," he once explained.[37] Mahathir also saw Proton as an opportunity to forward the NEP and his goal of the *Malayu Baru*. Its ranks would be filled with Malays eager to absorb the technical and managerial expertise he believed the Malay community needed.

In 1985, the first Proton car, the Saga, rolled off the assembly line. Far from the homemade Malaysian car Mahathir envisioned, the Saga was merely an adaptation of an existing Mitsubishi model.[38] Mahathir watched proudly nonetheless. A thankful Proton awarded him the first car off the line. "I felt that I had been vindicated," Mahathir recalls. The car showed that "we have arrived, that we can do what we promised to do."[39]

. . . .

DESPITE MAHATHIR'S EFFORTS, however, the Malaysian economy hit a serious wall in the mid-1980s. In 1985, the economy contracted by 1 percent.[40] Malaysia was still dependent on exports of commodities such as palm oil and rubber for growth, and global prices declined steeply. Malaysia's exports in 1985 were 40 percent smaller than policymakers had expected. Mahathir, in one of his standard diatribes, blamed the West for manipulating prices to the detriment of the developing world. Earlier, in a 1980 speech, he had called commodity trading on global exchanges a "sordid game."[41]

Yet, rhetoric aside, Mahathir realized that the economy needed serious reform. It was at this point that he showed that unexpected pragmatic side. Deviating from his earlier trajectory, Mahathir boldly began to liberalize the economy.

His partner in this effort was an eccentric businessman, Daim Zainuddin, who became finance minister in 1984. Daim grew up in the same town as Mahathir, though they did not know each other well in their youth. They met in 1947 when Daim joined his older brother, who was friendly with Mahathir, at the local train station to wish Mahathir farewell when he departed to Singapore for school.[42] Daim went on to study law in Great Britain and practice in Malaysia. Unhappy with his meager lifestyle, however, he gave up the law for property development, through which he made a substantial fortune.[43] Daim built a relationship with Mahathir in the late 1970s while studying urban planning at the University of California at Berkeley. He wrote letters to Mahathir with his thoughts on political events and economic policy.[44] The two were so tight by the mid-1980s that Daim became Mahathir's closest advisor on economic affairs, and they called each other almost daily.[45] Charming and affable, Daim became famous in international circles for dressing in flip-flops and a Hawaiian shirt to greet visitors.

The two friends' first target was the bloated state sector. The number of government-run firms had exploded by the mid-1980s to some eight hundred. Many were losing money, a worrisome drain on national finances.[46] Mahathir had been a proponent of these NEP-inspired public firms, but, sickened by the losses, he changed his position and decided to let private business take the lead. "At one stage before I became prime minister, I thought that government would be able to get both the tax and the profits, for itself" by developing its own enterprises, Mahathir explained. "But in fact what happened, you were not making any profits. . . . So I thought that this was completely wrong."[47] Mahathir and Daim began selling off state companies and projects to entrepreneurs or through the stock market beginning in 1984. By the mid-1990s,

most major government enterprises, including the country's largest port and the national telecommunications system, were in private hands.[48] Their performance for the most part improved.

Yet the privatization program caught flak nevertheless. Mahathir created the problems by mixing a policy based on sound
economic principle with a social agenda that was not. Most of the
divested government assets ended up in the hands of Malays.[49] Mahathir never gave up on his desire to craft a Malay business elite;
he just altered the methods of fostering one. His steadfast desire
to promote his own community mired the privatization drive in
charges of cronyism. State assets were sold to a relatively small
group of entrepreneurs and managers. Sometimes the procedures
for these divestments were murky with little public disclosure;[50]
other times, the entrepreneurs themselves recommended deals
to the government.[51] Daim, as finance minister, was point man
on the program,[52] and since the deals needed cabinet approval,
ultimately Mahathir had to give his nod as well. As a result, critics
claimed that contracts and assets went to companies and businessmen with close political connections to the Mahathir regime. Mahathir and Daim deny such nefarious dealings took place. What
looked like cronyism, they say, was sound commercial decision
making. The projects were large, the enterprises complex, and
only a few businessmen in the country had the skills and experience to successfully manage them, Mahathir argues. "We had to
be very selective about who takes on the projects. We must find
people who were capable," Mahathir complains. "The moment
you identify someone, he becomes your crony!"[53]

The most famous and controversial of these favored entrepreneurs was the cigar-chomping Halim Saad. At one time an obscure
accountant, Halim was a Daim protégé who managed UMNO-
linked companies in the mid-1980s. In 1987, a political dispute
forced UMNO to disgorge its business assets, and, through a
series of transactions, Halim ended up in control of many of them
as a private investor. One of the choicest assets was an engineering

firm called United Engineers, which had won a government contract to build the lion's share of a cross-country expressway in
1985. Halim consolidated some of UMNO's holdings into a company called Renong, which continued to make acquisitions and
win government contracts, including other major "national" projects such as a new road-link to Singapore.[54] By 1995, Renong was
the tenth-largest firm on the Kuala Lumpur stock market.[55]

While privatization was causing rancor, Mahathir's boldest
policy decision was yet to come. The main source of Malaysia's
economic malaise was a lack of investment. Malaysia was never
going to take off until Mahathir found a way of convincing investors, both foreign and domestic, to bet their money on his country.
Yet funds were flowing in the wrong direction. The wealthy Chinese community was pulling money out of Malaysia rather than
investing in new ventures at home.[56]

The stumbling block to reversing this trend was the NEP. Its
mandated quotas on share ownership for *bumiputera* was a disin-
centive for investors, who could find more attractive climates elsewhere in Asia. Why would an American multinational turn over
30 percent of its local operation to a Malay businessman when
it could open shop elsewhere and own 100 percent? Mahathir
came to see that the share-reservation policy was enriching a few
Malays who could afford to buy shares while depriving the masses
of the new jobs foreign investment would bring.

Mahathir and Daim huddled on the matter in 1986 and came
to a stark and politically dangerous conclusion: Parts of the NEP
had to go. Mahathir realized the consequences of this step. "I had
to make sure that my decisions wouldn't end up with my being
thrown out" of office, he says. "It was a hard decision, but it was
also realistic. I had to make it."[57] At the time, Mahathir was careful not to blame the NEP for the country's downturn. The NEP,
he said, was simply being held "in abeyance."[58] The cabinet approved the reforms, says Daim, because "if we cannot improve the
economy, we'd all go down together. We had to be brave."[59]

Mahathir announced the new policy during a lunch at New York's Waldorf-Astoria with U.S. business leaders in September 1986. The package of reforms suspended the 30 percent–*bumiputera* ownership requirement on certain foreign investments. (The new policy was meant to be temporary, but in the end, the NEP stipulations were never reinstated.[60]) "To achieve our goals, . . . Malaysia needs the help of our friends, especially those from the industrialized countries, in the East as well as the West," Mahathir told the assembled businessmen.[61] The response was spectacular. Over the next decade, Malaysia wooed $38 billion of foreign direct investment, nearly five times greater than that earned during the ten years before Mahathir's liberalization. Mahathir had propelled the economy forward by setting aside ideology and channeling the rationalism of Singapore's Lee Kuan Yew. The decision by Mahathir to reform the NEP solidified Malaysia's Miracle.

Mahathir's reform of the NEP brought about a massive increase in foreign investment and growth.

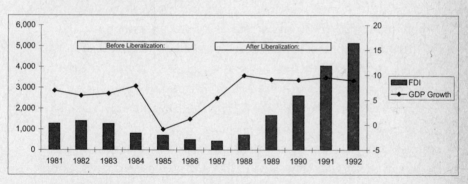

Source: International Monetary Fund, UNCTAD.

. . . .

MAHATHIR MAY HAVE ignored his critics, but they never came around to his economic thinking. While the cabinet approved of Mahathir's decisions, its meetings were not a forum for open debate. Ministers, including those closest to him, dared not disagree with Mahathir in public. Even Daim approached him gently and quietly when he wished to sway the prime minister's thinking. "Most fellows weren't able to argue with him. In the end they got scared," Daim says. "If you don't agree [with Mahathir], you resign."[62]

Underneath this false consensus, resentment was brewing. In 1987, Mahathir faced the greatest challenge to his leadership, and his economic policies were one of the chief targets of his critics. The forum was the UMNO General Assembly. His trade minister, Razaleigh Hamzah, contested Mahathir's position as party president. Mahathir's opponents criticized his liberalization efforts as counter to the spirit of the NEP, and attacked his big-ticket projects such as Proton as expensive and unnecessary.[63] "Money is misused, power abused," said Musa Hitam, who quit the government and allied himself with Mahathir's enemies. "We have to come out clean and open our books."[64]

Mahathir fiercely defended his record, even releasing minutes of cabinet meetings to show that all of the ministers—including his opponents—had approved of his policies.[65] In the end, Mahathir was victorious, but just barely. He defeated Razaleigh by only 1.5 percent of the vote. It was a stunning rebuke. But Mahathir did not take it that way. While challenged within the party, he was still prime minister, and he purged his cabinet of all the ministers in the opposing camp. Abdullah Badawi, one of the losers in this battle (but eventually Mahathir's successor), noted that Mahathir operated on "the corporate concept, whereby the majority shareholder gets his way."[66] That was the last real threat to Mahathir and his policies for another decade.

Some of the criticism leveled by Musa and his allies, however, was valid. Mahathir's favored heavy industrial projects showed few of the supposed economic benefits Mahathir had hoped. They were losing money and poorly managed. In 1988, Mahathir, fed up with Proton's mounting losses, fired its Malay manager and asked a Japanese Mitsubishi executive to take over.[67] The worst off was Perwaja, the steel joint venture. Originally founded in 1982, Perwaja's mill was set up with an imported Japanese production process that had not been tested commercially. It proved to be a disaster, producing at a cost significantly higher than the price of imported steel. In 1988, Mahathir brought in a new management team to try to engineer a turnaround,[68] but the situation only worsened. In 1996, the government admitted that Perwaja was insolvent, with accumulated losses of almost $1.2 billion and debts of $2.8 billion.[69] Even Mahathir confesses Perwaja was a failure.[70] Mahathir's Park Chung Hee–style industrialization drive never matched the success of Park's own.

Mahathir pressed on regardless, indulging in one megaproject after the next. In 1991, the government decided to build a glossy new international airport, which cost $3.8 billion. In 1993, he revived a project to build the largest dam in Southeast Asia, on the island of Borneo.[71] In 1995, he launched Putrajaya, a satellite city 16 miles (25 kilometers) outside of Kuala Lumpur to house the central government. When state oil company Petronas was planning a new headquarters in Kuala Lumpur's city center in the mid-1990s, Mahathir says he "casually" recommended to its managers, "Why not make it the highest towers in the world?" Such a monument, he believed, would serve as "a symbol for a growing country."[72] The result was the Petronas Twin Towers, the world's tallest buildings from 1996 to 2003. The Towers were just the trophy to satisfy Mahathir's passion to elevate the stature of his nation. "If you're a short person, you stand on a soapbox to speak to people," Mahathir says. "This is our soapbox."[73]

But again, concerns bubbled up inside the cabinet. Anwar Ibrahim, who became finance minister in 1991, worried Mahathir was going to blow out the national budget. He approached him privately to try to alter his plans. "Can we do this project in phases?" Anwar asked him. "Can we defer?" But once again,

Anwar feared confronting him directly. "I wouldn't approach it that way. I know him. He wouldn't accept that," Anwar says.[74]

Unbeknownst to Mahathir, or for that matter anyone else, the era of the intrusive "Asian model" was drawing to a close. Already under strain in Lost Decade Japan, the model was about to face a grave test throughout the countries that adopted it, as were its many proponents, including Mahathir Mohamad.

CHAPTER ELEVEN

EVERY STREET IS
PAVED WITH DEBT

There was nothing that could stop me. —KIM WOO CHOONG

K im Woo Choong was running out of options. In December
1998, Kim, the flamboyant founder and chairman of South
Korea's gargantuan Daewoo Group, flew to Hanoi for an urgent
meeting with Korea's president, Kim Dae Jung. Korea had finally
become a democracy in 1987 after massive street protests forced the
authoritarian regime to permit free elections. After two failed attempts, Kim Dae Jung—the man who had challenged Park Chung
Hee in the 1970s—was elected Korea's president in 1997. He was
on an official visit to Vietnam when Kim Woo Choong arrived in
Hanoi. Daewoo's problems were too severe to wait for the president's return. Daewoo, one of the country's high-flying *chaebols*,
was now teetering on the edge of bankruptcy. Kim Woo Choong
was scrambling to find new loans to pay off old ones. Amid the turmoil, he collapsed in Seoul with a brain aneurysm and was rushed
into emergency surgery only a month before his Hanoi trip.

Still not fully recovered, the Daewoo chief met the president
over breakfast at the Daewoo Hotel, one of the group's many investments in Vietnam. Kim Woo Choong outlined the precarious
state of Daewoo's finances and lobbied the president for a bailout.

Government-controlled banks, he said, had promised Daewoo loans that they were refusing to release. If he could get his hands on those funds, Daewoo could survive.[1]

In the old days, when Park lorded over the economy, such appeals might well have opened the government's financial spigot. After all, Daewoo was fulfilling the national priorities of building industry and expanding exports, goals that Park had supported at any cost. But what Kim Woo Choong could not accept was that Park's Korea Inc., which was responsible for Daewoo's dramatic ascent, was no longer functioning as it once had. In fact, those "Asian model" links between government and business were undergoing fundamental reform.

The catalyst for that change was the Asian Financial Crisis, a region-wide economic conflagration that was the worst Asia had experienced since World War II. Across the continent, several Asian Tigers faced national bankruptcy, their foreign currency coffers empty, their currencies in retreat, their economies contracting. Companies and banks were shuttering by the hundreds. In the past, *chaebols* like Daewoo could have expected continued support from the financial sector even in difficult times. The workings of the "Asian model" would protect a group like Daewoo under almost any circumstances.

However, the Asian Financial Crisis, just like the Lost Decade in Japan, was undermining that model—and with incredible speed. Korean banks were desperate to shore up their own deteriorating balance sheets. Instead of providing Daewoo with fresh funds, they called in Daewoo's loans. The political climate was changing just as rapidly. Kim Dae Jung believed Korea's "Asian model" of development required serious reform. It needed to become more open, decentralized, and market-oriented. The Crisis left the new president with no other option: Korea Inc. had to be put to rest once and for all.

So at that Hanoi breakfast meeting, the president refused to sanction a state bailout of Daewoo. What he offered was a stern lecture. Daewoo, the president said, had to reform itself if it wanted to avoid disaster. "You need to make your company lean and mean," he told Kim Woo Choong.[2]

The president's position sounded Daewoo's death knell. Eight months later, Daewoo's creditors took control of the group and dismantled it. With $75 billion in debt and other liabilities, the Daewoo debacle was one of the world's greatest corporate failures. Kim Woo Choong, disgraced, fled the country.

The collapse of Daewoo shook the Korean economy to its core. *Chaebols* like Daewoo were supposed to be sacred, the undisputed engines of the rapid growth Koreans had come to expect as a matter of course. Daewoo's astonishing end raised a question that would have been unthinkable only months earlier: *Could the Miracle be over?* Suddenly, the Tigers and their aggressive, voracious companies, which had once appeared so invincible, seemed just paper Tigers. "An 'Asian Miracle' Now Seems Like a Mirage," boomed one headline in the *New York Times*.[3] Many of the tremendous gains in income and industry of the previous three decades were being wiped out. Some of the region's proudest companies were on the edge of extinction; the frightening specter of poverty returned. So did social unrest and political upheaval. The Asian countries that succumbed to the Crisis—Korea, Malaysia, Indonesia, and Thailand—looked destined to follow Japan into their own lost decades.

The Crisis seemed to offer proof positive that the "Asian model" was just as toothless. Asia, many were now convinced, had not created a whole new and superior form of capitalism after all. "The Asian financial crisis may have finally put to rest the myth that the region's success has come about as a result of a unique system of capitalism rooted in Asian values—a system immune to the depressions and other troubles that economies in the West have to endure," commented Hong Kong professor Y. C. Richard Wong.[4] Many economists blamed the "Asian model" for *causing* the Crisis, in the same way it was supposedly at the root of Japan's Lost Decade. Asia's policymakers were no longer economic visionaries, but stubborn snake-oil salesmen, purveyors of phony, even dangerous, ideas. "When Asian economies delivered nothing but good news, it was possible to convince yourself that the alleged planners of those economies knew what they were doing," wrote economist Paul Krugman. "Now the truth is revealed: They don't have a clue."[5]

The Crisis was without doubt the greatest challenge the Miracle had ever faced. As the chaos settled, however, the result of the Crisis was not what anyone anticipated. The Crisis did not bring the Miracle to a close; it forced changes in Asian economic policy that ensured the Miracle's future. The fall of Kim Woo Choong was not a signal of the Miracle's end, but its transformation to a new, potentially more powerful stage of development.

To understand how that happened, we have to travel back in time to mid-1997, and across the continent to the Southeast Asian nation of Thailand, where the Crisis began in the halls of its beleaguered central bank.

. . . .

THE TRIGGER FOR the Crisis was a decision by the government of Thailand to allow its currency, the baht, to float. Thailand had kept the baht pegged to a basket of currencies, including the U.S. dollar. Currency traders, however, had been betting for months that the peg could not last; the dollar had been appreciating against other currencies. As the baht automatically strengthened with it, Thai exports became more expensive than those of its neighbors. The result was an increasing current account deficit—which means more money was flowing out of Thailand to pay for imports and other transactions than flowing in in the form of income on exports sold. Thai companies and banks, furthermore, had been borrowing heavily from overseas, and the country's foreign debt had expanded. International currency traders determined that this combination of factors would eventually force Thailand to allow the baht to depreciate. These traders helped speed matters along by shorting* baht, thus un-

---

* In "shorting," an investor signs a contract to trade currency in which he makes money if that currency depreciates.

dermining its value and putting further pressure on the Thai authorities to unpeg its currency.[6]

The Thai central bank furiously fought off the attacks and defended the value of the baht by selling dollars from its hard currency reserves. But by late June, the Thais had burned through nearly all of their $30 billion of reserves. Nearly bankrupt, the Thais threw in the towel. The day the government ended the peg—July 2, 1997—the baht lost more than 16 percent of its value.[7]

At the time, most experts believed that the decision would put an end to the Thais' problem. In Washington, U.S. Treasury Secretary Robert Rubin, a veteran of financial meltdowns from his experience with the collapse of the Mexican peso in 1994, thought that "after the country dealt with this disruption . . . healthy growth would return." The prospects for Asia were just too rosy, Rubin and others figured, for investors to lose confidence in the region overall and spread Thailand's difficulties to its neighbors.[8]

Such optimism proved misplaced. Currency traders assaulted Malaysia's ringgit, also linked to the dollar, as they had the baht, and the ringgit, too, began to lose value. Jittery foreign investors and international banks noticed that many other economies in the region shared the same imbalances and high debt as Thailand. They yanked out money by the billions. Indonesia's rupiah began to fall. By October, the virus hit South Korea. The financial community called the phenomenon "contagion." Like a virulent influenza, the Crisis spread from country to country.

. . . .

IN KUALA LUMPUR, Mahathir Mohamad was beside himself. The stock market was tanking, the currency sinking, and some of the country's most prominent corporations were spiraling toward bankruptcy. After sixteen years as prime minister, he believed his dream of a modern, industrialized Malaysia was in reach. Without warning, all of his hard work appeared to be vanishing. "No one seemed to understand what was happening," he later wrote.[9]

Mahathir came to his own conclusion: Greedy and unscrupulous currency speculators were behind the Crisis. He called them "rogues." "The currency manipulators with large amounts of borrowed funds were not interested in recognizing Malaysia's strength," he wrote. "They decided to make a profit on the back of this nebulous concept of contagion."[10] Mahathir placed special blame on American financier and democracy advocate George Soros, who he claimed was purposely undermining the currencies of Southeast Asian countries. "As much as people who produce and distribute drugs are criminals because they destroy nations, people who undermine the economies of poor countries [are too]," Mahathir ranted. "We spent our time building up these nations, trying to give our people a good life and trying to increase their income. But this man, in a matter of a few days, destroyed everything that we have done."[11]

Mahathir and Soros went head to head at the annual meeting of the World Bank and International Monetary Fund in Hong Kong in September 1997. Angry and bitter, Mahathir stood before the world's financial elite and issued a blistering rebuke. "It would seem that the old beggar-thy-neighbor instinct is still around, is still the guiding principle of a group of ultra-rich people," he blasted. "For them wealth must come from impoverishing others." The Crisis, he implied, was a concerted conspiracy by industrialized nations to undermine Asian economies that had become a threat to the dominance of the West.[12]

The next day, Soros took the same podium and fired right back. The source of Malaysia's problems was not some wild conspiracy, Soros said, but the faulty policies of Mahathir himself. "Dr. Mahathir is a menace to his own country," Soros said. "He is using me as a scapegoat to cover up his own failure." The *New York Times* quipped that Mahathir and Soros faced off "like gunfighters on a dust-blown street."[13] But behind the war of words was a very fundamental question: *Who really was to blame for the Crisis?*

Soros was expressing a view widely held within Western capitals, the International Monetary Fund, and the global financial community. The Crisis, the thinking went, was a result of misguided policymaking. Asian countries had embarked on expensive projects they could not afford, propped up weak and often politically connected companies, and, in the process, had taken on too much debt. The Tigers had made the mistake of intervening with market forces; their failings were, therefore, an outgrowth of the "Asian model." The Crisis erupted when free markets took hold and played the role of economic policeman. By fixing broken policies and punishing weak companies and banks, the international marketplace was scrubbing Asian economies clean and restoring them to health. This argument reflected the die-hard Western confidence in the sanctity of market forces.

Mahathir and some other Asian leaders believed the opposite. Asia's economies, they argued, were humming along before the Crisis hit. The disaster was caused when fickle foreign investors withdrew their support and their money. The supposedly poorly led Tiger economies and their equally inept corporations seemed perfectly sound investments only a few months before. What changed was not the real economic condition of Asia, but the perception of Asia among international financiers. The blame, therefore, should be fixed on the irrational behavior of the world's bankers and investors.

There is more than enough blame to pin on everyone involved. Both Asian policymakers and international financial institutions exhibited poor judgment that turned what should have been nothing more than a minor speed bump on the road of the Miracle into a region-wide catastrophe. The underlying cause of these mistakes was the same as in Japan—excessive optimism. The Miracle had been so miraculous that investors, executives, and government policymakers believed it would never end. Any project, any investment, no matter how outlandish, seemed a sure bet. As Robert Rubin later wrote, the large flows of capital into these emerging markets "were . . . a textbook example of the kind of speculative excesses that can take hold when investors become seized with some idea . . . and lose their discipline."[14]

The Tiger economies were, in fact, far riskier investments than most investors realized in the mid-1990s. Despite Mahathir's protests to the contrary, they had become riddled with imbalances and susceptible to outside shocks.[15] At the center of the problem were their financial sectors. Asian banks borrowed from overseas at a faster clip than their countries were stockpiling the currency reserves needed to pay down the loans, or they maintained a persistently high level of debt to available reserves, as in Indonesia.[16] They compounded the problem by lending these funds to local businessmen for ventures that proved uncompetitive and uneconomic. In Thailand, money rushed into speculative property development; in South Korea, funds were invested in excess manufacturing capacity. As these investments failed to generate profits, businessmen were not able to pay back their loans and the level of bad assets rose dangerously. When the external shock of the Crisis slammed into these fragile financial sectors, there was no cushion to buffer the blow.

Many of the Tigers' weaknesses were a legacy of the "Asian model." As in Japan, those close links between government and business and overbearing bureaucratic interference in the allocation of finance led to unproductive investments and unsustainable debt burdens. Even though by the 1990s the "Asian model" had undergone some reform—bureaucratic control was softened by liberalization—the practices and incentives the model had fostered, as in Japan, remained in place. Banks lent to politically connected companies simply because they always had, not because they were certain they would get paid back. Executives invested in the industrial capacity that their government overseers had always favored, whether it was profitable to do so or not. The result was a terminally ill Asian corporate sector. In South Korea, for example, the average debt-to-equity ratio at the thirty largest *chaebols* surpassed 300 percent by 1997; by contrast, American companies rarely maintain ratios of much more than 100 percent.

Meanwhile, the profits of these companies were practically non-existent. Thirteen of the thirty biggest Korean business groups lost money in 1997. Several went bankrupt in 1997 even before the Crisis hit Korea.[17] The problem with the "Asian model" was not the model itself, but the inability of Asia's policymakers to adapt it to new circumstances. What worked just fine when Asia was poor no longer had the same positive impact once its economies advanced. Then the state's meddling with markets hindered, not helped, development.

Still, whatever the defects of the "Asian model," the international financial community cannot escape criticism. As the saying goes, it takes two to tango, or, in this case, start a financial meltdown. If Asian banks and companies borrowed too heavily from abroad, someone, obviously, had to lend to them. Foreign bankers and investors, for all of their sanctimonious censure of Asian policy, had handed over billions of dollars to Asia before the Crisis. Once the Crisis began, these same foreign financial institutions withdrew that money at a fantastic pace. In 1996, $93 billion of foreign funds flowed into the five countries that the Crisis had the most impact on—South Korea, Thailand, Indonesia, Malaysia, and the Philippines; in 1997, $12 billion flowed out—a $105 billion swing. That represented some 11 percent of the GDP of those five countries. This mammoth shift in capital flows destabilized the region and made the Crisis much more severe than it otherwise should have been. Economists Steven Radelet and Jeffrey Sachs argued that panic by foreign investors and banks was as important a factor as, if not even more important than, suspect Asian policies and business practices in making the Crisis as disastrous as it became. "These imbalances [in Asian economies] were not severe enough to warrant a financial crisis of the magnitude that took place," they wrote. "The crisis is a testament to the shortcomings of the international capital markets and their vulnerability to sudden reversals of market confidence."[18]

Whatever blame deserves to be laid at the feet of the international financial community, Asian countries were forced to turn to this same community to stem the Crisis. The affected countries signed on for IMF-sponsored rescue packages—Thailand in August 1997 ($17 billion) and Indonesia in October ($43 billion). In return, their governments gave up control of their own economic policy and adopted a list of painful measures imposed by the IMF that, its economists believed, would restore confidence in their economies and halt the Crisis. These steps included hiking interest rates, slicing government budgets, and closing troubled banks. The policy gurus of Asia, once feted for their wisdom, ingenuity, and success, became the IMF's paper-pushers.

· · · ·

NOT MAHATHIR MOHAMAD, however. As the Malaysian economy continued to crumble, he became only more recalcitrant. In October 1997, he returned to one of his favorite subjects—the Jews. "We may suspect that [the Jews] have an agenda," he said while addressing villagers in Malaysia. "The Jews robbed the Palestinians of everything, but in Malaysia they could not do so, hence they do this, depress the ringgit."[19] His tirades did little to improve investor sentiment. A not-so-funny joke circulated that every time Mahathir opened his mouth, the ringgit's value fell further. Still, Mahathir resisted an IMF bailout. "We were not willing to surrender the management of our economy to the IMF," Mahathir later wrote. His position, he realized, was making Malaysia "a pariah nation to be avoided by everyone," but if East Asia succumbed to the dictates of foreigners, he believed, "the 21st century was not going to be the Asian Century."[20]

Mahathir's stubbornness was not just hubris. He had real concerns about the benefits of IMF programs. Anwar Ibrahim, the finance minister, had adopted similar policies to those advocated by the IMF to try to shore up the ringgit, including raising interest rates, restricting credit, and toughening accounting standards at Malaysian banks. Anwar even put some of Mahathir's beloved megaprojects on hold. Yet by early 1998, Mahathir believed these policies, which he derisively called a "virtual IMF" program, were making matters worse. The high interest rates and tight credit squeezed the private sector to the choking point, while consumption cuts further depressed growth. "The sum effect of all the measures . . . was that the banks and businesses which were already suffering from the currency crisis were pushed into a situation of due distress," Mahathir wrote. "Malaysia's economy plunged deeper in recession."

Mahathir and Anwar began to clash over the direction of policy. Anwar insisted his course was the right way to end the Crisis. Mahathir was rankled that the ringgit and stock market were still plunging despite Anwar's harsh policies. He wanted to ease credit and boost consumption to relieve the pressure on Malaysian companies and banks.[21] Simultaneously, Mahathir came under intense pressure from the international financial community to succumb to the IMF. Washington officials and international bankers had an evangelical faith in the sanctity of IMF expertise. Openly condemning the IMF, as Mahathir was doing, was a major affront to investor confidence.

Since then, however, this steadfast belief in the omnipotence of the IMF has wavered, to a great degree due to the fund's handling of the Crisis. New thinking has emerged that, in certain ways, Mahathir was correct. By deflating economies, the IMF tightened the already viselike grip strangling the private sector and made the Crisis and the resulting recession much worse than they had to be. The astronomical interest rates and demand-squashing measures mandated by IMF programs reduced revenues to companies while fattening their debt burden, shoving perfectly viable firms to the edge of a financial abyss.

How did the IMF go so wrong? Call it institutional inertia. The IMF imposed measures on Asia that were ideologically predetermined and applied without adapting them to the real problems facing Asian economies. Some conditions mandated by the IMF had nothing to do with the underlying causes of the Crisis and were unlikely to solve it—for example, forcing governments to liberalized import regulations and end domestic monopolies. The IMF was issuing prescriptions for the wrong disease. By focusing attention on the supposed structural flaws of Asian economies, the IMF also further undermined investor confidence in the region. Yet despite the mounting evidence that its policies were not working as designed, the IMF stuck to its agenda. "The IMF itself had become a part of the countries' problems rather than part of the solution," Joseph Stiglitz, chief economist at the World Bank during the Crisis, later wrote.[22]

Back in 1997, however, Mahathir was isolated, searching for his own way out of Malaysia's Crisis. He discovered one possible solution in an unlikely place: China. The Communist giant had remained unfazed by the Crisis. Mahathir noted that the country had an aspect to its economic structure absent from Malaysia, Thailand, and Indonesia—strict controls on capital flows and currency trading. Could this be the answer? He realized he did not understand enough about currency markets to know for sure. "I had this idea that money flowing out of the country means people carrying bags of money," he says. While on an official visit to Argentina in October 1997, Mahathir invited a Malaysian central banker to join him in Buenos Aires to give him a briefing on global currency markets. He realized that the speculators' trades were just marked in the books of the foreign institutions and local banks. Those stacks of ringgit he envisioned changing hands across the border never existed. The government, he figured, may not be able to control the speculators—but if Malaysian banks could be prevented from engaging in currency transactions, the speculators would be helpless. Mahathir decided Malaysia needed capital controls.

He proposed this idea to his policy team.[23] Everyone was opposed, including Anwar and Daim, who rejoined the government as an advisor and then a special minister in the cabinet. "We gave him forty reasons why it shouldn't be done," Daim says.[24] They feared that the foreign investors the country needed to sustain its

growth would flee. There was a chance the move would precipi-
tate total economic collapse.[25] In an era in which liberal financial
regimes were considered an absolute good, Mahathir's capital
controls idea was heresy. "We are going against the whole world,"
Mahathir realized.[26]

Mahathir stood his ground, however. "He was quite adamant,"
Daim recalls. For six months, the economic team wrangled over
capital controls. Daim eventually came around to Mahathir's
thinking, to a great degree by default. All other steps had failed
to stem the Crisis. "There was no option in the end. We had tried
everything," Daim says.[27]

On September 1, 1998, Mahathir took the plunge. The trading
of ringgit offshore was banned. Foreigners holding ringgit could
use it only for local transactions. Ringgit held outside of the country was worthless. The controls were not overly strict—foreign
investors who wanted to repatriate profits or sell assets could still
take their money out of the country. For these purposes, the ringgit was fixed at 3.8 to the U.S. dollar, one-third below its pre-
Crisis level.[28]

Mahathir's decision created outrage at home and abroad. The
governor of the central bank, never supportive of the idea, resigned.[29] Internationally, Malaysia became a leper. The *Wall Street
Journal* labeled the capital controls policy a "massive miscalcula-
tion" and warned that Malaysia "appears destined to spend an
unhappy period stumbling in the dark."[30]

The most powerful opponent of the controls was Anwar Ibrahim, the finance minister. Mahathir and Anwar had continued
to spar over the direction of Malaysia's Crisis policy, and the disagreement widened a rift between them. Anwar had been a protégé
of Mahathir's since the mid-1980s, and he was widely seen as the
most likely successor to the aging prime minister. Anwar, though,
was a much different personality than his mentor. An internation-
alist and intellectual, Anwar was considered a more democratic
figure than the heavy-handed Mahathir. He also possessed softer

views toward the West.[31] The two still somehow remained so close that Mahathir put Anwar in charge of the government when the prime minister took a two-month sabbatical in mid-1997.[32] By the time of the Crisis, Anwar was the most influential politician in the country, save for Mahathir himself.

As the Crisis deepened, however, a full-fledged contest for control ensued between the two men. Anwar says his break with Mahathir came over bailouts of companies. Some of the worst-affected corporations were those that had benefited from Mahathir's policies, such as Halim Saad's Renong and other politically connected firms. Mahathir and Anwar disagreed over how to handle these troubled companies. Anwar believed that the firms and their managers should take their lumps and be allowed to fail. Mahathir argued that corporate Malaysia was heading for disaster not of its own making and government support was necessary to preserve it. "Companies that can survive should be helped to survive," he says.[33] Beginning in late 1997, a series of financial deals raised cries among Mahathir's critics that he was bailing out his friends. In one controversial case in 1998, a state firm purchased the shipping assets of a debt-laden company controlled by Mahathir's son.[34] The situation became "unmanageable," Anwar says.[35] (Mahathir denies that there were any special favors granted by the government, adding that he personally did not have "one single cent" in any firm that got aid.)[36]

As the Crisis ate away at Malaysia's economy, public sentiment began turning against Mahathir. Anwar took advantage. He and his supporters believed that more than sound economic policy was needed to stem the Crisis. Malaysia required political reform as well, including a crackdown on corruption and improvements in civil rights.[37] The vulnerable Mahathir was aware that if he did not solve the Crisis, his long reign over Malaysia would end. "My job was on the line," he says.[38]

The battle between the two men burst into the public arena in UMNO meetings in June 1998. On the conference's first day, an Anwar loyalist gave a blistering speech denouncing corruption within the party—a not-so-veiled assault on Mahathir. But Mahathir's faction came well prepared. UMNO delegates received booklets titled *50 Reasons Why Anwar Cannot Become Prime Minister*. Included in the list were long-running accusations that Anwar engaged in sexual impropriety, including an illicit affair with his family's male chauffeur. Anwar's rebellion was squashed. Mahathir survived the meeting in control of UMNO.

The matter did not rest there. On September 2, one day after the announcement of capital controls, Anwar says Mahathir confronted him with a choice—resign or get sacked. Anwar refused to submit.[39] "You are obsolete in many of your views," he says he told Mahathir.[40] Later that day, Mahathir fired Anwar from his ministerial posts. That, however, only elevated Anwar's public standing as the champion of *reformasi*, a Malay word signifying political and social democratization. Protests against Mahathir broke out onto the streets of Kuala Lumpur. On September 20, Anwar spoke before a crowd of eighty thousand and demanded Mahathir's resignation. That same night, police kicked down the front door to Anwar's home and whisked him away while helicopters swirled overhead.[41] Anwar claims he was then handcuffed, blindfolded, and beaten until he passed out. Nine days later, Anwar appeared in court with a badly bruised black eye.[42] He was charged with abuse of power and sodomy, both of which he denied. That made little difference. Anwar was found guilty on both charges and sentenced to fifteen years in prison.[43]*

In the end, Mahathir's heretical economic policies were vindicated. The capital controls he devised stemmed the collapse of the currency and the economy began to revive.[44] "The objective fact is that whatever you think of Mahathir, Malaysia has gotten away with its economic apostasy," wrote Paul Krugman. "You can question whether that apostasy was necessary, but you cannot claim that it has been a disaster—and you cannot disguise the fact that those who predicted disaster were letting politics and ideology

---

* *Anwar, eventually vindicated in 2004, was freed from prison and the guilty verdict on the sodomy charge against him was overturned.*

cloud their judgment."[45] Even the IMF admitted the wisdom of the move. One year after controls were imposed, the IMF announced "that the regime of capital controls . . . had produced more positive results than many observers had initially expected."[46]

. . . .

IN INDONESIA, SUHARTO was fighting for his political life as well. By late October 1997, the Indonesian rupiah had lost a third of its value in only four months. Confidence in the economy continued to dwindle. Suharto looked to the Mafia for guidance. He put Widjojo Nitisastro, the old chief of the Mafia, in charge of overseeing the negotiations with the IMF and implementing a reform program.[47] The agreement for a rescue package, reached on October 31, committed Suharto to drastic and mandatory reforms, including cutting the budget, liberalizing trade, ending certain monopolies, and liquidating troubled banks.[48] Widjojo had saved Indonesia in a time of crisis again and again, much to the betterment of Suharto's New Order, but this time he put his boss in a politically impossible position. If Suharto implemented the IMF reforms, they would eat away at the patronage networks underpinning his regime and sabotage the business interests of his family and cronies. On the other hand, if he dragged his feet, he would be unable to rebuild confidence in the economy, the Crisis would worsen, and that, too, could destabilize the New Order. The highly personalized nature of Suharto's rule was coming to haunt him. He chose a middle course that satisfied no one—to talk reform while protecting those close to him. In one especially embarrassing case, the government shut a failing bank controlled by Suharto's son Bambang called Bank Andromeda only to allow him to acquire another bank and effectively reopen under a different corporate name, simply switching the signs on the office doors.[49]

The consequences for dodging the IMF's reforms were severe. On January 8, concerns that the IMF would punish Suharto by cutting off support sent the rupiah plunging 26 percent.[50] That same day, U.S. President Bill Clinton called Suharto to urge him to work with the IMF, specifically mentioning the sleight of hand with Bambang's bank. Suharto did not heed Clinton's advice and responded with a rant about foreign "speculators" depressing the rupiah.[51] Nevertheless, on January 15, with the pressure mounting, Suharto signed another accord with the IMF that demanded even stiffer reforms. The IMF stipulated that the government dismantle his son Tommy's controversial clove monopoly and Bob Hasan's plywood cartel, and cease all state aid for Habibie's prized, but subsidized, airplane maker.[52]

Despite the growing turmoil, a controlled convention voted Suharto to his seventh term as president in March 1998. The cabinet he selected showed his oblivion to the precarious position of his regime. It included one of his unpopular business-minded daughters and his favorite crony, Bob Hasan, as trade minister. Suharto had been nagging Hasan to become a minister for the previous two decades, but Hasan had always turned him down. "I am your crony," he told Suharto, "so it's not right that I become a minister." That March, however, Hasan changed his mind. "I felt that he needed my help. I felt I had to stand by him as a friend," Hasan says.[53]

It was a disastrous decision. Hasan's appointment further fueled criticism of Suharto at home and abroad. He dissolved the controversial cabinet. Massive protests against the New Order began to fill the streets of Jakarta led by university students—ironically, the same group that had brought Suharto to power in 1966. Now they vented their ire at Suharto and demanded his resignation. The protests degenerated into violence. On May 12, six students were killed when police opened fire on protestors from Jakarta's Trisakti University.[54] Two days later, a mob took out their fury on the Chinese minority, resented for the wealth and power they commanded under the New Order, by ransacking Jakarta's Chinatown, looting and burning buildings. Journalist Mark Landler of the *New York Times* reported Chinatown "looked as if it had been bombed, with debris piled high on the

sidewalks and charred hulks of cars, trucks and motorcycles forming a grim obstacle course on the main street."[55]

The chaos finally convinced Suharto that his regime was
coming to an end, but he did not move quickly enough. On May
19, he met with nine leading Islamic figures and presented a plan
for holding new elections and gradually handing over power. Their
response was firm. "What everyone understands to be reform
is that you step down," they told him.[56] The next day, Habibie,
then the country's vice president, appeared at Suharto's home for
their daily evening meeting. He found Suharto in his office with a
large sheet of paper; he was selecting ministers for a new cabinet.
The two debated over the appointments. Then Suharto dropped
a bombshell. After the cabinet was sworn in, Suharto intended to
resign from the presidency. As Habibie departed, Suharto hugged
him and then said: "There's not much time left." Habibie prayed
on the drive back to his residence.[57]

There was a lot less time than either of them thought. Over the
course of that day, the pressure on Suharto grew to an unbear-
able level. The speaker of parliament threatened to start impeach-
ment proceedings if Suharto had not resigned within two days,
and the commander of the armed forces convened a meeting of
top generals who recommended Suharto step down. The pillars of
Suharto's regime had crumbled.[58]

On May 21, 1998, the New Order ended in a brief, subdued
ceremony. Wearing a gold government employee pin, Suharto
slipped on a pair of glasses and read a prepared statement that announced his resignation after thirty years as president. "I am sorry
for my mistakes," he said, "and I hope the Indonesian country
will live forever." He gave a small salute to the assembled officials
and journalists, then departed.[59] When Bob Hasan asked Suharto
why he decided to resign, he answered that he feared even more
violence in the unstable nation. "It is better that I get hurt than the
students," he told Hasan.[60]

A short time later, Emil Salim, Suharto's long-serving economic
advisor, visited the former president's home. Salim found Suharto

disillusioned, still perplexed about why his reign, with all of its tremendous economic achievements, had collapsed in such acrimony and embarrassment. "Is there something we did wrong?" Suharto asked Salim. The wise economist knew what had happened. Suharto had clung to power for too long. Salim could not bring himself to say that to his old friend. Instead, Salim simply answered: "Times have changed."[61]

. . . .

KOREA, HOWEVER, PRESENTED the biggest threat to the global financial order. Korea was not only the largest Asian economy to fall into the Crisis, it was also tightly woven into international capital markets and manufacturing systems. Robert Rubin, the U.S. Treasury secretary, woke to the seriousness of the situation in late November 1997, shortly after the Korean government had called in the IMF for a rescue. IMF officials discovered Korea's central bank had burned through nearly all of its $30 billion in reserves to help Korean commercial banks cover their foreign debts. The revelation "ushered in a period of grave danger for the world economy," Rubin later wrote.

He decided Washington had to act. Throughout Thanksgiving Day in 1997, Rubin held a series of intense conference calls with President Bill Clinton, National Security Advisor Sandy Berger, and officials from the Federal Reserve to formulate a policy response. Secretary of State Madeleine Albright basted a turkey in the middle of one conversation. Rubin feared that the loss of investor confidence in South Korea could spread well beyond Asia to Russia, Eastern Europe, the entire developing world. He argued that the United States should put together its own funds to support the Korean economy, beyond what the IMF would offer. But those funds alone, he argued, would not solve the problem. In return for a rescue, Rubin intended to force the Korean government into a far-reaching reform program. As they continued to talk in coming days, Rubin's view hardened.

Korea, he believed, needed to end government-directed lending by commercial banks and open the economy up to more
competition and foreign investment.[62] In other words, Rubin
aimed to dismantle Korea's "Asian model."

Would the Korean government go for it? On December 3, the
Koreans inked a $58 billion rescue deal with the IMF, its largest
bailout ever. The government had accepted—reluctantly—most
of the policy measures Rubin had demanded. But, as in Thailand,
the program did little to ease the Crisis. After a few days' respite,
the won resumed its downward plunge. About $1 billion of for-
eign currency was flowing out of Korea *every day*.[63]

A big part of the problem was political uncertainty. With a
presidential election in Korea days away, the administration
that signed the IMF deal was not going to remain in office much
longer. Kim Dae Jung was the front-runner, and he was not inspiring confidence. He sounded much like Mahathir, and the won,
like the ringgit, was suffering as a result. In early December, Kim
told voters he would "surmount the IMF humiliation." If elected,
he promised to "pursue new negotiations with the IMF in order
to regain our economic autonomy."[64] The international financial
community trembled, but voters in South Korea elected Kim on
December 18, an amazing feat in itself. Democracy was still new
in South Korea, and the fact that a free election was held amid the
country's Crisis was a testament to how quickly democratic ideals
had taken hold. For Kim Dae Jung, the victory crowned three decades of sacrifice and struggle. His reward, however, was to step
into the Blue House at the country's lowest point since the Korean
War. "I was lamenting my fate," he says.[65]

Korea's economic situation worsened after his election and the
value of the won reached new lows. With some $15 billion in for-
eign loans coming due by late December, the possibility that Korea
would default or impose a moratorium on debt payments became
real. Kim warned the public that Korea "may go bankrupt."[66]
However, now in power, he woke up to the turmoil caused by his
campaign rhetoric and, in contrast to Mahathir, began moderat-

ing his views toward the IMF. After his election, Kim received a congratulatory phone call from President Bill Clinton, who used the opportunity to press Kim to reform the economy. Kim promised to work closely with the IMF. "If there is any necessary action we need to take, we will take it," Kim told Clinton. "Don't worry about it."[67]

The worrying in Washington only intensified, however. Rubin came to the conclusion that Korea required drastic action. He cobbled together the outline of a dramatic plan. The IMF, United States, and other countries would rush emergency funds to Korea to shore up confidence while private banks would roll over their loans to stave off a default. This complex maneuver was not assured of success. With Korea's creditors stretched across the globe, convincing enough banks and governments to participate in Rubin's scheme was a Herculean task. As compensation, Rubin insisted that Korea promise even more painful and fundamental reforms. That meant extracting a pledge from Kim Dae Jung, even though his inauguration was still two months away, since any agreement with the outgoing administration was effectively meaningless. Rubin dispatched Treasury official David Lipton to Seoul to sound out the president-elect's willingness to accept Washington's plan.

Kim was wise enough to realize Lipton had come to test him. "If my policies sounded hopeful, the U.S. would support and help Korea," Kim knew, "but if not, [the U.S.] would have left Korea to go bankrupt." Kim promised Lipton he would open up the economy to foreign firms and convince Korea's powerful labor unions to allow big companies to restructure. Most of all, Kim assured Lipton he would cut the close relationships among government, business, and finance that were a legacy of Park Chung Hee's MITI-style economic system. "I will sever the collusive ties between politicians and businesses so that there would not be any corrupt activities," Kim says he told Lipton. In short, he vowed to dismantle the "Asian model." Lipton emerged from the meeting encouraged that Kim intended to pursue the reform plan Rubin wanted.[68]

With Kim on board, Rubin had to convince foreign governments to accelerate their promised loans to Korea. His deputy, Larry Summers, worked the phones, lobbying his counterparts in Europe and Japan to build support for the Korea rescue. "We must have set some kind of record that holiday for disturbing the slumber of finance ministers and central bankers all over the world," Rubin wrote. The effort paid off. On Christmas Eve, the IMF, United States, and twelve other countries[69] announced they would rush $10 billion of loans to Korea by early January.[70] Kim called it "a Christmas gift."[71]

The last piece of the package was the trickiest. A massive international effort, led to a great degree by the Federal Reserve Bank of New York and Rubin's Treasury department, was undertaken to coordinate a multibillion-dollar restructuring of Korea's foreign debt in which the world's major banks would collectively roll over their loans to the country. From a conference table in Summers's office, Rubin tracked down executives at U.S. banks on their winter holidays to convince them to join the rollover arrangement. William McDonough, president of the Federal Reserve of New York, convened a meeting of bank chiefs in his office and impressed upon them that such an agreement would benefit the financial position of the banks and their shareholders. This task was delicate. Rubin and McDonough had to be careful not to be seen as abusing their authority. "I had to be persuasive about the banks' collective self-interest . . . without overstepping an uncertain line," Rubin later wrote.

In the end, Rubin's plan worked. Korea's currency and stock markets began to stabilize. The international banking community agreed to restructure $24 billion in Korean external debt in January, all of which got paid back. The worst, at least for Korea, was over.[72]

· · · ·

AS KIM DAE Jung fought to save Korea, Kim Woo Choong at Daewoo acted as if there were nothing unusual happening. On

January 1, 1998, he outlined his vision for the future in a company newsletter. "Daewoo will overcome the crisis through expansionist measures," he wrote. "We cannot embrace the future if we flinch at a time of recession." He was a man of his word. A month earlier, Daewoo had absorbed a failed Korean automaker, Ssangyong Motor, from a competing *chaebol*. Kim had also just finalized a contract with Ukraine's AvtoZAZ to form a $1.3 billion automaking joint venture. "We are in a better position than others," Kim said confidently in his office at the top of Seoul's Hilton Hotel, which he also owned.[73]

Not everyone agreed. The *Wall Street Journal* warned Kim's strategy "may risk corporate suicide."[74] The *chaebols*, with their penchant for overinvestment and monstrous, debt-heavy projects—fostered by the practices of the "Asian model"—were being criticized inside and outside Korea as the main culprits of the country's Crisis. All of the big *chaebols* were scaling back. Over at Hyundai, Chung Ju Yung postponed the construction of a coveted steel mill,[75] while the motor company eventually laid off 25 percent of its workforce.[76] The *chaebols* had no option. Korean banks, strapped for cash, were reluctant to lend, while the loss of external financing combined with the high interest rates and tight monetary policies imposed by the IMF sent the economy into recession.

Meanwhile, Kim Dae Jung kept his promise to Rubin and went to work reforming the "Asian model." On January 13, he had breakfast with the leaders of four top *chaebols*, who promised to improve their accounting practices, cut debt, and shed affiliates. Kim Woo Choong, however, made no such promises. He was away on business and missed the meeting.[77] While Hyundai and other big *chaebols* publicly announced major reforms of their finances and structure, Daewoo made only token gestures toward abiding by Kim Dae Jung's policies. Kim Woo Choong's mistake was that he saw the Crisis as just another trifling annoyance in Daewoo's ascent to world greatness, not a fundamental shift in the entire way the Korean economy operated.

The reason was Kim's unrelenting optimism, which was a natural outgrowth of his amazing life story. Born in Taegu in December 1936, Kim, like Chung Ju Yung, was a self-made entrepreneur, a poor boy who succeeded through hard work and political connections. During the Korean War, his father, a teacher, was kidnapped by the North Koreans. At a mere fourteen years old, Kim became responsible for feeding his mother and two younger brothers. He sold newspapers in the local Taegu market, but, like many Koreans at the time, the family had little to eat. "On some days I had only a few extra coins to give the family for the day's meals," Kim later wrote. After the war, the intelligent Kim attended prestigious Yonsei University in Seoul, where he studied economics. The campus was six miles from his house, a trek that took him two hours. "I did not have a single coin in my pocket, but I had dreams," he later wrote. "I still cannot forget the feeling that would come over me when I stepped out of the library late at night, or when I looked up at the sky on the long trudge home. . . . There was nothing that could stop me."

In 1967, Kim and four colleagues raised $10,000 and started a company in a small room in a corner of a Seoul office building. He called it the Daewoo Industrial Company. The name was a sign of his ambition. "Daewoo" in Korean means "great universe." At first the firm exported clothing; later he set up factories to manufacture his own products. From an office in New York, Kim made sales calls personally, often knocking on doors with his sample cases without appointments. "Instead of seeing three or four customers a day, I could see ten," he once said. Kim's big break came, like Chung Ju Yung's, from his close connection to Park Chung Hee. Park had been a student of Kim's father while in school in Taegu. In 1976, the government asked Kim to take over a debt-ridden machinery factory that had been losing money for thirty-seven years. Kim slept and ate in the factory for months trying to figure out what was wrong. He determined the problem was an unproductive workforce. Unable to survive on their regular wages, the staff purposely slowed down the factory's output to charge the company for overtime. "The machinery was turning, but it wasn't producing anything," Kim recalled. Kim struck a deal with the workers—higher pay for greater productivity. The factory quickly turned to profit, and it became the base for Daewoo Heavy Industries.

That success opened the way to more government-backed deals. Kim convinced the government to allow him to purchase 50 percent of a car company partially owned by General Motors. He eventually bought out GM, and the carmaker became Daewoo Motor. In 1978, Park's government asked Kim to take on a financially troubled shipyard. The job was too perilous even for Kim, and he turned the offer down. Such niceties never concerned Park. The government simply waited for Kim to leave town on a business trip and then announced the transfer to Daewoo in his absence. The company became one of Daewoo's most important businesses.

By 1997, Daewoo had become a sprawling global enterprise. Kim made cars, ships, electronics, trucks, telecom equipment, and machinery. The group brokered stocks, managed hotels, and built highways. Along the way, Kim had made some highly risky investments. He opened a tire factory in the Sudan, built railways in Iran during the Iran-Iraq War, and completed $10 billion of construction projects in Libya. Journalist Louis Kraar compared Kim to Andrew Carnegie and John D. Rockefeller. He even penned his own management guide, *Every Street Is Paved with Gold,* a compendium of homilies and down-home advice on the secrets of making money and building businesses. "When others start counting the impossibilities, I start counting the possibilities," Kim wrote.[78]

In the mid-1990s, Daewoo Motor went on an expansion binge perhaps unseen in the history of the global car industry. His strategy was to penetrate emerging markets with great potential but few competitors. Factories went up in Iran, Vietnam, and India. In 1995, Kim outbid GM to forge a $1.1 billion joint venture with a Polish state auto company. Daewoo even opened a plant in Uzbekistan (where he invested so much money that the country became nicknamed "Daewooistan").[79] Though his plans were fantastically risky, many skeptics were won over. Kim would wax on for hours, bursting with enthusiasm, about the untapped customers, the high growth potential, and his sleek new models. Unlike Chung at Hyundai and other *chaebol* chiefs, who became imperial and secretive, Kim remained the unpretentious, hustling apparel salesman. He could often be found chatting on a mobile phone by himself on the streets near Seoul's City Hall or in the lobby of the Hilton.

The reality, however, was that Kim's emerging-markets strategy was flawed. He was building large factories in countries with growing but still low income levels. "I tried to do in five years what usually took 10 to 15 years," Kim once explained. "To gain economies of scale we made investments without the markets' being there and then had to find ways to sell the cars." It was a classic case of "Asian model" overinvestment. Debt-financed factories were built too quickly and too big; they then achieved poor returns and required more loans to keep them going. Kim amassed $20 billion of debt from his automobile expansion alone. When the Crisis hit Korea, Daewoo's debt load became unsustainable. Yet Kim refused to change course. His car ventures, he believed, were too far along to delay or cancel.

As his financial position weakened, Kim kept expecting the government to step in and bail him out. He was especially confident due to his close relationship with Kim Dae Jung.[80] Upon entering office, the new president recommended Daewoo's Kim to head the Federation of Korean Industries, the powerful *chaebol* business association, and invited him to monthly meetings of his economic advisors. Kim Woo Choong, the president believed, could help him guide the country through the Crisis.[81] After a few months, however, these sessions deteriorated into shouting matches between Daewoo's Kim and the president's economic team. "They blamed everything on overborrowing by companies," Kim Woo Choong later said of the government's policymakers. "This was a financial crisis, not an industrial crisis. In this emergency we needed short-term government help."[82] The president, though, stuck to his reform program.

Daewoo's Kim looked for another white knight. He turned to General Motors. The two companies signed a memorandum of understanding in February 1998 in which GM agreed to purchase a stake in Daewoo Motor. Kim expected as much as $7 billion.[83] The Daewoo chief begged the president for more time to restructure his group. The money from GM would save the day, he insisted. An annoyed Kim Dae Jung gave him until October.[84]

By September, the negotiations with GM had stalled, with the two parties unable to agree on a valuation of Daewoo's car operations. With no place else to turn, Daewoo borrowed more money. In 1998, Daewoo companies issued over $10 billion in short-term corporate notes in Korea. Their overall debt increased by 40 percent.[85] The government began to worry about the danger the collapse of Daewoo could pose to the financial system. In a confidential 1998 report, Kim Dae Jung's economic advisors warned that Daewoo's operating profits could barely cover its interest payments.

In early 1999, Kim Woo Choong grasped the true scale of the financial catastrophe he had created. In March, consolidated financial reports revealed Daewoo was close to bankruptcy.[86] Kim Dae Jung was not only altering the government's relationship with big business, he was also forcing market-oriented reforms onto the financial sector. In return for taxpayer money to buy up bad loans and strengthen balance sheets, banks were held to strict capital requirements. The government stopped meddling in bank management and ordered them to install independent directors and audit committees to monitor lending practices.[87] The banks were, therefore, no longer conduits of government-directed funds to the *chaebols* as they had been since Park Chung Hee's days. Kim Woo Choong could not count on the unquestioning support of Korean financial institutions as he had in the past. The cash flow to Daewoo reversed. In the first half of 1999 alone, creditors demanded payment on $5 billion of Daewoo bonds.[88] New funds were harder and harder for Daewoo to attract, even at the 30 percent yields then common on corporate bonds.[89] "All the world's financial institutions were asking us to pay," Kim said later, "but there was no way."[90]

Daewoo had entered its death throes. In April, a subdued Kim Woo Choong announced a sweeping reform plan in which he promised to sell off affiliates, including his prized shipyard. It was too little, too late. In July, Daewoo appealed to its creditors for help. They promised to roll over some debt and extend $3 billion of new loans in return for fresh collateral, including $1 billion of Kim's personal fortune. Even that was not enough. In mid-August, Daewoo's creditors, many of them state-owned, voted to break up Daewoo and sell off most of the pieces. Kim vowed to the public that he would resolve Daewoo's woes and "retire in honor."[91]

That, too, was not to be. Kim clashed with the bankers sent into Daewoo's companies by its creditors to oversee the restructuring plan. "Those bankers promised to leave our companies operating but didn't know much about anything except collecting money," he said.[92] Daewoo executives were torn between the dictates from the bankers and their loyalty to Kim. Government technocrats, who hoped a smooth restructuring would soften the impact on the economy, became impatient with Kim.[93]

Kim Dae Jung intervened. He began to realize that nothing would change at Daewoo until its companies came under new management and became more independent. The president phoned Kim Woo Choong and suggested "it would be better for you to leave the nation" and allow the break-up of Daewoo to proceed unhindered. "Even though it was not his right to intervene, [Kim Woo Choong] continued to be involved in the restructuring, and eventually it did not go smoothly," Kim Dae Jung says.[94] Shortly thereafter, in October 1999, Kim Woo Choong visited the town of Yantai in China for the opening of three auto-parts factories—and did not return home. "In the Orient, face is very important," Kim explained to *Fortune* magazine. "So if I made Daewoo bankrupt, how could I meet people?" In November, he sent an emotional farewell address to Daewoo employees, in which he said Daewoo's problems had left him "feeling pains with my entire body."[95] With that, he vanished.

The Asian Crisis hit all of its victims hard, but some recovered more quickly than others.

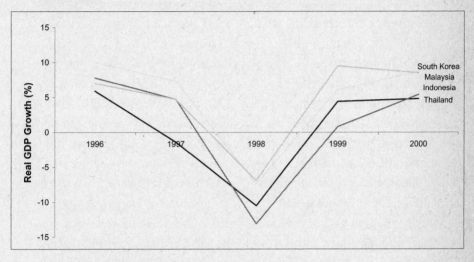

Source: International Monetary Fund.

. . . .

THE CRISIS TOOK a terrible toll on Asia. In 1998, the economy of South Korea contracted by nearly 7 percent. Thailand's shrank by more than 10 percent and Indonesia's by a staggering 13 percent. Unemployment tripled in Thailand, quadrupled in South Korea, and skyrocketed tenfold in Indonesia. Suharto's astonishing record of alleviating poverty was thrown backward, as the number of Indonesians living in poverty doubled.[96] Hopelessness gripped the continent. The Miracle seemed doomed.

But it was not. The economies of Korea and Malaysia returned to solid growth as quickly as they had tumbled. Thailand eventually staged a strong comeback as well. Only Indonesia retained the scars of the Crisis for the next decade. Because of poor policy and widespread corruption, foreign investment and growth in Indonesia did not return to pre-Crisis levels until 2007. Other high-growth Asian countries remained generally untouched by the Crisis, especially China and India.

The Miracle lived on, and the Daewoo debacle provides the reason why. The Crisis swept away the bad debts, overbearing bureaucrats, white-elephant projects, and egotistical management created by the "Asian model." Though elements of the "Asian model" remain, enough free-market reform has taken place to allow the Tigers to reach a new level of development, with stronger financial systems, more profitable companies, and better regulation and risk management. Even many of the pieces of Daewoo, financially restructured and under new management, sprang back to vivid life. Daewoo's shipyard remains one of the world's most competitive, while GM eventually absorbed parts of Daewoo Motor. Kim Woo Choong's failure represented the most dramatic event in a period of painful reform that set the stage for the Miracle's continuation.

For Kim Woo Choong, however, the Crisis was truly an end. After fleeing Korea, Kim checked himself into a hospital near Frankfurt to get treatment for a heart ailment. He cut off all contact with Korea, not even reading Korean newspapers or speaking with his wife back in Seoul. After several months in the hospital, he moved into a small apartment. A Vietnamese chef from the Daewoo Hotel in Hanoi cooked his meals. At the end of 2000, he turned up in Sudan. The goodwill his tire factory created paid big returns. Omar Hassan Ahmad al-Bashir gave Kim a house, secretary, and chauffeured car.[97]

After some further wandering in Asia and Europe, in June 2005, after six years in exile, Kim Woo Choong returned to Korea. It was a true act of contrition, knowing full well that prosecution awaited him. Police and protestors holding banners that read "Punish the Thief" greeted him at the airport.[98] In a handwritten statement, Kim admitted that he was "entirely responsible for imposing a burden on the national economy." To explain his return, he invoked a Korean proverb: "An old fox looks homeward when it is about to die."[99]

In May 2006, Kim was found guilty of accounting fraud and embezzlement, sentenced to ten years in prison and ordered to forfeit $23 billion in penalties.[100] He was pardoned in 2007 by South Korea President Roh Moo Hyun.[101]

CHAPTER TWELVE

A FISH JUMPS THROUGH THE DRAGON GATE

I had a strong vision in my mind that we could do something to make this country a better country. —LIU CHUANZHI

Liu Chuanzhi's phone rang in late 2004 with news that would rock the global economy. On the other end was Mary Ma, chief financial officer of Chinese PC maker Lenovo. She had been negotiating intensively with IBM for more than four months to acquire the American company's PC division. The talks had been arduous, but over the previous few weeks, Liu's excitement had been mounting as Ma ironed out the last remaining details. Ma phoned to tell Liu, Lenovo's chairman and founder, that the final sticking point—concerning intellectual property rights—had been resolved. "The road is clear," she said.

Liu's mind was already preoccupied with the challenges ahead. For Liu, the IBM acquisition was the crowning achievement of two decades of devotion, relentless work, bare-knuckled competition, and flashes of well-timed ingenuity that had built Lenovo from a minor start-up to China's largest PC company. The IBM deal would transform the Chinese outfit, still little known outside of its home nation, into the world's third-largest computer maker. In 1985, when Lenovo was only one year old, its main business was selling IBM PCs in China. Liu recalls attending a conference IBM held for its distributors at the ritzy Great Wall Sheraton Hotel in Beijing. Liu did not have a suit to wear, so he borrowed one from his father. His most vivid memory of the conference was the cookies IBM lavishly served to the participants. In those early days of Chinese reform, luxuries like cookies were rare. "I was startled that this company was so big it could afford so many cookies!" Liu recalls. "I never thought I'd ever sit at the same table as IBM."[1] Only twenty years later, he owned that very company.

The acquisition's significance was even more monumental for China. Liu placed the IBM deal in the context of the previous two hundred years of Chinese history—the humiliations China suffered at the hands of Western imperialists, the civil wars, the harsh days of hard-core Communism, the miserable reputation of China in the global economy. Now all that was in the past. China was in the ascendancy, and Liu's PC company was leading the way.

Lenovo's acquisition got the world's attention. No other single event better encapsulated the rising fortunes of China and the shifting roles of China and the United States in the global economy. IBM, after all, was American corporate royalty, its PC business a symbol of American economic and technological prowess. In 1981, IBM invented the PC and forever altered the lifestyles and work habits of billions of people around the planet. Now this industrial gem was in the hands of China. Lenovo's success showed how the Chinese economy was transforming from one that simply churned out cheap toys and T-shirts with bargain-basement labor into a more modern economy that produced its own products under its own brands. China's cheap labor, as in Taiwan, Hong Kong, and South Korea, would not stay cheap for long under conditions of rapid industrialization. Developing new comparative advantages is a necessary ingredient for a country to perpetuate its Miracle. Japan, South Korea, and Taiwan had already undertaken this important shift as their economies became more advanced. They had progressed from assemblers of clothes and basic electronics to manufacturers of cars, chemicals, heavy equipment, semiconductors, and LCD panels. China was, once again, following in their footsteps and poised to make an even greater global impact.

It is no surprise then that the IBM deal created confusion, concern, and even fear in the United States. The reaction echoed the paranoia sparked by Japan's acquisitions in the United States in the 1980s. Lenovo's purchase woke up Americans to China's global ambitions—in the same fashion that Morita's Columbia Pictures grab had alerted Americans to the growing power of Japan two decades earlier. It gave notice that China's companies were advancing on the world stage, as Honda and other Japanese firms had done in the 1970s and 1980s. Once again, the American economy appeared to be under threat from the East. After the IBM acquisition, warned the *Christian Science Monitor*, "the gathering might of the Chinese economy became as imposing and obvious as the Great Wall." The deal, it continued, "does point to the seemingly inevitable rise of a challenger to the economic hegemony America has enjoyed for nearly a century."[2] In Washington, Lenovo's acquisition raised a cacophony of protest from politicians convinced that IBM was handing China crucial American technology. U.S. Congressman Thomas Reynolds complained that the IBM sale to Lenovo could give the Chinese "sensitive information and technologies, many with military applications that could, in turn, be used against the United States."[3]

Back in China, on the other hand, the deal generated great pride and confidence. "With this brave act, Lenovo has overthrown people's traditional notions about Chinese enterprise, the idea that it is happy with a small amount of wealth," boasted the *Beijing Daily Messenger*. The deal "is also a starting point for the PC world to welcome the China era."[4] Liu's personal celebration was much less boastful. Three days after the deal's December 8 announcement, as the brouhaha was settling down, Liu relaxed in his Beijing home, uncorked a bottle of wine, and poured a glass for himself and his wife.

The self-congratulatory mood, however, did not last long. His wife and son began peppering him with questions about the future. They had serious concerns about the IBM acquisition. Would Americans and Chinese be able to work together peacefully in the same company? his wife wondered. How much value would the IBM unit have after it became part of a Chinese company? But most of all, she was concerned that Liu was taking too big a chance so late in his career. "You're risking all of your achievements," she told him.

Liu was well aware of the risks and had at one point shared his family's doubts about the wisdom of the deal.[5] Lenovo now faced the most daunting management challenge in the history of the company. The IBM business was three times larger than Lenovo and had lost a staggering $1 billion in the three-and-a-half years prior to Lenovo's acquisition.[6] The IBM deal was Lenovo's greatest opportunity, a chance to become China's first true global multinational enterprise and show how far China's economy had developed in the short time since Deng Xiaoping's first reforms. Or it would expose the inexperience of China's top businessmen and put on international display the long road China's economy still had to travel to match the West.

Liu tried to remain confident, telling his wife that the management team had considered all of her questions before pursuing the deal. Liu accepted this new challenge because it was just that—a challenge, and one that could benefit not only Lenovo, but also the entire country. The IBM deal, he says, "was a once in a lifetime chance and you have to take it. Not everyone is as lucky as me to have such an opportunity. It was my honor for me to do it."[7]

. . . .

THE STORY OF Lenovo shows the messy nature of China's conversion from Communist command economy to market economy. That transition created a tangled mix of unfettered capitalism and state control that presented both unprecedented opportunities to entrepreneurs like Liu but also countless obstacles in his attempts to build a modern company. China's rise in the global economy might have been meteoric, but it has not been smooth.

Liu and his family had operated in this strange netherworld between the realms of capitalism and Communism long before Deng's reforms. Liu was born on April 29, 1944, in Shanghai. Liu's father, Gushu, was an employee at the Shanghai branch of the Bank of China. Bankers were considered evil capitalists after Mao's conquest, but Gushu was a secret sympathizer and had made contacts in the underground Communist movement in Shanghai during the civil war. These connections helped protect the family. Transferred to Beijing, they lost most of their wealth but retained enough to move into a house in a desirable section of the city center. Gushu kept his job at the Bank of China, which was reconstituted as a state-owned enterprise, and joined the Communist Party.

The family's history, still suspect to class-conscious Communists, dogged Liu in his early days. As a student, Liu was a fan of military novels and dreamed of being a fighter pilot, a coveted job in early Communist China. After graduating from high school in 1962, Liu passed all of the exams necessary to become a candidate,[8] but he was rejected anyway. An uncle had been labeled a "rightist," and that was enough to make Liu ideologically unfit for duty.[9] His career in aviation thwarted, Liu began studying at a military institute in Xi'an that specialized in atomic weapons and missile technologies. But again, Liu was considered of questionable loyalty and banned from work on sensitive projects. Instead, he was assigned to conduct research on radar systems, which brought him into contact with the field of computers for the first time.[10]

Then in 1966, as the Cultural Revolution began, Liu's life, like Deng Xiaoping's, was thrown into turmoil. At first Liu joined the Red Guards and was an active organizer and speaker in their effort to weed out "rightists" and "capitalist roaders." "We really worshipped Mao and believed whatever he said," Liu recalls. His enchantment with the Cultural Revolution, however, was dashed when the movement became violent. Riots on campus broke out, and professors considered "enemies" were beaten and humiliated. A horrified Liu withdrew from Red Guard activities. "I realized the nature of this Cultural Revolution. It wasn't for the development of the country," Liu says. Mao and his allies "were using the innocent students' minds" for their own purposes, Liu says.[11] His stand made him a target of Red Guard criticism. One commander denounced him as a "retreatist from revolutionary consciousness."

Liu managed to graduate in 1968 and began work improving China's radar systems at a research institute in Chengdu.[12] Soon after, though, came a major turning point in his life. Mao decreed that all "intellectuals" be sent to the countryside to join the peasants in manual labor to cleanse them of "capitalist" thinking. Many students and professionals were posted to collectivized farms, but Liu was banished to an isolated work camp run by the military on an island off the coast of Guangdong province in China's south. There he spent long hours standing in muddy rice paddies planting seedlings, cut off from contact with the outside world. Each morning, Liu and the other inmates would "report" to a picture of Mao on the wall about their work plans for the day. When they returned from the paddies at night, they recounted to the same picture on that day's achievements. Amid the drudgery and loneliness, Liu became overwhelmed by hopelessness. "We didn't know when the situation would get better," he says. "We couldn't see the future."

It was at this time of uncertainty that Liu decided upon his life's course. Politics, he decided, was a risky, dangerous game best avoided. In business he might be able to have greater freedom and accomplish more for the country. "I was really determined to be an entrepreneur," he recalls.[13] After nearly two years in the camp—which was later relocated from the southern island to Hunan province in central China—Liu was rehabilitated, allowed to return to Beijing and given a job at the computer research institute of the prestigious Chinese Academy of Sciences. This institute was developing massive mainframe computer systems, which were used primarily for military purposes. Life was much better than in the camp, but by the mid-1970s, Liu again felt repressed. "All day long you had to be totally quiet. It was intolerable," Liu once recalled. "If you were to mention what was going on inside yourself, how you felt about things, someone might report you. If anything got out, you would not just be in trouble but in danger."[14]

Even worse from Liu's perspective was the institute's tremendous waste of talent and effort. The computer systems developed at the institute were never used to help the economy or society. As soon as one project was done, the machine was set aside and a new one initiated. Nothing was every commercialized. Watching their efforts come to naught frustrated Liu. "I felt strangled, like someone was wringing my throat and I couldn't breathe," Liu says.

Relief came with Deng Xiaoping's reforms of the early 1980s. The new spirit swept through the Chinese Academy of Sciences. Fearful of funding cuts as Deng scaled back the state sector, administrators encouraged researchers to start their own enterprises and transform their scientific expertise into real-world product development. Liu saw an opportunity to launch the company he had thought of while planting rice during the Cultural Revolution. He volunteered to strike out on his own.[15] The grateful Academy gave him some $25,000 in seed money.[16]

Liu's move was risky. Deng's reforms were brand new, and no one was sure they would stick. If Chinese politics again swung to the left, Liu could be criticized as a "capitalist roader." Liu, though, felt he had little choice. "There is a Chinese saying that a barefoot man working beside a river won't be afraid of getting his shoes wet," Liu explains. "The only other option was to stay the same as before, which I didn't like."

Though his venture was an outgrowth of a government academy, Liu bristled at the idea of being the manager of a state-owned enterprise. Government companies in China, he believed, were bloated, inefficient affairs where the managers had little control over decision making. Liu knew he could never be successful under such conditions. Before he started his new venture, he laid down some stiff ground rules for his government financiers. He demanded full management control of the company, the right to hire whom he wanted and to choose the businesses the firm would pursue. In return, Liu promised not to ask the Academy for further funding. The Academy's leadership, simply happy to find a researcher enthusiastic enough to become an entrepreneur, consented to Liu's demands.[17] In 1984, Liu founded the company that became Lenovo. From its roots, Lenovo was an oddball in the Chinese economy, a privately run but state-owned firm. Liu was stuck, like he always had been, between Communist and capitalist systems.

He recruited ten other researchers from the computer institute to join his new company, and in October they held their first meeting. The institute had donated a two-room guardhouse outside its offices as a headquarters. The barren rooms were covered in dust, so before starting their first business planning session, they had to sweep the floor and bring in benches and tables. Liu and his colleagues, all scientists raised as Communists, had no idea how to start a company.[18] Liu admits that he was not even sure what he wanted his new company to do. "In the first year, there was no vision," he says.[19] Much of that initial meeting was spent debating the company's name. They eventually all agreed on the "New Technology Developer Inc."[20] (Liu's firm later changed its name to Legend, and in 2004, to Lenovo.)

In the beginning, Liu traded ice skates, digital watches, and pocket calculators. Inevitably for a bunch of technical experts, Lenovo gravitated toward computers. Shortly after Lenovo's launch, the Academy granted the start-up a contract to test and maintain five hundred IBM PCs it had purchased. The computers showed up in too many crates to fit into Lenovo's two-room headquarters. The middle-aged men donned shoulder poles and lugged the crates into a borrowed room at the Academy, huffing and puffing on a sizzling hot Beijing summer day.[21]

Liu wanted to sell the coveted IBMs on his own account. "If you had a source of IBM machines, you had a source of money," Liu recalls. China in the mid-1980s, however, was still a tightly controlled economy. Liu needed an import license to become an IBM sales agent. A true state-controlled company might have been able to extract one from China's bureaucrats, but an independent outfit like Liu's did not have the clout. A former colleague working at the Hong Kong branch of the Bank of China tipped him off that the computer division there possessed such an import license. Liu worked out a deal whereby the bank bought and imported the machines and Lenovo marketed them in China.[22] Liu was in the PC business.

Before long, Liu began thinking of making his own computers. Though his business selling foreign machines was growing and profitable, he also realized that most of the profits were going into the pockets of foreign firms. The Lenovo team, all computer experts, "had a lot of emotion about selling our own brand," Liu says. There was also an element of patriotism in Liu's dream of making a Lenovo PC. Foreign brands were charging a premium on their computers in China, sucking up more profit while pricing PCs out of range for most Chinese. A Chinese PC would also, he believed, help develop Chinese technology, strengthening the entire economy.[23] From the beginning, Liu always equated Lenovo's success with China's.

A number of hurdles stood between Liu and a homegrown computer business. The difficulties stemmed from Lenovo's precarious position between the state and private sectors. Liu did not have the political connections to get a production license from the Chinese government.[24] Once again, he had to circumvent the rules. Liu decided to set up shop in less regulated Hong Kong, ironically, just as Hong Kong companies were moving factories into China. In 1988, in the British colony, he launched a subsidiary that was a joint venture with a Hong Kong computer firm and a Chinese state company controlled by his father. Liu spent $100,000 on an office in eastern Hong Kong that acted as a headquarters and dormitory. Visiting executives from Beijing, with little money to stay in expensive hotels, slept in the office, sometimes on rugs laid out in the hallways. Liu had grand plans for the operation. The Hong Kong company was a crucial part of a campaign he called the "Three Marching Songs for the Battle Plan to Advance Overseas." He even held a staff meeting at the prestigious Great Hall of the People in Beijing to "swear in the troops who are launching the overseas advance."[25]

It was at this time that Mary Ma had her first experience with Lenovo. Ma was managing a World Bank program at the Chinese Academy of Sciences and she accompanied the academy's president—still Lenovo's lone shareholder—to the opening ceremony of the Hong Kong subsidiary. Afterward, Liu invited them to visit his new Hong Kong office. Ma was appalled at what she saw. The office was in an old, dark industrial building. Ma, formally clad in a business suit, got squished to the back of a cargo elevator by crates shoved about by shirtless and sweaty laborers. "How could this company tell a big, inspiring story about going abroad when they have such a humble office?" she asked herself. Liu, though, was unperturbed. He told the president about his plans for the future, to manufacture computers, to compete with foreign multinationals. Ma was impressed. "They wanted to leverage the opening of the Chinese economy," she says. "He was the head of a small company but he had a big dream and a big strategy." In 1989, after the Tiananmen massacre, the World Bank canceled Ma's program, and Ma, looking for something to do, remembered Liu and Lenovo. She joined in 1990 as an assistant to the general manager in Hong Kong.[26]

Meanwhile, Lenovo engineers were working furiously on a homemade PC, the prototype of which was ready by early 1989. Lenovo patched together a makeshift PC factory in Hong Kong, hiring poorly educated local women, giving them each a bit of training and a pair of gloves, and setting them to work assembling the 286s by hand. Liu sent a team with the new machine to a huge computer fair in Hanover, Germany, where it took orders for more than two thousand PCs. Liu was making a Chinese PC.[27]

. . . .

AS LIU STRUGGLED to uplift Chinese technology, Deng Xiaoping struggled to find ways to help him. The aged reformer had
already begun to worry about the Chinese economy before the
Tiananmen massacre. He still thought the powerful bureaucracy
and its irrepressible penchant for control was stifling entrepreneurship, even after his extensive reforms. At the same time, he
feared that further market reform would cause Beijing to lose its
grip over the economic direction of the country. In that event, the
gap between rich and poor could expand to the point where social
stability would be threatened. Deng also knew there could be no
backsliding on his reforms. The government had to reach a delicate balance.

These issues were on Deng's mind when he visited Shanghai
in early 1991 and met with Zhu Rongji, the city's mayor. Deng
had always been impressed by Zhu. The mayor had a Clintonian
ability to command huge quantities of data and he never bothered reading from notes when discussing economic matters. Deng
also thought Zhu seemed full of fresh ideas. He planned to apply
Deng's SEZ concept in Shanghai's undeveloped Pudong district,
but with a twist. Zhu's SEZ focused on finance, trade, and infrastructure, not manufacturing, as the zones had in the south. It was
just the type of creativity that Deng believed the nation's economic
policymaking required.

During their meeting, Deng shared with Zhu some of his own
thoughts on the future of his cherished reform program. "Reform
should have new ideas," he told Zhu. "Reform should adopt different measures from what has been used over the past decade, ex-
ploring new ideas to use in the new situation." Deng had decided.
Zhu was the man to take the Chinese economy to the next level.

Zhu Rongji was born in Changsha in Hunan province on October 1, 1928. Orphaned as a young child, he was raised by his father's brother. In China's highly structured Confucian order, such
wayward children usually had little chance of success, but Zhu

proved a superior student. He was a popular regular at Changsha's antique bookshops and a diligent scholar of Chinese literature. (As a politician later in life, he wowed diplomats and colleagues by belting out Peking opera arias and quoting Abraham Lincoln verbatim.) Zhu was a Communist Party member by the time he was a student at Beijing's prestigious Tsinghua University, and after he graduated, he was dispatched to a Manchurian province to work at its state planning commission in 1951. The province was undertaking an experiment in Soviet-style command economics. When the concept caught on throughout China, Zhu was assigned to a newly formed national commission in 1952. Thus, at an early age, Zhu was at the center of China's new power elite.

Yet even at this time, Zhu's ideas were different than those of most of his colleagues. He was interested in trying to merge theories of planned and market economies, and he often argued with other policymakers about China's economic direction, especially after the catastrophic Great Leap Forward. His outspokenness came back to haunt him. In 1958, he was declared a "rightist," kicked out of the Communist Party, and sent to the countryside, where he bred pigs and cleaned toilets for five years. His fortunes revived with Deng's. By 1979, he was back in Beijing, devising policy to revive the economy at a state commission. In 1991, Deng elevated him to vice-premier of the State Council. His growing authority was made clear during a visit Deng made in 1992 to a state steel complex in the suburbs of Beijing. Deng ranted to the assembled dignitaries that too many of China's senior leaders still did not understand the importance of economic reform. "Zhu Rongji," Deng proclaimed, "is the only one who understands economics."

From that point on, no one questioned Zhu's stewardship of the economy. In 1998, he became premier of China. Perhaps no other single person has had more influence over the modern economy of China than Zhu, aside from Deng himself. Zhu squashed runaway inflation and set the groundwork for more stable, yet still hyperactive, growth; began cleaning up China's bad loan-burdened financial sector; promoted stock markets; and stream-lined state enterprises, in the process allowing private business to flourish.[28]

Zhu's most important policy decision was steering China into the World Trade Organization. He fast-tracked WTO entry after discussing the matter with Alan Greenspan during the Federal Reserve chairman's 1999 visit to Beijing. Zhu believed the reforms required by the WTO could help China generate more jobs, an important concern since his overhaul of state-owned companies was producing massive layoffs. He was especially influenced by Greenspan's arguments that the liberalization of China's capital and banking sectors mandated by WTO admission would pro-vide more financial muscle for the country's private enterprises. In Zhu's mind, WTO reforms would put in place the final piece China needed to become a full-fledged market economy—com-petition. By opening up the domestic market to international companies, Chinese firms would be forged into top-notch com-petitors through the fierce struggle for customers with the West's best firms, just as the entrepreneurs of Japan and the Tigers had been in the 1960s and 1970s. WTO entry would "give certain in-dustries a serious attack," he said. But "challenges will be trans-formed to opportunities, pressure transformed into motivation."

Yet reaching this goal was a slow, painful process. China had already been negotiating to join the WTO and its predecessor organization since the mid-1980s, but the plan faced serious po-litical opposition in Beijing from officials who feared that Chi-nese companies could not survive the dramatic market opening the WTO would create. Meanwhile, U.S. officials pressed for more and more market access as a requirement for China's ad-mission. Zhu visited the United States in April 1999 with hopes of finalizing a WTO deal with President Clinton, but he returned home empty-handed and disappointed.

Zhu did not give up. The U.S. trade representative Charlene Barshefsky flew to Beijing six months later to restart negotiations, but the talks still deadlocked over several politically sensitive issues, including Chinese reluctance to open its financial and telecommunications sectors to U.S. companies and Washington's insistence on maintaining the right to use antidumping laws* against Chinese imports. Barshefsky was despondent, and on November 13, resigned herself to returning home without an agreement. However, only hours before her departure, she was invited into a meeting with Zhu himself. The premier had taken over the negotiations personally, and his involvement brought progress in renewed talks—but only for a few hours. By the end of the next day, the stalemate returned. On the morning of November 15, a frustrated Barshefsky sent her bags to the airport to signal to the Chinese her willingness to walk away.

Zhu saved the day again. Barshefsky was summoned into another last-minute meeting with the premier. The U.S. negotiators described Zhu's role at that session as "Solomonic." He overcame the remaining differences by pledging to resolve them in the future. His comments caught the Americans off guard, but they decided to move forward anyway. By the afternoon, China and the United States had signed their agreement on China's admission to the WTO.[29] That deal between Zhu and Barshefsky basically ensured China's entry, and the country formally joined the WTO in 2001. It also had a tremendous impact on Liu and Lenovo.

. . . .

"WE HOPE WE will see goldfish leaping through the Dragon-Gate to become dragons," Liu was quoted saying in a 1992 company newsletter.[30] A play on a Chinese idiom, the saying was employed to describe an ordinary man who ascended to a higher social status. That was what Liu intended for Lenovo. "Many of the employees and management were more than satisfied" with the company's stature at the time, he says. "But I had even higher

---

* *"Dumping" occurs when a company sells a product below its cost of production in an effort to claim market share from its competitors. U.S. "antidumping" laws placed penalties on such goods to protect American industry.*

goals. I wanted to tell them that there will be a better, a higher goal for us to achieve in the future. I wanted the company to be a dragon instead of staying in a small pond and being happy with being a fish."[31]

Liu's optimism seemed misplaced. Lenovo was heading into one of its darkest periods. Its PC sales overseas were stagnating. In 1990, Lenovo sold its first branded computers inside China. But there, too, Liu was at a serious disadvantage. Lenovo was not even a top-ten computer brand in China in the early 1990s. Meanwhile, the government, in its continued efforts to liberalize the economy, announced a sweeping reform plan that would open the Chinese market for foreign PC makers. All of those American and Japanese companies Liu could not contend with abroad were stampeding onto his home turf. To counter the heightened competition, the government put in place a support program for some Chinese PC makers, which included large new investments. But Lenovo, again suffering due to its strange public-private status, was left out.[32] The aid did not help the industry much anyway. The Chinese companies did not have the technology and marketing prowess to compete with IBM, Hewlett-Packard, and Compaq. In 1989, foreign brands held only a third of the China market; by 1993, their share had risen to nearly 80 percent.[33]

By then, the survival of the Lenovo PC was in serious doubt. The company turned a profit on distributing foreign computers, but its own PC business was losing money. Colossal debates took place among Lenovo's managers over what to do. Liu, his stress level beyond control, suffered from constant headaches and ended up in the hospital with a bout of Ménière's disease, an inner-ear condition he had been battling on and off for many years. For more than two months in early 1994, Liu held management conferences from his hospital bed, searching for ways out of the crisis. Some advocated abandoning the Lenovo computer altogether. The PC unit was a mess, with high costs, low quality, bureaucratic management, and poor R&D. In the end, Liu refused to take that route. Ending Lenovo's PC program would make the company no more than an agent of foreign brands,[34] incongruous with his vision of a technologically advanced China. Liu chose to focus the majority of his resources on his own PC, and to live or die by it. His decision was perhaps the most important Liu had taken since starting the company.

Drastic changes were badly needed, however, if the PC business had any shot at success. He resolved that the problem was mainly one of management. The different aspects of the PC business—manufacturing, research, sales—were all run independently, creating inefficiencies and a lack of coordination. No one person oversaw the entire process. Lenovo needed a PC czar, someone to take control of every part of the operation and weld them together into a working whole.

His choice for this crucial position was an unlikely one—Yang Yuanqing, a young, aggressive salesman. Liu gave Yang full authority over the Lenovo PC and the responsibility for turning the business around. The step was unprecedented. Aside from Liu himself, no one within Lenovo had ever held so much power. Liu's decision ruffled a lot of feathers. Yang was a mere twenty-nine years old and the more experienced executives balked at taking orders from him. Liu stood his ground. Yang had performed exceptionally at a division in the company that sold specialized Hewlett-Packard equipment, always meeting his sales targets no matter what. Liu was convinced Yang, whom he considered "trustworthy" and "a very good leader," was the right choice. "He never failed the company," Liu said.[35]

Liu proved prophetic. The appointment of Yang was a major turning point in Lenovo's history. Yang discovered a way to compete with, and eventually overtake, foreign computer makers in China. He borrowed the sales tactics and management techniques of foreign companies with which Lenovo had done business, and combined that experience with a knowledge of the China market outsiders could not match. The strategy turned Lenovo into one of China's most successful and modern companies, setting the stage for its eventual purchase of IBM.

Yang, blunt and tough, imposed his vision with an iron will. Staffers were fearful of even entering his office.[36] Yet he was also bold and decisive. He consolidated the disparate divisions that handled the PC operation into one unit under his control in March 1994. Believing Lenovo had become too bureaucratic, he reduced the staff by two-thirds. There was, however, a method in his madness. Yang, tapping into his in-depth knowledge of the Chinese computer market, divined the secret to expanding Lenovo's presence in China. Most computers, with a price tag of about $6,000, were far out of the range of the average Chinese. Those who did not have the money but wanted a computer went to small shops that sold the individual components and pieced them together at a fraction of the cost rather than splurge on a branded machine. Yang knew he had to reduce his prices to compete. Lenovo had already tried such a strategy by creating a bargain, "home-use" computer called a "1+1" that sold for as little as 10 percent of the price of regular machines. These were bare-bones affairs—one model did not even have a hard drive—and sales were sluggish. The way forward, Yang realized, was to pair higher technology with lower prices.

To get there, he reformed Lenovo's operations. Engineers cut production costs in half. Yang purchased components in bulk to save money, and he capitalized on the competition between Intel and AMD to get his hands on cheaper, faster microprocessors. Imported components were replaced when possible with locally made parts. Yang substituted thin steel sheets for plastic computer cases, which were not available in China. These metal containers did not look that great, but they brought down the price. Inventories were controlled. To measure progress, Yang called two meetings a month simply to monitor cash flow and inventories. His staff called these sessions "going to court." Yang would berate and humiliate any manager who failed to meet targets. His employees may have been terrorized, but so were Lenovo's competitors. Yang began marketing his low-priced computers in

May 1994, and Lenovo's PC business started to thrive. By early 1996, Lenovo marketed a $1,200 Pentium machine. Never before had a computer of such quality been sold for so little in China.[37] Foreign computer makers were slow to pick up on the new threat from Lenovo. "We didn't give [the foreign companies] a break," Yang once said. They "were far away and couldn't follow us fast enough."[38]

Yang made equally dramatic changes to Lenovo's sales and marketing system. Here, his experience with foreign PC makers proved invaluable. During his time selling Hewlett-Packard products in China, he absorbed its distribution strategy of creating a network of sales agents. Lenovo had always sold computers with its own sales force. Yang believed this strategy limited Lenovo's flexibility and ability to penetrate markets. Agents had better local knowledge of conditions in each city. Yang traveled around the country beginning in 1994 in search of agents, enticing them with promises of wider margins on sales of Lenovo computers than they received from other PC companies. Here Yang was aided by the continuing reforms in China. "Middlemen," like agents, were anathema to the old Maoist system, parasites who fed off the honorable working class. As the economy liberalized, more and more Chinese wanted to start their own businesses, and becoming an agent was an easy way to get off the ground. Meanwhile, Yang dismantled Lenovo's existing sales operation, firing all but eighteen of the one hundred salesmen on the payroll. "If we don't get rid of the old, there's no room to deploy the new," Yang said unsympathetically at the time.[39]

Yang's strategy worked miracles. At the end of 1997, Lenovo became the No. 1 PC brand in China (with IBM running second).[40] Liu showed that his Lenovo could compete head on with American multinationals—and win. Yet he realized Lenovo was not the global enterprise he envisioned. "We can't be called a real dragon," Liu said in 1995. "We're just a dragonette."[41] Lenovo's opportunity to reach "dragon" status would come, and more quickly than Liu could have imagined.

. . . .

Lenovo has not been the only Asian company with dreams of jumping through the Dragon Gate. One of the major stories in international business over the next several decades will be the tremendous number of Asian firms that manage to make that leap.

Even now, the list of Asian companies that have become global competitors is no longer limited to Sony, Honda, and a handful of other Japanese competitors. The most aggressive jumpers are from South Korea. Some of Park Chung Hee's creations, laid low by the Asian Financial Crisis, mismanagement, and hubris, have achieved revivals that once seemed impossible. The impact of the Crisis and the reforms it forced on Korea are, ironically, among the main reasons for this turnaround. *Chaebol* managers had no choice but to streamline bloated operations, produce internationally competitive products, and ditch nonperforming operations. Market forces and a reduction in bureaucratic control provided new discipline that raised Korean companies to a higher level of competitiveness. The result has been remarkable. Korean companies have exploded onto the world stage, terrifying their Japanese, American, and European rivals.

A prime example is Chung Ju Yung's car company, Hyundai Motor. Chung first tried competing with the global auto industry's best in 1986 when he exported his Excel sedan to the American market. The fuel-efficient Excel with its $4,995 price tag was an instant hit with frugal drivers. But customers soon discovered they got what they paid for: Excels suffered breakdowns and needed parts replaced frequently. Sales tanked, and the Hyundai name became a synonym for "shoddy." In 1998, *Late Show* TV host David Letterman listed his "Top 10 Hilarious Mischief Night Pranks to Play in Space"; "Paste a 'Hyundai' logo on the main control panel" came in at No. 8.

The comeback began in the late 1990s, led by an unlikely figure, Chung's son, Chung Mong Koo. In an effort to divvy up the Hyundai empire among his squabbling sons, Chung planted

Mong Koo at the motor company in 1998, and two years later, the son broke it off from the rest of the Hyundai Group. It was not a welcome move. The conservative, chain-smoking Chung had limited experience in the car business but a penchant for micromanagement. One Hyundai executive once quipped that he "makes the decision on how big a Christmas tree to put in the lobby."

As it turned out, his skills were underestimated. Mong Koo grasped that Hyundai would remain stalled until it overcame its reputation for making cars more popular with mechanics than drivers. In 2000, Chung suddenly burst into the company president's office and barked: "Quality is crucial to our survival. We have to get it right no matter what the cost!" Though this was obvious to everyone outside the company, inside its Seoul headquarters there had always been a premium placed on making cars cheaply and quickly, but not necessarily well. Mong Koo, like his father, squeezed the company into his iron grip and pounded home the new quality mantra. He boosted Hyundai's R&D budget, forced car designers and engineers to purge defects from new models while still on the drawing board, and encouraged assembly-line workers to speak out with ideas for improving the manufacturing process, as Taiichi Ohno had done at Toyota. Hyundai cars began climbing up J.D. Power initial quality surveys and by 2004, they matched Honda at No. 2. U.S. sales revived. In 2007, Hyundai, together with its Kia affiliate, sold 772,482 vehicles in the United States, 91 percent more than in 2000. "We will make ourselves an invincible competitor," Mong Koo promised in 2005.[42]

Hyundai had jumped through the Dragon Gate. Now it was Lenovo's turn.

. . . .

IN 2001, JOHN Joyce, the chief financial officer of IBM, arrived at Lenovo's Beijing headquarters. Joyce, an avid mountain climber who once almost reached the summit of Mt. Everest, had an offer for Liu and Yang that was equally adventurous. Would

Lenovo, he asked them, be interested in buying IBM's PC business? The typically aggressive Yang was intrigued. Such a deal would give Lenovo the largest international presence of any Chinese company. Liu, however, thought it risky. The IBM unit was too big and unwieldy for Lenovo to swallow, Liu thought, and he turned Joyce's offer down. When Joyce reported Liu's response to Louis Gerstner, the prominent CEO was impressed by Liu's caution. "That's why he's the chairman," Gerstner told Joyce.[43]

Liu's initial rejection did not dissuade Joyce. He had become convinced that selling the PC unit was crucial for IBM's survival. The operation had become the unwanted stepchild, a commodity business starved of capital and attention amid IBM's more cutting-edge divisions. Two years later, Joyce approached Lenovo again[44]—and this time, Joyce caught the company at just the right moment.

Yang and Ma were engaged in an exhaustive study of Lenovo's corporate strategy. Lenovo had become the undisputed champion of China's PC industry, with more than a quarter of the expanding market. Liu was heralded as a national hero, the Steve Jobs of China. "No one—Chinese or foreign—thought a Chinese company could beat the respected international brands," Edward Tian, CEO of telecom firm China Netcom, said in 2002. Lenovo "is heroic because it gave confidence to Chinese people that our technology could be as good as any in the world."[45] Lenovo had also reached a crossroads. In recent years the company had tried to diversify within China into non-PC businesses, including dotcoms, MP3 players, and IT services. None of them proved successful, causing Yang and Ma to rethink the company's direction altogether. They invited industry analysts to give presentations to management on how Lenovo was viewed in the stock market. These experts explained that investors demanded more than just profitability, but high returns on equity and investment. "These kinds of concepts were actually quite new at that time to the management team," Ma says. "We thought as long as we make money it's okay."

Ma also examined the global PC industry and noticed it was

changing in ways that could put Lenovo at risk. With the PC increasingly commoditized, scale became crucial to profitability and survival. Lenovo was a huge player in China, which, though the fastest-growing large market in the world, was not big enough to ensure the firm's future. The company had little presence outside of China. A key factor in Ma's analysis was Zhu Rongji's reform program, especially China's WTO entry. The remaining barriers to foreign companies in China were being dismantled. Ma realized she had to start thinking about Lenovo as a competitor to Hewlett-Packard and Dell both inside and outside of China. "After WTO, the whole China situation was changed totally," Ma says. Lenovo had to go international, to become one of the three largest PC firms in the world if it was to compete.

That was easier said than done. Creating sales and distribution networks around the world was expensive and time-consuming. So was attracting the right talent to staff such operations and building a recognizable brand name in a crowded PC market. Lenovo experimented with sales offices in three European countries. The results only proved Ma's concerns were justified. Lenovo's Chinese management, though highly successful at home, had no experience operating on a large scale outside of China. No company in China had such expertise. Building an international presence from scratch was "almost impossible," Ma decided. Acquiring an overseas business would prove much cheaper and easier.

Enter IBM. Liu, Yang, and Ma decided to pursue IBM's offer, at least on a preliminary basis. Ma sent fact-finding teams to the United States in November 2003 and March 2004 to meet with IBM executives. What they learned was encouraging. IBM had an experienced global sales team, excellent technology, and, of course, a famous brand name.

Not everyone agreed with Ma. In April, Ma had just arrived in Shanghai on a business trip when Yang phoned her from Beijing. "Mary, you've got to come back. The board said no," Yang told her. Liu had again nixed IBM's offer. Ma was shocked. She immediately returned to Beijing headquarters and went on a lobbying campaign with Lenovo's board. Calling Liu, she pleaded: "Why don't you give us another chance."[46]

Her pleas worked. Later that month, Yang, Ma, Liu, and the board held a series of intense meetings over the course of a week. The two sides were looking at the IBM opportunity from opposite perspectives. Liu was, as before, focused on the risks. He worried that some of the benefits IBM would bring to Lenovo—especially the talented staff and well-known brand name—would evaporate once the unit was in Chinese hands. The IBMers might just flee to Lenovo's competitors, and the value of the IBM brand could deteriorate. That potential problem was linked to his biggest worry—could Lenovo's Chinese executives manage Americans? The cultural differences between Liu's former Communists and IBM's independent-minded Americans could prove insurmountable.

Yang and Ma set about alleviating Liu's apprehensions. They debated whether or not Lenovo's current management team could integrate IBM's worldwide operations, and came to the startling conclusion that the answer was no. "We didn't have the faintest idea of how to manage a global business," Liu says. Lenovo would need help from the existing management at IBM, and in the end, the combined firm would have to forge a joint team of Lenovo and IBM executives. With the guidance of McKinsey & Company, they began crafting different scenarios for accommodating a new management structure and eventually agreed on an unexpected formula: appoint an IBMer as Lenovo's post-acquisition CEO.

Both Liu and Yang fell on their swords for the company. Liu said he would resign from the chairmanship but remain on the board. He doubted he had the energy to manage such a gargantuan task anyway. Yang made a bigger sacrifice. Though in the prime of his career, Yang agreed to give up his CEO post and take Liu's place as executive chairman. Yang also devised a three-word formula for smoothing out cultural tensions in the merged firm—"respect, openness, and compromise." If managers focused on these values, the differences, he believed, could be overcome. Liu was swayed and the board changed its position. The IBM deal was back on.[47]

What followed were long and stressful negotiations between IBM and Lenovo. From late July until late November, the Lenovo team, led by Ma, haggled with IBM executives in sessions in New York and Hong Kong. One of the biggest sticking points was price. The two sides were about $250 million apart—not a huge gap, but each clung to its position. The other major hurdle was intellectual property. How much proprietary technology would Lenovo acquire along with the IBM unit, and what royalties could Lenovo collect on it? Joyce ratcheted up the pressure on Ma by refusing to negotiate exclusively with Lenovo. Another serious bidder was in the wings, which the Lenovo executives originally knew only as "Plan B." They eventually discovered it was the private-equity fund Texas Pacific Group, led by financier David Bonderman. Joyce took advantage of the competition between Lenovo and Texas Pacific to gain leverage over Ma. Every time Texas Pacific made a concession, IBMers revealed the details to Ma to force her to match the offer.

Slowly the two sides hammered out a deal. Joyce flew to Beijing on several occasions to break through hurdles personally. To resolve especially touchy issues, he sent everyone out of the negotiating room except for Liu and Yang. The three then talked privately to achieve solutions. In the end, the two companies agreed on a $1.25 billion purchase price, roughly in the middle of their original positions. The intellectual property issues dragged on to the bitter end. After Thanksgiving in 2004, as Ma flew back to Beijing from New York to await the paperwork on what she thought was the final agreement, she got a phone call on the airplane from IBM demanding a one-word change to the document language, a change Lenovo's lawyer rejected. By early December, IBM told Texas Pacific they had no deal. Lenovo would be buying the IBM PC unit.[48]

Ma could afford to relax and even allow herself a minor celebration. She decided to treat herself to some jewelry. She thought about the fish jumping through the Dragon Gate. Lenovo had made the jump. It was now a dragon. She wondered how attractive a dragon-shaped piece of jewelry would be. Instead, she bought a brooch in the form of a butterfly, a prominent element in Chinese art. For Ma it symbolized "a beautiful dream." As she stood with Liu and Joyce on December 8 to make the formal announcement of Lenovo's acquisition, she wore the brooch proudly.[49]

. . . .

LIU, YANG, AND Ma managed to meld with IBM's top executives. Lenovo is, as Ma predicted, now competing head-on around the world with Hewlett-Packard and Dell, and the Chinese company has found its role as a multinational a difficult one. In early 2009, Liu and Yang had to return to their old posts of chairman and CEO, respectively, to reenergize the company, which had been struggling to succeed in the international marketplace. Liu, though, is confident that his creation will win out. Even more, Liu believes that Lenovo's great experiment is contributing to his most important goal—the economic development of China. "I had a strong vision in my mind that we could do something to make this country a better country," Liu says.[50]

CHAPTER THIRTEEN

AN UNEXPECTED JOURNEY FROM SHORTENING TO SOFTWARE

*It didn't require Einstein to decide which was the best
industry to be in.* —AZIM PREMJI

In June 2005, Azim Premji, chairman of Indian IT giant Wipro Ltd., faced a crucial management decision. Wipro's talented vice chairman, who had overseen the firm's growing technology services division, had resigned.[1] Premji had to find a replacement. The division, though the newest of Wipro's businesses, had become its most dominant. What was merely a $50 million operation in 1996 took in revenues of $1.35 billion that year.[2] Almost overnight, Wipro had become a major force in global IT, writing software, designing new products, undertaking research and development projects, and integrating computer systems for the largest multinationals in the world.

Premji believed Wipro was at a critical juncture. Fresh opportunities were appearing every day in the heady world of technology outsourcing. The IT industry in India had been a curious sideline, where multinationals dumped a few nonessential programming tasks to take advantage of the country's army of cheap talent. But by 2005, a combination of low wages, well-trained engineers, top-notch professional corporations, and escalating demand for computer services had remade the sector into an indispensable component of the global economy. Every American CEO needed his India strategy; if not, he would lose out on the profitability and productivity gains his competition was enjoying by utilizing India's IT expertise. Premji wanted Wipro to be his first choice, and in order for that to happen, he believed Wipro had to become even more aggressive. The firm needed to market and brand itself more forcefully, expand the depth of the services it offered, and continue making acquisitions around the world. In simple terms, Premji thought Wipro required a few swift kicks in the pants, the kind of kicks he had been inflicting on his executives for the previous forty years. In the end, Premji resolved that there was only one person qualified for the crucial post—himself.[3]

Premji made this choice at a point when most entrepreneurs are preparing to ride off into the sunset. About to turn sixty, Premji—with his drooping gray moustache and dignified crop of white hair—was already an iconic figure in India's IT industry, one of its founding fathers and a symbol of India's growing international economic influence. Known as the Bill Gates of India, Premji is also one of the richest tycoons in the country, with a fortune estimated at $12.7 billion.[4]

Adding to this already sizable nest egg was not Premji's motivation for taking on his new responsibilities. He is a notorious penny-pincher, a man with no taste for indulging himself with the money he has so dearly earned. For nine years, he puttered about his home city of Bangalore in a Ford Escort compact car. In 2005, he finally splurged—on a Toyota Corolla. He switches off the lights in unused conference rooms while walking through Wipro's Bangalore headquarters, and he flies economy class on Indian business trips like the rest of his employees. When visiting New York City, Premji prefers a street-side vendor hot dog to the culinary delights of Le Cirque. Such cost consciousness adds to Wipro's bottom line—and Premji's wealth. He maintains 80 percent ownership of the New York Stock Exchange–listed firm.[5] Wipro, he says flatly, "is a good investment."[6]

What does drive Premji, however, is something much grander than personal wealth: to make Wipro a formidable multinational enterprise, a service provider in the league of IBM, a firm the global economy cannot do without. Wipro is well on its way. It is the largest independent R&D lab in the world. Its engineers design MP3 players and computer printers for consumer electronics firms, customize information systems for companies in businesses from finance to retail, and write the software on many mobile phones. Premji also does back-office work for multinationals in a service called "business-process outsourcing," abbreviated as BPO. Wipro staffers handle credit-card applications and medical insurance claims, enter data, and take customer phone calls. All of this work is done on contract for giant, often American, companies. Each year the services become more advanced. Wipro even designs semiconductors and writes software for airplance navigation systems.

The success of Premji and India's other IT tycoons has taken the Miracle in a new direction. Until the Miracle reached India, the rise of Asia was a manufacturing story. South Korea, Taiwan, Hong Kong, Singapore, and especially China capitalized on high-quality, low-wage labor to vacuum up manufacturing production from around the world. India is doing the same today, but, for the first time, with IT and business services. The underlying forces making this happen are similar to the ones that generated the Miracle in East Asia—a combination of low costs, available talent, and improved infrastructure in transport and communications. Just as your average clothing manufacturer or computer maker could not survive without transferring at least some production to China, the same financial necessity is pressuring multinationals, especially from the United States, to outsource IT and other services to India. Through this process, India's IT sector is reorganizing the way the world economy operates. The rise of China forever altered how blue jeans, stuffed toys, and PCs were made; the rise of India has forever altered how software gets written, R&D is conducted, and insurance claims are processed.

The impact of the rise of India on the U.S. economy may one day be even more significant than that of China. The Chinese economy has tended to absorb low-paying, low-skill jobs from the United States. As a result, the United States has continued to enjoy strong growth and minute unemployment even as manufacturing jobs were transited to Asia. The American workforce advanced into higher-wage careers, often in sectors like financial services or technology. India, meanwhile, is attracting highly skilled, large-salary positions from the United States. Indian firms are competing not only in IT industries, but in legal, accounting, and medical services as well. Thanks to the Internet, types of work that could never in the past have been done outside of the United States can now be completed just about anywhere. College graduates in India compete directly for jobs with college graduates in the United States. Aside from Indian firms such as Wipro, American multinationals, including Intel, Microsoft, IBM, and Texas Instruments, are also investing billions in research centers and other operations in India to take advantage of its low-cost engineering talent.

The potential upheaval India can cause for the U.S. economy has given even die-hard free traders second thoughts. Alan Blinder, Princeton economist, presidential advisor, and free-trade advocate, raised eyebrows in the business world when he determined that the downside of services outsourcing could be much more severe than many laissez-faire economists believe. He estimates that as many as 40 million American jobs could be at risk of being shipped overseas over the next ten to twenty years—twice the current workforce in manufacturing.[7] India, with its English-speaking population and giant head start, would most likely gobble up the largest share of these jobs. If China is the Workshop of the World, India is quickly becoming its Service Center.

The Indian IT industry is having an equally transformative effect on India. If Manmohan Singh laid the groundwork for India's take-off with his liberalizing reforms, businessmen such as Premji have hit the ignition switch. Their success has convinced Indian companies of all types that they, too, can become major international powerhouses. "We really turbo-charged the ambition levels and the confidence levels of many business leaders in multiple industries," says Premji. "Their interpretation clearly was: If these fools in software can achieve this, why can't we?"[8] Expanding industries like IT services and BPO are also offering college graduates more job opportunities and higher salaries than ever before in the nation's history. This injection of spending power is spawning shopping malls, multiplex cinemas, new media, and other modern businesses that are creating yet more jobs.[9] The city of Bangalore, the home base of India's IT sector, was a quiet provincial town in the early 1990s. When Texas Instruments set up its first research lab there in 1985, it had to haul a satellite dish through the city by oxcart.[10] Today, Bangalore is a traffic-clogged metropolis of over six million people stuffed with luxury restaurants and buzzing shopping centers. On its outskirts sit the sprawling campuses of Wipro and other tech giants, where the best and brightest of India are altering Asia's economic relationship with the West.

India became an IT behemoth through the efforts of a handful of visionary entrepreneurs, including Premji, who fought against the constraints imposed by their own country to achieve what seemed almost impossible. Ironically, the engineer who started it all would rather have been doing something else.

. . . .

F. C. KOHLI WAS less than enthralled with his new job. By the late 1960s, Kohli had become a highly trusted manager for the Tata family. There were few more enviable positions in all of Indian business. The Tatas are one of India's most admired corporate clans. Their empire began in the 1860s with a trading company and expanded into steel, autos, tea, telecom, finance, hotels, chemicals, and retail. Kohli, an engineer, served them as a senior executive at an electric company the family controlled, now called Tata Power.

In 1969, his career took an unexpected turn. The Tatas asked

Kohli to take the helm of a fledgling venture they had launched a year earlier. Called Tata Consultancy Services, or TCS, the outfit was a computer programming and consulting firm. At that time in India, where many people still needed regular electricity, the venture bordered on science fiction. The forward-looking Tatas figured that computerization was the wave of the future. Kohli, who knew little about software, was reluctant to leave the power company for this odd start-up. Kohli accepted the post, but arranged an option to return to his old job after one year. The Tatas generously agreed that he could return anytime he chose.[11]

As things panned out, Kohli spent the next twenty-seven years at TCS and became known as the father of India's IT services industry. "If anyone should get the credit for building this industry from a white sheet of paper, he should," Premji says of Kohli. When Kohli joined TCS, the company was primarily handling basic data processing and software programming for other Tata companies. Kohli realized he needed more than internal jobs to turn TCS into a viable, independent business. He began shopping around his staff's services to other Indian firms. Over the next several years he won a few major contracts, including one to computerize the giant Mumbai phonebook. Expansion in India, however, was a gargantuan task. The country was then at the height of the License Raj, which hamstrung Kohli's ability to adopt the latest international technology. Importing anything into the country was a nightmare of red tape, especially expensive computers that consumed fistfuls of scarce hard currency. The government feared computers would replace workers and increase unemployment, and was in no rush to adopt the latest technology. Kohli often waited two years for permission to import a new machine.[12]

Despite these constraints, Kohli was convinced India could become a global IT powerhouse. His vision, radical at the time, proved prophetic, as he predicted how India would one day succeed. Unlike in industry, which required large sums for investment and would force India to play catch up to the West, Kohli argued,

India could compete in IT on a level playing field with industrialized countries. "Many years ago, there was an Industrial Revolution. We missed it due to reasons over which we had no control," Kohli told a computer conference in India in 1975. "Today, there is a new revolution, a revolution in information technology, which requires the capability to think clearly. This we have in abundance."[13]

However, Kohli was not able to achieve this vision locked up inside the License Raj. "We had to work outside, to learn about technology and bring technology" back to India, Kohli says. He crisscrossed the United States in search of new technologies and potential customers for TCS's services. His first success came in 1974 with a computer maker named Burroughs, then a rival to IBM. He visited its Detroit headquarters, talking up TCS's experience in programming on Burroughs computers, which Kohli had managed to import into India. After about four visits, Kohli convinced Burroughs that his team had the skills to take on a project to design a health care software system for a new Burroughs machine.[14] The era of the global Indian IT firm began.

TCS's focus on drumming up U.S. business intensified with the arrival of Subramanian Ramadorai. The computer scientist had a plush job at NCR in the United States writing diagnostic programs, but family matters compelled him to give it up and return to India. His parents had found him a young bride, and, almost simultaneously, the opportunity to join TCS arose. Though reluctant to leave the United States, the two offers were too tempting. In the end, he returned home.[15]

Ramadorai reported to work in 1972, where he fell under the thumb of the no-nonsense, hard-driving Kohli. Premji says Kohli is a "military general" who is "so full of himself" and "pisses people off."[16] Ramadorai more gently calls Kohli a "tough taskmaster" and "a man of few words," but one who "had a soft heart." Kohli "threw challenge after challenge. . . . A part of me wanted to just walk away," Ramadorai recalls. "I stuck on and faced them" and became an "excellent foot soldier."[17] The tightly controlled, poorly paid programmers later became known as "cyber coolies."

By the late 1970s, TCS had hit a major transition point. The Burroughs business was spun off into a separate Tata joint venture with the U.S. firm. With this large chunk of revenues gone, Kohli realized his company required a much wider roster of clients. "We needed to build a market," says Ramadorai. Kohli asked Ramadorai to open a TCS office in New York in 1979 to push for other customers, figuring Ramadorai's previous experience in the United States would come in handy. Much like Chan Chin Bock of Singapore had done a decade earlier in his quest for foreign investment for his home island, Ramadorai set off to find potential customers for TCS from a single desk at Tata's offices in Manhattan. He was a one-man show, typing his own letters and searching for contacts in the phone book and computer magazines. His biggest hurdle was the miserable image U.S. businessmen had of India. Few CEOs had ever visited the country. All they knew about was its grinding poverty and pro-Soviet tendencies. Yet several months after he arrived in New York, he landed a major client. Over about four months of meetings, Ramadorai convinced American Express in 1980 to hire TCS to undertake software programming work. The deal showed that TCS might create a global business.[18]

. . . .

WHILE RAMADORAI HUSTLED for customers in New York, another Indian engineer, Narayana Murthy, launched one of TCS's major competitors from his apartment in the Indian city of Pune. His journey to entrepreneurship began, oddly enough, in a tiny, dark cell in a Bulgarian train station.

Born August 20, 1946, Murthy was from a standard middle-class family, but he swung far to the left in his politics. Devoted to socialism, he once said, because its "primary tenet" held that "wealth should be distributed among all members of society," he changed his thinking radically as he backpacked from France to India through the Soviet Bloc in 1974.[19] One night he arrived in Yugoslavia from Bulgaria at the town of Nis. He was hungry and tired, but it was past 9:30 at night and Nis was shut down tight. With no place else to go, he laid out his sleeping bag on the train platform—his "normal hotel," he says—and slept until morning. Even then, he could not get a meal or a room. It was Sunday, the one bank in town was closed, and restaurants refused to serve him unless he paid in local currency. He returned to his sleeping bag on the train platform and slept through the day, waiting for his onward train to arrive that evening. When it pulled into the station, all he could think about was getting a hot meal. He sat across from a young woman, an economist, who began detailing the various hardships she had faced under the Communist regime. A man, eavesdropping nearby, reported this suspicious conversation to the police, who hauled Murthy off the train and locked him into a small room at the train station. He sat there alone, with only a bit of light creeping through a tiny window, for three days. Finally, the police released him and dumped him on a cargo train bound for Istanbul. He was being let go, they explained, because he was from a "friendly" nation. "If this system treats friends like this, I don't want to be their enemy," Murthy told himself. His belief in communism shaken forever, he vowed instead to enter "an experiment in entrepreneurship."[20] Murthy became "determined to someday create a venture that embodied the best principles of capitalism and socialism—by creating wealth for all."[21]

In 1980, Murthy was the head of the software group at an Indian technology firm called Patni Computer Systems. He noted some fundamental shifts in global technology, shifts he believed could offer an opportunity to launch that socialist/capitalist venture. By the early 1980s, computers were becoming more powerful at smaller sizes and lower prices. New software like spreadsheets and higher quality operating systems were coming to market. "We realized that here was a confluence of events that was going to make computing power ubiquitous," Murthy says. His idea was to create a software services firm that would ride this wave of tech-

nological advancement.[22] In 1981, he and six other Patni employees met in his apartment, anted up a total of $250,[23] and founded
Infosys Technologies.

Infosys saw itself as a global enterprise at its inception.
"There was absolutely no opportunity in India," Murthy explains. "And we said in some sense it is good because it will force
us to have an export orientation." Their first target, as it had
been with so many Asian entrepreneurs, was the United States.
While Murthy stayed in India and managed the operation, the
six other founders fanned out across America to drum up business. Their first client was a now-defunct U.S. firm called Data
Basics. Infosys convinced Data Basics to outsource work upgrading its software. A few other big-name clients followed, including Digital Equipment. Little of the programming at that
time was done in India. Communications to the country were too
unreliable and the U.S. companies that hired Infosys were more
comfortable having the tasks completed on site at home. Infosys
dispatched experts to its clients' offices, where they stayed until
the project was complete.

Murthy's special venture, however, had a shaky start. In 1989,
Infosys had a mere $1 million in revenue. Murthy's partners began
to doubt the viability of their business model. Could an Indian
start-up like Infosys become an international IT firm? They were
spending weeks at a time away from their families and homes,
living on the road in the United States on meager salaries, and
they were getting tired and fed up. Their way out materialized
in a $1 million buyout offer. The seven founders held a crucial
meeting, and, after a long discussion, all of them voted to take
the buyout—except Murthy. He sat quietly through most of the
debate, then offered to purchase the shares of the other founders himself. Murthy's resolve bolstered the confidence of everyone
else. They changed their minds and rejected the takeover bid.[24]
Just as Infosys was struggling to survive, Wipro charged into
Murthy's industry.

. . . .

AZIM PREMJI WAS studying for summer session exams at Stanford University in 1966 when a phone call changed his life. It was his distraught mother, Gulbanoo, from Mumbai. His father had died of a massive heart attack at only fifty-one years old. Premji packed up a few things and headed for home. With only two quarters remaining to complete his bachelor's degree in engineering, he expected to return soon.

He never did.* His father had named Premji his successor at the helm of the troubled family business, Western India Vegetable Products, a manufacturer and marketer of vegetable oil. (The corporate name Wipro was introduced in 1977.) It was not Premji's dream job. He had his heart set on a career at the World Bank, not peddling tins of peanut oil at Mumbai grocery stalls,[25] but family duty called. Nor could he bear to leave his mother alone. A medical doctor, she opened India's first hospital for children with polio. "You had very, very poor people," Premji remembers, "who couldn't afford to pay anything, coming from all over India." The hospital, he says, was a complex organization with three hundred staff members and was always desperately in search of new funds. Gulbanoo was firm yet generous with her staff and patient yet perseverant in wrangling subsidies from the government. Premji says he has tried to adopt her management techniques at Wipro.[26]

Premji, at only twenty-one, settled in at the family firm's Mumbai headquarters. He was not made welcome. The company was losing money, and its investors were irate. "My strong recommendation," scolded one vocal investor at Premji's first shareholders meeting, "is that you should sell your shares to somebody who is more mature and more capable of managing this company." The attack only strengthened his resolve to take his father's place.[27]

The belligerent shareholder, however, had a point. Premji, with no management experience or knowledge of the business,

---

* Premji finished his degree by correspondence in 2000.

was ill prepared to run a food company. He put himself on a crash course. Premji got recommendations for a reading list of management guides from a Mumbai professor and started cramming, usually late at night after long hours at the office.[28] He also did a lot of hands-on market research. About ten days a month, he would wander through local bazaars for hours, quizzing forty or more shopkeepers a day about his products and what his competitors were doing.[29] Internally, he imposed new procedures that transformed the firm into a more professional, focused operation. Before Premji's arrival, buyers traveled through the countryside, visited farmers' fields, chewed on a few peanuts, assessed the oil content by taste, and then set a price for buying the crop. Premji ditched these old-fashioned, imprecise methods. He ordered the company to collect samples of peanuts from farmers, dry and weigh them, determine the exact oil content, and set prices based on the results. He also began holding management meetings each Monday (still a Wipro tradition). With direct-dialing a novelty at that time in India, operators connected calls to managers in the field to gather real-time intelligence.[30] Wipro became profitable, and Premji expanded into soaps and beauty products and built a factory to manufacture hydraulic components for construction equipment.

In the late 1970s, Premji smelled an exciting opportunity. A new government had come into office, one aggressively opposed to foreign companies and investment. It passed a law requiring foreign firms to take on an Indian investor as a majority shareholder in their India units. Rather than become minorities in their own companies, some multinationals packed up and left. One of them was IBM. With IBM gone, India would need its computers from somewhere else. Premji recognized a hole to fill. "It didn't require Einstein to decide which was the best industry to be in," he says.[31]

Premji did not know the first thing about computers. He hired people who did. One of them was Sridhar Mitta, a manager at state-owned Electronics Corporation of India. In 1980, a Premji lieutenant first contacted Mitta about joining Wipro as head of R&D. Mitta was ready for a change—the government firm, he believed, was out-of-date—but he did not consider Wipro a better option. He told the Wipro executive Premji should stay clear of computers. "I don't think you're going to make it," he said. But Wipro persisted. "Join for two years," the executive implored. "If we make it, you get the experience of starting a business. If we fail, you learn what *not* to do." Mitta signed on.

His reward was the daunting task of building a computer business from scratch. He rented an office in Bangalore—one of the first Indian technology firms to do so—where he could tap several top technical schools in the area for talented staff. He stole eight colleagues from the Electronics Corp. and added another four young college grads as his initial employees. After studying the computer business for months, Mitta licensed an operating system from a U.S. firm and bought his microprocessors from Intel. A simple factory with about ten employees was set up in the nearby town of Mysore.[32] In 1981, Wipro introduced its first computer, the S-86.

Wipro was nothing close to a glitzy Silicon Valley start-up. Sudip Banerjee remembers working in sales for a Wipro rival in 1983, when he visited a former colleague at his new job in Wipro's office in the Bengali town of Kolkata (then called Calcutta). It was on the twentieth floor of an office tower that had an elevator that rose only to the tenth. He had to climb the rest of the way in Kolkata's stifling heat. Scribbled in chalk on a blackboard in the office were the names of different oilseeds and their latest prices. The computer salesmen were working next to the peanut oil sellers. "I walked in, and almost walked out," Banerjee recalls. His friend was visiting a customer, so the office manager offered him a much-needed drink of water. "Your friend has talked to me a lot about you. You know, we're looking for people," the manager said. Banerjee, that sweaty climb up ten flights of stairs very fresh in his mind, was not receptive. But the manager convinced him to at least go to Wipro headquarters and find out more about the company.

Shortly thereafter, Banerjee was immersed in a grueling interview process at Wipro's Mumbai office. He had to examine a
case study on a food company, take a written test, and conduct
a role-playing exercise in which he made a mock sales call. The
grand finale was what Banerjee calls a "marathon interview" with
Premji himself. Banerjee describes Premji at that time as "very
engaging, very sophisticated," and "strikingly handsome, almost
like a movie star." At the end of the interview, Premji huddled with
some executives, then gave Banerjee an offer—and a hard sell to
join the company. Premji weaved a tale of an exciting campaign to
build a technology empire from scratch. Banerjee was convinced.
"He was selling a vision," Banerjee says.[33]

. . . .

WIPRO BECAME A leading computer maker in India, but as the
company entered the 1990s, the changing economy threatened the
existence of Premji's technology business. India's foreign exchange
crunch hit the computer operation hard. Wipro had to import core
components, like microchips, from the United States, but could not
get enough foreign exchange from the cash-strapped government.
Without sufficient parts, production of new computers ground
to a halt. Matters only worsened with the coming of Manmohan
Singh's reform program. As the License Raj on trade and foreign
investment liberalized, the major PC makers marched back into
India. IBM returned in 1992. Premji's computer business developed
due to government restrictions that kept foreign competition to a
minimum. With those barriers gone, there was no way his small
outfit could compete in technology or resources with the international giants. He was manufacturing a measly ten thousand PCs a
year. Wipro would have to find something else to do.

The solution was already percolating within the company's research labs. Back in 1984, Premji launched a unit called Wipro
Systems to develop packaged software for export. Wipro had
some success in the United States with project-management soft-

ware called InstaPlan, but with limited resources compared to bigger international competitors, Wipro Systems did not have the marketing muscle to break into foreign markets with its software products. In the late 1980s, the business model of the operation began to shift into one much more akin to that of TCS and Infosys—Premji started hiring out his programmers to firms in the United States for software development and other services.

One of the main proponents of this shift to a business model based on outsourcing was Sridhar Mitta. Around 1989, Mitta, too, began to press Premji to allow the engineers at his computer R&D lab to take on work for foreign companies. Premji rejected the idea, thinking that Mitta was stepping on the toes of Wipro Systems. But Mitta would not let the matter drop. He says that Premji "got angry" with his insistence, but eventually gave him the go-ahead anyway. "That's the kind of company Wipro is," Mitta says. "Anywhere else I would have gotten thrown out."

Mitta became even more convinced outsourcing was Wipro's future with the coming of the Internet. Fascinated by the potential of the newly forming World Wide Web, Mitta installed an expensive Internet connection at his computer lab. At that time, India had no Internet service provider, so he had to connect directly to the United States. One day in 1991, he got a note from a man named John Graves based in San Diego. Graves had some ideas for educational software products, but he did not have the money to hire programmers in California. He heard that India had lots of good computer programmers. Could Mitta do the project for a fee? he inquired. Mitta assigned a team to develop Graves's product—a tool to assist in software design—and shipped it to him over the Internet. The deal was unusual at the time. Unlike much of the work done at that time by Indian firms, Mitta's project was completed entirely in India. The only communication with the client took place over the Internet. It opened Mitta's mind to new possibilities. "I realized the world was changing," he says. "Anything that can be digitized can be sent around the globe without hindrance." Mitta believed he had stumbled upon a major new business opportunity. Wipro could become a "lab for hire," completing R&D work for multinationals around the globe from Bangalore.[34]

Mitta's idea looked more and more attractive as Wipro's position in India became more and more precarious. Liberalization was making Wipro's existing business model untenable, but Premji and his managers could not agree on a strategy. Mitta and others advocated shifting more and more resources into IT services outsourcing. Many of Wipro's managers had worked tirelessly to build up the computer operation and were reluctant to abandon it as the company's primary focus.[35]

In the end, though, Premji had no other choice. By 1992, the entire company altered course as Premji relaunched Wipro as a global services provider. "The decision was forced on us," says Banerjee. "We didn't have a business otherwise."[36] Salesmen and managers who had served the Indian market were flying to the United States and hustling for deals. "It was like starting the business all over again," says Sambuddha Deb, a senior Wipro executive who then marketed the company's IT services in the United States.

The early going was rough on the entire company. To cut costs, Deb and his colleagues stayed in cheap hotels and flew economy class. In cities where Wipro had staff based full-time, Deb stocked up on groceries at a local supermarket or invited himself over for dinner. The employees' wives cooked up the meals; for compensation, Deb made sure to bring a stack of Indian women's magazines from home.[37] Premji joined in the marketing efforts, but even he had trouble convincing U.S. executives to make a bet on India. "To get a meeting with an assistant to an assistant of a vice-president used to be a huge challenge," Premji says. "You had to virtually wait in corridors. All of those companies had no knowledge of India." Premji calls his business trips to the United States at that time "exhausting and humiliating. They couldn't believe India could do R&D work. They couldn't believe their intellectual property would be safe with us."[38] Meanwhile, back in India, Wipro was burning through cash to develop the new services business and beef up on technology, while the business coming in was still meager. Girish Paranjpe, treasurer of Wipro in the early 1990s, says he faced a week-to-week scramble for funds to keep the operation going. Wipro began taking on debt. The shift "strained our financial resources." Paranjpe says. Premji and the other senior managers met every two days to discuss the financial situation. Premji tried to appear confident and calm, but he would still sometimes call Paranjpe twice a day for updates.[39]

As Wipro struggled, changes were afoot both at home and abroad that gave the new IT services business a fighting chance. Manmohan Singh's reforms might have undermined Wipro's computer business, but they also allowed Wipro, Infosys, and TCS to more easily open offices, send staff overseas, and import the latest technologies into India more easily. Meanwhile, the rise of the Internet boosted the demand for software services and improved communications. The cost benefits of outsourcing work to Indian firms were also becoming too great for U.S. CEOs to ignore.

Perhaps no single person did more to enhance the credibility of India than Jack Welch, the heralded former CEO of General Electric. On a 1989 visit to India, Welch was feted by everyone from Rajiv Gandhi to the maharaja of Jaipur, who threw him a lavish dinner at his opulent palace. Afterward, they reclined together on carpets and pillows on the palace roof and watched a spectacular fireworks display. Welch described it as "pinch-me stuff." He was most impressed by the Indian people, their technical skills, entrepreneurship, and high level of education. "We saw all kinds of opportunities there. After that trip, I became the champion for India," he later wrote. The next month, at GE's annual officers' conference, Welch "portrayed the country as a great place to make a bet. I wanted to gamble on India."[40] Welch ordered every division within GE to devise its own India strategy, and managers throughout the conglomerate began shifting technical work to the country. "India's market wasn't ready at the time, but their brains were," Welch says. "My strategy was all about how we can use India's intellect."[41]

Welch had also forged a relationship with Premji on that 1989 trip. The two formed a joint venture to sell GE medical equipment in India. When Wipro shifted into IT services, Welch became one of Wipro's earliest and most important clients. The GE connection gave Wipro the credentials it needed to reel in other customers. In the 1990s, Banerjee traveled at least twice a year to Boston to tap that area's dense crop of technology outfits. He checked into the Ramada Inn near Logan Airport, opened the local yellow pages and started cold-calling companies. Most did not call back; if they did, there was only one sure way to keep them listening: "Within the first 60 seconds, you had to say GE," Banerjee says. Intel, Nortel, Sun Microsystems, and Tandem Computers were early clients. Slowly, Premji, Banerjee, and Deb began building the business that would become Wipro's future.

. . . .

RAMAN ROY THOUGHT he had "reached nirvana." It was 1992, and he was head of operations and technology for American Express in India. Perhaps it was not the adventurous career many might hope for, but as a teenager growing up in New Delhi, he had dreamed of working for a big American multinational. "They might give you a car and a house. What else would you want?" he recalls thinking.

His career, though, was about to take an unexpected turn. Roy oversaw the staff that processed credit-card applications and managed the accounts. He noted that his workers were as efficient as their counterparts in the United States and elsewhere—but performed their tasks at a fraction of the cost. He hit upon a novel idea. If Amex transferred some of this credit-card work to India from more expensive countries, the company could save a lot of money. He began pestering his superiors in New York with the idea but got nowhere. The executives at headquarters did not think India had the necessary infrastructure to make such work feasible. Telecommunications were so poor that Roy and his bosses in New York could barely speak by phone at all.

Then one day Roy's secretary told him that John McDonnell, the comptroller of Amex, was on the phone. "I thought I was in some kind of trouble," Roy recalls. "Why else would McDonnell be calling *me*?" It ended up that McDonnell wanted to start an evaluation of the potential of India as a base for back-office operations, as Roy had suggested. India was on Amex's map. A short time later, Roy pitched India to be one of three locations at which Amex planned to consolidate the accounting offices for its global credit-card business. Amex, impressed by the cost efficiency of Roy's operation, awarded India the privilege and put Roy in charge. Roy's experiment at Amex is the first example of business-process outsourcing in India, the spark that launched what was to become a major Indian service industry.

The stubborn Indian bureaucracy, however, came very close to squashing this inventive new business before it even got started. Though Manmohan Singh had done much to strip down red tape, the web of regulations created by the License Raj was so thick that, like a nasty cobweb, they could not be quickly brushed away. Roy spent long hours waiting for government officials in stifling hot corridors in ministry buildings, sitting on hard benches and sipping sickly sweet, milk-laden Indian tea. The main problem he needed to solve concerned proprietary telephone-line allocation. In order to make the accounting operation a success, Roy had to capture more dedicated access than most companies required. Without it, communicating with headquarters and sending and receiving information would be too cumbersome. His application to the government, however, was rejected. Roy says the officials suspected that he was attempting "to do espionage" for the Americans. With the entire project on the line, Roy did not give up. He lectured the officials that the new operation would create jobs and earn much-needed foreign exchange. "I want India to be doing more," he implored them. After six months of lobbying, the government reversed its position. In 1993, Roy's operation was up and running.[42]

Amex's BPO operation, however, remained limited in scope, as did similar programs instituted by a handful of other international companies, including British Airways. That changed when GE threw its weight behind the idea. In 1996, Pramod Bhasin, the top executive at the conglomerate's finance arm, GE Capital, in India, began thinking along the same lines as Roy—that his team of office clerks could process credit-card data and do other paperwork for the company's global operations. Bhasin figured he could perform these duties for as little as one-third the cost in the United States. Bhasin prodded his skeptical superiors into giving his plan a go. His first phone call went to Raman Roy. Roy's progress at Amex made him the premier expert on this odd new industry, and thus an irresistible target for GE. Bhasin offered Roy a job, and in 1996 Roy began building GE's BPO operation in India.[43]

Bhasin and Roy started by handling some back-office work for GE Capital's global credit-card business. The U.S. headquarters couriered customer correspondence to India, where Roy's staff updated databases, changed account addresses, and performed other simple tasks. Roy wanted to expand the experiment into call centers for GE. His plan was to reroute customer-service phone calls from the United States to India, where staff could be trained to handle their complaints and queries. To Roy, the concept was a natural for India, with its combination of English-speaking workers and low costs. Bhasin was skeptical, but Roy's perseverance convinced him to try out a call center. Opened in 1998, it was India's first. Bhasin and Roy set up the center in an old building in Gurgaon, a suburb of New Delhi, with a staff of about twenty people. To soundproof the room, the workers brought in dusty, old curtains from home. "We were flying by the seat of our pants," Bhasin says. The center "was very much a pilot experiment."[44]

Bhasin, though, felt he was onto something big. As Roy proved the call center could work efficiently, more and more GE back-office business poured into India. Welch was thrilled. Calling the results "sensational," he boasted that he had "moved the GE 'back rooms' in the United States to the 'front room' in India."[45] Welch invited Bhasin to speak at GE management conferences in the United States to convince officers throughout the conglomerate to shift work to India. At one meeting in 1998, Welch followed up Bhasin's presentation with comments of his own, telling the assembled executives that they were crazy to miss out on the opportunities offered in India. When Bhasin returned to his Delhi office, "my inbox was flooded with e-mails from people wanting to visit India."[46]

. . . .

BY THE EARLY years of this century, India had become the global IT powerhouse F. C. Kohli had predicted thirty years earlier. In India's 2000 fiscal year, the revenue of the entire IT and BPO services industry in India was $8 billion. Eight years later, the sector had grown to $64 billion, with two million employees. Kohli's Tata Consultancy, Murthy's Infosys, and Premji's Wipro are the titans of the industry. Infosys has ridden the outsourcing wave to revenues of $4.2 billion. Along the way, Murthy realized his dream of creating a company that generated wealth for all. In 1994, Infosys introduced India's first large-scale employee stock option scheme, which spread the wealth generated by the successful firm among its many workers. Today the firm that began in Murthy's bedroom is housed on an 80-acre office compound outside of Bangalore that is a cross between a university campus and Disneyland. The menagerie of unusual buildings includes odd replicas of an Egyptian pyramid and the Sydney Opera House.[47]

Premji has been equally successful. The IT and BPO services business he launched with reluctance pulled in revenues of $3.7 billion in fiscal 2007–08. (Another $668 million still comes from Wipro's original businesses, including vegetable oil. Premji never sold them because they are "fun," he says. "You can touch and feel" the consumer operations, while with IT, "all you can touch and feel is the people.")[48] For Premji, though, Wipro is only at the beginning of what it can achieve. He is no longer content to scrounge for the crumbs of the global IT business, or happy to get any contracts he can. His goal is to provide services for every aspect of corporate activity—taking customer queries in call centers, entering data, programming software, designing products, and consulting CEOs on the best technology to use. What skills and expertise Wipro cannot develop quickly enough on its own, Premji is buying. Wipro has been on a major global acquisition binge that has included U.S. consulting firms, an Austrian semiconductor developer, a Portuguese retail IT services firm, and a Finnish telecom design outfit.

One of Premji's targets was Raman Roy. In 2000, the restless Roy resigned from GE, took a few executives with him, and founded Spectramind, which grew into one of the largest independent BPO service providers in India.[49] Beginning in 2002, Premji acquired 100 percent of Spectramind in a series of share purchases. Roy stayed in charge of the division for more than three years, but, accustomed to running his own show, he left to found yet another BPO firm in January 2006. Seeing it as his fourth start-up, he named it Quatrro.

The Indian IT services and BPO industries have exploded at a fantastic pace this decade.

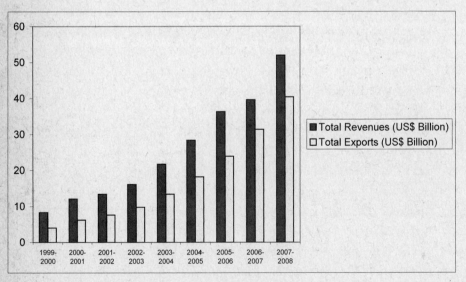

Source: National Association of Software and Service Companies (NASSCOM).

. . . .

INDIAN BUSINESSMEN SUCH as Premji and Murthy have added India to the list of Asia's ascending economic powerhouses. Now that Asia has regained its rightful place at the forefront of the global economy, one big question remains: How will the United States react to the challenge?

EPILOGUE
LESSONS FROM A REFRIGERATOR FACTORY

I don't care where they're from.
They're bringing jobs. —GERALD REEVES

A road trip with Rick Franklin shook my faith in free trade. We were driving in June 2007 on a two-lane road in a white Honda through rural South Carolina past dense woods, picturesque horse and cow pastures, and small towns with rows of quaint shops and aged houses. Franklin, a chatty local with basset-hound cheeks and an obsession with Isaac Asimov, was recounting a litany of woes that had battered the area's citizens. "When I was younger, if you graduated from school and could do some math, you could walk right into a job," he explained. "Now you can't find jobs, and when you do, you can't live on them." Depressed and mired in hopelessness, many residents had turned to drugs, both selling and using them. Houses that were once home to happy families were now crack dens. "If we keep going like this," Franklin warned, "there's gonna be nothing left."

Franklin turned off the main road onto lumpy backstreets to show me what had gone so wrong. Behind the old houses were the ruins of textile mills. Some of the factories were standing silent, empty, and unkempt, like dinosaur skeletons—dusty, leftover reminders of a different era. Other mills had been demolished into

piles of broken brick and glass in abandoned lots. The towns of
this section of South Carolina had been dependent on these mills
for jobs and taxes. Whole communities sprouted up around them.
But no matter how important they once were, these mills could
not survive competition from China and other countries with
much lower wages. With the mills gone, the life in these small
towns was lost as well. Franklin drove me down the forlorn main
streets, where many of the shops and restaurants were shut. Their
owners posted "For Rent" signs in the windows in the vain hope
of finding new tenants. Other storefronts were simply boarded up.
The Miracle, it turns out, had not been kind to South Carolina.

Whatever my economics training taught me about the inevitable vicissitudes of capitalism, it was impossible to witness the
damage done to the American workforce by globalization and the
rise of Asia and not be profoundly affected. It is easy to sit in
my Hong Kong office overlooking spectacular Victoria Harbor,
buried in my economic statistics and theories, and expound with
great conviction on the benefits of free trade. It is easy to watch
the fantastic pace of development and growth of wealth in Bangalore, Shanghai, and Seoul and focus only on the positive results of
today's international economic system.

I began to question my own economic beliefs. Is Asia stripping
the United States of its future? Are free trade and globalization
impoverishing the American middle class? Does America need to
protect its economy from an ascending Asia? *Could I be wrong?*

But then we arrived at our final destination, a white boxy factory in the town of Camden. Upon entering the building, I could
tell this was no ordinary factory. A banner next to the reception
desk boasted giant Chinese characters, with the cryptic English
translation "Everlasting Sincere Heart." Inside the plant, an American flag hung over the assembly lines side-by-side with the red flag
of China. Below, Americans were manufacturing refrigerators for
the U.S. market. The walls were covered with more unusual banners and posters with pithy sayings. "It is easier to be critical of

others; it is easier to see others' shortcomings," read one, penned by a Li Xin of the "Freezer Department." "1% quality defect leads to 100% disaster for the customers!!!" said another, written by the oddly named "Karwen Brandery." (It ends up that the American assembly-line worker who devised the proverb is actually Kevin Bradshaw, but the non-English-speaking executives at the company's headquarters botched the spelling.) The name of the company might be equally unfamiliar to many reading this page: Haier.

What makes this refrigerator factory much more noteworthy than the average refrigerator factory is that it is the first manufacturing plant opened by a Chinese company in America.[1] Haier, China's largest appliance manufacturer, invested $40 million in this operation. All of the two hundred people employed here are Americans, from the plant manager on down. And it is just a start. With grand designs on U.S. consumers, Haier envisions this 110-acre plot in rural South Carolina as a $100 million industrial complex, with five factories making air conditioners, dishwashers, and clothes dryers, and employing one thousand people. The production already contributes to American exports. Refrigerators are shipped from Camden to Latin America and the Middle East.

Haier is not the only Asian firm that has come to small-town South Carolina. Elsewhere in the state, Japan's Honda operates a factory making personal watercraft and all-terrain vehicles. Its Japanese suppliers have set up shop as well. In all, a full one-third of the workers in Kershaw County, where Haier's plant is located, are employed by foreign companies that have invested in the United States.

As I walked through Haier's factory, watching one refrigerator after another roll off the assembly line, I thought how truly remarkable the international economy is today. While jobs are being lost in one industry to Asia, jobs are being re-created in the same place by growing Asian companies in entirely different industries. Even companies controlled by the government of Communist China.

. . . .

AT FIRST GLANCE, there may appear to be some irony in the Haier factory. American businessmen are closing down factories in America and shipping production overseas or outsourcing to foreign companies, while foreign companies are opening factories in America. Why do Chinese firms see the advantages of manufacturing in the United States while American companies do not? It is a question antitrade populists ask repeatedly. Of course, the reality is not so simple. In an ever-changing global economy, different companies in different industries have different priorities at different times. There is, however, one constant that bodes well for the future of Asia-U.S. economic ties: it is as true today as in the era of Akio Morita and Soichiro Honda that the United States is the first place in which every up-and-coming businessman wants to succeed.

The story of Haier makes this fact clear. In the early 1980s, Haier, based in the coastal city of Qingdao (famous for its beer), was a typically bloated, inefficient Chinese state company. Its products were shoddy; its workers dozed on the job and even urinated on the assembly lines. In 1984, with reform sweeping the country, Qingdao city civil servant Zhang Ruimin was given the task of fixing the mess. One day in the summer of 1985, after watching a customer arrive at Haier's factory with a recently purchased fridge that did not work, an annoyed Zhang examined four hundred finished refrigerators in the factory warehouse waiting for shipment to customers. He determined seventy-six of them had such serious flaws that he refused to release them to the public. Instead, Zhang rolled the faulty fridges in front of the company's six hundred staff and handed around a sledgehammer. "Destroy them!" he barked. Soon the floor was covered in shattered bits of refrigerator.[2] Zhang even tore into one himself. (The sledgehammer is preserved today in Haier's museum.) Haier had made a violent and dramatic break with its incompetent past.

Born in 1949, just before Mao's Red Army conquered all

of China, Zhang was, like Lenovo's Liu Chuanzhi, a Chinese oddity—a man who had grown up in a Communist world but held strong capitalist concepts of business. The only son of a textile-factory worker, Zhang was an avid reader of both Western management texts and Chinese philosophers, such as Daoism founder Lao-tzu. When Zhang took over the struggling Haier, it produced a paltry eighty-four refrigerators a month. At first, Zhang did not even have the funds to buy coal to heat the factory during Qingdao's icy winters; workers stripped the factory's window frames and burned the wood instead. Zhang employed a carrot-and-stick approach to motivating the staff to work harder. He invested in a bus to ferry workers to the factory each day, a major luxury at the time that endeared him to the staff. Workers who slacked off felt his ire. In a Maoist form of punishment, those deemed responsible for mistakes were forced to stand on a painted circle on the factory floor in full view of their comrades, a grave humiliation in face-conscious China.

As Zhang improved quality and productivity, he also acquired other appliance makers and the company grew in scale.[3] Haier came to dominate the Chinese white goods market. Like Akio Morita, Chung Ju Yung, and all the rest of the titans of Asian industry who came before him, Zhang inevitably looked for new business in the global market. By 1995, Haier began exporting to the United States. Its first big product in America was the small, square fridge that is a staple feature of college dorm rooms and hotel minibars. Haier's distributor was a U.S. company called Welbilt Appliances run by American businessman Michael Jemal. Haier's U.S. business was minuscule at the time, but Jemal believed Haier could be doing much more. "I saw desire to win. I saw the desire to have the brand grow throughout the world," Jemal says of Zhang's Haier. The two formed a joint venture, Haier America, in 1999.[4]

Simultaneously, Haier was looking to build a factory in the United States. Though the cost base is significantly lower in China than the United States, shipping large appliances—with their hollow interiors—across the Pacific in containers is expensive, eliminating some of the advantages of Chinese production. Haier also realized that its business would hit a ceiling if the company only sold Chinese-made fridges on the U.S. market. Haier's products would have to be adapted, and even developed, especially for the American consumer.[5] A U.S. factory appeared crucial if Zhang had any hope of expanding his presence in America.

Haier hired a husband-and-wife consulting team to scout possible locations for a refrigerator factory. At first, Camden was not one of them, but that changed at a 1998 cocktail party in the town. A former chairman of the local economic development board began chatting with the couple and learned the wife was originally from Camden. Wasting no time, he asked if she would consider her hometown as a site for Haier's factory. The county government, smelling a unique opportunity, rolled out the red carpet for the Communist investors. Just as Japanese companies such as Honda have invested large sums in factories in the United States since the 1980s, an emerging China, the officials figured, would do exactly the same. When a delegation from Haier arrived in Camden later that year to explore possible sites, they saw "Welcome Haier" banners hung throughout the town. Local business leaders wrote letters to the Haier executives expressing support.[6] The enthusiasm worked. In 1999, Haier began the process of building a refrigerator factory in South Carolina.

. . . .

DESPITE HAIER'S GREAT success, Jemal believes that "the best is yet to come." And that is not just true for Haier. The Camden refrigerator factory is almost definitely the first drop in a coming wave of Chinese investment in the United States. In this regard, China, once again, is simply following other Asian countries that have staked out a major presence in the American economy. By mid-2008, Honda had invested $9 billion in the United States, built 10 plants, and hired 27,000 employees. Japanese carmakers, in fact, have invested nearly $33 billion in America, and the firms and their dealers employ 425,000 people. In 2005, Chung Ju Yung's Hyundai Motor opened its first factory in the United States in Alabama; its Kia affiliate will follow in 2009 in Georgia.

Asian investment in America is just one way the United States will continue to benefit from the Miracle. The richer Asians become, the better customers they are for American companies. Asia in coming years will be the fastest growing source of new sales for everything from plane tickets and café lattes to cars and mobile phones. That means the Intels, Motorolas, Starbucks, Coca-Colas, and Boeings, the cream of American business, will find eager new customers in an ascending Asia at a faster rate than anywhere else in the world. The twenty-first century may prove to be the Asian Century, but that does not mean the United States cannot profit from it.

America has always reaped great rewards from the Miracle. The cost savings gained by corporate America through outsourcing or offshoring to Asia has kept U.S. firms highly competitive. This shift of production has also reduced prices on necessary consumer goods such as clothing, toys, and electronics to a level far below what could have been possible if their manufacture remained in the United States. The rise of Asia has thus allowed Americans to enjoy a higher quality of life. Most of all, the Miracle has proven an uncontested victory for American ideals. Capitalism is the dominant force everywhere. China has, in essence, been "reconquered" by the ideas of Chiang Kai-shek's Nationalists. South Korea has far outpaced its North Korean rival. India has rejected its socialist leanings. In many societies, such as Indonesia, South Korea, and Taiwan, democracy has taken hold. Like the crumbling of the Berlin Wall, the Miracle is one of America's greatest triumphs.

There is an irony, then, in the American reaction to its success in Asia. Instead of embracing the strong, capitalist Asia that Americans worked so hard to create, we too often recoil in fear and horror at the potential challenges that Asia presents. First,

Americans panicked at the ascendance of Japan; today the threat has switched to China. India, too, has become a target of American concern. Asian countries are "stealing" American jobs and employing "unfair" trade practices to undermine American industries; Asian firms are "buying up" crucial parts of the American economy. The reaction against China has been especially paranoid. In 2005, state-owned China National Offshore Oil Corp. scuttled its bid to buy midsize American energy firm Unocal due to fierce opposition from Washington politicians who feared the acquisition would hand China important reserves of oil and deal a blow to U.S. national security.[7]

Even in Camden, not everyone thought the coming of the Chinese was such a grand idea. To some in this conservative swath of the South, the Chinese were still the dangerous, godless Reds of the Cold War. Gerald Reeves, the Haier factory's human resources director, says that a few of his friends "thought I had lost my mind" to "work for a Chinese company owned by a Communist government we didn't get along with."[8] Rick Franklin's mother refused to sit next to her own son in church for two weeks after Haier hired him as a transportation manager.[9] Fortunately for Camden, this resistance was conquered by rational economic thinking. "I don't care where they're from," Reeves says of Haier. "They're bringing jobs." When the Haier plant opened, it required only twenty-eight workers. Reeves chose them from among several thousand eager applicants.[10]

The inevitable result of growing anti-Asia sentiment is talk of retaliation, protectionism, new tariffs, and the implementation of laws restricting the free flow of production, goods, and services. One of the chief proponents of such steps is CNN anchorman Lou Dobbs, who rallies investors to dump the shares of American companies that outsource to Asia. In his book *Exporting America*, Dobbs makes the incredible recommendation that, in order to preserve American employment, U.S. multinationals should be barred from freely manufacturing goods overseas for shipment back to the United States, a practice he labels the "exploitation of our trade policies." The gap between American wages and those in China is so great, he argues that "pursuing free trade policies that force the American worker to compete against third world workers . . . is patently unfair and absurd."[11]

Dobbs is advocating the kind of insular policies that the likes of Deng Xiaoping and Manmohan Singh rejected. The mistake pundits and populists make about the Miracle is that it has set up a global contest for economic greatness. It is "us against them," a zero-sum game of winners and losers. A growing Asia means a declining America. But this thinking is flawed. The United States, and the world economy in general, has benefited as much from Asia's fantastic economic boom as Asia has itself. America will continue to discover new benefits from the Miracle as the epic story of Asia's quest for wealth continues, as long as we see a rising Asia as an opportunity, not a threat, and a partner, not a competitor.

Yet as I write the final words of this book in February 2009, the "forces of obscurantism," in Singh's words, are gathering strength. The world is engulfed in what may prove to be the worst global economic catastrophe since the Great Depression of the 1930s. And it is a very dangerous time for the pro-trade philosophy of the Miracle. In a desperate attempt to preserve jobs and rescue companies, governments are turning inward and nationalistic, bailing out industries and implementing export promotion drives and "buy local" campaigns. Even more, the downturn has fomented doubts about the virtues of globalization itself. As the subprime mortgage meltdown on Wall Street morphed into a global recession, everyone from Persian Gulf emirs to Chinese assembly-line workers woke up to the reality that globalization can bring hardship as well as prosperity. The tight ties of trade and investment that have proven so successful in uplifting the poor can suddenly reverse, destroying the same wealth they had created and sending millions right back under the poverty line. Even in Asia, economists are questioning the very export-led model that sparked the Miracle. The economies most affected by the recession are those that are most integrated into the world economy—especially the early movers—South Korea, Singapore, Taiwan, and Hong Kong. In China, tens of thousands of export factories—the best hope for a new life for hundreds of millions of poor Chinese—have shut as credit tightened and orders shrank. Tens of millions are losing their jobs.

But that does not mean the Miracle is over. Clearly, the globalization-led development method divined by Lee Kuan Yew, Park Chung Hee, and the other early Miracle leaders needs reform. The problem lies in the Miracle's spectacular success. The invest-and-export route to wealth has worked so well that policymakers have not fostered other potential sources of growth in their own domestic economies, leading to overdependence on trade. In China, for example, the farmers of the vast hinterland—who had launched the Chinese reform process in the communes of Anhui province—have generally been ignored in recent years as the country rushed to industrialize. Only now, as China's manufacturing machine sputters, has Beijing refocused its attention on agricultural development. Nor have China and other Miracle nations encouraged domestic consumption, which could act as another pillar of economic growth. They have failed to put in place the welfare programs—proper health care systems and unemployment insurance, for example—that would persuade their citizens, usually endemic savers, to spend more of their newfound riches. The leaders of Asia have been complacent in utilizing the vast wealth generated by globalization to find new ways to perpetuate the Miracle. Hopefully, the 2008–09 recession will wake them from their slumber and, like the 1997 Asian Financial Crisis, force much-needed change that allows the Miracle to reach yet another stronger level.

The problems Asia faces today, however, do not negate the power of globalization to create Miracles. The story told in the preceding pages provides irrefutable proof that free trade, foreign investment, and free enterprise produce wealth and alleviate poverty on a scale that cannot be matched by any other mix of policies. These tools forged superpowers from some of the poorest nations on earth. Once the 2008–09 recession comes to end—which it inevitably will—the forces of globalization will once again become the catalyst for improving human welfare. The world's political and economic leadership should not sacrifice the long-term prospects for the global economy by imposing protectionist, beggar-thy-neighbor policies in response to an economic downturn today. The consequences of rejecting the lessons of the Miracle would be disastrous. The World Bank estimates that in 2005, 1.4 billion people still lived in absolute poverty. There is every reason to believe that the pro-trade, pro-investment policies used by Asia to rapidly increase incomes can be deployed by governments in Africa and the Middle East in their own quests for wealth. If destitute Bangladesh or Ethiopia or Haiti set in place a similar policy framework as Taiwan or South Korea, it is almost certain that they, too, could spark their own Miracles.

The poor nations of the world cannot achieve Miracles on their own, however. As the story of Asia makes clear, the support for trade and foreign investment in Washington and American corporate boardrooms was an indispensable factor in making the Miracle happen. The United States has an important part to play in ensuring that the policies necessary to keep the Miracle alive remain firmly in place. As the world sinks into recession, to a great degree due to faulty American economic policy and behavior, the global community needs Washington to step up and point out the correct path to recovery and renewal more than ever. The new administration of Barack Obama has the responsibility to find ways of preserving the benefits of globalization while minimizing its detriments.

The importance of spreading the Miracle around the globe should be a priority for Americans, and not just for altruistic reasons. As the 2008–09 recession proved with devastating force, we all rise and fall together in today's highly integrated world. Slower global income growth means fewer customers for American products and services, and fewer jobs for Americans back home. The fallout for the United States from a world without Miracles is not limited to the realm of economics. The story of the Miracle in Asia tells that there is a connection between rising wealth and democracy. Dictatorships may have launched the Miracle in most Asian nations, but almost everywhere, economic progress undermined their legitimacy and vibrant democracies have taken their place. Even in China, where Deng Xiaoping and his successors have maintained the dominance of the Communist Party despite the nation's economic reforms, the demands of a market-oriented economy have given the Chinese people far more freedom—over how they live, work, and communicate—than they had during the harsh days under Mao. The continuation of the Miracle will create a freer world, and therefore a world more favorable for American national security and diplomatic interests.

It is in the continued creation of prosperity that America can find its future role in the world. The United States has already helped Asia achieve a Miracle, but its mission is incomplete. In the words of Nehru, there are still many tears in many eyes, and our work will not be over until they are all wiped away.

ACKNOWLEDGMENTS

The number of people I need to thank for their cooperation in this project seems nearly as vast as the population of Asia itself. With research in ten countries, I managed to impose myself on the kindness of friends, colleagues, executives, and politicians from rural South Carolina to the halls of the Indian finance ministry.

My first thanks must go to my editor, Michael Elliott of *Time* magazine. Without his support, I would never have had the time and opportunity to complete this project. His encouragement of my career and my growth as a writer has simply been invaluable. A former *Time* editor, Hanna Kite, also played a crucial role in this project by reading the entire manuscript and providing insights and advice that greatly improved the book. Another *Time* editor, Zoher Abdoolcarim, made the mistake of volunteering to read my chapters as they were produced and his guidance was equally priceless. A friend and former colleague, Neil Weinberg, also took time from his work and family to read my manuscript, and his careful eye saved me from embarrassing errors.

Other colleagues donated their time to assist with specific sections of the book based on their expertise. Susan Jakes, one of the most knowledgeable people I know about China, kindly helped with my chapter on Deng Xiaoping. Simon Elegant lent his expertise to my chapters on Malaysia.

There were also many people who provided great assistance in helping me gain access to key figures in this story. Former Hasbro chairman Alan Hassenfeld voluntarily asked his friend Hong Kong entrepreneur Li Ka-shing to contribute to my book, and due to his intervention, I was able to include fresh, personal anecdotes from Mr. Li in this narrative. In India, Deepak Puri employed his boundless contacts and influence to get me in to see important government figures. In Indonesia, Jason Tedjasukmana employed his connections to get me access to Suharto's former ministers.

In each country, there were many people who wasted their valuable time assisting me with appointments, contacts, and information. On China, Jason Zhou and Matthew Forney; on Hong Kong, Laura Cheung, Godfrey Scotchbrook, and Tom Mitchell; on India, Sanjeev Kapur, Kumar Kandaswami, Jessie Paul, Swapna Pillai, and Pradipta Bagchi; on Indonesia, Puspa Madani and Zamira Loebis; on Japan, Yu Wada, Shin Tanaka, Norihiko Shirouzu, Jathon Sapsford, Yuki Oda, and Toko Sekiguchi; on Malaysia, Leslie Lopez, S. Jayasankaran, and Sufi Yusoff; on Singapore, Yeong Ying Yoon and Pang Kim Poh; on South Korea, Lina Yoon, Jeffrey Jones, and Mark Clifford; on Taiwan, Teresa Chen, Don Shapiro, Joyce Huang, and Ting-i Tsai; on the United States, Rick Franklin and Teresa Justice.

Then of course there is my agent, Michelle Tessler, who kindly puts up with all of my incessant questions and mini–panic attacks, and my editor at HarperCollins, Ben Loehnen, whose careful and thoughtful work on the manuscript greatly improved the work.

On a personal level, I must of course give great thanks to my wife, Eunice Yoon. Not only were her insights on my chapters highly valuable, but she also patiently suffered through the manic and obsessive behavior I exhibited when researching this project. And I cannot forget my family: my father, Herbert; my sister, Sheri; and my mother, Emily. It was my mother, an English teacher for most of her life, who originally taught me how to write. One day I came home from second grade with an assignment to write a paper on Booker T. Washington. I had no idea how to proceed, but my mom told me to approach the process of writing as an inquisitive reader. Make a list of questions I'd like to ask about Washington, she suggested, find the answers, and then use that information as the basis for the paper. I still use a similar process in my writing today.

INTERVIEWS

Montek Singh Ahluwalia, deputy chairman of the Planning Commission and former commerce and finance secretaries, India

Anwar Ibrahim, former deputy prime minister and finance minister, Malaysia

Sudip Banerjee, chief executive officer of L&T Infotech and a former senior executive at Wipro Ltd., India

Pramod Bhasin, chief executive officer, Genpact, India

Stephen Bosworth, former U.S. ambassador to South Korea

Chan Chin Bock, former chairman of the Economic Development Board, Singapore

Morris Chang, founder, Taiwan Semiconductor Manufacturing Company, Taiwan

B. K. Chaturvedi, former cabinet secretary to Prime Minister Manmohan Singh, India

P. Chidambaram, finance minister and former commerce minister, India

William "Chip" Connor, chairman, W.E. Connor & Associates, Hong Kong

Daim Zainuddin, former finance minister, Malaysia

Sambuddha Deb, chief global delivery officer, Wipro Ltd., India

Victor Fung, chairman, Li & Fung, Hong Kong

Mohamad "Bob" Hasan, timber tycoon, Indonesia

Alan Hassenfeld, former chairman, Hasbro, United States

Nobuyuki Idei, former chief executive officer, Sony, Japan

Shoichiro Irimajiri, former president Honda Manufacturing of America, Japan

Michael Jemal, chief executive officer, Haier America, United States

John Joyce, former chief financial officer, IBM, United States

Kim Chung Yum, former finance minister and chief of staff to President Park Chung Hee, South Korea

Kim Dae Jung, former president, South Korea

Yotaro Kobayashi, former chairman, Fuji Xerox, Japan

F. C. Kohli, former deputy chairman, Tata Consultancy Services, India

K. Y. Lee, chief executive officer, BenQ, Taiwan

Lee Kuan Yew, minister mentor and former prime minister, Singapore

Nelson Lindsay, director, Economic Development Office of Kershaw County in South Carolina, United States

Liu Chuanzhi, founder, Lenovo, China

Mary Ma, former chief financial officer, Lenovo, China

Mahaleel Ariff, former chief executive officer, Proton, Malaysia

Mahathir Mohamad, former prime minister, Malaysia

Sridhar Mitta, managing director, e4e, and a former senior executive at Wipro Ltd., India

Simon Murray, former chief executive officer, Hutchison Whampoa, Hong Kong

Narayana Murthy, co-founder, Infosys Technologies, India

Deepak Nayyar, former economic advisor to the government, India

Park Tae Joon, founder, POSCO, South Korea

David Parks, former president, Haier America Refrigerator Co., United States

Azim Premji, chairman, Wipro Ltd., India

S. Ramadorai, chief executive officer, Tata Consultancy Services, India

Gerald Reeves, human resources director, Haier America Refrigerator Co., United States

Raman Roy, founder, Spectramind and Quatrro, India

Ruan Ming, former deputy director of the Theoretical Research Department at the Central Party School of the Chinese Communist Party, Taiwan

Emil Salim, former cabinet minister and economic advisor to Suharto, Indonesia

Carolyn Shih, co-founder, Acer Computer, Taiwan

Stan Shih, co-founder, Acer Computer, Taiwan

Joseph and Lucy Sun, son and daughter of Sun Yun-suan, former premier of Taiwan

Kenneth Ting, chairman, Kader Industrial, Hong Kong

Ali Wardhana, former finance minister, Indonesia

Jack Welch, former CEO, General Electric, United States

NOTES

Introduction: A Few Thoughts on How Miracles Happen

1. For the complete study on global poverty, see the World Bank report by Chen, Shaohua, and Martin Ravallion, "The Developing World Is Poorer Than We Thought but No Less Successful in the Fight against Poverty," August 26, 2008.
2. Ferguson, Niall. *The War of the World: History's Age of Hatred*. London: Penguin, 2007, p. lxviii.
3. Prestowitz, Clyde. *Three Billion New Capitalists: The Great Shift of Wealth and Power to the East*. New York: Basic Books, 2005, pp. xii, xiv, and 255. His earlier book on the threat from Japan is *Trading Places: How We Allowed Japan to Take the Lead*. New York: Basic Books, 1988.
4. Sachs, Jeffrey D. "Welcome to the Asian Century," *Fortune*, January 12, 2004.
5. Wilson, Dominic, and Roopa Purushothaman. "Dreaming with BRICs: The Path to 2050," Goldman Sachs Global Economics Paper No. 99, October 1, 2003.
6. Schuman, Michael. "Hey, Big Spenders," *Time* (Asia edition), May 9, 2005. Other details from author's notes.
7. Dower, John W. *Embracing Defeat: Japan in the Wake of World War II*. New York: W. W. Norton, 2000, pp. 44–47 and 89–93.
8. Maddison, Angus. *The World Economy: A Millennial Perspective*. Paris: Development Centre of the Organization for Economic Cooperation and Development, 2001, p. 263.
9. Keay, John. *India: A History*. London: HarperCollins, 2001, pp. 326–327.
10. MacFarquhar, Roderick. "The Post-Confucian Challenge," *Economist*, February 9, 1980, p. 68.
11. World Bank. *The East Asian Miracle: Economic Growth and Public Policy*. New York: Oxford University Press, 1993, p. 5.
12. Goh Keng Swee. *The Practice of Economic Growth*. Singapore: Marshall Cavendish, 2004, p. 257.
13. Park Chung Hee. *Korea Reborn: A Model for Development*. Englewood Cliffs, N.J.: Prentice-Hall, 1979, pp. 91–92.

14. Speech by Jawaharlal Nehru, August 14, 1947. In Norman, Dorothy, ed. *Nehru: The First Sixty Years*. Vol. 2. Mumbai: Asia Publishing House, 1965, p. 336.
15. Krugman, Paul. "Why Adam Smith Would Love Asia," *Time* (Asia edition), August 23–30, 1999.
16. Author's interview with Lee Kuan Yew.

Chapter One: The Radio That Changed the World

1. Morita, Akio. *Made in Japan: Akio Morita and Sony*. With Edwin M. Reingold and Mitsuko Shimomura. London: HarperCollins, 1994, pp. 2–4, 50, 52, and 69.
2. A translation of the Founding Prospectus can be found on Sony's website, at http://www.sony.net/SonyInfo/CorporateInfo/History/prospectus.html.
3. Morita, pp. 68–70.
4. Watch the commercial on YouTube at http://www.youtube.com/watch?v=MG_k7dmt0FQ.
5. Nathan, John. *Sony: The Private Life*. London: HarperCollins, 1999, pp. 71 and 76.
6. This quote is from an internal commemorative booklet prepared by Sony after Morita's death in 1999 and provided to the author, entitled "In Memory of Mr. Morita," p. 67.
7. Nathan, pp. 1–2.
8. "Japan, Inc: Winning the Most Important Battle," *Time*, May 10, 1971.
9. "In Memory of Mr. Morita," pp. 63 and 80.
10. Author's interview with Yotaro Kobayashi.
11. Ohmae, Kenichi. "Akio Morita," *Time*, December 7, 1998.
12. Morita, pp. 66–67.
13. Sony's official history.
14. Nathan, p. 32.
15. Johnson, Chalmers. *MITI and the Japanese Miracle: The Growth of Industrial Policy 1925–1975*. Stanford, Calif.: Stanford University Press, 1982, p. 240.
16. Nathan, p. 31.
17. Sony's official history.
18. Morita, p. 69.
19. Nathan, p. 33.
20. Morita, p. 69.
21. Feifer, George. *Breaking Open Japan: Commodore Perry, Lord Abe, and American Imperialism in 1853*. New York: Smithsonian Books, 2006, p. 68.
22. Feifer, pp. 106 and 110.
23. Beasley, William G. *The Meiji Restoration*. Stanford, Calif.: Stanford University Press, 1972, pp. 89 and 96.
24. Pyle, Kenneth B. *The Making of Modern Japan*. 2nd ed. Lexington, Mass.: D. C. Heath, 1996, p. 101.
25. Macpherson, W. J. *The Economic Development of Japan, 1868–1941*. Cambridge, U.K.: Cambridge University Press, 1995, p. 29.
26. Pyle, pp. 99–100.
27. Johnson, p. 20.

28. Johnson, p. 12.
29. Many of the details about Sahashi in this section are from his autobiography *Ishoku Kanryo* or "An Extraordinary Bureaucrat." Published by Shakaishi-sosha in Tokyo in 1994, the book has unfortunately been released only in Japanese. The information and quotes from the book were translated specifically for the author by Yu Wada. These specifics are from pp. 162 and 179.
30. Johnson, pp. 243 and 272.
31. Sahashi, p. 41.
32. Sahashi, p. 45.
33. Sahashi, p. 162.
34. Chernow, Ron. *Alexander Hamilton.* New York: Penguin, 2005, p. 377.
35. Johnson, p. 199.
36. My description of how Japan's industrial policy worked is from several sources but I relied heavily on Johnson's *MITI and the Japanese Miracle,* especially pp. 19–33 and 200–273.
37. Johnson, pp. 9–10.
38. Sahashi, pp. 290–292; and Johnson, pp. 269–271.
39. Hartcher, Peter. *The Ministry: The Inside Story of Japan's Ministry of Finance.* London: HarperCollins, 1998, p. 2.
40. Sahashi, p. 217; and Johnson, pp. 246–247.
41. Ingrassia, Paul, and Joseph B. White. *Comeback: The Fall & Rise of the American Automobile Industry.* New York: Simon & Schuster, 1994, pp. 31–32.
42. For one study of MITI's success and failures, see Porter, Michael E., and Hirotaka Takeuchi, "Fixing What Really Ails Japan," *Foreign Affairs,* May/June 1999.
43. Morita, p. 69.
44. Johnson, p. 240.
45. Nakamura, Takafusa. *The Postwar Japanese Economy: Its Development and Structure 1937–1994.* 2nd ed. Tokyo: University of Tokyo Press, 1995, p. 91.
46. Kosai, Yutaka. Jacqueline Kaminski, trans. *The Era of High Speed Growth: Notes on the Postwar Japanese Economy.* Tokyo: University of Tokyo Press, 1986, p. 203.
47. Patrick, Hugh, and Henry Rosovsky, eds. *Asia's New Giant: How the Japanese Economy Works.* Washington, D.C.: Brookings Institution, 1976, pp. 47–48.
48. Okimoto, Daniel I. *Between MITI and the Market: Japanese Industrial Policy for High Technology.* Stanford, Calif.: Stanford University Press, 1989, p. 65.
49. Johnson, p. 236.
50. Author's interview with Nobuyuki Idei.
51. This information is from an interview Nobutoshi Kihara conducted in 1994 for the Center for the History of Electrical Engineering.
52. Author's interview with Nobuyuki Idei.
53. Fallows, James. *Looking at the Sun: The Rise of the New East Asian Economic and Political System.* New York: Vintage, 1995, pp. xvii and 176.

54. The Fallows quote is from an episode of ABC News *Nightline* on Akio Morita, which aired April 24, 1990.
55. Morita, pp. 1, 4, 6, 12, 15–17, and 31–32.
56. Nathan, pp. 35–36.
57. "In Memory of Mr. Morita," p. 56.
58. Morita, pp. 45–51.
59. "In Memory of Mr. Morita," p. 56.
60. Nathan, pp. 27–28.
61. Morita, pp. 58–62 and 70–71.
62. Nathan, pp. 33–35. Also see Sony's official history.
63. Sony's official history.
64. Nathan, p. 35; also see Sony's official history.
65. Morita, p. 74.
66. "In Memory of Mr. Morita," p. 76.
67. Author's interview with Nobuyuki Idei.
68. Morita, p. 78.
69. Author's interview with Nobuyuki Idei; and Nathan, p. 54.
70. Morita, p. 88; and Sony's official history.
71. Morita, pp. 97–98.
72. Nathan, pp. 59–60.
73. Morita, p. 102.
74. "In Memory of Mr. Morita," p. 80.
75. Morita, p. 102.
76. Nathan, p. 67.
77. Kosai, p. 130.
78. Nakamura, pp. 87–88.
79. Johnson, p. 202.
80. Kosai, p. 153.
81. Johnson, p. 236.
82. Nakamura, p. 95.
83. Kosai, p. 130.
84. "Consider Japan," *Economist*, September 1 and 8, 1962.
85. Quoted in "Japan, Inc."

Chapter Two: Why Koreans Want to Clone a Dictator

1. This story of Park's actions during the coup is from Keon, Michael, *Korean Phoenix: A Nation from the Ashes*. Englewood Cliffs, N.J.: Prentice Hall, 1977, p. 61.
2. Park Chung Hee. *To Build a Nation*. Washington, D.C.: Acropolis Books, 1971, p. 100.
3. Park Chung Hee. Leon Sinder, trans. *The Country, the Revolution and I*. Seoul: Hollym, 1970, p. 22.
4. Park, *The Country*, pp. 27 and 43.
5. Amsden, Alice H. *Asia's Next Giant: South Korea and Late Industrialization*. New York: Oxford University Press, 1989, p. 3.
6. Park Chung Hee. *Our Nation's Path: Ideology of Social Reconstruction*. Seoul: Hollym, 1970, p. 196.

7. Cho, Namju. "Forget Madonna, Donald Trump; Koreans Would Clone a Dictator," *Wall Street Journal*, March 14, 1997.

8. Kim Chong Shin. *Seven Years with Korea's Park Chung Hee*. Seoul: Hollym, 1967, p. 17.

9. Oberdorfer, Don. *The Two Koreas: A Contemporary History*. Rev. ed. New York: Basic Books, 2001, p. 31.

10. Keon, p. 8.

11. The story of the assassination attempt is from Oberdorfer, pp. 47–48, and Keon, pp. 198–199.

12. From speech titled "Production, Export, and Construction," delivered January 16, 1965, and reprinted in *Major Speeches by Korea's Park Chung Hee*. Seoul: Hollym, 1970, p. 300.

13. From "Modernization of Korea Is Not Far Away," speech given January 18, 1966, and reprinted in *Major Speeches*, p. 322.

14. Kim Chong Shin, p. 171.

15. Kim Chung Yum. *Policymaking on the Front Lines: Memoirs of a Korean Practitioner 1945–79*. Washington, D.C.: World Bank, 1994, pp. 116–117.

16. Kim Chong Shin, p. 82.

17. Amsden, p. 205.

18. Author's interview with Park Tae Joon.

19. Park, *The Country*, pp. 58–59.

20. Keon, pp. 41–45.

21. Oberdorfer, p. 32.

22. Park, *The Country*, pp. 20–21.

23. Park, *To Build a Nation*, p. 96.

24. Eckert, Carter J., et al. *Korea Old and New: A History*. Seoul: Ilchokak Publishers, 1990, p. 355.

25. Park, *To Build a Nation*, pp. 96–97.

26. Park, *The Country*, pp. 50 and 62.

27. Eckert, p. 360.

28. Park, *The Country*, pp. 27, 29, and 61–62.

29. Park, *To Build a Nation*, p. 105.

30. Park, *The Country*, pp. 26–27 and 29.

31. Woo Jung En. *Race to the Swift: State and Finance in Korean Industrialization*. New York: Columbia University Press, 1991, p. 81.

32. Park, *To Build a Nation*, pp. 107 and 113.

33. Vogel, Ezra F. *The Four Little Dragons: The Spread of Industrialization in East Asia*. Cambridge, Mass.: Harvard University Press, 1991, pp. 50 and 53–54. Other details provided to the author by South Korea's Ministry of Strategy and Finance.

34. Lee Byeong Cheon, ed. *Developmental Dictatorship and the Park Chung Hee Era: The Shaping of Modernity in the Republic of Korea*. Translated by Kim Eungsoo and Cho Jaehyun. Paramus, N.J.: Homa & Sekey Books, 2006, p. 71.

35. Amsden, p. 84.

36. Vogel, *Four Little Dragons*, p. 51.

37. Amsden, pp. 72–73.

38. From "Production, Export, and Construction," speech reprinted in *Major Speeches*, p. 305.
39. Kim Chung Yum, pp. 38–40 and 51–52.
40. Amsden, pp. 13–14.
41. Vogel, *Four Little Dragons*, p. 52.
42. Kim Chung Yum, pp. 30 and 116.
43. Park, *The Country*, p. 33.
44. Author's interview with Kim Chung Yum.
45. Kim Chung Yum, pp. 25–27; and Woo, pp. 82–83.
46. Kim Chung Yum, pp. 103–107 and 113–114.
47. Keon, pp. 78–79.
48. Kim Chung Yum, p. 110.
49. Author's interview with Park Tae Joon.
50. Amsden, p. 291.
51. Seo, K. K. *The Steel King: The Story of T. J. Park*. New York: Simon & Schuster, 1997, pp. 89–90. Also see Kim Chung Yum, pp. 53–64.
52. Clifford, Mark L. *Troubled Tiger: Businessmen, Bureaucrats, and Generals in South Korea*. Armonk, N.Y.: M. E. Sharpe, 1994, pp. 68–69. Also see the biography of Park Tae Joon on South Korea prime minister's office website.
53. Author's interview with Park Tae Joon.
54. Seo, pp. 113–114, 127, and 159–166.
55. Author's interview with Park Tae Joon.
56. Author's interview with Park Tae Joon; and Seo, pp. 174–175.
57. Author's interview with Park Tae Joon.
58. Seo, pp. 189–205; and Kim Chung Yum, pp. 54–56.
59. Seo, pp. 261–262.
60. Author's interview with Park Tae Joon.
61. Clifford, pp. 71–72.
62. Seo, p. 265.
63. Clifford, p. 101.
64. Author's interview with Kim Chung Yum.
65. Woo, pp. 128–131.
66. Amsden discusses the disciplinary role of the state in detail; see, for example, *Asia's Next Giant*, p. 8.
67. Glain, Steve. "Can-Do Contender: Chung's Populist Flair Raises Stakes in Korean Campaign," *Asian Wall Street Journal*, December 14, 1992.
68. Sanger, David E. "Seoul Journal: Wealthy Like Croesus and Running a la Perot," *New York Times*, October 29, 1992.
69. Steers, Richard M. *Made in Korea: Chung Ju Yung and the Rise of Hyundai*. New York: Routledge, 1999, pp. 28–57, 67, and 229.
70. Kim Chung Yum, p. 107.
71. Steers, pp. 68 and 229.
72. Clifford, p. 115.
73. Steers, p. 69.
74. Clifford, p. 116.
75. Steers, pp. 73–80.
76. Steers, pp. 1–3.

77. Jones, Leroy P., and Sakong Il. *Government, Business, and Entrepreneurship in Economic Development: The Korea Case.* Cambridge, Mass.: Harvard University Press, 1980, p. 119.

78. The story of Hyundai's start in the ship business is from Steers, pp. 5 and 95–96; Clifford, pp. 116–117; and Schuman, Michael, "The Miracle Workers," *Time* (Asia edition), August 6, 2005. Also see Amsden, p. 269.

79. Jones and Sakong, p. 358.

80. World Bank, pp. 309 and 312–313.

81. Eckert, pp. 361–365.

82. Oberdorfer, pp. 42–43.

83. Eckert, pp. 368–371

84. Details of Park's assassination are from Clifford, pp. 138–139; and Oberdorfer, pp. 109–110.

85. Oberdorfer, pp. 113–115.

86. Park, *Korea Reborn*, pp. 12–13.

Chapter Three: Minister Mentor's Asian Values

1. Lee Kuan Yew. *The Singapore Story.* Singapore: Prentice Hall, 1998, pp. 15–16, 21, 23, and 646–648. Other details of the press conference from Josey, Alex, *Lee Kuan Yew: The Crucial Years.* Singapore: Times Books International, 1980, pp. 285–286.

2. Lee Kuan Yew. *From Third World to First: The Singapore Story, 1965–2000.* New York: HarperCollins, 2000, pp. 3 and 7.

3. These quotes are from testimonials to Lee at the opening of *Singapore Story.*

4. Lee, *Singapore Story*, p. 316.

5. Josey, p. 4.

6. Elegant, Simon, and Michael Elliott. "The Man Who Saw It All," *Time* (Asia edition), December 12, 2005.

7. "Brilliant, but a Bit of a Thug," *Life*, July 16, 1965, p. 43.

8. Author's interview with Lee Kuan Yew.

9. Zakaria, Fareed. "A Conversation with Lee Kuan Yew," *Foreign Affairs* March/April 1994, pp. 109–127.

10. U.S. State Department Singapore Country Report on Human Rights Practices 2006, released March 6, 2007.

11. Reporters Without Borders 2008 Press Freedom Index, which can be found at http://www.rsf.org/article.php3?id_article=29031.

12. United Nations report titled "Capital Punishment and Implementation of the Safeguards Guaranteeing Protection of the Rights of Those Facing the Death Penalty," March 9, 2005, p. 14.

13. Han Fook Kwang, Warren Fernandez, and Sumiko Tan. *Lee Kuan Yew: The Man and His Ideas.* Singapore: Times Editions, 1998, p. 229.

14. Patten, Chris. *East and West: The Last Governor of Hong Kong on Power, Freedom and the Future.* London: Macmillan, 1998, p. 149.

15. Han, Fernandez, and Tan, *Lee Kuan Yew*, p. 380.

16. Lee, *From Third*, p. 491.

17. Han, Fernandez, and Tan, *Lee Kuan Yew*, p. 383.

18. Lee, *From Third*, p. 491.

19. Barr, Michael D. *Lee Kuan Yew: The Beliefs behind the Man*. London: Curzon Press, 2000, p. 2.
20. Patten, p. 155.
21. Kim Dae Jung. "Is Culture Destiny? The Myth of Asia's Anti-Democratic Values," *Foreign Affairs*, November/December 1994.
22. Lee, *From Third*, pp. 3 and 8–9; and Lee, *Singapore Story*, pp. 18–19.
23. Lee, *Singapore Story*, pp. 25–28, 36–38, 44–46, and 50–53.
24. Barr, pp. 13–14.
25. Barr, pp. 16–17.
26. Han, p. 262.
27. Barr, pp. 17–19.
28. Han, p. 129.
29. Barr, pp. 20–23.
30. Barr, p. 29.
31. Lee, *From Third*, p. 50.
32. "Brilliant, but a Bit of a Thug," p. 48.
33. Author's interview with Lee Kuan Yew.
34. Tan Siok Sun. *Goh Keng Swee: A Portrait*. Singapore: Editions Didier Millet, 2007, pp. 12, 27–28, 38, 57, and 63.
35. Goh, pp. 56 and 109.
36. Chan Chin Bock et al. *Heart Work: Stories of How EDB Steered the Singapore Economy from 1961 to the 21st Century*. Singapore: Singapore Economic Development Board and EDB Society, 2002, pp. 16–19.
37. Tan, Sumiko, "Singapore's Trusted Guide," *Straits Times*, December 7, 2006.
38. Tan, *Goh Keng Swee,* p. 90.
39. Lee, *Singapore Story*, p. 347.
40. Chan, p. 19.
41. Lee, *From Third*, p. 58. Also author's interview with Chan Chin Bock.
42. Lee, *From Third*, pp. 50–51 and 61; and Chan, p. 21.
43. Tan, *Goh Keng Swee*, pp. 94–96.
44. Vogel, *Four Little Dragons*, pp. 80–81; and Lee, *From Third*, pp. 59 and 66.
45. Lee, *From Third*, p. 52.
46. Lee, *From Third*, pp. 57 and 66.
47. Author's interview with Lee Kuan Yew.
48. Lee, *From Third*, p. 57.
49. Author's interview with Lee Kuan Yew.
50. Lee, *From Third*, pp. 55–56.
51. Author's interview with Lee Kuan Yew.
52. Author's interview with Chan Chin Bock; and Chan, pp. 32 and 42–43.
53. Lee, *From Third*, p. 59.
54. Lee, *From Third*, pp. 56–57; Chan, p. 51; and author's interview with Chan Chin Bock.
55. Lee, *From Third*, p. 62; and Chan, p. 46.
56. Author's interview with Lee Kuan Yew.
57. Author's interview with Chan Chin Bock; and Chan, p. 46.
58. Author's interview with Chan Chin Bock; and Chan, p. 47.

59. Chan, pp. 46, 49, and 57–58.
60. Lee, *From Third*, pp.83–87.
61. Goh, p. 10.
62. Lee, *From Third*, p. 62.
63. Author's interview with Lee Kuan Yew.
64. Lee, *From Third*, p. 58.

Chapter Four: The Early Days of Superman

1. The story of the G.I. Joe heads was sent to the author in written form by Li Ka-shing.
2. Author's interview with Alan Hassenfeld.
3. Author's interview with Alan Hassenfeld.
4. Peet, Richard. "Relations of Production and the Relocation of United States Manufacturing Industry Since 1960," *Economic Geography*, vol. 59, no.2, April 1983, p. 134.
5. Author's interview with Alan Hassenfeld.
6. Author's interview with Alan Hassenfeld. Not all of Hasbro's toy manufacturing has departed America. It still makes Milton Bradley board games like Monopoly and Clue in a Massachusetts plant.
7. Vogel, *Four Little Dragons*, p. 71.
8. Friedman, Milton, and Rose Friedman. *Free to Choose: A Personal Statement*. San Diego: Harcourt Brace, 1990, pp. 33–34.
9. Kraar, Louis. "The Legend of Li Ka-shing," *Asiaweek*, July 17, 1992.
10. Kraar, Louis. "A Billionaire's Global Strategy," *Fortune*, July 12, 1992.
11. Schuman, Michael. "Can He Follow the $7.8 Billion Man?" *Time*, December 1, 2003.
12. Kraar, "The Legend."
13. Kraar, "The Legend."
14. Rafferty, Kevin. *City on the Rocks: Hong Kong's Uncertain Future*. New York: Viking, 1989, p. 294.
15. This information on Li was provided to the author by the Li Ka-shing Foundation.
16. Chan, Anthony. *Li Ka-shing: Hong Kong's Elusive Billionaire*. Hong Kong: Oxford University Press, 1996, p. 45.
17. This information on Li was provided to the author by the Li Ka-shing Foundation.
18. Kraar, "The Legend."
19. This information on Li was provided to the author by the Li Ka-shing Foundation.
20. Kraar, "The Legend."
21. This information on Li was provided to the author by the Li Ka-shing Foundation.
22. The story of Li's American client was sent to the author in written form by Li Ka-shing.
23. This information was sent to author in written form by Li Ka-shing.
24. Lam Kit Chun and Liu Pak Wai. *Immigration and the Economy of Hong Kong*. Hong Kong: City University of Hong Kong Press, 1998, p. 8.

25. Chan, *Li Ka-shing*, p. 35.
26. Author's interview with Kenneth Ting.
27. The story of Li & Fung is from the author's interview with Victor Fung and from Feng Bang-yan. *100 Years of Li & Fung: Rise from Family Business to Multinational*. Singapore: Thomson Asia, 2007, pp. 21–38. Other details provided by Chang Ka-mun, managing director of Li & Fung's research center.
28. Author's interview with Kenneth Ting.
29. This anecdote is from Chan, *Li Ka-shing*, p. 83; and Kraar, "The Legend." Purves's quote is from Rafferty, p. 296.
30. Kraar, "The Legend."
31. Rafferty, p. 296.
32. Chan, *Li Ka-shing*, p. 73.
33. This information provided to the author in written form by Li Ka-shing.
34. This information was provided to the author by the Li Ka-shing Foundation.
35. Kraar, "The Legend."
36. Kraar, "The Legend."

Chapter Five: A Tale of Duck Eggs and Dragon Dreams

1. Author's interview with Stan Shih. Other details from Chen, Robert H., *Made in Taiwan: The Story of Acer Computers*. Taipei: McGraw-Hill, 1997, p. 54.
2. Chen, p. 55.
3. Author's interview with Stan Shih.
4. Chen, p. 60.
5. Shih, Stan. *Me Too Is Not My Style*. 2nd ed. Taipei: Aspire Academy, 2004, pp. 11–12.
6. Author's interview with Stan Shih.
7. Chen, pp. 279–287.
8. Otellini, Paul. "60 Years of Heroes: Stan Shih," *Time* (Asia edition), November 12, 2006.
9. Author's interview with Stan Shih.
10. For a more comprehensive comparison between the Taiwan and Hong Kong electronics sectors and the supposed impact of the state, see Tuan, Chyau, and Linda F. Y. Ng, "Evolution of Hong Kong's Electronics Industry under a Passive Industrial Policy," *Managerial and Decision Economics*, vol. 16, 1995, pp. 509–523.
11. Li Kuo-ting. *Economic Transformation of Taiwan, ROC*. London: Shepheard-Walwyn, 1988, p. 19.
12. Shih, p. xiv.
13. Author's interview with Stan Shih.
14. Author's interview with K. Y. Lee.
15. Author's interview with Stan Shih.
16. Shih, pp. 11–12.
17. Author's interview with Stan Shih.
18. Shih, p. xi.
19. Author's interview with Carolyn Shih.

20. Chen, p. 63.
21. Shih, p. 12.
22. Author's interview with Carolyn Shih.
23. Author's interview with K. Y. Lee.
24. Author's interview with Stan Shih.
25. Shih, p. 12.
26. Fenby, Jonathan. *Chiang Kai-shek: China's Generalissimo and the Nation He Lost*. New York: Carroll & Graf, 2004, pp. 400, 480, and 495–498.
27. Wang, Lutao Sophia Kang. *K. T. Li and the Taiwan Experience*. Taipei: National Tsing Hua University Press, 2006, pp. 31–33, 41, 52–53, 58, 61, 64–65, 71, and 82.
28. Author's interview with Y. C. Li, son of Li Kuo-ting.
29. Li Kuo-ting. *The Evolution of Policy behind Taiwan's Development Success*. 2nd ed. Singapore: World Scientific, 1995, pp. 71 and 261.
30. Li, *The Evolution of Policy*, p. 260.
31. For a full study of Taiwan's land reform policies and their impact on the economy, see Chen Cheng. *Land Reform in Taiwan*. Taipei: China Publishing, 1961. Chen's quote is from p. x.
32. Hsueh, Li-min, Chen-kuo Hsu, and Dwight H. Perkins, eds. *Industrialization and the State: The Changing Role of the Taiwan Government in the Economy, 1945–1998*. Cambridge, Mass.: Harvard University Press, 2001, pp. 20–21; and Vogel, *Four Little Dragons*, pp. 22–23.
33. Sun Yat-sen. *The Three Principles of the People*. Taipei: China Publishing, 1981, p. 132.
34. Vogel, *Four Little Dragons*, p. 22; and Hsueh, p. 15.
35. Li, *The Evolution of Policy*, p. 61.
36. Hsueh, pp. 19–26; and Wang, pp. 127–128.
37. Li, *The Evolution of Policy*, pp. 159–163 and 165.
38. Hsueh, p. 270.
39. Li, *The Evolution of Policy*, p. 57.
40. Li, *Economic Transformation*, p. 233.
41. Chen, pp. 2 and 12–13.
42. Author's interview with Stan Shih.
43. Shih, p. 105.
44. Author's interview with Stan Shih.
45. Shih, pp. 14–16 and 28; and author's interview with Stan Shih.
46. Author's interview with Stan Shih and Chen, pp. 91–97.
47. Chen, pp. 108–111.
48. Li, *Economic Transformation*, p. 225.
49. "Y. S. Sun: The Vision to Guide a Nation," DVD documentary on Sun Yun-suan.
50. Author's interview with Lucy and Joseph Sun.
51. Chen, p. 104.
52. Author's interview with Stan Shih.
53. Author's interview with Stan Shih; and Chen, pp. 113–114.
54. Shih, pp. 62–63.
55. Chen, p. 115.

56. Author's interview with Stan Shih; and Shih, p. 63.
57. Author's interview with Stan Shih.
58. Shao, Maria. "Stan Shih Wants 'Made in Taiwan' to Mean First-Rate," *Businessweek*, June 8, 1987, p. 109.
59. Rice, Faye. "On the Rise: Stan Shih," *Fortune*, November 9, 1987.
60. Shao, p. 109.
61. Author's interview with Stan Shih.
62. Chen, pp. 150–151.
63. Author's interview with Stan Shih. Also see Chen, p. 149.
64. Author's interview with Stan Shih.
65. Author's interview with Stan Shih.
66. Chen, p. 152.
67. Shih, p. 81.
68. Sanger, David. "PC Powerhouse (Made in Taiwan)," *New York Times*, September 28, 1988.
69. The story of the founding of TSMC is from the author's interview with Morris Chang, except where noted otherwise. Some biographical details from an "Oral History of Morris Chang," from the Computer History Museum, 2007.
70. Quote from Harvard Business School case study on TSMC, April, 2000, p. 4.
71. Harvard case study, p. 6.
72. Harvard case study, p. 6.

Chapter Six: To Get Rich Is Glorious

1. Author's interview with Ruan Ming; and Ruan Ming. Nancy Liu, Peter Rand, and Lawrence R. Sullivan, trans. *Deng Xiaoping: Chronicle of an Empire*. Boulder, Colo.: Westview, 1994, pp. 6–8.
2. Deng Xiaoping's December 13, 1978, speech is in his *Selected Works* under the title "Emancipate the Mind, Seek Truth from Facts and Unite as One in Looking to the Future." The *People's Daily* was kind enough to put all three volumes of Deng's *Selected Works* on the Internet at http://english.peopledaily.com.cn/dengxp/.
3. Deng Maomao. *Deng Xiaoping: My Father*. New York: Basic Books, 1995, p. 4.
4. Fewsmith, Joseph. *Dilemmas of Reform in China: Political Conflict and Economic Debate*. Armonk, N.Y.: M. E. Sharpe, 1994, p. 17.
5. Deng Xiaoping. "Answers to the Italian Journalist Oriana Fallaci," August 21 and 23, 1980, from *Selected Works*.
6. Fewsmith, pp. 11–12.
7. Lee Kuan Yew, *From Third World to First*, p. 601.
8. Deng Xiaoping. "Restore Agricultural Production," July 7, 1962, from *Selected Works*.
9. Naughton, Barry. "Deng Xiaoping: The Economist." *China Quarterly*, September 1993, p. 491.
10. Lee Khoon Choy. *Pioneers of Modern China: Understanding the Inscrutable Chinese*. Singapore: World Scientific, 2005, p. 250.

11. Salisbury, Harrison E. "Zhao Ziyang, on Mao and China's Future," *New York Times*, November 14, 1987.

12. Burns, John F. "Peking Has Seen the Future—and It Lacks Chopsticks," *New York Times*, December 24, 1984.

13. Kristof, Nicholas. "Hu Yaobang, 73, Dies in China," *New York Times*, April 16, 1989.

14. Ruan, p. 10.

15. Baum, Richard. *Burying Mao: Chinese Politics in the Age of Deng Xiaoping*. Princeton, N.J.: Princeton University Press, 1994, p. 179.

16. Naughton, p. 491.

17. Shirk, Susan L. *The Political Logic of Economic Reform in China*. Berkeley: University of California Press, 1993, p. 28.

18. Deng, "Emancipate the Mind."

19. Shirk, pp. 35–36.

20. Fewsmith, p. 11.

21. Naughton, p. 509.

22. Deng Xiaoping. "Some Comments on Economic Work," October 4, 1979, from *Selected Works*.

23. Fewsmith, p. 36.

24. Deng Xiaoping. "To Build Socialism We Must First Develop the Productive Forces," April 12, 1980, from *Selected Works*.

25. Deng Xiaoping. "China's Goal Is to Achieve Comparative Prosperity by the End of the Century," December 6, 1979, from *Selected Works*.

26. Naughton, p. 505.

27. Deng Xiaoping. "The Working Class Should Make Outstanding Contributions to the Four Modernizations," October 11, 1978, from *Selected Works*.

28. Deng Xiaoping. "We Can Develop a Market Economy under Socialism," November 26, 1979, from *Selected Works*.

29. Author's interview with Ruan Ming.

30. Deng Xiaoping, "Answers to the Italian Journalist Oriana Fallaci."

31. Deng Xiaoping, "We Can Develop a Market Economy under Socialism."

32. Deng Xiaoping. "Opening Speech at the Twelfth National Congress of the Communist Party of China," September 1, 1982, from *Selected Works*.

33. Deng Maomao, pp. 12 and 40.

34. Evans, Richard. *Deng Xiaoping and the Making of Modern China*. Rev. ed. London; New York: Penguin, 1997, pp. 1 and 4; and Goodman, David S. G. *Deng Xiaoping and the Chinese Revolution: A Political Biography*. London: Routledge, 1994, p. 23.

35. Deng Maomao, pp. 41, 49–51, and 58–60; Evans, pp. 6, 10, and 15.

36. Deng Maomao, pp. 61–62.

37. Goodman, pp. 25–26.

38. Deng Maomao, p. 71.

39. Deng Maomao, p. 60.

40. Deng Maomao, pp. 77 and 80.

41. Deng Xiaoping, "Answers to the Italian Journalist Oriana Fallaci."

42. Deng Maomao, p. 100; Evans, pp. 18–19; and Goodman, pp. 25 and 27.

43. Deng Maomao, p. 102; and Goodman, p. 25.
44. Evans, pp. 113–115.
45. Evans, pp. 162–164.
46. Deng Xiaoping, "Restore Agricultural Production."
47. Evans, pp. 179–184.
48. Deng Maomao, p. 14.
49. Evans, pp. 185–187, 189, and 202–203.
50. Deng Xiaoping. "The Whole Party Should Take the Overall Interest into Account and Push the Economy Forward," March 5, 1975, from *Selected Works*.
51. Evans, pp. 206–207 and 210–213.
52. For a complete explanation of Deng's rise to power, see Baum, pp. 41–64.
53. Fewsmith, pp. 20 and 22–28. Also see Kelliher, Daniel, *Peasant Power in China: The Era of Rural Reform 1979–1989*. New Haven, Conn.: Yale University Press, 1992, p. 61; and Ruan, p. 66.
54. Lee Khoon Choy, p. 283.
55. Fewsmith, pp. 20 and 23.
56. Kelliher, pp. 57 and 62.
57. Fewsmith, p. 29.
58. Baum, p. 399.
59. Naughton, p. 507.
60. Fewsmith, pp. 32–33 and 41–42.
61. Deng Xiaoping. "On Questions of Rural Policy," May 31, 1980, from *Selected Works*.
62. Fewsmith, pp. 47–48.
63. Wan Li's speech appeared on the BBC Summary of World Broadcasts on January 24, 1984.
64. Deng Xiaoping. "Carry Out the Policy of Opening to the Outside World and Learn Advanced Science and Technology from Other Countries," October 10, 1978, from *Selected Works*.
65. Deng Xiaoping, "Update Enterprises with Advanced Technology and Managerial Expertise."
66. Deng Xiaoping, "Some Comments on Economic Work."
67. Most of the details of Deng's visit to the United States are from Deming, Angus, "Bearbaiting," *Newsweek*, February 12, 1979. The immigration story is from Oberdorfer, Don, "During Week in U.S., Teng Proves His Mastery of Political Positioning," *Washington Post*, February 4, 1979.
68. Jao, Y. C., and C. K. Leung, eds. *China's Special Economic Zones: Politics, Problems and Prospects*. New York: Oxford University Press, 1986, p. 88; and Vogel, Ezra F. *One Step Ahead in China: Guangdong under Reform*. Cambridge, Mass.: Harvard University Press, 1989, pp. 130–132.
69. Deng Xiaoping, *Fundamental Issues*, p. 190.
70. Naughton, p. 509.
71. Jao and Leung, p. 88; and Marti, Michael E. *China and the Legacy of Deng Xiaoping: From Communist Revolution to Capitalist Evolution*. Washington, D.C.: Brassey's, 2002, p. 7.
72. Vogel, *One Step Ahead in China*, p. 137.
73. Vogel, *One Step Ahead in China*, pp. 151–153.

74. Yu, Tony Fu-lai. *Entrepreneurship and Economic Development in Hong Kong.* London: Routledge, 1997, p. 81.

75. Author's interview with Kenneth Ting.

76. Author's interview with Victor Fung. Also see Schuman, Michael, "Hong Kong at the Center of the World," *Time* (Asia edition), January 18, 2007, and "60 Years of Asian Heroes: Victor & William Fung," *Time* (Asia edition), November 13, 2006.

77. Fewsmith, p. 108.

78. Baum, pp. 160 and 182.

79. Deng Xiaoping. "The Party's Urgent Tasks on the Organizational and Ideological Fronts," October 12, 1983, from *Selected Works.*

80. Baum, pp. 159–162.

81. Deng Xiaoping. "Make a Success of Special Economic Zones and Open More Cities to the Outside World," February 24, 1984, from *Selected Works.*

82. Baum, pp. 164–165.

83. Deng, "Emancipate the Mind."

84. Fewsmith, pp. 76, 78–79, and 99.

85. Fewsmith, p. 109.

86. Baum, pp. 170–171.

87. Sterba, James P., and Amanda Bennett. "Deng's Tune: Peking Turns Sharply down Capitalist Road in New Economic Plan," *Wall Street Journal*, October 25, 1984.

88. Shirk, p. 12.

89. The details of the debate over martial law between Deng and Zhao, as well as Zhao's Tiananmen Square speech and self-defense, are from Zhang Liang, *The Tiananmen Papers.* Edited by Andrew J. Nathan and Perry Link. London: Little, Brown and Company, 2001, pp. 187–189, 192–193, 210, 217, 264, and 441–442.

Chapter Seven: The Father of Development and His Mafia

1. Author's interview with Ali Wardhana.

2. Radius Prawiro. *Indonesia's Struggle for Economic Development: Pragmatism in Action.* Kuala Lumpur: Oxford University Press, 1998, p. 264.

3. Details of the customs reform are from the author's interview with Ali Wardhana and from Radius, p. 265.

4. Abdulgani-Knapp, Retnowati. *Soeharto: The Life and Legacy of Indonesia's Second President.* Singapore: Marshall Cavendish, 2007, p. 300.

5. Soeharto. *My Thoughts, Words and Deeds.* Translated by Sumadi. Jakarta: Citra Lamtoro Gung Persada, 1991, p. 252.

6. Author's interview with Ali Wardhana.

7. Radius, p. 265.

8. Poverty statistics are from the World Bank website.

9. Soeharto, p. 3.

10. Radius, p. 150.

11. Elson, R. E. *Suharto: A Political Biography.* Cambridge, U.K.: Cambridge University Press, 2001, p. 236.

12. Author's interview with Emil Salim.

13. Soeharto, pp. 197 and 199.
14. Lee, *From Third*, pp. 267–268 and 271.
15. Author's interview with Emil Salim.
16. Author's interview with Ali Wardhana.
17. Author's interview with Emil Salim.
18. Author's interview with Emil Salim.
19. Author's interview with Ali Wardhana.
20. Abdulgani-Knapp, pp. 82–83.
21. Author's interview with Emil Salim.
22. Radius, p. 83.
23. For a discussion of these competing policy interests, see Schwarz, Adam, *A Nation in Waiting: Indonesia's Search for Stability*. St. Leonards, Australia: Allen & Unwin, 1999, pp. 52–56.
24. Author's interview with Emil Salim.
25. Author's interview with Ali Wardhana.
26. Abdulgani-Knapp, pp. 19–21.
27. Soeharto, p. 196.
28. The early life of Suharto is from Soeharto, pp. 5–21.
29. "Djago, the Rooster," *Time*, March 10, 1958.
30. Brown, Colin. *A Short History of Indonesia: The Unlikely Nation?* Crows Nest, Australia: Allen & Unwin, 2003, p. 199.
31. Soeharto, pp. 99–102.
32. Elson, pp. 106, 110–111, and 125.
33. Soeharto, p. 113.
34. Soeharto, p. 141.
35. The account of the cabinet meeting is from Vittachi, Tarzie, *The Fall of Sukarno*. London: Andre Deutsch, 1967, pp. 168–170. A similar version is in Elson, p. 135.
36. This quote is from Suharto's own account in Seoharto, p. 145.
37. There are different versions of the story of the meeting with Sukarno. This version is from Machmud and is recounted at length in Elson, pp. 136–137.
38. Radius, pp. 7–8. The details of Indonesia's economic decline are from Radius, pp. 4–8 and 47.
39. Author's interview with Emil Salim.
40. Author's interview with Ali Wardhana.
41. Radius, pp. 85–86 and 260.
42. Author's interview with Emil Salim.
43. Elson, p. 149.
44. Author's interview with Emil Salim.
45. Radius, pp. 27 and 45. The explanation of the stabilization and reform plan is from pp. 25–45.
46. Soeharto, p. 198.
47. Author's interview with Bob Hasan.
48. Radius, p. 80.
49. Author's interview with Ali Wardhana.
50. Author's interview with Ali Wardhana.
51. Radius, pp. 46–47 and pp. 51–69.

52. Soeharto, p. 64.
53. Sulfikar, Amir. "Symbolic Power in a Technocratic Regime: The Reign of B. J. Habibie in New Order Indonesia," *Journal of Social Issues in Southeast Asia*, April 1, 2007.
54. Soeharto, p. 241.
55. Sulfikar, "Symbolic Power."
56. Schwarz, p. 88.
57. Schwarz, p. 86.
58. Soeharto, p. 241.
59. Sulfikar, "Symbolic Power"; and Pura, Raphael. "Habibie Moves Center Stage in Jakarta," *Asian Wall Street Journal*, November 11, 1994.
60. Author's interview with Emil Salim.
61. Soeharto, p. 392.
62. Soeharto, p. 391.
63. Soeharto, p. 240.
64. Soeharto, p. 242.
65. Soeharto, p. 389.
66. Author's interview with Emil Salim.
67. Pura, Raphael. "Indonesian Aircraft Industry Tries to Make a Flight of Fancy Reality," *Wall Street Journal*, December 26, 1985.
68. Hill, Hal. *Indonesia's Industrial Transformation*. Singapore: Institute of Southeast Asia Studies, 1997, pp. 127–131.
69. Soeharto, pp. 389–390.
70. Pura, Raphael. "Plywood Power: Bob Hasan Builds an Empire in the Forest," *Asian Wall Street Journal*, January 20, 1995.
71. Author's interview with Bob Hasan.
72. Abdulgani-Knapp, pp. 35–36.
73. Author's interview with Bob Hasan.
74. Pura, "Plywood Power."
75. Author's interview with Bob Hasan.
76. My discussion of Hasan's control over the plywood business is mostly from Barr, Christopher M., "Bob Hasan, the Rise of Apkindo, and the Shifting Dynamics of Control in Indonesia's Timber Sector," *Indonesia*, vol. 65, April 1998; and Pura, "Plywood Power."
77. Pura, "Plywood Power."
78. Author's interview with Bob Hasan.
79. Elson, pp. 248–249; Jones, Stephen, and Raphael Pura. "All in the Family: Indonesian Decrees Help Suharto's Friends and Relatives Prosper," *Wall Street Journal*, November 24, 1986. Other details from Schwarz, pp. 133–134.
80. Schwarz, pp. 143 and 153–157.
81. Borsuk, Richard. "Suharto Son Shrugs Off His Many Critics," *Asian Wall Street Journal*, July 1, 1992.
82. Elson, pp. 249–250.
83. Soeharto, pp. 77 and 195.
84. Author's interview with Ali Wardhana.
85. Author's interview with Emil Salim.

86. Radius, p. 100.
87. Radius, p. 219.
88. Author's interview with Ali Wardhana.
89. Author's interview with Ali Wardhana.
90. Radius, p. 256.
91. Radius, pp. 269–270.
92. Schwarz, p. 50.
93. Radius, pp. 272–273.
94. Radius, p. 225.
95. Radius, p. 274.
96. UNCTAD statistics.
97. Schwarz, p. 73.
98. McBeth, John, and Nigel Holloway. "Aviation: Will It Fly?" *Far Eastern Economic Review*, November 24, 1994, p. 122.
99. Shari, Michael. "Flying on a Wing, a Prayer and a Blank Check," *Businessweek*, March 18, 1996, p. 18.
100. Schwarz, p. 87.
101. McBeth and Holloway, "Will It Fly?"; and Shari, "Flying on a Wing."
102. Elson, p. 275.
103. Pura, "Habibie Moves Center Stage in Jakarta."
104. Elson, p. 270.

Chapter Eight: Mr. Thunder's American Dream

1. The story of Soichiro Honda and the cake is from the author's interview with Shin Tanaka.
2. NHK Group. *Good Mileage: The High-Performance Business Philosophy of Soichiro Honda*. New York: NHK Publishing, 1996, p. 160.
3. Japan Automobile Manufacturers Assocation. "The Motor Industry of Japan Annual Report 2007," pp. 58–59.
4. Womack, James P., Daniel T. Jones, and Daniel Roos. *The Machine That Changed the World*. New York: Rawson Associates, 1990, p. 245.
5. Author's interview with Shin Tanaka.
6. Vogel, Ezra F. *Japan as Number One: Lessons for America*. New York: toExcel, 1999 (originally published by Harvard University Press in 1979), pp. 10–11.
7. Wood, Christopher. *The Bubble Economy: Japan's Extraordinary Speculative Boom of the '80s and the Dramatic Bust of the '90s*. New York: Atlantic Monthly Press, 1992, pp. 7–8 and 50.
8. Foreign trade statistics, U.S. Census Bureau.
9. Kennedy, Paul. *The Rise and Fall of the Great Powers: Economic Change and Military Conflict 1500 to 2000*. London: Unwin Hyman, 1988, pp. 432–436 and 515.
10. Vogel, *Japan as Number One*, p. 8.
11. Associated Press. "Americans More Concerned about Japan Than about Soviet Union," July 28, 1989.
12. Kearns, Robert L. *Zaibatsu America: How Japanese Firms Are Colonizing Vital U.S. Industries*. New York: Free Press, 1992, pp. 2 and 10–11.

13. Crichton, Michael. *Rising Sun*. New York: Ballantine, 1992, p. 207.
14. Standish, Frederick. "Mr. Honda Visits Detroit," Associated Press, October 9, 1989.
15. Sakiya, Tetsuo. Kiyoshi Ikemi, trans. *Honda Motor: The Men, the Management, the Machines*. Tokyo: Kodansha, 1982, pp. 52–53; and Honda's official history.
16. Sato, Masaaki. Hiroko Yoda, trans. *The Honda Myth: The Genius and His Wake*. New York: Vertical, 2006, p. 64.
17. Sakiya, pp. 69–70.
18. Author's interview with Toshikata Amino.
19. NHK Group, p. 154.
20. NHK Group, p. 11.
21. Honda's official history.
22. Johnson, Richard A. *Six Men Who Built the Modern Auto Industry*. St. Paul, Minn.: Motorbooks, 2005, p. 53.
23. Johnson, p. 49.
24. NHK Group, pp. 39–40.
25. Sato, pp. 66 and 68.
26. Sakiya, pp. 69–72.
27. NHK Group, pp. 21–22 and 25–27.
28. Honda's official history.
29. NHK Group, p. 16.
30. Author's interview with Shoichiro Irimajiri.
31. Shook, Robert L. *Honda: An American Success Story*. New York: Prentice Hall, 1988, pp. 25–35.
32. Johnson, p. 54.
33. Sato, p. 164.
34. Johnson, pp. 55–59; Sato, pp. 199–200; and Sakiya, pp. 180–181.
35. I am indebted for the story of Honda's plant opening in Ohio to Robert Shook, who detailed it in his book *Honda: An American Success Story*, pp. 38–51.
36. Togo, Yukiyasu, and William Wartman. *Against All Odds: The Story of the Toyota Motor Corporation and the Family That Created It*. New York: St. Martin's Press, 1993, p. 216; and Ingrassia and White, p. 41.
37. Toyoda, Eiji. *Toyota: Fifty Years in Motion*. Tokyo: Kodansha International, 1987, pp. 106–109.
38. Ingrassia and White, p. 38.
39. Togo, p. 216; and Ingrassia and White, pp. 41–42.
40. Ingrassia and White, pp. 35–36 and 41–42.
41. Ohno, Taiichi. *Toyota Production System: Beyond Large-Scale Production*. New York: Productivity Press, 1988, pp. 3 and 13.
42. Womack, pp. 48–69.
43. Ohno, pp. 14–15.
44. Womack, pp. 80–82.
45. Ingrassia and White, p. 328; and author's interview with Stan Shih.
46. Sato, p. 23.
47. Shook, pp. 20–22.

48. Shook, pp. 89–91.
49. Author's interview with Toshikata Amino.
50. Author's interview with Shoichiro Irimajiri.
51. Author's interview with Shoichiro Irimajiri.
52. The excellent anecdotes about Irimajiri are from Ingrassia and White, pp. 328–330.
53. Author's interview with Shoichiro Irimajiri.
54. Ingrassia and White, p. 330.
55. Author's interview with Shoichiro Irimajiri.
56. Johnson, Richard Tanner, and William G. Ouchi. "Made in America (under Japanese Management)," *Harvard Business Review*, vol. 52, September/October 1974, pp. 61–69. Quote from p. 69.
57. Vogel, *Japan As Number One*, pp. 56, 65, 74, 232–236, and 253–254.
58. Prestowitz, Clyde. *Trading Places: How We Allowed Japan to Take the Lead*. New York: Basic Books, 1988, p. 13.
59. Iacocca, Lee. *Iacocca: An Autobiography*. With William Novak. New York: Bantam, 1986, pp. 331–334 and 339.
60. Alexander, Charles P. " 'Buy More Foreign Goods,' " *Time*, April 22, 1985.
61. Russell, George. "Trade Face-Off," *Time*, April 13, 1987.
62. Morita, Akio, and Shintaro Ishihara. *The Japan That Can Say "No."* Washington, D.C.: Jefferson Educational Foundation, 1990, pp. 42–43.
63. Nathan, pp. 189–190.
64. Goodwin, Richard N. "Sold Off by a Greedy Few, to Our Vast Harm," *Los Angeles Times*, September 29, 1989.
65. Barron, James. "Huge Japanese Realty Deals Breeding Jokes and Anger," *New York Times*, December 18, 1989.
66. "Will the Rockettes Wear Kimonos?" editorial in the *Christian Science Monitor*, November 7, 1989.
67. Hiatt, Fred. "Sony Chairman Seeks to Send Friendly Signals to U.S. on Columbia Deal," *Washington Post*, October 4, 1989.
68. Morita and Ishihara, pp. 13–14.
69. Nathan, pp. 54 and 217–218.
70. Flanigan, James. "U.S.-Bashing Book by Sony's Chief Costs Him Credibility," *Los Angeles Times*, October 11, 1989.
71. Wood, pp. 7–8.
72. Saxonhouse, Gary R., and Robert M. Stern, eds. *Japan's Lost Decade: Origins, Consequences and Prospects for Recovery*. Oxford, U.K.: Blackwell Publishing, 2004, pp. 1–2 and 17.
73. My explanation of the causes and effects of Japan's Bubble Economy and its subsequent crash is condensed from several sources, including Mikuni, Akio, and R. Taggart Murphy, *Japan's Policy Trap: Dollars, Deflation, and the Crisis of Japanese Finance*. Washington, D.C.: Brookings Institution Press, 2002, especially pp. 145–188. Also see Saxonhouse and Stern, *Japan's Lost Decade*; Wood, *The Bubble Economy*; and Freedman, Craig, ed. *Why Did Japan Stumble? Causes and Cures*. Cheltenham, U.K.; Edward Elgar, 1999.
74. Porter and Takeuchi, p. 67.
75. Fallows, p. 70.

76. Wood, p. 2.
77. Johnson, Chalmers. "Economic Crisis in East Asia: The Clash of Capitalisms," *Cambridge Journal of Economics*, no. 22, 1998, pp. 655.
78. Tamamoto, Masaru. "Japan and Its Discontents: A Letter from Yokohama," *World Policy Journal*, October 1, 2000.
79. Gigot, Paul. "The Great Japan Debate Is Over; Guess Who Won?" *Wall Street Journal*, January 31, 1997.
80. Vogel, Ezra F. *Is Japan Still Number One?* Selangor Darul Edsan, Malaysia: Pelanduk, 2000, p. 8.

Chapter Nine: The Man in the Blue Turban

1. The details of the Singh meeting are from the author's interview with Montek Singh Ahluwalia and from Chakravarti, Sudeep, "Bold Gamble," *India Today*, July 31, 1991, pp. 22–23.
2. Cassen, Robert, and Vijay Joshi, eds. *India: The Future of Economic Reform*. Oxford, U.K.: Oxford University Press, 1995, p. 27.
3. Quote from Singh is from an interview published in *India Today*, July 31, 1991, p. 25.
4. Nath, Kamal. *India's Century*. New York: McGraw-Hill, 2008, p. 54.
5. Tharoor, Shashi. *Nehru: The Invention of India*. New York: Arcade Publications, 2001, p. 239.
6. Bhagwati, Jagdish. *India in Transition: Freeing the Economy*. New York: Oxford University Press, 1995, p. 21.
7. From the transcript of Singh's interview with Charlie Rose on PBS, September 21, 2004.
8. Reddy, Sheela. "Read His Lips," *Outlook*, September 13, 2004.
9. Das, Gurcharan. *India Unbound*. London: Profile Books, 2002, p. 225.
10. Jha, Prem Shankar. *The Perilous Road to the Market: The Political Economy of Reform in Russia, India and China*. London: Pluto Press, 2002, p. 166.
11. Author's interview with B. K. Chaturvedi.
12. Housego, David, and Alexander Nicoll. "Monday Interview: India's Financial Architect," *Financial Times*, September 2, 1991.
13. From Singh's interview with Charlie Rose on February 27, 2006.
14. From Singh's interview with Charlie Rose on September 21, 2004.
15. Ahuja, Ajay, ed. *Manmohan Singh: The Sterling Sardar*. New Delhi: Pentagon Press, 2004, p. 85.
16. Ahuja, pp. 79–80.
17. Bhagwati, pp. 17, 50, and 58–59.
18. From Singh's interview with Rose, 2004.
19. Ahuja, p. 90.
20. Ahuja, pp. 188–189.
21. The details of Singh's early life are from his daughter, Upinder Singh.
22. *Our India* can be read on the Internet at http://www.vidyaonline.net/arvindgupta/OUR%20INDIA%20-%20Minoo%20Masani.pdf.
23. From Singh's interview with Charlie Rose, 2004.
24. Singh, Manmohan. *India's Export Trends and the Prospects for Self-Sustained Growth*. Oxford, U.K.: Clarendon Press, 1964, p. v.

25. Thakurta, Paranjoy Guha. "Who Is the Real Manmohan Singh?" *Hindu Business Line*, June 1, 2004.
26. Housego and Nicoll, "Monday Interview."
27. Weinraub, Bernard. "India Is Now in a New Ball Game," *New York Times*, July 8, 1991.
28. Ahuja, p. 82.
29. Ahuja, p. 90.
30. Thakurta, "Who Is the Real Manmohan Singh?"
31. Walsh, James. "India: Death's Return Visit," *Time*, June 4, 1991.
32. Author's interview with Deepak Nayyar.
33. Agha, Zafar. "Back to the Old Guard," *India Today*, July 15, 1991.
34. Bhaduri, Amit, and Deepak Nayyar. *The Intelligent Person's Guide to Liberalization*. New Delhi: Penguin, 1996, pp. 27 and 29.
35. Details of Nayyar's briefing are from the author's interview with Deepak Nayyar.
36. Author's interview with Deepak Nayyar.
37. Associated Press. "New Prime Minister Warns of Tough Economic Decisions," June 22, 1991.
38. Ahuja, p. 84.
39. Ahuja, p. 93.
40. Quote from Singh is from an interview in *India Today*, July 31, 1991.
41. Ahuja, p. 84.
42. Ahuja, p. 83.
43. Author's interview with P. Chidambaram.
44. Ahuja, p. 149.
45. Author's interview with Deepak Nayyar. Quote from Singh is in Ahuja, p. 152.
46. Ahuja, pp. 152–153.
47. Author's interviews with Montek Singh Ahluwalia and P. Chidambaram. Other details from Das, pp. 215–217; and Penna, Anil, "India Announces Sweeping Trade Reforms," AFP, July 4, 1991.
48. Das, p. 218.
49. Author's interview with P. Chidambaram.
50. "Statement on Industrial Policy," Ministry of Industry, July 24, 1991.
51. Nath, p. 55.
52. Speech by Singh to Parliament, July 24, 1991.
53. Author's interview with Deepak Nayyar.
54. Quoted in Nath, p. 57.
55. *India Today*, July 31, 1991, pp. 22–23.
56. Chakravarty, "Bold Gamble," p. 32.
57. Das, p. 215.
58. Details of Singh's fertilizer plan are from his July 24, 1991, budget speech to Parliament.
59. Agha, Zafar. "Political Pressure," *India Today*, August 31, 1991.
60. Montek Singh Ahluwalia wrote a clear summary of India's early reforms in Cassen, pp. 13–27. Other details from Jha, pp. 180–181.
61. Jha, pp. 183 and 192–199.

62. Ahuja, p. 127.
63. Jha, pp. 191–192.
64. Tharoor, p. 245.
65. Speech by Manmohan Singh to India's parliament on July 24, 1991.

Chapter Ten: A Dose of Dr. M's Tough Medicine
1. The details of Mahaleel's meeting are from the author's interview with Tengku Mahaleel.
2. Lehner, Urban C. "Interview with Mahathir Mohamad," *Asian Wall Street Journal*, March 26, 1996.
3. Spaeth, Anthony. "Bound for Glory," *Time* (Asia edition), December 9, 1996.
4. Quotes from speech by Mahathir Mohamad at UMNO General Assembly on June 19, 2003.
5. Quotes on Jews from speeches by Mahathir Mohamad at the Opening of the Tenth Session of the Islamic Summit Conference, October 16, 2003, and at the 8th conference of the heads of state of the Non-Aligned Movement on September 1, 1986.
6. Author's interview with Mahathir Mohamad.
7. Mahathir Mohamad. *A New Deal for Asia*. Selangor Darul Ehsan, Malaysia: Pelanduk, 1999, pp. 13–14. Other details from author's interview with Mahathir Mohamad.
8. Mahathir, *A New Deal*, p. 14.
9. Author's interview with Mahathir Mohamad.
10. Mahathir, *A New Deal*, pp. 15–17.
11. Keay, John. *Last Post: The End of Empire in the Far East*. London: John Murray, 1997, pp. 229–235.
12. Mahathir, *A New Deal*, p. 17.
13. Author's interview with Mahathir Mohamad.
14. Mahathir, *A New Deal*, p. 18.
15. Keay, pp. 234–236.
16. Mahathir, *A New Deal*, p. 18.
17. Author's interview with Mahathir Mohamad.
18. Mahathir, *A New Deal*, p. 20.
19. Keay, pp. 315–316.
20. Mahathir, *A New Deal*, p. 20.
21. Author's interview with Mahathir Mohamad.
22. Khoo Boo Teik. *Paradoxes of Mahathirism: An Intellectual Biography of Mahathir Mohamad*. New York: Oxford University Press, 1995, pp. 21–22.
23. Hooker, Virginia Matheson. *A Short History of Malaysia: Linking East and West*. Crows Nest, Australia: Allen & Unwin, 2003, pp. 251–252.
24. Mahathir, *A New Deal*, p. 22. Also see Khoo Boo Teik, *Paradoxes of Mahathirism*, pp. 22–23.
25. Mahathir Mohamad. *The Malay Dilemma*. Singapore: Marshall Cavendish, 1970, pp. 29–30 and 103–114.

26. Poon Wai Ching. *The Development of Malaysian Economy*. Selangor, Malaysia: Prentice Hall, 2005, pp. 21 and 222.
27. Mahathir Mohamad. *The Way Forward*. London: Weidenfeld & Nicolson, 1998, p. 8. The explanation of the policies of the NEP is also from *The Way Forward*, especially pp. 11–19.
28. Mahathir, *The Way Forward*, p. 7.
29. Khoo, p. 127.
30. Khoo, p. 128.
31. Mahathir, *The Way Forward*, p. 12.
32. Mahathir, *A New Deal*, p. 39.
33. Mahathir, *A New Deal*, pp. 84–90.
34. Lehner, "Interview with Mahathir Mohamad."
35. Khoo, p. 119.
36. Author's interview with Mahathir Mohamad. Other details from Jomo, K. S., ed. *Industrializing Malaysia: Policy, Performance, Prospects*. London: Routledge, 1993, pp. 272–273 and 276–277.
37. Khoo, pp. 120–123.
38. Jomo, p. 277.
39. Author's interview with Mahathir Mohamad.
40. Poon, p. 187.
41. Khoo, pp. 116–117.
42. Author's interview with Daim Zainuddin.
43. Milne, R. S., and Diane K. Mauzy. *Malaysian Politics under Mahathir*. London: Routledge, 1999, p. 70; and Cheong Mei Sui and Adibah Amin. *Daim: The Man behind the Enigma*. Selangor Darul Ehsan, Malaysia: Pelanduk, 1995, pp. 14–15.
44. Author's interview with Daim Zainuddin.
45. Milne, p. 71.
46. World Bank, p. 311; and Mahathir, *The Way Forward*, pp. 13–14.
47. Lehner, "Interview with Mahathir Mohamad."
48. Rohwer, Jim. *Asia Rising: Why America Will Prosper as Asia's Economies Boom*. New York: Touchstone, 1996, p. 272.
49. Jayasankaran, S. "The Chosen Few: Privatization Allows Mahathir to Pick Winners," *Far Eastern Economic Review*, December 21, 1995; and Mahathir, *The Way Forward*, pp. 26 and 96.
50. Jayasankaran, "The Chosen Few."
51. Author's interview with Mahathir Mohamad.
52. Author's interview with Daim Zainuddin.
53. Author's interview with Mahathir Mohamad.
54. Pura, Raphael. "How Renong Followed a Road to Riches," *Asian Wall Street Journal*, January 19, 1998. Other details from Khoo, p. 278.
55. Jayasankaran, S. "Policies—It's Our Pleasure," *Far Eastern Economic Review*, January 19, 1995.
56. Khoo, p. 137.
57. Author's interview with Mahathir Mohamad.
58. Khoo, p. 140.

59. Author's interview with Daim Zainuddin.
60. Mahathir, *The Way Forward*, pp. 20–22; and Milne, p. 73.
61. Speech by Mahathir on September 30, 1986, in New York City.
62. Author's interview with Daim Zainnudin.
63. Khoo, pp. 262–266.
64. Crossette, Barbara. "Malaysia's Leader Facing Major Revolt in His Party," *New York Times*, March 28, 1987.
65. Khoo, pp. 264–266.
66. Khoo, pp. 269–271.
67. Author's interview with Mahathir Mohamad; and Jomo, p. 282.
68. Milne, p. 66.
69. Lopez, Leslie, and Raphael Pura. "Malaysia Says Perwaja Faces Financial Crisis," *Asian Wall Street Journal*, May 22, 1996.
70. Author's interview with Mahathir Mohamad.
71. Sime Engineering corporate website.
72. Author's interview with Mahathir Mohamad.
73. Author's interview with Mahathir Mohamad.
74. Author's interview with Anwar Ibrahim.

Chapter Eleven: Every Street Is Paved with Debt
1. Kraar, Louis. "Wanted," *Fortune* (Asian edition), February 3, 2003.
2. Author's interview with Kim Dae Jung.
3. Mydans, Seth. "An 'Asian Miracle' Now Seems Like a Mirage," *New York Times*, October 22, 1997.
4. Wong, Y. C. Richard. "Lessons from the Asian Financial Crisis," *Cato Journal*, vol. 18, no. 3 (Winter 1999), p. 391.
5. Krugman, Paul. "What Ever Happened to the Asian Miracle?" *Fortune*, August 18, 1997.
6. For one clear explanation of the Thai currency crisis, see Moreno, Ramon, "Lessons from Thailand," Federal Reserve Bank of San Francisco Economic letter, November 7, 1997.
7. "Thailand Finally Lets Its Currency Float," *Wall Street Journal*, July 3, 1997.
8. Rubin, Robert, and Jacob Weisberg. *In an Uncertain World: Tough Choices from Wall Street to Washington.* New York: Random House, 2003, p. 218.
9. Mahathir Mohamad, *The Malaysian Currency Crisis: How and Why It Happened.* Selangor Darul Ehsan, Malaysia: Pelanduk, 2000, p. 9.
10. Mahathir, *The Malaysian Currency Crisis*, p. 18.
11. Abdullah, Ashraf. "Dr. M: It's George Soros," *New Straits Times*, July 27, 1997; Maniam, Hari. "Soros Blamed for Currency Attacks," Associated Press, July 26, 1997; and Associated Press. "Malaysian PM: Anti-Burma American behind Regional Currency Crisis," July 22, 1997.
12. Mahathir Mohamad, speech at the annual seminar of the IMF and World Bank, Hong Kong, September 20, 1997.
13. Gargan, Edward A. "Premier of Malaysia Spars with Currency Dealer," *New York Times*, September 22, 1997.
14. Rubin, p. 217.

15. For an exhaustive discussion of Asia's imbalances see Corsetti, Giancarlo, Paolo Pesenti, and Nouriel Roubini, "What Caused the Asian Currency and Financial Crisis? Part I: A Macroeconomic Overview," National Bureau of Economic Research Working Paper No. 6833.

16. Corsetti, see tables 23 and 26.

17. Statistics on Korea corporations from Corsetti, pp. 14–15.

18. Radelet, Steven, and Jeffrey Sachs. "The Onset of the East Asian Financial Crisis," Harvard Institute for International Development, March 30, 1998, pp. 1–2 and 5.

19. Mydans, Seth. "Malaysian Premier Sees Jews behind Nation's Money Crisis," *New York Times*, October 16, 1997.

20. Mahathir, *The Malaysian Currency Crisis*, p. 19.

21. Mahathir, *The Malaysian Currency Crisis*, pp. 23–26. Other details from author's interviews with Mahathir Mohamad and Anwar Ibrahim. For a list of the megaprojects deferred, see Chen May Yee, "Asian Economic Survey 1997–98: Malaysia," *Asian Wall Street Journal*, October 20, 1997.

22. Stiglitz, Joseph E. *Globalization and Its Discontents*. New York: W. W. Norton, 2002, p. 97.

23. Author's interview with Mahathir Mohamad.

24. Author's interview with Daim Zainnudin.

25. Mahathir, *The Malaysian Currency Crisis*, p. 36.

26. Author's interview with Mahathir Mohamad.

27. Author's interview with Daim Zainnudin.

28. Mahathir, *The Malaysian Currency Crisis*, pp. 43–46.

29. Author's interview with Mahathir Mohamad.

30. "Malaysia's Self-Isolation," *Wall Street Journal*, September 3, 1998.

31. Pura, Raphael, and Leslie Lopez. "Mahathir Fires Deputy Prime Minister as Malaysia's Political Tensions Escalate," *Asian Wall Street Journal*, September 3, 1998. For a summary of the Anwar-Mahathir relationship and the eventual conflict between the two men, see Milne, pp. 144–157.

32. Milne, p. 151

33. Author's interview with Mahathir Mohamad.

34. Lopez, Leslie. "Petronas's Purchase Plan Fuels Questions," *Asian Wall Street Journal*, March 9, 1998; and Pura, Raphael. "Malaysia Can't Kick the Bailout Habit," *Asian Wall Street Journal*, April 8, 1998.

35. Author's interview with Anwar Ibrahim.

36. Author's interview with Mahathir Mohamad.

37. Spaeth, Anthony. "He's the Boss," *Time* (Asia edition), September 14, 1998.

38. Author's interview with Mahathir Mohamad.

39. Spaeth, "He's the Boss."

40. Interview with Anwar Ibrahim printed in *Time* (Asia edition), September 14, 1998.

41. Hajari, Nisid. "Out of the Bottle," *Time* (Asia edition), October 5, 1998.

42. Larimer, Tim. "Blackest Hours," *Time* (Asia edition), October 12, 1998, p. 20.

43. Chen May Yee. "Anwar Receives Six Years in Jail," *Asian Wall Street Journal,* April 15, 1999; Lopez, Leslie. "Court Gives Anwar a Nine-Year Jail

Term," *Asian Wall Street Journal,* August 9, 2000; and Spaeth, Anthony. "Rough Justice," *Time* (Asia edition), August 21–28, 2000, p. 14.

44. Stiglitz, p. 93.
45. Krugman, Paul. "Capital Control Freaks: How Malaysia Got Away with Economic Heresy," *Slate,* September 27, 1999.
46. Phillips, Michael M. "IMF Concedes That Malaysia's Controls over Capital Produced Positive Results," *Wall Street Journal,* September 9, 1999.
47. Pura, Raphael. "Suharto Hands Economy to Veteran Trouble-Shooter," *Asian Wall Street Journal,* October 13, 1997
48. IMF Letter of Intent with the government of Indonesia, October 31, 1997.
49. Rubin, p. 244; and Tripathi, Salil. "Companies: A Moment of Truth," *Far Eastern Economic Review,* January 8, 1998.
50. Borsuk, Richard, Jay Solomon, and Darren McDermott. "Shock Waves: Indonesia Falls Prey to Hoarding, Loss of Public Confidence," *Wall Street Journal,* January 9, 1998.
51. Rubin, p. 245.
52. "Statement by the Managing Director on the IMF Program with Indonesia," January 15, 1998; Borsuk, Richard. "Sweeping Reforms Unveiled by Jakarta and IMF Fail to Impress Markets in Asia," *Asian Wall Street Journal,* January 16, 1998; McDermott, Darren, et al. "Indonesia Reaches IMF Pact to Speed Reforms," *Wall Street Journal,* January 15, 1998; and Della-Giacoma, Jim. "Indonesia Plane Maker Staggering after IMF Deal," Reuters, January 16, 1998.
53. Author's interview with Bob Hasan.
54. Liebhold, David. "An Eyewitness Account: The Moment Things Snapped," *Time* (Asia edition), May 25, 1998, p. 22.
55. Landler, Mark. "The Chinese: The Target of Violence in a Time of Wrath," *New York Times,* May 16, 1998.
56. McCarthy, Terry. "End of an Era," *Time* (Asia edition), June 1, 1998.
57. Habibie, Bacharuddin Jusuf. *Decisive Moments: Indonesia's Long Road to Democracy.* Jakarta: Ilthabi Rekatama, 2006, pp. 33–36.
58. McCarthy, "End of an Era"; and Habibie, p. 31.
59. Mydans, Seth. "Suharto, Besieged, Steps Down after 32-Year Rule in Indonesia," *New York Times,* May 21, 1998.
60. Author's interview with Bob Hasan.
61. Author's interview with Emil Salim.
62. Rubin, pp. 228 and 231–234.
63. Rubin, pp. 234–235.
64. Schuman, Michael, and Namju Cho. "Seoul's Markets Rebound ahead of Election," *Wall Street Journal,* December 16, 1997.
65. Author's interview with Kim Dae Jung.
66. Wessel, David, et al. "U.S. Weighs Short-Term Loan to South Korea," *Wall Street Journal,* December 24, 1997.
67. Author's interview with Kim Dae Jung.
68. Author's interview with Kim Dae Jung and Rubin, pp. 238–239.
69. Rubin, p. 340.

70. Schuman, Michael, et al. "Korea to Get Quick Release of $10 Billion in Aid," *Wall Street Journal*, December 26, 1997.
71. Author's interview with Kim Dae Jung.
72. Rubin, pp. 240–241. Other details from Wessel, David, and Stephen E. Frank, "Korea Loan Deal Looks Favorable for Seoul," *Wall Street Journal*, January 30, 1998.
73. Schuman, Michael. "Daewoo Group Takes Expansionist Tack amid Crisis," *Wall Street Journal*, April 22, 1998.
74. The author wrote this comment during his coverage of the Daewoo collapse in 1999. See Schuman, "Daewoo Group Takes Expansionist Tack."
75. Schuman, "Daewoo Group Takes Expansionist Tack."
76. Schuman, Michael. "Hyundai Revs Up," *Time* (Asia edition), April 18, 2005.
77. Nam In Soo. "Chaebol Heads Agree to Drastic Reforms at Meeting with Kim Dae Jung," *Korea Herald*, January 14, 1998.
78. Kim Woo Choong. *Every Street Is Paved with Gold: The Road to Real Success*. New York: William Morrow, 1992, pp. 14–15, 18–24, 31–33, 37–38, and 62–63.
79. Kraar, "Wanted"; and Michaels, Daniel. "Daewoo Boosts Its Investment in Poland, Buying a 2nd Car Plant," *Asian Wall Street Journal*, November 15, 1995.
80. Kraar, "Wanted."
81. Author's interview with Kim Dae Jung; and Kraar, "Wanted."
82. Kraar, "Wanted."
83. Kraar, "Wanted."
84. Author's interview with Kim Dae Jung.
85. Schuman, Michael, and Jane L. Lee. "Won World: Dismantling of Daewoo Shows How Radically Korea Is Changing," *Wall Street Journal*, August 17, 1999.
86. Kraar, "Wanted."
87. Author's interview with Oh Kap Soo, former financial regulatory official.
88. Schuman and Lee, "Won World."
89. Author's interview with Oh Kap Soo.
90. Kraar, "Wanted."
91. Schuman and Lee, "Won World."
92. Kraar, "Wanted."
93. Author's interview with Kim Dae Jung.
94. Author's interview with Kim Dae Jung. Also see Kraar, "Wanted."
95. Kraar, "Wanted."
96. Stiglitz, p. 97.
97. Kraar, "Wanted."
98. Kraar, Louis. "A Fugitive Boss Faces the Music," *Fortune* (Asia edition), July 11, 2005, p. 13.
99. Choe Sang Hun. "Ex-Fugitive Gets Hostile Reception in South Korea," *New York Times*, June 15, 2005.
100. Choe Sang Hun. "Daewoo's Founder Is Given 10-Year Sentence for Fraud," *New York Times*, May 31, 2006.

101. Associated Press. "Former Daewoo Chairman among 75 People Who Receive South Korea Amnesty," December 31, 2007.

Chapter Twelve: A Fish Jumps through the Dragon Gate
1. Author's interview with Liu Chuanzhi.
2. Sappenfield, Mark. "A Landmark Move for China Inc.," *Christian Science Monitor*, December 9, 2004.
3. Statement from Representative Thomas Reynolds on *US Fed News*.
4. Quote is from Coonan, Clifford, "Newspapers Express the State's Approval of Lenovo-IBM Deal," *The Times*, December 10, 2004.
5. Author's interview with Liu Chuanzhi.
6. Lenovo public relations.
7. Author's interview with Liu Chuanzhi.
8. Ling, Zhijun. Martha Avery, trans. *The Lenovo Affair: The Growth of China's Computer Giant and Its Takeover of IBM PC*. Singapore: John Wiley & Sons, 2006, pp. 2–9.
9. Feng Shan and Janet Elfring. *The Legend behind Lenovo: The Chinese IT Company That Dares to Succeed*. Hong Kong: Asia 2000, 2004, p. 23.
10. Ling, pp. 9–10.
11. Author's interview with Liu Chuanzhi.
12. Ling, p. 11.
13. Author's interview with Liu Chuanzhi.
14. Ling, pp. 11 and 14.
15. Author's interview with Liu Chuanzhi.
16. Lenovo corporate website.
17. Author's interview with Liu Chuanzhi.
18. Ling, pp. 22–25.
19. Author's interview with Liu Chuanzhi.
20. Ling, pp. 25–26. The original name of Lenovo is translated differently in other sources. This version is from the Lenovo corporate website.
21. Ling, p. 48.
22. Author's interview with Liu Chuanzhi.
23. Author's interview with Liu Chuanzhi.
24. Ling, p. 85.
25. Ling, pp. 61–66.
26. Author's interview with Mary Ma.
27. Ling, pp. 83–85 and 101–102.
28. The background on Zhu's career and its importance, as well as Zhu's 1991 meeting with Deng Xiaoping, is from Brahm, Laurence J., *Zhu Rongji and the Transformation of Modern China*. Singapore: John Wiley & Sons, 2002, mainly from pp. xx–xxxiv.
29. The details of Zhu and China's entry into the WTO are from Brahm, pp. 261–280. Other details on the specifics of the Beijing negotiations are from Mann, Jim, "U.S. Negotiators Conduct Harmony from Discord," *Los Angeles Times*, November 16, 1999.

30. Ling, p. 136.
31. Author's interview with Liu Chuanzhi.
32. Ling, pp. 132–134.
33. Ling, p. 164.
34. Ling, pp. 165–167.
35. Author's interview with Liu Chuanzhi.
36. Feng, p. 51.
37. Ling, pp. 171–174 and 240–241; and Feng, pp. 58–59 and 62–63.
38. Feng, p. 93.
39. Ling, pp. 190–191.
40. Ling, p. 273.
41. Ling, p. 199.
42. Schuman, Michael. "Hyundai Revs Up." Sales statistics are from Hyundai Motor public relations. Other details from author's notes.
43. Author's interviews with John Joyce, Liu Chuanzhi, and Mary Ma.
44. Author's interview with John Joyce.
45. Sheff, David. "Enter the Dragon," *Wired*, issue 10.08 (August 2002).
46. Lenovo's analysis of the deal and Ma's relations with the board are from the author's interview with Mary Ma.
47. The information on the meetings between Lenovo management and the board are from the author's interview with Liu Chuanzhi and Mary Ma.
48. The specifics of the negotiations come mainly from the author's interview with Mary Ma, with some details from John Joyce.
49. Author's interview with Mary Ma.
50. Author's interview with Liu Chuanzhi.

Chapter Thirteen: An Unexpected Journey from Shortening to Software
1. Wipro, Ltd. U.S. Securities and Exchange Commission filing 6-K for July 2005.
2. Wipro, Ltd. Annual Report 2005–2006.
3. Author's interview with Azim Premji.
4. *Forbes* magazine estimate.
5. Author's interview with Jesse Paul, Wipro marketing manager.
6. Author's interview with Azim Premji.
7. Wessel, David, and Bob Davis. "Pain from Free Trade Spurs Second Thoughts," *Wall Street Journal*, March 28, 2007.
8. Author's interview with Azim Premji.
9. Schuman, Michael. "Hey, Big Spenders," *Time*, August 25, 2003.
10. From Texas Instruments public relations.
11. Author's interview with F. C. Kohli and "IT Takes Vision and Wisdom," essay written by F. C. Kohli on Tata corporate website.
12. Details of F. C. Kohli's early days at TCS from author's interview with Kohli. Also see Kohli, "IT Takes Vision and Wisdom."
13. Quote from Kohli, "IT Revolution in India: An Assessment."
14. Author's interview with F. C. Kohli.
15. Author's interview with S. Ramadorai and speech by Ramadorai reprinted in *Business India*, issue dated March 28 to April 10, 2005.

16. Author's interview with Azim Premji.
17. Speech by Ramadorai in *Business India*.
18. Author's interview with S. Ramadorai. Other details from speech by Ramadorai in *Business India*.
19. Wharton Business School case study written by Jithendra V. Singh, 1999, pp. 5–6.
20. Author's interview with Narayana Murthy. See also Singh, Wharton case study, p. 6.
21. Singh, Wharton case study, p. 6.
22. Author's interview with Narayana Murthy.
23. Infosys public relations.
24. Author's interview with Narayana Murthy. Also see Wharton case study, pp. 4–5.
25. Hamm, Steve. *Bangalore Tiger: How Indian Tech Upstart Wipro Is Rewriting the Rules of Global Competition*. New York: McGraw-Hill, 2007, pp. 31–32.
26. Author's interview with Azim Premji.
27. Author's interview with Azim Premji.
28. Hamm, p. 33.
29. Author's interview with Azim Premji.
30. Hamm, pp. 33–34.
31. Author's interview with Azim Premji.
32. Author's interview with Sridhar Mitta.
33. Author's interview with Sudip Banerjee.
34. Author's interview with Sridhar Mitta.
35. Author's interview with Sudip Banerjee.
36. Author's interview with Sudip Banerjee.
37. Author's interview with Sambuddha Deb.
38. Author's interview with Azim Premji.
39. Author's interview with Girish Paranjpe.
40. Welch, Jack, with John A. Byrne. *Jack: Straight from the Gut*. New York: Warner Books, 2001, pp. 307–310.
41. Author's interview with Jack Welch.
42. Author's interview with Raman Roy.
43. Author's interview with Pramod Bhasin.
44. Author's interview with Pramod Bhasin.
45. Welch, p. 314.
46. Author's interview with Pramod Bhasin.
47. Infosys corporate website.
48. Author's interview with Azim Premji.
49. Author's interview with Raman Roy.

Epilogue: Lessons from a Refrigerator Factory

1. According to the South Carolina Department of Commerce and Michael Jemal.
2. Paul, Anthony. "China's Haier Power," *Fortune* (Asia edition), February 15, 1999, p. 54.

3. Paul, "China's Haier Power."
4. Author's interview with Michael Jemal.
5. Author's interview with David Parks.
6. Author's interview with Nelson Lindsay.
7. White, Ben. "Chinese Drop Bid to Buy U.S. Oil Firm," *Washington Post*, August 3, 2005.
8. Author's interview with Gerald Reeves.
9. Author's interview with Rick Franklin.
10. Author's interview with Gerald Reeves.
11. Dobbs, Lou. *Exporting America: Why Corporate Greed Is Shipping American Jobs Overseas*. New York: Warner, 2004, pp. 76 and 156–157.

BIBLIOGRAPHY

Abdulgani-Knapp, Retnowati. *Soeharto: The Life and Legacy of Indonesia's Second President*. Singapore: Marshall Cavendish, 2007.

Ahearne, Alan G., and Naoki Shinada. "Zombie Firms and Economic Stagnation in Japan." Institute of Economic Research, Hitotsubashi University, June 2005.

Ahuja, Ajay, ed. *Manmohan Singh: The Sterling Sardar*. New Delhi: Pentagon Press, 2004.

Alten, Florian von. *The Role of Government in the Singapore Economy*. Frankfurt: Peter Lang, 1995.

Amsden, Alice H. *Asia's Next Giant: South Korea and Late Industrialization*. New York: Oxford University Press, 1989.

Barr, Christopher M. "Bob Hasan, the Rise of Apkindo, and the Shifting Dynamics of Control in Indonesia's Timber Sector." *Indonesia* 65 (April 1998).

Barr, Michael D. *Lee Kuan Yew: The Beliefs behind the Man*. London: Curzon Press, 2000.

Baum, Richard. *Burying Mao: Chinese Politics in the Age of Deng Xiaoping*. Princeton, N.J.: Princeton University Press, 1994.

Beasley, William G. *The Meiji Restoration*. Stanford, Calif.: Stanford University Press, 1972.

Berger, Suzanne, and Richard K. Lester, eds. *Made by Hong Kong*. Hong Kong: Oxford University Press, 1997.

Bhaduri, Amit, and Deepak Nayyar. *The Intelligent Person's Guide to Liberalization*. New Delhi: Penguin, 1996.

Bhagwati, Jagdish. *India in Transition: Freeing the Economy*. New York: Oxford University Press, 1995.

Brahm, Laurence J. *Zhu Rongji and the Transformation of Modern China*. Singapore: John Wiley & Sons, 2002.

Brown, Colin. *A Short History of Indonesia: The Unlikely Nation?* Crows Nest, Australia: Allen & Unwin, 2003.

Bryan, Michael F., and Michael W. Dvorak. "American Automobile Manufacturing: It's Turning Japanese." *Economic Commentary*, Federal Reserve Bank of Cleveland, March 1, 1986.

Cassen, Robert, and Vijay Joshi, eds. *India: The Future of Economic Reform.* Oxford, U.K.: Oxford University Press, 1995.

Chai, Joseph C. H., and Kartik C. Roy. *Economic Reform in China and India: Development Experience in a Comparative Perspective.* Cheltenham, U.K.: Edward Elgar, 2006.

Chan, Anthony. *Li Ka-shing: Hong Kong's Elusive Billionaire.* Hong Kong: Oxford University Press, 1996.

Chan Chin Bock et al. *Heart Work: Stories of How EDB Steered the Singapore Economy from 1961 to the 21st Century.* Singapore: Singapore Economic Development Board and EDB Society, 2002.

Chang, Chun-yen, and Yu Po-lung, eds. *Made by Taiwan.* Singapore: World Scientific Publishing, 2001.

Chang, David Wen-wei. *China under Deng Xiaoping: Political and Economic Reform.* London: Macmillan, 1988.

Chen Cheng. *Land Reform in Taiwan.* Taipei: China Publishing, 1961.

Chen, Robert H. *Made in Taiwan: The Story of Acer Computers.* Taipei: McGraw-Hill, 1997.

Cheong Mei Sui and Adibah Amin. *Daim: The Man behind the Enigma.* Selangor Darul Ehsan, Malaysia: Pelanduk, 1995.

Clifford, Mark L. *Troubled Tiger: Businessmen, Bureaucrats, and Generals in South Korea.* Armonk, N.Y.: M. E. Sharpe, 1994.

Clifford, Mark L., and Pete Engardio. *Meltdown: Asia's Boom, Bust, and Beyond.* Paramus, N.J.: Prentice Hall, 2000.

Corsetti, Giancarlo, Paolo Pesenti, and Nouriel Roubini. "What Caused the Asian Currency and Financial Crisis? Part I: A Macroeconomic Overview." National Bureau of Economic Research Working Paper No. 6833. Cambridge, Mass.: National Bureau of Economic Research, 1998.

Daim Zainuddin. *Daim Speaks His Mind.* Selangor Darul Ehsan, Malaysia: Pelanduk, 1996.

Das, Gurcharan. *India Unbound.* London: Profile Books, 2002.

Deng Maomao. *Deng Xiaoping: My Father.* New York: Basic Books, 1995.

Deng Xiaoping. *Fundamental Issues in Present-Day China.* Oxford: Pergamon Press, 1987.

Deng Xiaoping. *Selected Works of Deng Xiaoping.* 3 vols. Beijing: Foreign Languages Press, 1983–1994. Volume 2 (1975–1982) printed 1984, volume 3 (1982–1992) printed 1994.

Dick, Howard, et al. *The Emergence of a National Economy: An Economic History of Indonesia, 1800–2000.* Crows Nest, Australia: Asian Studies Association of Australia and Allen & Unwin, 2002.

Dobbs, Lou. *Exporting America: Why Corporate Greed Is Shipping American Jobs Overseas.* New York: Warner, 2004.

Dower, John W. *Embracing Defeat: Japan in the Wake of World War II.* New York: W. W. Norton, 2000.

Dreze, Jean, and Amartya Sen. *India: Development and Participation*. New Delhi: Oxford University Press, 2005.

Eckert, Carter J., et al. *Korea Old and New: A History*. Seoul: Ilchokak Publishers, 1990.

Elson, R. E. *Suharto: A Political Biography*. Cambridge, U.K.: Cambridge University Press, 2001.

Enright, Michael J., Edith E. Scott, and Ka-mun Chang. *Regional Powerhouse: The Greater Pearl River Delta and the Rise of China*. Singapore: John Wiley & Sons, 2005.

Evans, Richard. *Deng Xiaoping and the Making of Modern China*. Rev. ed. London: Penguin, 1997.

Fallows, James. *Looking at the Sun: The Rise of the New East Asian Economic and Political System*. New York: Vintage, 1995.

Feifer, George. *Breaking Open Japan: Commodore Perry, Lord Abe, and American Imperialism in 1853*. New York: Smithsonian Books, 2006.

Fenby, Jonathan. *Chiang Kai-shek: China's Generalissimo and the Nation He Lost*. New York: Carroll & Graf, 2004.

Feng Bang-yan. *100 Years of Li & Fung: Rise from Family Business to Multinational*. Singapore: Thomson Asia, 2007.

Feng Shan and Janet Elfring. *The Legend behind Lenovo: The Chinese IT Company That Dares to Succeed*. Hong Kong: Asia 2000, 2004.

Ferguson, Niall. *The War of the World: History's Age of Hatred*. London: Penguin, 2007.

Fewsmith, Joseph. *Dilemmas of Reform in China: Political Conflict and Economic Debate*. Armonk, N.Y.: M. E. Sharpe, 1994.

Freedman, Craig, ed. *Why Did Japan Stumble? Causes and Cures*. Cheltenham, U.K.: Edward Elgar, 1999.

Friedman, Milton, and Rose Friedman. *Free to Choose: A Personal Statement*. San Diego: Harcourt Brace, 1990.

Goh Keng Swee. *The Practice of Economic Growth*. Singapore: Marshall Cavendish, 2004.

Goh Keng Swee. *The Wealth of East Asian Nations: Speeches and Writings*. Edited by Linda Low. Singapore: Federal Publications, 1995.

Gomez, Edmund Terence, and K. S. Jomo. *Malaysia's Political Economy: Politics, Patronage, and Profits*. Cambridge, U.K.: Cambridge University Press, 1997.

Goodman, David S. G. *Deng Xiaoping and the Chinese Revolution: A Political Biography*. London: Routledge, 1994.

Habibie, Bacharuddin Jusuf (B. J.). *Decisive Moments: Indonesia's Long Road to Democracy*. Jakarta: Ilthabi Rekatama, 2006.

Hamm, Steve. *Bangalore Tiger: How Indian Tech Upstart Wipro Is Rewriting the Rules of Global Competition*. New York: McGraw-Hill, 2007.

Han Fook Kwang, Warren Fernandez, and Sumiko Tan. *Lee Kuan Yew: The Man and His Ideas*. Singapore: Times Editions, 1998.

Hartcher, Peter. *The Ministry: The Inside Story of Japan's Ministry of Finance*. London: HarperCollins, 1998.

Hill, Hal. *Indonesia's Industrial Transformation*. Singapore: Institute of Southeast Asia Studies, 1997.

Hsueh, Li-min, Chen-kuo Hsu, and Dwight H. Perkins, eds. *Industrialization and the State: The Changing Role of the Taiwan Government in the Economy, 1945–1998*. Cambridge, Mass.: Harvard University Press, 2001.

Huntington, Samuel P. "The U.S.—Decline or Renewal?" *Foreign Affairs* (Winter 1988/89): 76–96.

Iacocca, Lee. *Iacocca: An Autobiography*. With William Novak. New York: Bantam, 1986.

Iacocca, Lee. *Talking Straight*. With Sonny Kleinfield. New York: Bantam, 1988.

Ingrassia, Paul, and Joseph B. White. *Comeback: The Fall and Rise of the American Automobile Industry*. New York: Simon & Schuster, 1994.

Jao, Y. C., and C. K. Leung, eds. *China's Special Economic Zones: Politics, Problems, and Prospects*. New York: Oxford University Press, 1986.

Jenkins, Rob. *Democratic Politics and Economic Reform in India*. New York: Cambridge University Press, 1999.

Jha, Prem Shankar. *The Perilous Road to the Market: The Political Economy of Reform in Russia, India and China*. London: Pluto Press, 2002.

Johnson, Chalmers. "Economic Crisis in East Asia: The Clash of Capitalisms." *Cambridge Journal of Economics* 22 (1998): 653–661.

Johnson, Chalmers. *Japanese "Capitalism" Revisited*. Japan Policy Research Institute, Occasional Paper, no. 22. Cardiff, Calif.: Japan Policy Research Institute, 2001.

Johnson, Chalmers. *MITI and the Japanese Miracle: The Growth of Industrial Policy, 1925–1975*. Stanford, Calif.: Stanford University Press, 1982.

Johnson, Richard A. *Six Men Who Built the Modern Auto Industry*. St. Paul, Minn.: Motorbooks, 2005.

Johnson, Richard Tanner, and William G. Ouchi. "Made in America (under Japanese Management)." *Harvard Business Review* 52 (Sept./Oct. 1974): 61–69.

Jomo, K. S., ed. *Industrializing Malaysia: Policy, Performance, Prospects*. New York: Routledge, 1993.

Jomo, K. S., ed. *Manufacturing Competitiveness in Asia: How Internationally Competitive National Firms and Industries Developed in East Asia*. London: Routledge, 2003.

Jones, Leroy P., and Sakong Il. *Government, Business, and Entrepreneurship in Economic Development: The Korea Case*. Cambridge, Mass.: Harvard University Press, 1980.

Josey, Alex. *Lee Kuan Yew: The Crucial Years*. Singapore: Times Books International, 1980.

Kearns, Robert L. *Zaibatsu America: How Japanese Firms Are Colonizing Vital U.S. Industries*. New York: Free Press, 1992.

Keay, John. *India: A History*. London: HarperCollins, 2001.

Keay, John. *Last Post: The End of Empire in the Far East*. London: John Murray, 1997.

Kelliher, Daniel. *Peasant Power in China: The Era of Rural Reform 1979–1989*. New Haven, Conn.: Yale University Press, 1992.

Kennedy, Paul. *The Rise and Fall of the Great Powers: Economic Change and Military Conflict, 1500 to 2000.* London: Unwin Hyman, 1988.

Keon, Michael. *Korean Phoenix: A Nation from the Ashes.* Englewood Cliffs, N.J.: Prentice Hall, 1977.

Khoo Boo Teik. *Paradoxes of Mahathirism: An Intellectual Biography of Mahathir Mohamad.* New York: Oxford University Press, 1995.

Kim Chong Shin. *Seven Years with Korea's Park Chung Hee.* Seoul: Hollym, 1967.

Kim Chung Yum. *Policymaking on the Front Lines: Memoirs of a Korean Practitioner, 1945–79.* Washington, D.C.: World Bank, 1994.

Kim Dae Jung. "Is Culture Destiny? The Myth of Asia's Anti-Democratic Values." *Foreign Affairs* (November/December 1994).

Kim Kihwan. *Korea: A Case of Government-Led Development.* Washington, D.C.: World Bank, 1993.

Kim Woo Choong. *Every Street Is Paved with Gold: The Road to Real Success.* New York: William Morrow, 1992.

Kobayashi-Hillary, Mark. *Outsourcing to India: The Offshore Advantage.* 2nd ed. New York: Springer, 2005.

Kohli, F. C. *The IT Revolution in India: Selected Speeches and Writings.* 2nd ed. New Delhi: Rupa, 2005.

Kosai, Yutaka. *The Era of High Speed Growth: Notes on the Postwar Japanese Economy.* Translated by Jacqueline Kaminski. Tokyo: University of Tokyo Press, 1986.

Kwong, Kai-sun, et al. *Industrial Development in Singapore, Taiwan, and South Korea.* Hackensack, N.J.: World Scientific, 2001.

Lam Kit Chun and Liu Pak Wai. *Immigration and the Economy of Hong Kong.* Hong Kong: City University of Hong Kong Press, 1998.

Lee Byeong Cheon, ed. *Developmental Dictatorship and the Park Chung Hee Era: The Shaping of Modernity in the Republic of Korea.* Translated by Kim Eungsoo and Cho Jaehyun. Paramus, N.J.: Homa & Sekey Books, 2006.

Lee Khoon Choy. *Pioneers of Modern China: Understanding the Inscrutable Chinese.* Singapore: World Scientific, 2005.

Lee Kuan Yew. *From Third World to First: The Singapore Story, 1965–2000.* New York: HarperCollins, 2000.

Lee Kuan Yew. *The Singapore Story.* Singapore: Prentice Hall, 1998.

Legge, J. D. *Sukarno: A Political Biography.* 3rd ed. Singapore: Archipelago Press, 2003.

Li Kuo-ting. *Economic Transformation of Taiwan, ROC.* London: Shepheard-Walwyn, 1988.

Li Kuo-ting. *The Evolution of Policy behind Taiwan's Development Success.* 2nd ed. Singapore: World Scientific, 1995.

Ling, Zhijun. *The Lenovo Affair: The Growth of China's Computer Giant and Its Takeover of IBM PC.* Translated by Martha Avery. Singapore: John Wiley & Sons, 2006.

Lu Yunyuan, ed. *Li Ka-shing.* Beijing: Xinhua Publishing, 1996.

Macpherson, W. J. *The Economic Development of Japan 1868–1941.* Cambridge, U.K.: Cambridge University Press, 1995.

Maddison, Angus. *The World Economy: A Millennial Perspective*. Paris: Development Centre of the Organization for Economic Cooperation and Development, 2001.

Maguire, Keith. *The Rise of Modern Taiwan*. Aldershot, U.K.: Ashgate, 1998.

Mahathir Mohamad. *The Challenge*. Selangor Darul Ehsan, Malaysia: Pelanduk, 1986.

Mahathir Mohamad. *The Malay Dilemma*. Singapore: Marshall Cavendish, 1970.

Mahathir Mohamad. *The Malaysian Currency Crisis: How and Why It Happened*. Selangor Darul Ehsan, Malaysia: Pelanduk, 2000.

Mahathir Mohamad. *A New Deal for Asia*. Selangor Darul Ehsan, Malaysia: Pelanduk, 1999.

Mahathir Mohamad. *The Way Forward*. London: Weidenfeld & Nicolson, 1998.

Marti, Michael E. *China and the Legacy of Deng Xiaoping: From Communist Revolution to Capitalist Evolution*. Washington, D.C.: Brassey's, 2002.

Mathews, John A. *Dragon Multinational: A New Model for Global Growth*. Oxford, U.K.: Oxford University Press, 2002.

Mikuni, Akio, and R. Taggart Murphy. *Japan's Policy Trap: Dollars, Deflation, and the Crisis of Japanese Finance*. Washington, D.C.: Brookings Institution Press, 2002.

Milne, R. S., and Diane K. Mauzy. *Malaysian Politics under Mahathir*. London: Routledge, 1999.

Mirza, Hafiz. *Multinationals and the Growth of the Singapore Economy*. London: Croom Helm, 1986.

Morita, Akio. *Made in Japan: Akio Morita and Sony*. With Edwin M. Reingold and Mitsuko Shimomura. London: HarperCollins, 1994.

Morita, Akio, and Shintaro Ishihara. *The Japan That Can Say "No."* Washington, D.C.: Jefferson Educational Foundation, 1990.

Nakamura, Takafusa. *The Postwar Japanese Economy: Its Development and Structure 1937–1994*. 2nd ed. Tokyo: University of Tokyo Press, 1995.

Nath, Kamal. *India's Century*. New York: McGraw-Hill, 2008.

Nathan, John. *Sony: The Private Life*. London: HarperCollins, 1999.

Naughton, Barry. "Deng Xiaoping: The Economist." *China Quarterly* 135 (September 1993): 491–514.

NHK Group. *Good Mileage: The High-Performance Business Philosophy of Soichiro Honda*. New York: NHK Publishing, 1996.

Norman, Dorothy, ed. *Nehru: The First Sixty Years*. Vol. 2. Mumbai: Asia Publishing House, 1965.

Oberdorfer, Don. *The Two Koreas: A Contemporary History*. Rev. ed. New York: Basic Books, 2001.

Ohno, Taiichi. *Toyota Production System: Beyond Large-Scale Production*. New York: Productivity Press, 1988.

Okazaki, Tetsuji, and Masahiro Okuno-Fujiwara, eds. *The Japanese Economic System and Its Historical Origins*. Oxford: Oxford University Press, 1999.

Okimoto, Daniel I. *Between MITI and the Market: Japanese Industrial Policy for High Technology*. Stanford, Calif.: Stanford University Press, 1989.

Park Chung Hee. *The Country, the Revolution, and I*. Translated by Leon Sinder. Seoul: Hollym, 1970.

Park Chung Hee. *Korea Reborn: A Model for Development*. Englewood Cliffs, N.J.: Prentice Hall, 1979.

Park Chung Hee. *Major Speeches by Korea's Park Chung Hee*. Seoul: Hollym, 1970.

Park Chung Hee. *Our Nation's Path: Ideology of Social Reconstruction*. Seoul: Hollym, 1970.

Park Chung Hee. *To Build a Nation*. Washington, D.C.: Acropolis Books, 1971.

Patrick, Hugh, and Henry Rosovsky, eds. *Asia's New Giant: How the Japanese Economy Works*. Washington, D.C.: Brookings Institution, 1976.

Patten, Chris. *East and West: The Last Governor of Hong Kong on Power, Freedom, and the Future*. London: Macmillan, 1998.

Peebles, Gavin, and Peter Wilson. *Economic Growth and Development in Singapore: Past and Future*. Cheltenham, U.K.: Edward Elgar, 2002.

Peet, Richard. "Relations of Production and the Relocation of United States Manufacturing Industry Since 1960," *Economic Geography* 59, no.2 (April 1983): 112–143.

Poon Wai Ching. *The Development of Malaysian Economy*. Selangor, Malaysia: Prentice Hall, 2005.

Porter, Michael E., and Hirotaka Takeuchi. "Fixing What Really Ails Japan." *Foreign Affairs* (May/June 1999): 66–81.

Prestowitz, Clyde. *Three Billion New Capitalists: The Great Shift of Wealth and Power to the East*. New York: Basic Books, 2005.

Prestowitz, Clyde. *Trading Places: How We Allowed Japan to Take the Lead*. New York: Basic Books, 1988.

Pyle, Kenneth B. *The Making of Modern Japan*. 2nd ed. Lexington, Mass.: D.C. Heath, 1996.

Radelet, Steven, and Jeffrey Sachs. "The Onset of the East Asian Financial Crisis." Unpublished paper, Harvard Institute for International Development, March 30, 1998.

Radius Prawiro. *Indonesia's Struggle for Economic Development: Pragmatism in Action*. Kuala Lumpur: Oxford University Press, 1998.

Rafferty, Kevin. *City on the Rocks: Hong Kong's Uncertain Future*. New York: Viking, 1989.

Riedel, James Charles. *The Industrialization of Hong Kong*. London: University Microfilms International, 1981.

Rohwer, Jim. *Asia Rising: Why America Will Prosper as Asia's Economies Boom*. New York: Touchstone, 1996.

Ruan Ming. *Deng Xiaoping: Chronicle of an Empire*. Translated by Nancy Liu, Peter Rand, and Lawrence R. Sullivan. Boulder, Colo.: Westview, 1994.

Rubenstein, Murray A., ed. *Taiwan: A New History*. Armonk, N.Y.: M. E. Sharpe, 1998.

Rubin, Robert, and Jacob Weisberg. *In an Uncertain World: Tough Choices from Wall Street to Washington*. New York: Random House, 2003.

Sakiya, Tetsuo. *Honda Motor: The Men, the Management, the Machines*. Translated by Kiyoshi Ikemi. Tokyo: Kodansha, 1982.

Sakong Il. *Korea in the World Economy.* Washington, D.C.: Institute for International Economics, 1993.

Sato, Masaaki. *The Honda Myth: The Genius and His Wake.* Translated by Hiroko Yoda. New York: Vertical, 2006.

Sato, Ryuzo, and John A. Rizzo, eds. *Unkept Promises, Unclear Consequences: U.S. Economic Policy and the Japanese Response.* New York: Cambridge University Press, 1988. Reprint, 2006.

Saxonhouse, Gary R., and Robert M. Stern, eds. *Japan's Lost Decade: Origins, Consequences, and Prospects for Recovery.* Oxford: Blackwell Publishing, 2004.

Schwarz, Adam. *A Nation in Waiting: Indonesia's Search for Stability.* St. Leonards, Australia: Allen & Unwin, 1999.

Seo, K. K. *The Steel King: The Story of T. J. Park.* New York: Simon & Schuster, 1997.

Seoharto. *My Thoughts, Words, and Deeds.* Translated by Sumadi. Jakarta: Citra Lamtoro Gung Persada, 1991.

Shigeru Sahashi. *Ishoku Kanryo.* Tokyo: Shakaishisosha, 1994. This book is in Japanese. The English name is "An Extraordinary Bureaucrat" and it is the autobiography of Sahashi. The book was analyzed and parts were translated specifically for this project by Yu Wada.

Shih, Stan. *Me Too Is Not My Style.* 2nd ed. Taipei: Aspire Academy, 2004.

Shirk, Susan L. *How China Opened Its Door: The Political Success of the PRC's Foreign Trade and Investment Reforms.* Washington, D.C.: Brookings Institution, 1994.

Shirk, Susan L. *The Political Logic of Economic Reform in China.* Berkeley: University of California Press, 1993.

Shook, Robert L. *Honda: An American Success Story.* New York: Prentice Hall, 1988.

Singh, Manmohan. *India's Export Trends and the Prospects for Self-Sustained Growth.* Oxford: Clarendon Press, 1964.

Somun, Hajrudin. *Mahathir: The Secret of the Malaysian Success.* Translated by Lejla Somun Krupalija. Selangor Darul Ehsan, Malaysia: Pelanduk, 2003.

Steers, Richard M. *Made in Korea: Chung Ju Yung and the Rise of Hyundai.* New York: Routledge, 1999.

Stiglitz, Joseph E. *Globalization and Its Discontents.* New York: W. W. Norton, 2002.

Stone, P. B. *Japan Surges Ahead: Japan's Economic Rebirth.* London: Weidenfeld & Nicolson, 1969.

Studwell, Joe. *Asian Godfathers: Money and Power in Hong Kong and South-East Asia.* London: Profile Books, 2007.

Sun Yat-sen. *The Three Principles of the People.* Taipei: China Publishing, 1981.

Tamamoto, Masaru. "Japan and Its Discontents: A Letter from Yokohama." *World Policy Journal* (October 1, 2000): 41–49.

Tan Siok Sun. *Goh Keng Swee: A Portrait.* Singapore: Editions Didier Millet, 2007.

Tharoor, Shashi. *Nehru: The Invention of India.* New York: Arcade Publications, 2001.

Togo, Yukiyasu, and William Wartman. *Against All Odds: The Story of the Toyota Motor Corporation and the Family That Created It.* New York: St. Martin's Press, 1993.

Toyoda, Eiji. *Toyota: Fifty Years in Motion.* Tokyo: Kodansha International, 1987.

Tuan, Chyau, and Linda F. Y. Ng. "Evolution of Hong Kong's Electronics Industry under a Passive Industrial Policy." *Managerial and Decision Economics* 16 (1995): 509–523.

Vatikiotis, Michael R. J. *Indonesian Politics under Suharto: Order, Development, and Pressure for Change.* Rev. ed. London: Routledge, 1994.

Vittachi, Tarzie. *The Fall of Sukarno.* London: Andre Deutsch, 1967.

Vogel, Ezra F. *The Four Little Dragons: The Spread of Industrialization in East Asia.* Cambridge, Mass.: Harvard University Press, 1991.

Vogel, Ezra F. *Is Japan Still Number One?* Selangor Darul Edsan, Malaysia: Pelanduk, 2000.

Vogel, Ezra F. *Japan as Number One: Lessons for America.* New York: toExcel, 1999. First published 1979 by Harvard University Press.

Vogel, Ezra F. *One Step Ahead in China: Guangdong under Reform.* Cambridge, Mass.: Harvard University Press, 1989.

Wang, Lutao Sophia Kang. *K. T. Li and the Taiwan Experience.* Taipei: National Tsing Hua University Press, 2006.

Welch, Jack. *Jack: Straight from the Gut.* With John A. Byrne. New York: Warner Books, 2001.

Wolferen, Karel van. *The Enigma of Japanese Power.* London: Macmillan, 1989.

Womack, James P., Daniel T. Jones, and Daniel Roos. *The Machine That Changed the World.* New York: Rawson Associates, 1990.

Woo Jung En. *Race to the Swift: State and Finance in Korean Industrialization.* New York: Columbia University Press, 1991.

Wood, Christopher. *The Bubble Economy: Japan's Extraordinary Speculative Boom of the '80s and the Dramatic Bust of the '90s.* New York: Atlantic Monthly Press, 1992.

World Bank. *The East Asian Miracle: Economic Growth and Public Policy.* New York: Oxford University Press, 1993.

Yergin, Daniel, and Joseph Stanislaw. *The Commanding Heights: The Battle for the World Economy.* New York: Touchstone, 1998.

Yu, Tony Fu-lai. *Entrepreneurship and Economic Development in Hong Kong.* London: Routledge, 1997.

Zakaria, Fareed. "A Conversation with Lee Kuan Yew." *Foreign Affairs* (March–April 1994): 109–127.

Zhang Liang. *The Tiananmen Papers.* Edited by Andrew J. Nathan and Perry Link. London: Little, Brown and Company, 2001.

INDEX